# Exploring Apple iPhone

## iOS 15 Edition

Kevin Wilson

Elluminet Press
www.elluminetpress.com

# Exploring Apple iPhone: iOS 15 Ed



Publisher: Elluminet Press
Director: Kevin Wilson
Lead Editor: Steven Ashmore
Technical Reviewer: Mike Taylor, Robert Ashcroft
Copy Editors: Joanne Taylor, James Marsh
Proof Reader: Steven Ashmore
Indexer: James Marsh
Cover Designer: Kevin Wilson

eBook versions and licenses are also available for most titles. Any source code or other supplementary materials referenced by the author in this text is available to readers at

`www.elluminetpress.com/resources`

For detailed information about how to locate your book's resources, go to

`www.elluminetpress.com/resources`

# Table of Contents

# About the Author

With over 20 years' experience in the computer industry, Kevin Wilson has made a career out of technology and showing others how to use it. After earning a master's degree in computer science, software engineering, and multimedia systems, Kevin has held various positions in the IT industry including graphic & web design, programming, building & managing corporate networks, and IT support.

He serves as senior writer and director at Elluminet Press Ltd, he periodically teaches computer science at college, and works as an IT trainer in England while researching for his PhD. His books have become a valuable resource among the students in England, South Africa, Canada, and in the United States.

Kevin's motto is clear: "If you can't explain something simply, then you haven't understood it well enough." To that end, he has created the Exploring Tech Computing series, in which he breaks down complex technological subjects into smaller, easy-to-follow steps that students and ordinary computer users can put into practice.

# Acknowledgements

Thanks to all the staff at Luminescent Media & Elluminet Press for their passion, dedication and hard work in the preparation and production of this book.

To all my friends and family for their continued support and encouragement in all my writing projects.

To all my colleagues, students and testers who took the time to test procedures and offer feedback on the book

Finally thanks to you the reader for choosing this book. I hope it helps you to use your iPhone with greater understanding.

Have fun!

# 1 iPhones

The iPhone is a smart phone developed by Apple, first introduced in 2007. The interface is a touch screen, meaning you can manipulate sliders, switches, buttons and icons using your finger.

The main screen is called the home screen and contains icons that represent apps. You can download countless apps from the App Store - you'll find an app for almost anything you can think of.

The iPhone runs an operating system called iOS, and can connect to cellular networks/Wi-Fi, make calls, send/receive text messages, browse the web, take pictures, record videos, play music, video chat, and send/receive emails.

Up until 2017, the iPhone included a single button on the front panel called the home button that returns the user to the home screen. Since 2017, with the introduction of iPhone X, the design switched to a bezel-less front panel which removed the home button.

In this chapter, we'll take a look at

- What's New in iOS 15
- A few Technical Terms

# What's New in iOS 15?

iOS 15 introduces a few new features and improvements, let's take a look at some of the main ones.

You can now place widgets among the apps on your Home Screen.

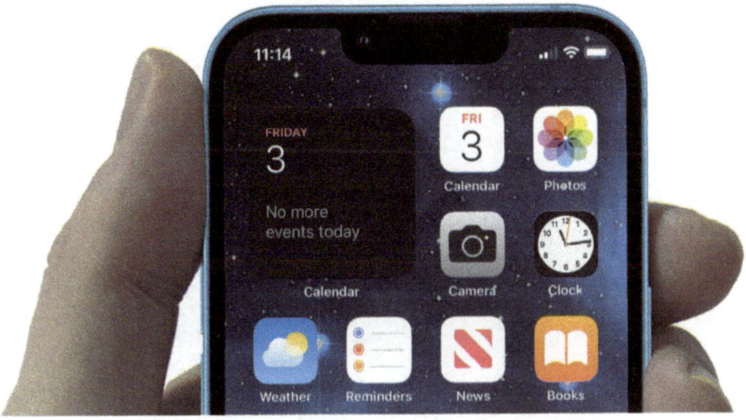


You can use Live Text to copy text out of an image and paste it into another app, or translate the text into another language.

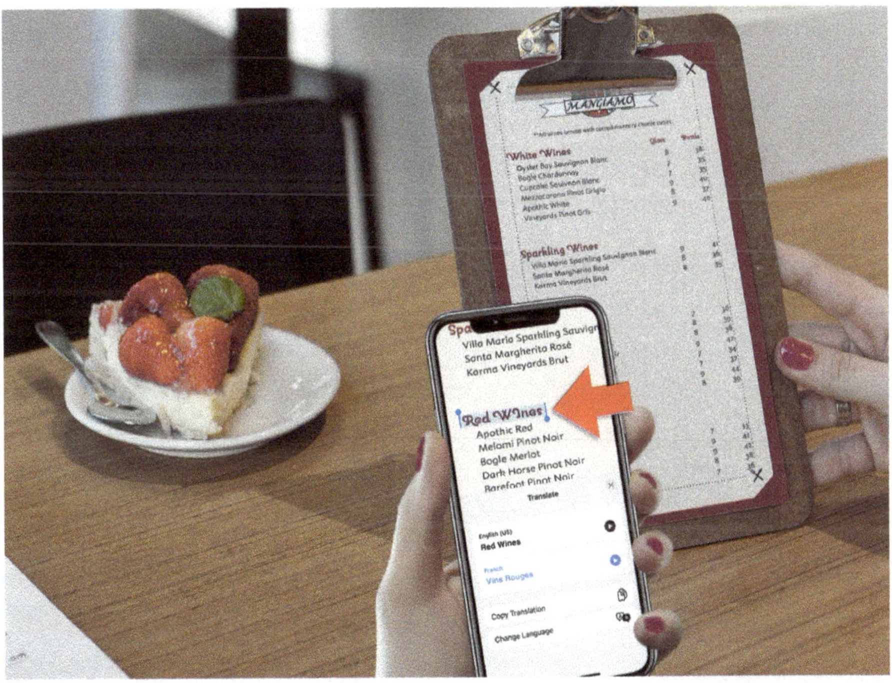


You'll need an iPhone XS, XR or later.

You can also look up information. Visual Lookup identifies objects and landmarks in photos. Here in the photo below, visual lookup has identified my dog as a dachshund, and offers extra photos and info.

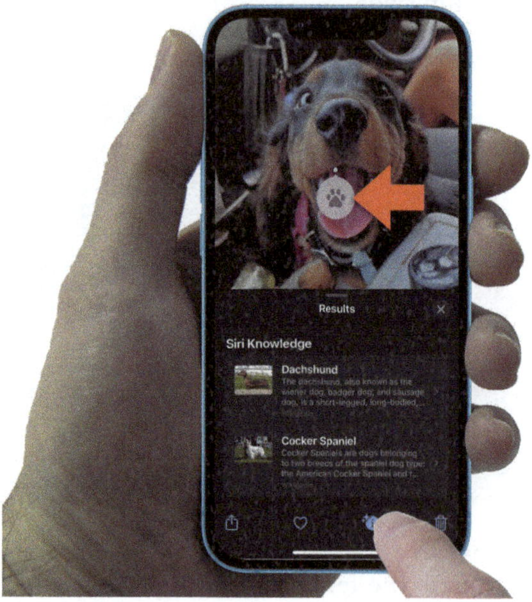


SharePlay allows you to watch and listen to music in your FaceTime calls with your friends.

Memojis now includes clothing, new headgear and glasses. You can customise these with colours and styles to suit your tastes. You can use your memojis in the messages app as well as facetime.

Focus mode allows you to concentrate on a task and minimise distractions. You can turn on 'do not disturb' to switch off all apps & notifications, or choose from pre-defined focus modes for work, sleep, fitness, gaming, reading or driving. You can select only the apps, people or notifications related to a particular task such as work. You can also configure your own focus modes.

In Safari, the tab bar is now at the bottom making it a bit easier to control.

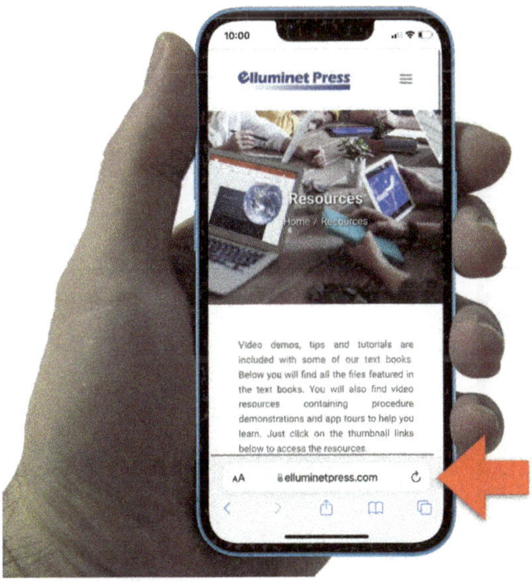

The maps app now has an interactive globe but this only works on an iPhone XS or later.

With wallet, you can add home, hotel, office and car keys.

The 'find my' app now has live locations so you can see where your family and friends are.

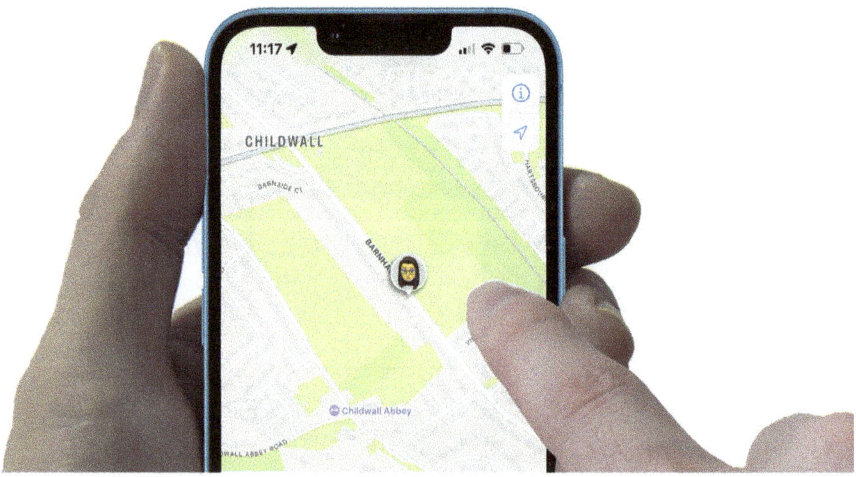

# A Series Chip

The Apple A series is a series of microprocessors known as a system on a chip (SoC) used to power iPhones and iPads. The A series chips combine the CPU, Graphics Processor (or GPU), memory (or RAM), flash storage, and a neural engine which is a component designed to use machine learning and artificial intelligence for tasks such identifying objects in photos, or applying an automatic filter to a picture, analysing videos, voice recognition, and so on.

# Liquid Retina Displays

A Retina Display is a screen with a high pixel density - meaning there are a lot more pixels per inch than a standard computer screen. This generates a high resolution, crystal clear image. The image on the left is a standard LCD screen, while the image on the right is a retina screen.

Liquid Retina XDR display is lit by multiple mini-LEDs, and supports resolutions of 2732x2048 pixels for a total of 5.6 million pixels with 264 pixels per inch, and delivers P3 wide colour giving richer and more vibrant colours.

ProMotion technology automatically adjusts the display refresh rate up to 120 Hz (twice the rate of typical LCD displays) to the optimal rate for the content.

High Dynamic Range (HDR) delivers detail in extremely bright parts of the image along with the subtle details in the darkest parts of the image.

True Tone uses multiple sensors to adjust the colour temperature of the display on your iPhone depending on the ambient light, to make the display look more natural.

A nit is measurement of the brightness of light. Computer monitors usually range from 200 - 600 nits. Higher nits allow you to brighten the display so you can see the screen clearly on a sunny day.

# 2

# Setting up iPhone

If you've just bought your new iPhone and taken it out the box, the process to set it up to use for the first time is very simple. You don't even have to connect it to your computer.

In this chapter, we'll take a look at

- Insert your SIM
- Power Up
- Charging your iPhone's Battery
- Unlock & Wake iPhone
- Initial Setup
- Upgrading your iPhone to iOS 15
- Language & Region
- Settings
- Apple ID
- FaceID
- Passcode
- Privacy
- Notifications
- Adding Email Accounts
- Add Social Media Accounts
- Connecting Devices

Take a look at the video resources, open your web browser and navigate to the following website.

`elluminetpress.com/using-iphone`

# Insert your SIM

**Make sure your device is off before doing this.** To insert a SIM card from your network provider. Find the SIM Card Tray. This is on the side edge of your phone, next to the volume buttons (or the opposite side button on older models).

Push the end of a paper clip into the release hole on the side of your device. The tray will pop out.

Pull out the little tray and insert your SIM.

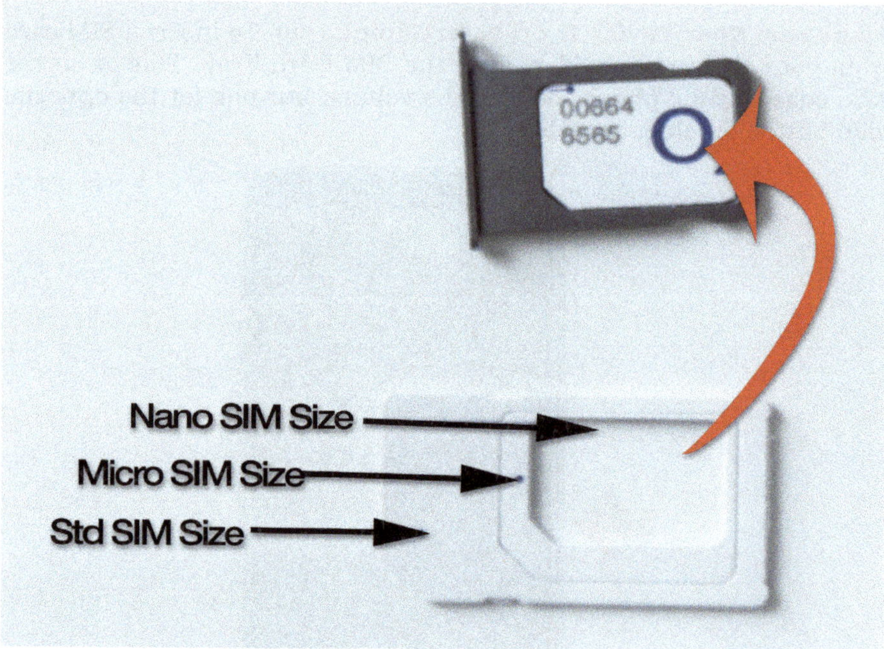


The SIM will only go one way around, so make sure it clips firmly into the cutout in the tray.

Slide the little tray back into your phone, until it clips firmly into place against the side.

# Power Up

To power on your iPhone, press and hold the side button on the right hand edge of the device until you see the Apple logo on the screen.

Once your iPhone powers up, you'll land on the lock screen, see .

If you have a new iPhone, you'll need to run through the initial setup. See .

# Charging your iPhone's Battery

Plug your iPhone directly into the charger to charge the battery. Plug one end of the lightning cable into the charger.

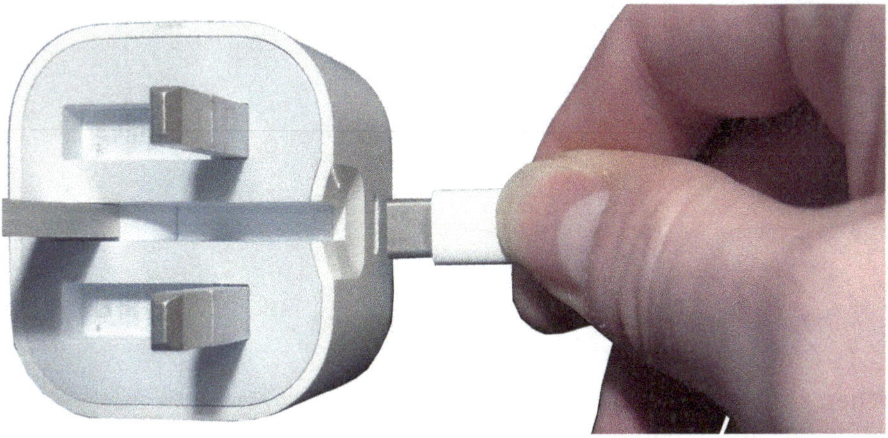

Plug the other end of the lightning cable into the port on the bottom of your iPhone.

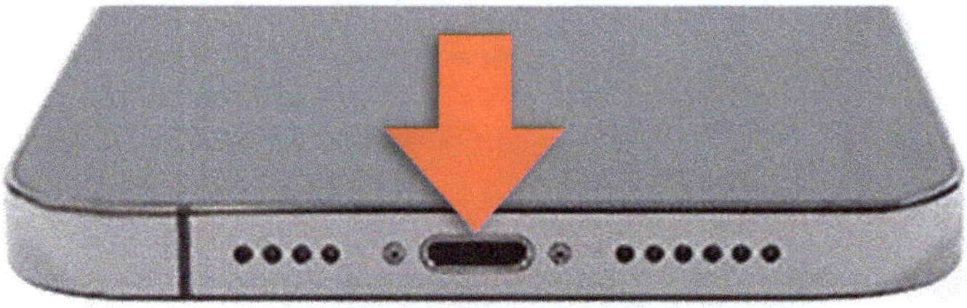

Your battery will take a few hours to charge. Best practice is not to let your battery deplete completely, charge it up when you still have about 20% charge left.

# Unlock & Wake iPhone

To unlock and wake your phone, press the side button while looking at the iPhone screen. This will allow the True Depth camera and Face ID to identify you to unlock your phone.

When you see the lock icon at the top unlock, swipe upwards on the white bar at the bottom of the screen.

If you haven't set up your Face ID you'll be prompted for your passcode. This is the code you enter during the initial setup procedure.

# Initial Setup

To use iPhone, you need an internet connection and your Apple ID. In iOS 11, Apple introduced an automated setup feature that allows you to transfer settings from another device, such as an iPhone. Both devices must be running iOS 11 or later. If you don't have this, you can still set up your iPhone manually. First lets take a look at the auto setup feature.

## Auto Setup

If you have iOS 11 or later set up on another device such as another iPhone or iPad, you can use it to transfer your settings to your new iPhone.

On your iPhone, slide or press the home button to start, then select your language.

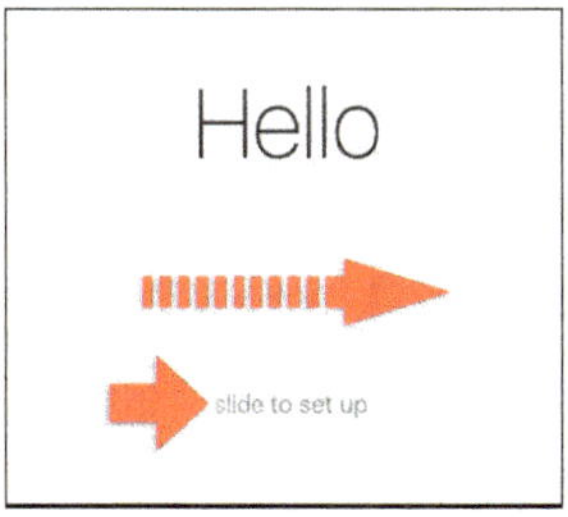

Scroll down the list, select your region or country.

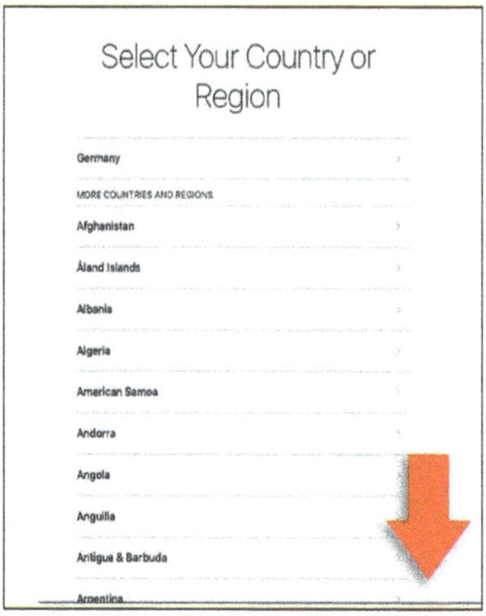


Now, if you have iOS 11 or 12 set up on your old iPhone, bring it over to your new iPhone. You'll see a prompt on your old iPhone. Tap 'continue'.

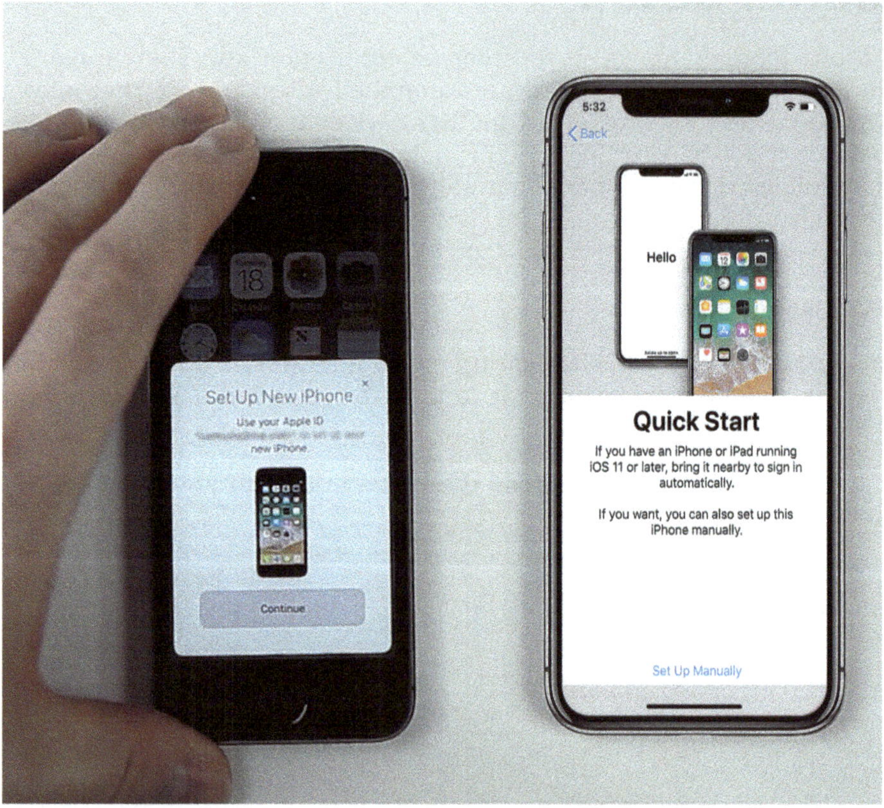

Your new iPhone will display a strange pattern, like the one shown below.

Using the camera on your old iPhone, position the blue pattern in the circle shown on the bottom of your old iPhone's screen.

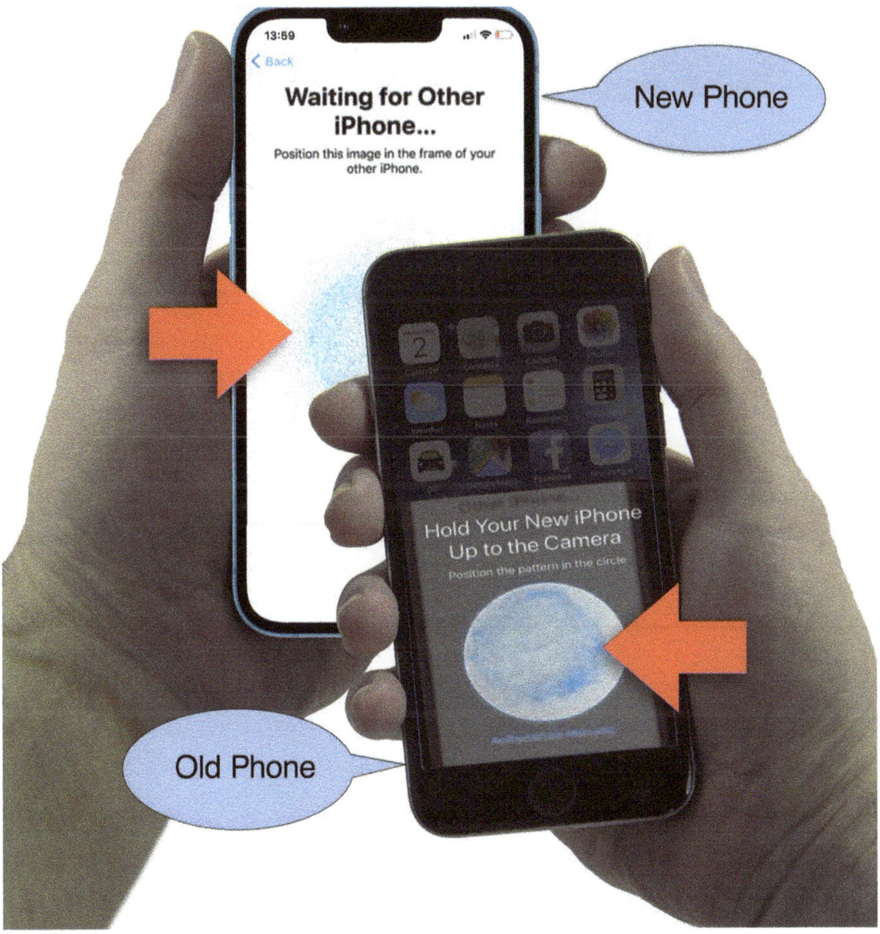

Now leave your old iPhone next to your new iPhone until the set up process is complete. Your new iPhone will activate, you may need to enter your passcode, the same one you use to unlock your iPhone.

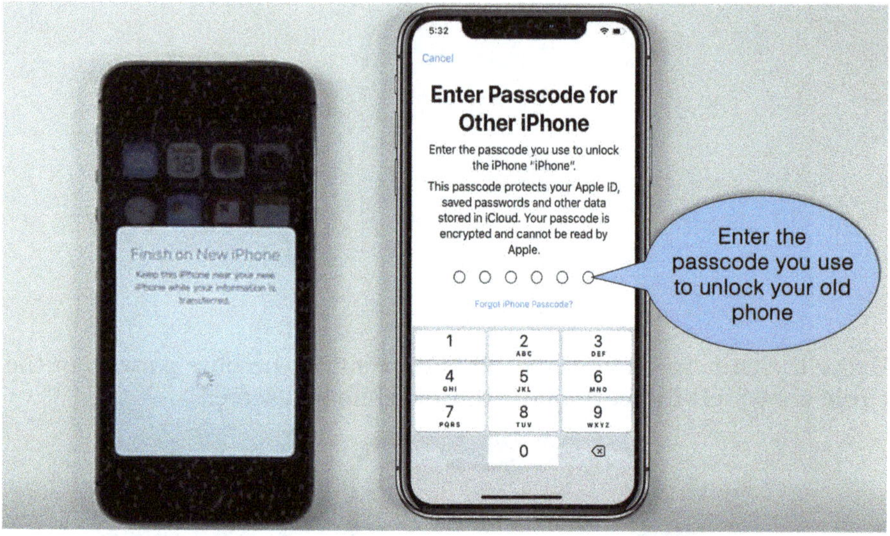


Follow the prompts on your iPhone to set up Face ID. See page 30.

## Manual Setup

Turn iPhone on and follow the Setup Assistant. This will guide you through the process

Swipe your finger across the bottom of the screen.

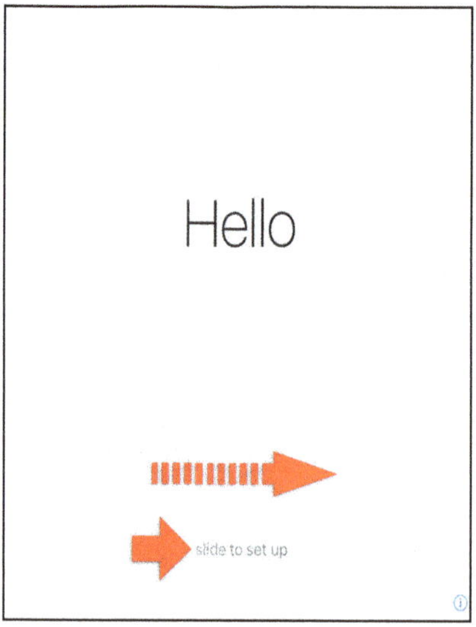

Select your language from the list. Scroll down, select your country or region.

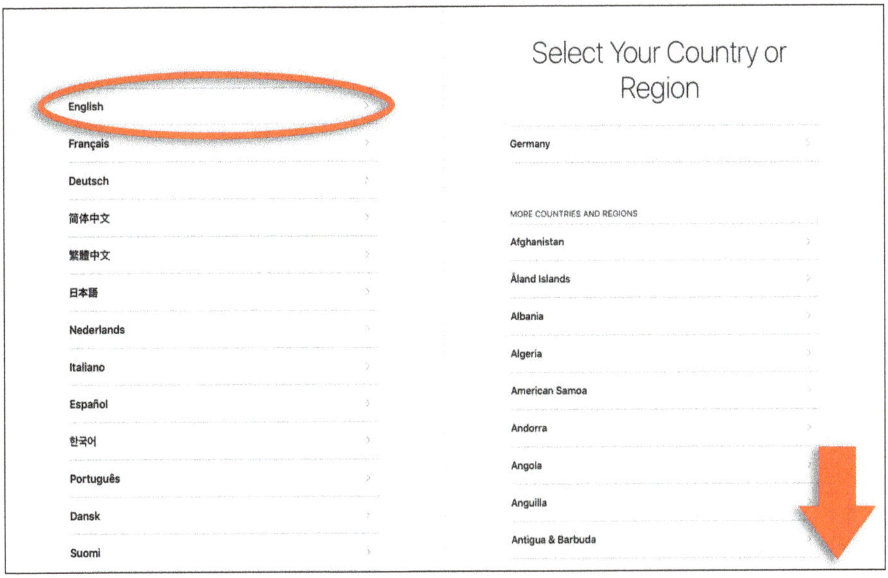


Tap 'set up manually' at the bottom of the screen.

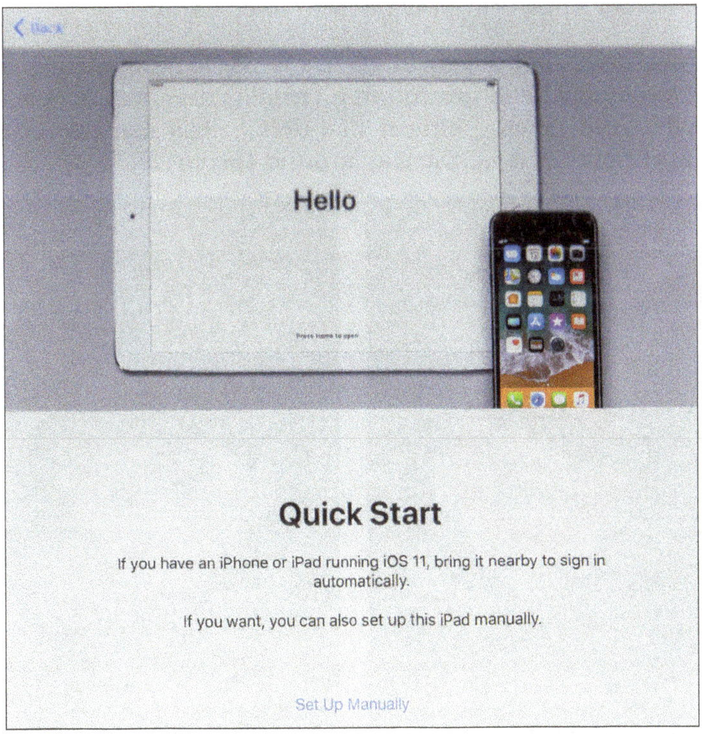

Tap on the name of your WiFi Network. Enter your WiFi password or network key when prompted.

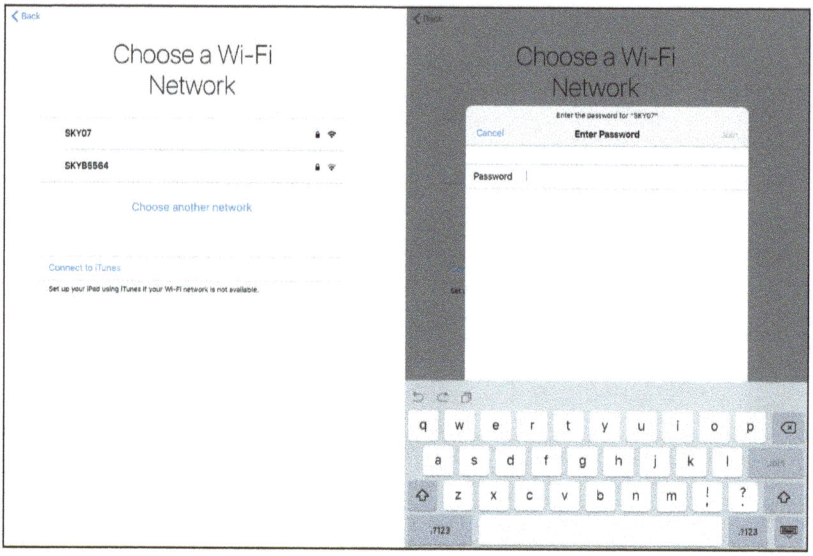


Tap 'Enable Location Services'. The location services allow your iPhone to determine your current physical location. Some apps require this; maps and other apps that provide local information.

Enter a passcode and set up Face ID. While looking straight at your phone, rotate your head around in a circular manner - to the left, up, to the right, and down - almost like doing neck exercises, until the green marker makes it all the way around the circle.

Tap 'done' to accept.

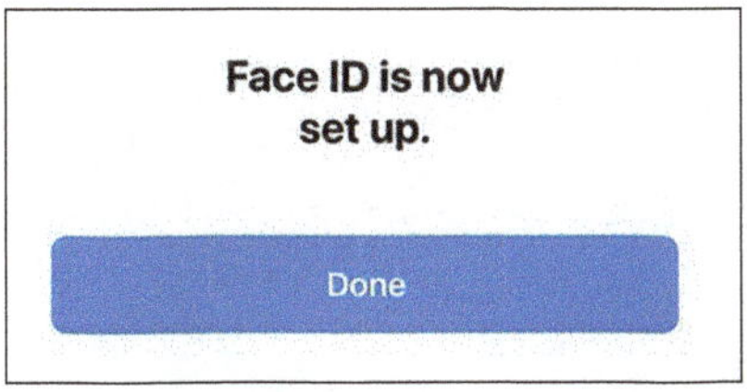


Tap 'set up as New iPhone'. This will create a clean iPhone. *If you have upgraded to a new iPhone, you can tap 'restore from iCloud backup' and select the latest backup. This will set up your iPhone using your previous settings and data.*

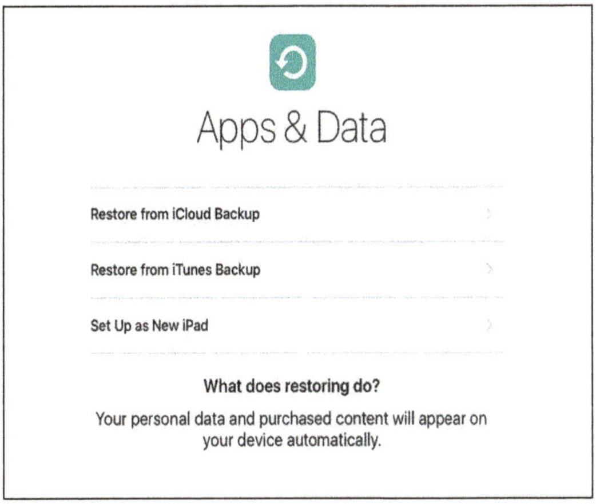


Tap sign in with your Apple ID. Enter your username and password.

Hit 'continue' to set up Siri. Follow the instructions on the screen to initialise Siri.

Tap "don't send" or "don't share" on 'Apple Diagnostics' and 'App Analytics'.

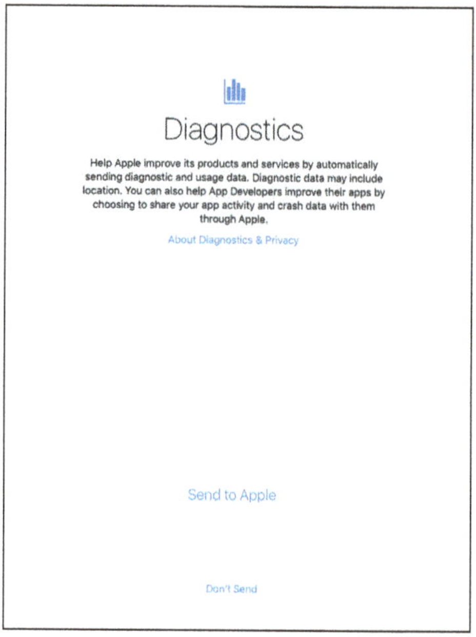


Tap OK to get started.

# Upgrading your iPhone to iOS 15

Make sure your iPhone is plugged into a power charger and that it is connected to your WiFi.

Once you have done that, go to the settings app then tap 'General'.

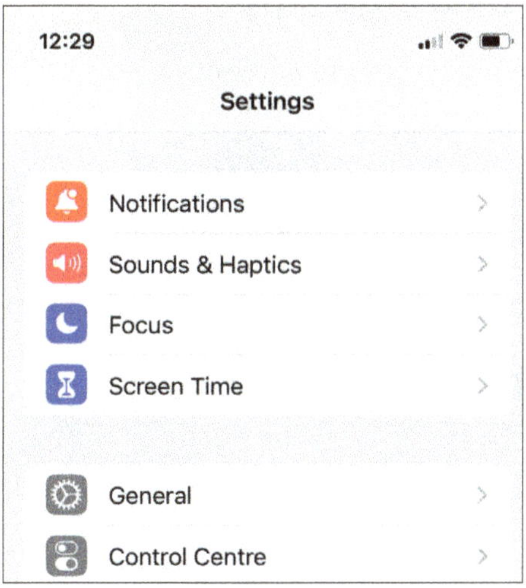


Select 'Software Update'.

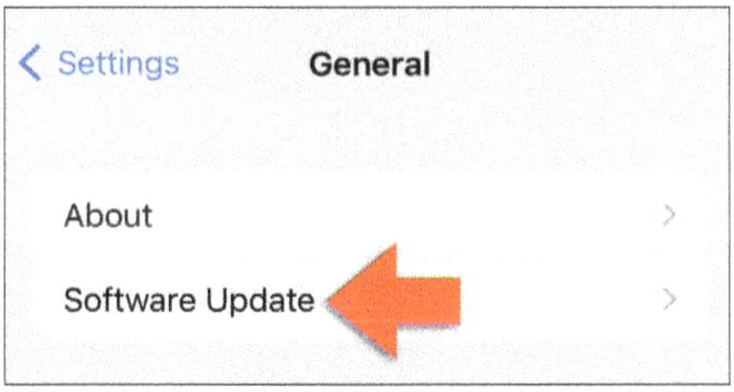


If there are any updates available, you'll see them listed here, Tap 'Download and Install'.

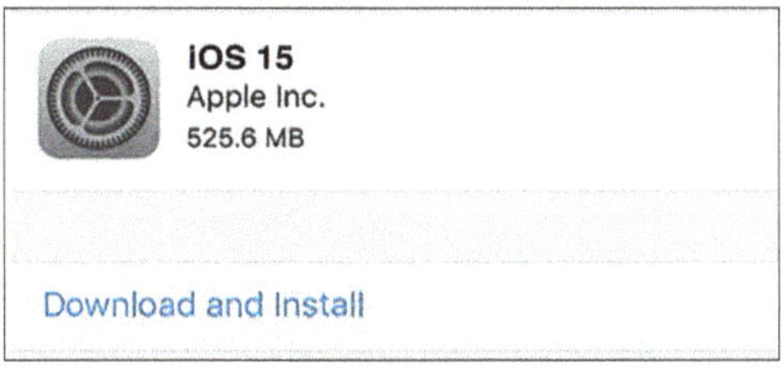


To update now, tap 'download and install'. Enter your passcode when prompted. Your iPhone will restart and the update will install. This might take a while.

# Adjusting Settings

To adjust any settings on your iPhone, you'll need to use the settings app.

## Opening the Settings App

You'll find the icon on the home screen.

Settings are grouped into sections based on the feature the settings control. You'll find a section for display, sound, or home screen settings among many others.

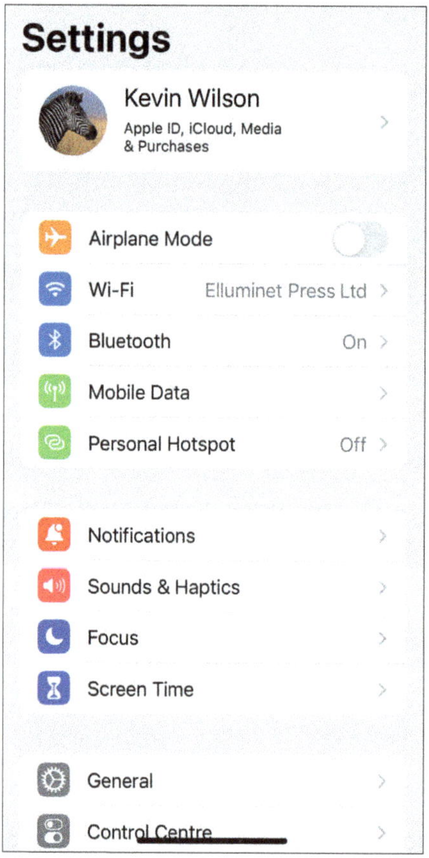


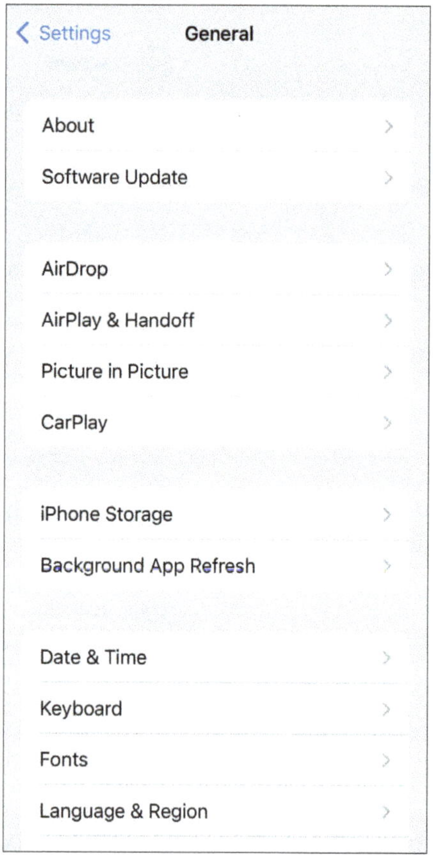


When you select a section, the settings in that section appear.

## Searching for Settings

On the top left of the settings app, you'll see a search field. Drag the list on the left downwards if the field doesn't show.

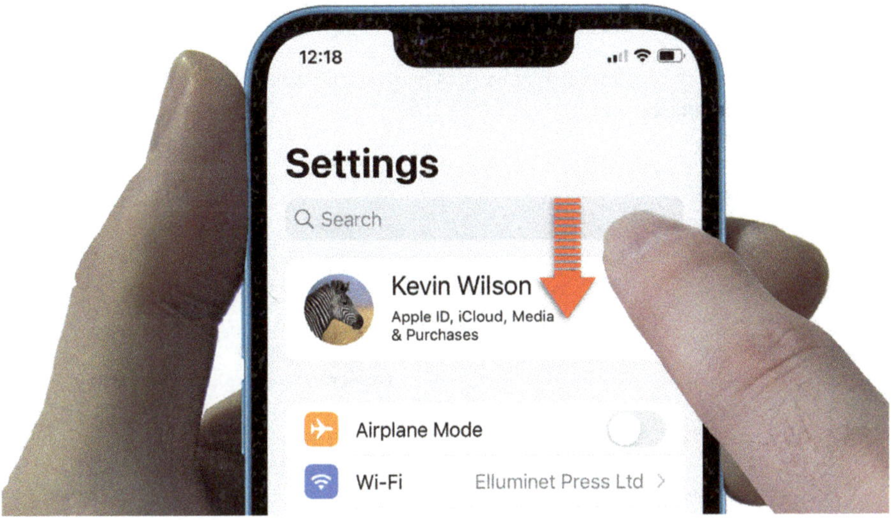


Type in the name of the setting or device you want to change.

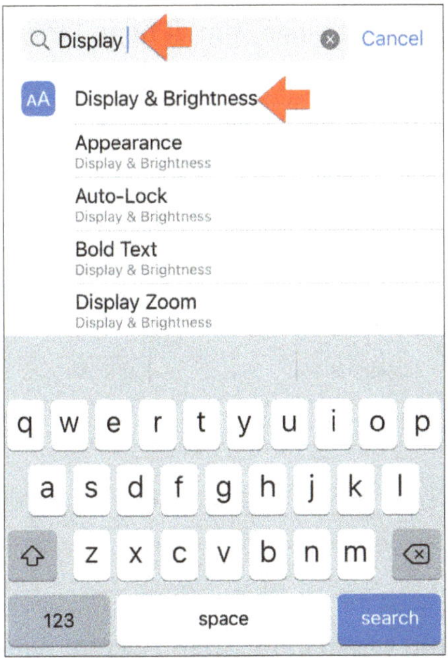


In the drop down list, you'll see suggested settings. Select the closest match from the drop down list.

# Language & Region

You can change the language of your iPhone, and the region if it's incorrect or if you've accidentally changed it. To do this, open the settings app, then select 'general' from the list, then tap on 'language & region'.

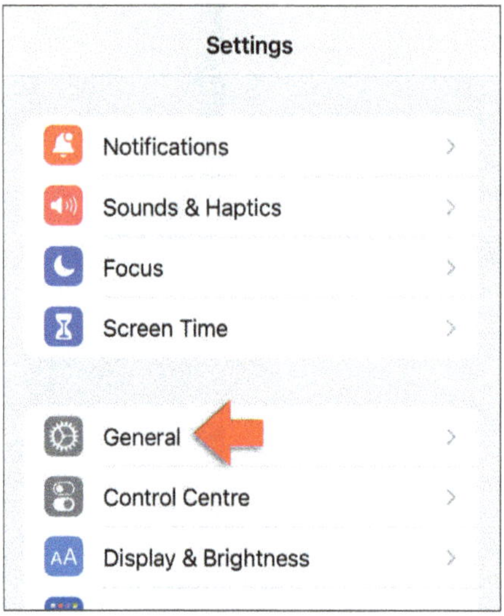


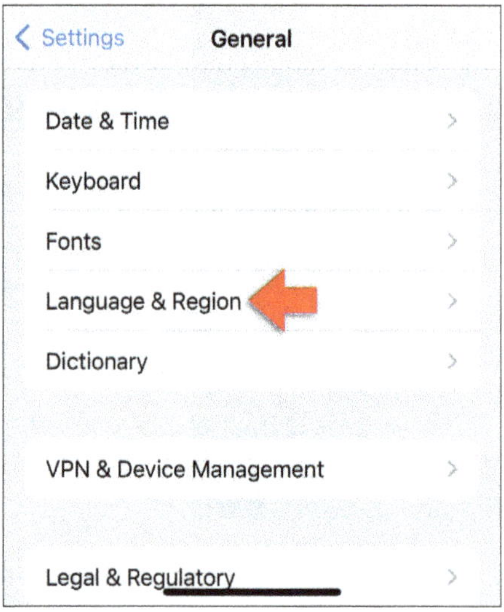


To change the display language, tap 'iPhone language', then select a language from the list.

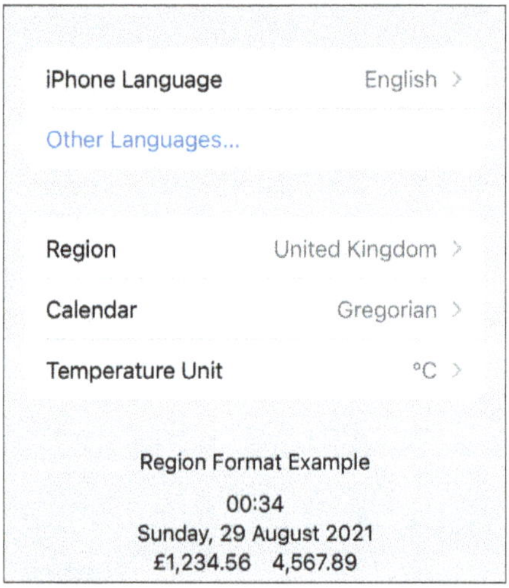


To change the region, tap 'region', then select a region from the list. If you use a different calendar, tap 'calendar', select a calendar from the list. To change the temperature units, click 'temperature unit', then select F for Fahrenheit, or C for Celsius.

# Keyboard

To adjust keyboard settings, open the settings app, select 'general' from the list on the left, then select 'keyboard

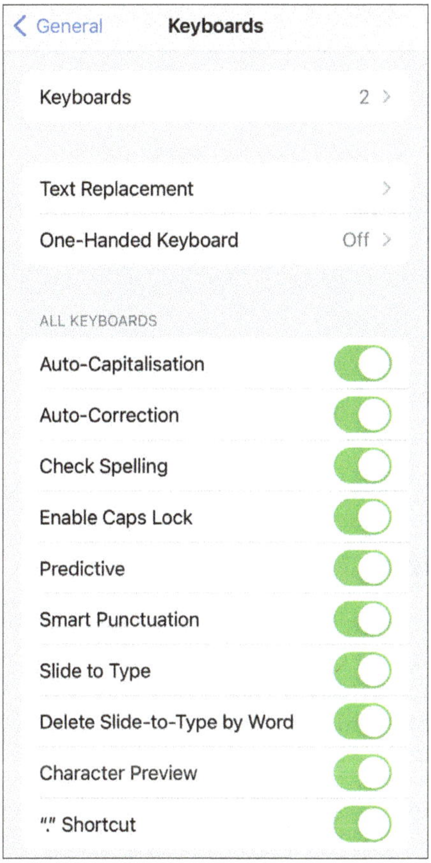


You can add keyboards for other languages, you can also enable or disable typing features, such as spell check, auto capitalisation which captitalizes the first letter in a new sentence, predictive text which tries to predict the next word in your sentence, or auto-correct which corrects common misspelled words, and smart punctuation.

## Change or Add Keyboard

In the keyboard settings, tap on 'keyboards' at the top of the page.

Tap 'add new keyboard'.

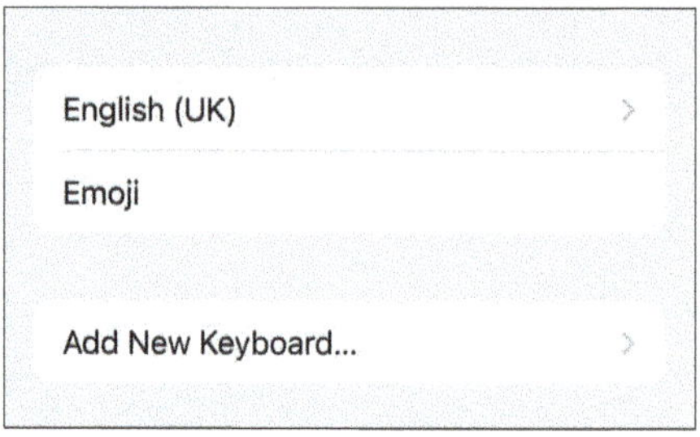


Select a keyboard from the list, or search for your keyboard

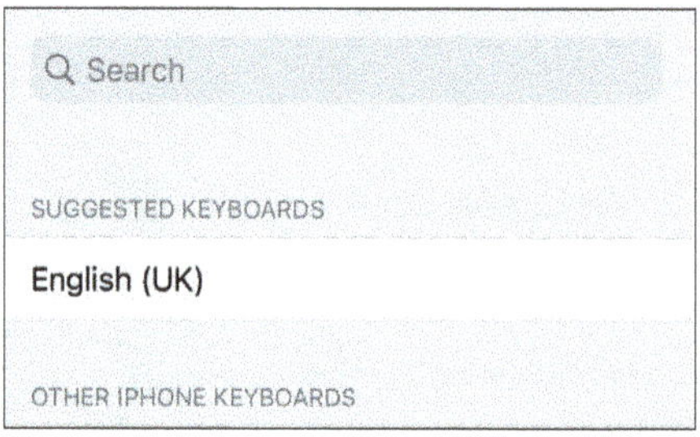


## Text Shortcuts

You can create shortcuts for sentences or phrases you use most often. So for example, you can create a shortcut for "I'm on my way, see you in a bit". So instead of typing that out every time, you can shorten it to perhaps OMY, then all you need to do is type, OMY each time you want to use the phrase.

To do this in the keyboard settings, tap 'text replacement'.

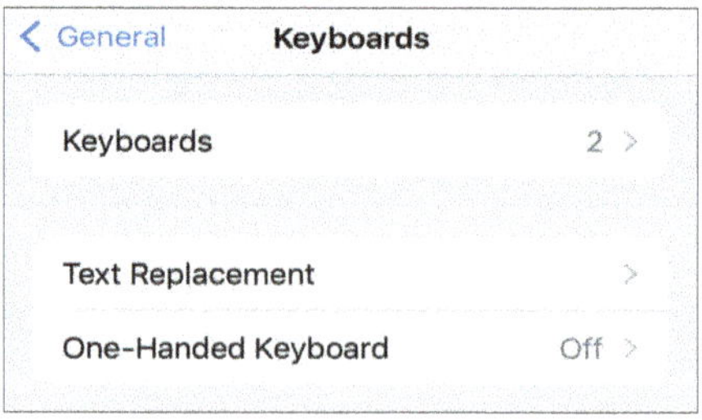


Tap the '+' icon on the top right to create a new shortcut.

Type your sentence into the field marked 'phrase'. Then type in the shortcut. Tap 'save' when you're done.

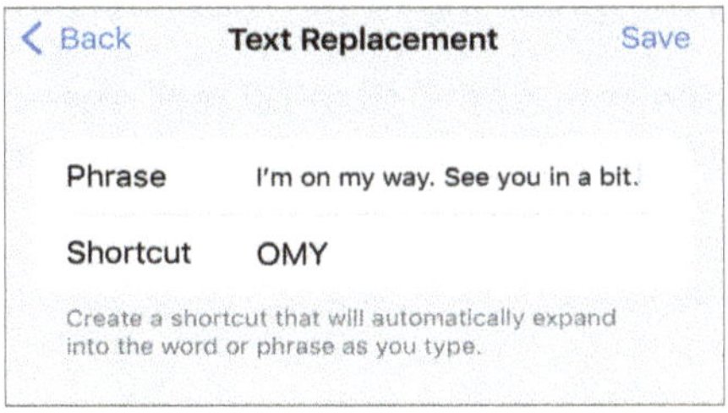


Now, when you're typing, all you need to type when you want to use the phrase is the shortcut.

# Date & Time

The date and time is usually set automatically for you depending on your location. However, sometimes you want to change these if you're travelling or in another country.

To do this, open the settings app then select 'general' from the list, then tap 'date and time'.

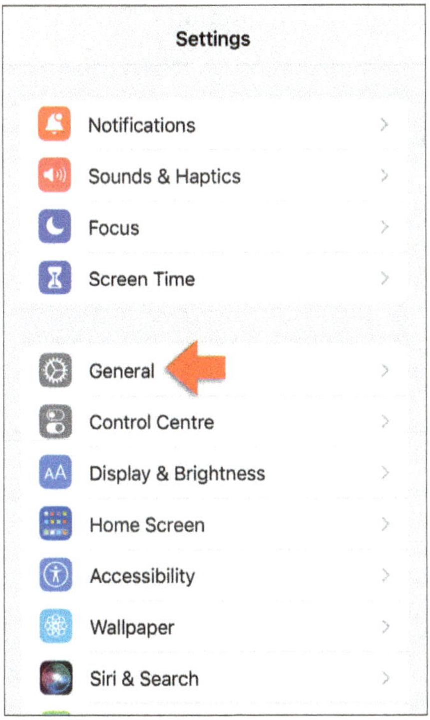


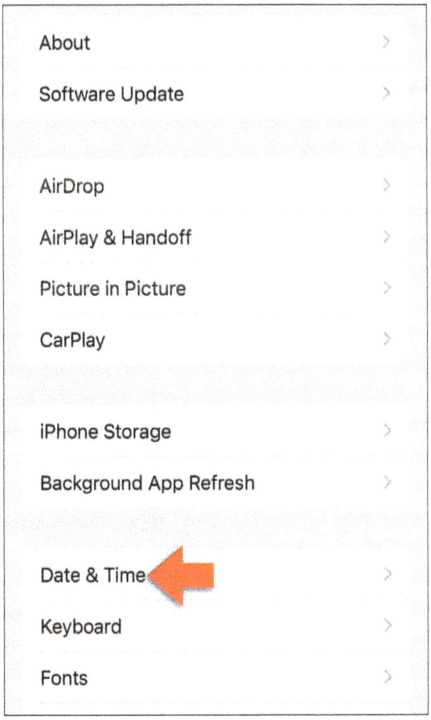

Here, you can change to 24 hour clock, add or remove the AM/PM markers or remove/show the date on the status bar on the top left of your iPhone screen or on the top of the lock screen.

To set your time zone manually, turn off 'set automatically', then tap on the time zone location. Type in the country you're in or want to use.

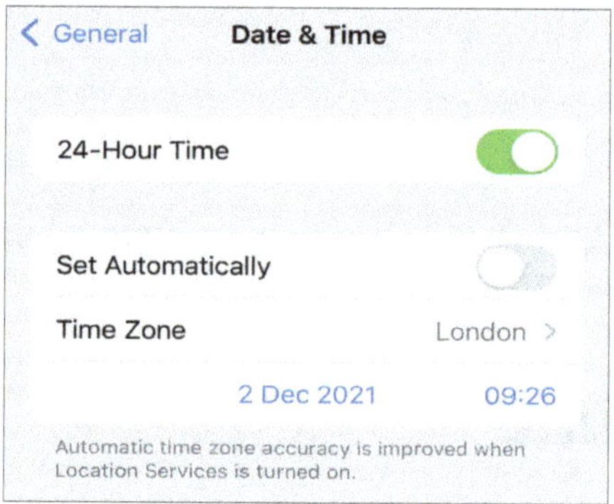


Tap on the country in the search results.

# Display

Using the display settings you can change various options. To do this, open the settings app, scroll down, select 'display & brightness' from the list.

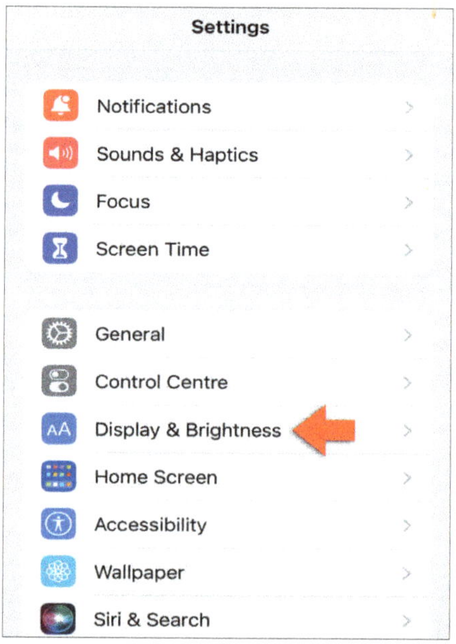

Here, you can switch between dark and light mode... Dark mode reduces the amount of white on the screen and is perfect for low-light environments making it easier on your eyes. Here below, you can see light mode on the left, and dark mode on the right.

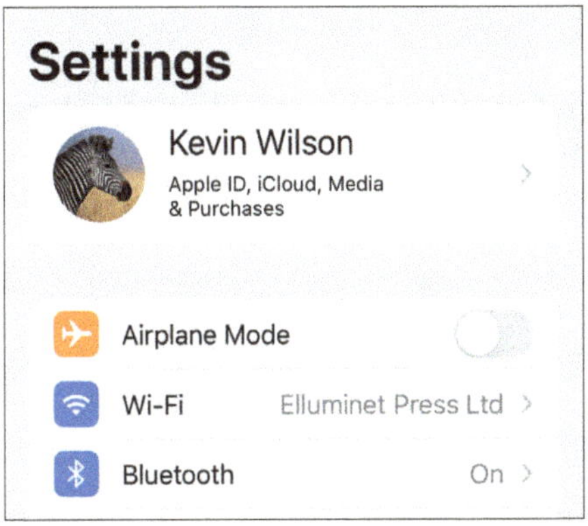


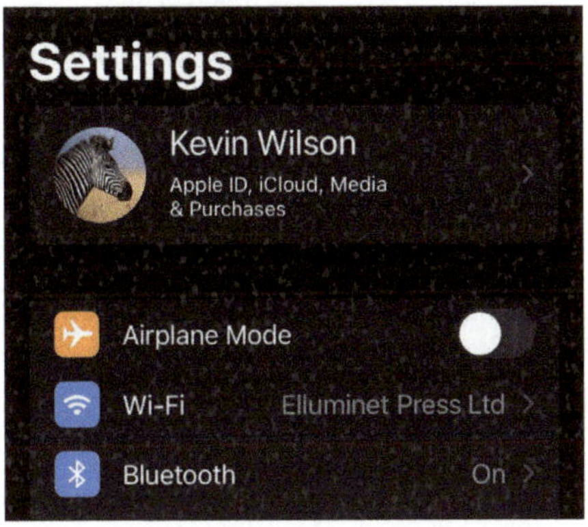


You can turn on 'automatic' which will turn on light mode until sunset, then switch to dark mode. If you tap 'options', then 'custom schedule', you can enter a time to use light mode, and a time to switch to dark mode.

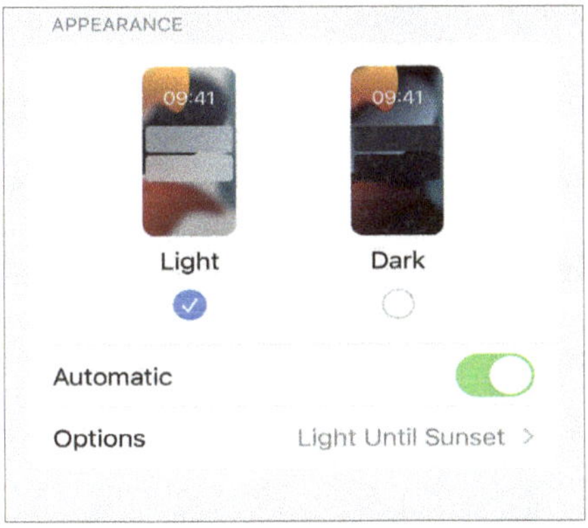


Further down you can change the screen brightness and enable/ disable true tone. Now true tone is a feature that adapts the screen colour, brightness and contrast according to the ambient light in the room you're physically in.

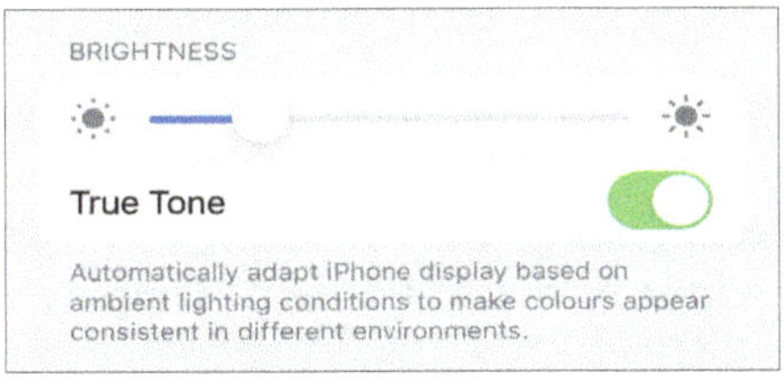

Under 'night shift', you can remove the bright blue light from your screen. This gives your screen a orange tint that is supposed to make it easier on your eyes.

To do this tap on 'night shift'. Under 'scheduled', turn this on, then select the time you want night shift to start and when you want it to end.

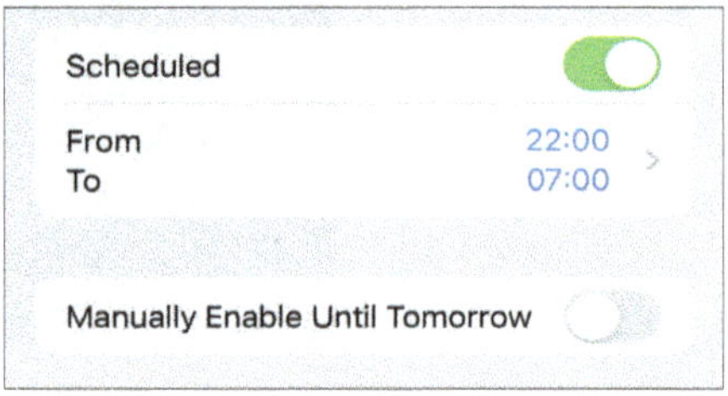


To change the amount of blue or orange, use the slider under 'colour temperature'. When you slide this to the right, you'll see the screen go orange. If you slide to the left, you'll see the screen go more blue.

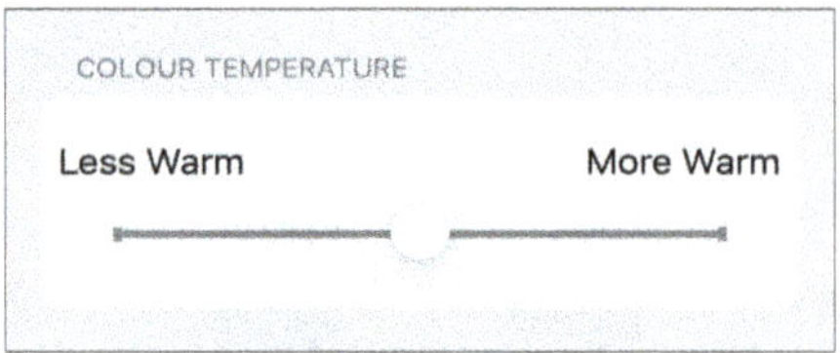


At the bottom of the screen, you'll see 'auto lock', this allows you to change the time it takes for your screen to lock after you stop using your iPhone. Tap on the time to change.

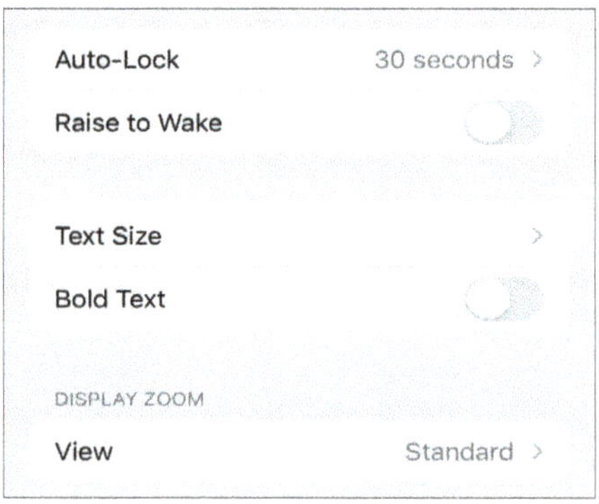


At the bottom, you can change the text size. To do this just tap on 'text size' then drag the slider to resize the text. Display zoom, enlarges the display.

# Wallpaper

You can set a photograph as a background on your lock screen and home screen.

## Adjusting your Wallpaper

First, open the settings app, then select ‘wallpaper’ from the list.

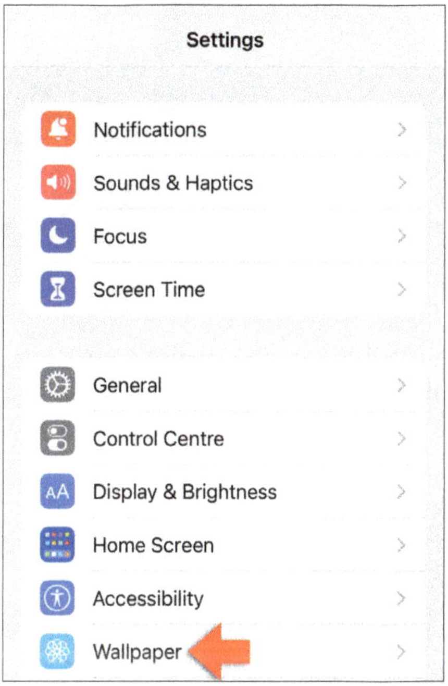


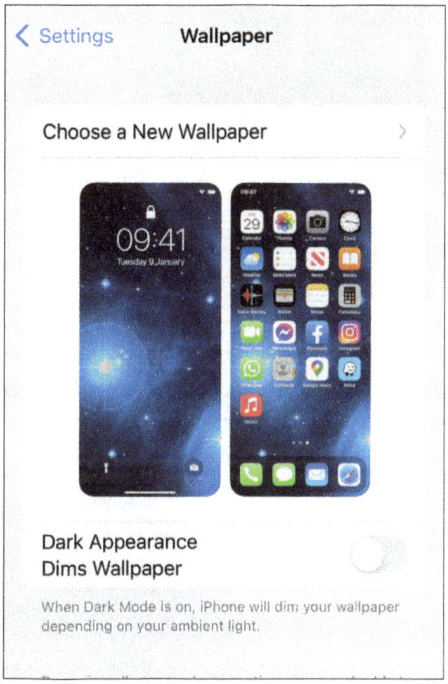


Here, you’ll see two previews, the one on the left is your lock screen, the one on the right is your home screen. You can reposition the wallpapers using these previews. Just tap on the one you want to reposition, then drag the image.

Underneath you’ll see a setting called ‘dark appearance dims wallpaper. This, as the name suggests, reduces the brightness of the wallpaper to match dark mode.

## Changing your Wallpaper

To change the wallpaper image, on the wallpaper section of the settings app, click ‘choose a new wallpaper’.

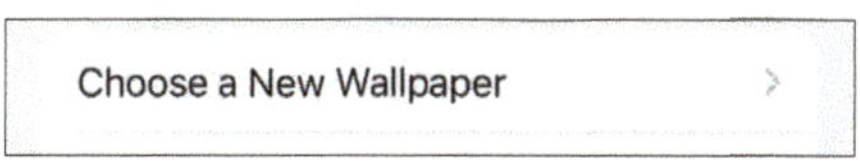

Choose one of the presets at the top, or tap 'all photos' if you want to select one of your own photographs. Select the photo you want to use.

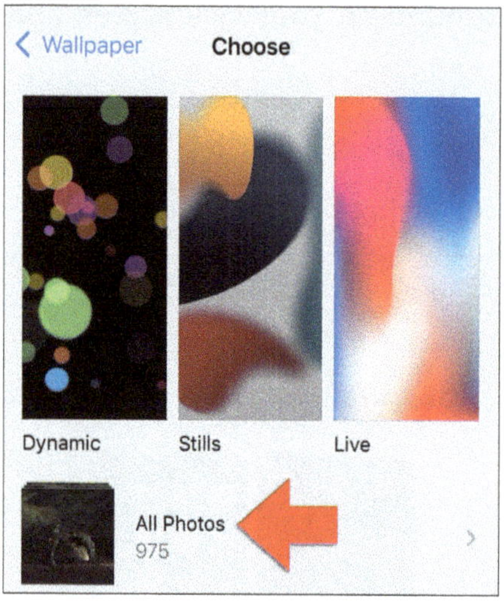

Drag the photograph with your finger until it's in the desired position. You can also make the photograph bigger or smaller by pinching the screen with your thumb and forefinger. Tap 'set' on the bottom right when you're done.

To set as both home and lock screen tap 'set both'. If you just want the photo on your home screen, tap 'set home screen'. Likewise for lock screen.

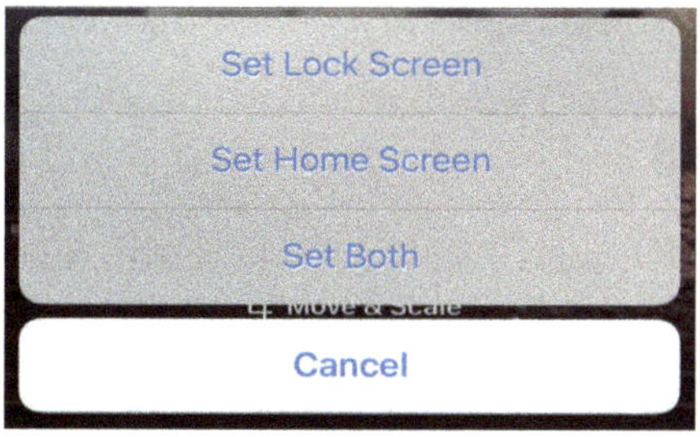


# Home Screen

You can change the size of the apps on your dock, you can also select where you want new apps to appear (on home screen or in library). You can choose to show app library link on the dock or recent apps you've either used or downloaded, as well as show the notification badges on the icons in the library. To change these settings, open the settings app, then select 'home screen & dock' from the list.

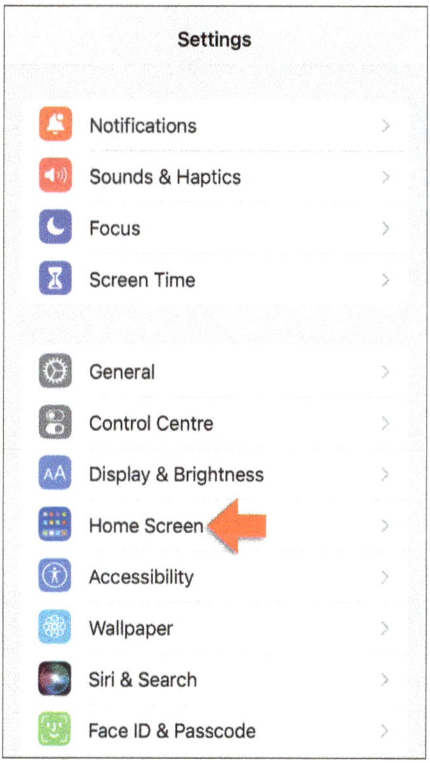

# Apple ID

Your Apple ID contains all your personal information, messages, calendar, contacts, email, and various settings.

## Creating an ID

To create an Apple ID open safari and go to the following website:

`appleid.apple.com`

From the website click 'Create your Apple ID' on the top right.

Fill in the form with your details, scroll down to the bottom and click 'continue'.

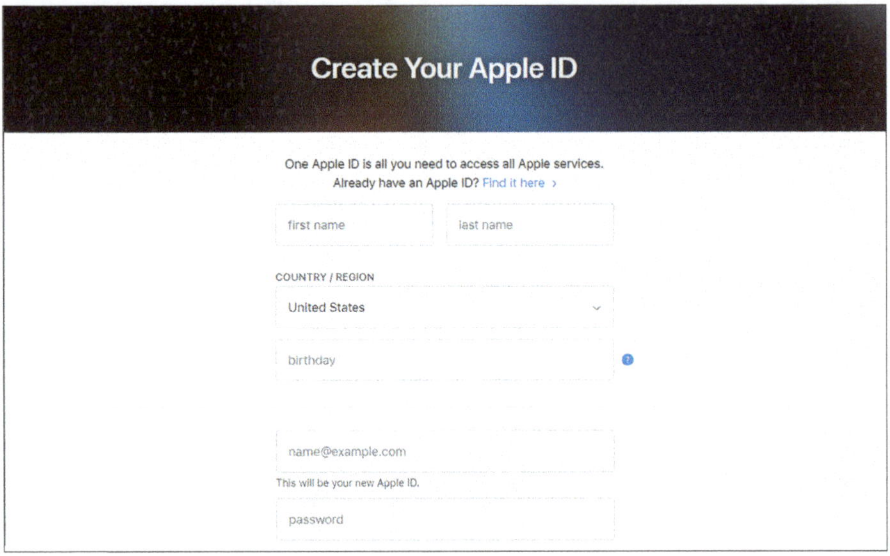


Keep a note of the email address and password you entered. You will need this Apple ID if you want to purchase Apps from the App Store, use iCloud, Apple Email, or purchase songs from iTunes Store.

# FaceID

Face ID is available on the iPhone X or later, and uses the TrueDepth HD camera to take a digital scan of your face to unlock your device.

## Setup

To setup FaceID, open your settings app, select 'Face ID & Passcode' from the list on the left. Enter your passcode when prompted. Tap 'Set Up Face ID'.

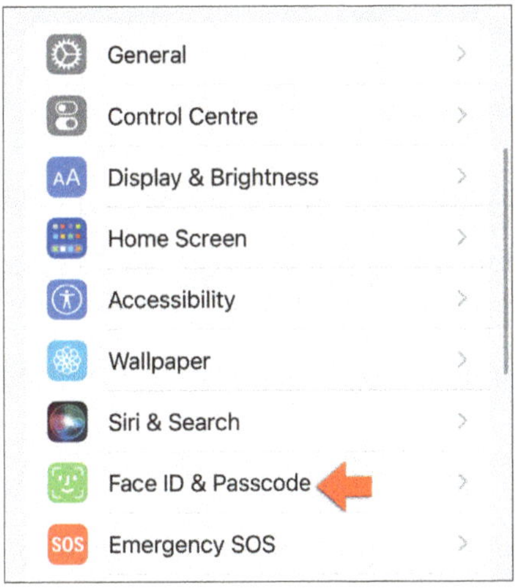


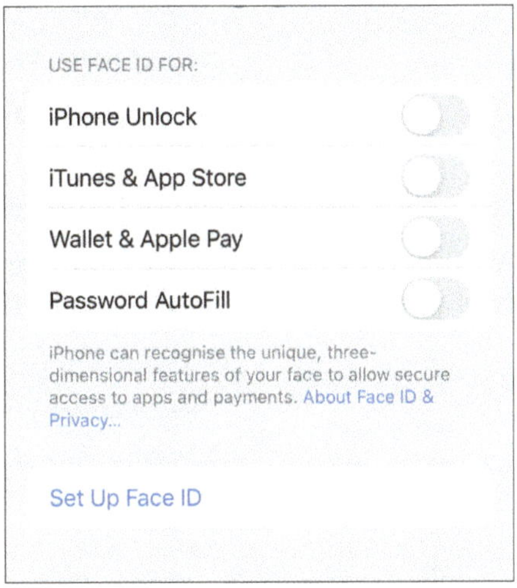


Now, look straight at your device. Rotate your head around in a circular manner - keep looking at your device, rotate your head left, then down, then right, then up, until the green marker makes it all the way around the circle. Tap 'done' to accept.

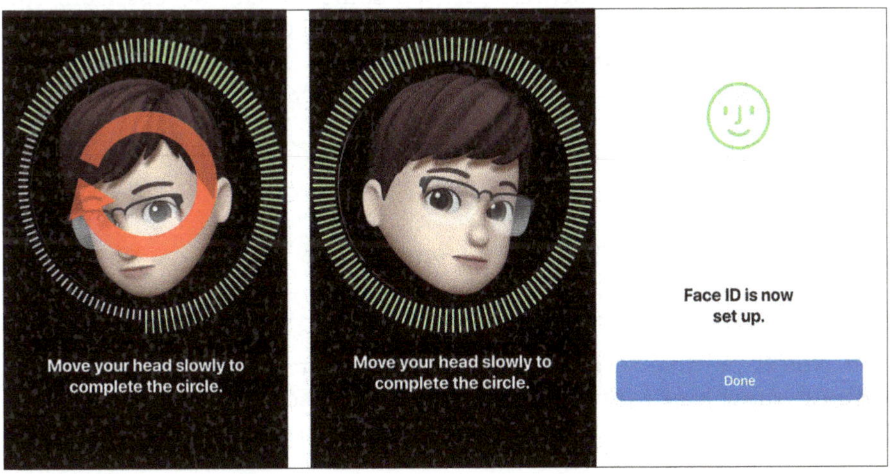

# FaceID Unlock Settings

You can use FaceID to unlock your iPhone, authenticate a purchase in the iTunes or App store, or Apple Pay. You can also use FaceID to authenticate password autofill in Safari or another app. To enable these turn on the green switches next to the settings.

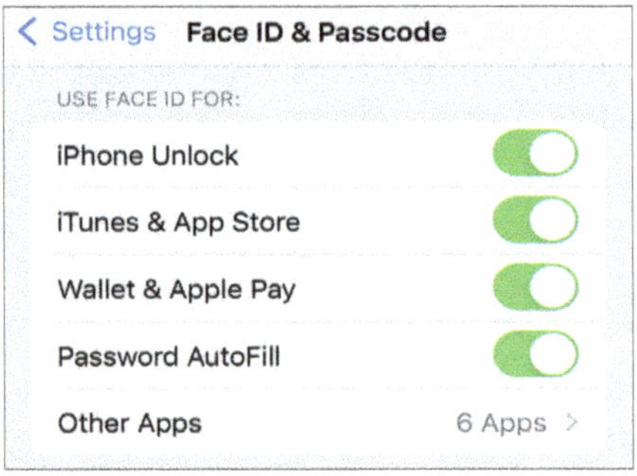


At the bottom, you can change your attention settings. Read the explanations underneath the settings for details on what they do.

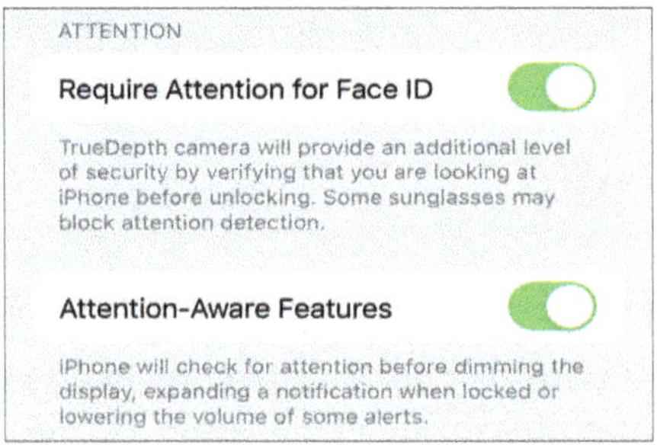


At the bottom, you can allow or disallow access to features when your iPhone is locked. This means features someone can access from the lock screen. For example, if we enabled control center, or search using the green switches below

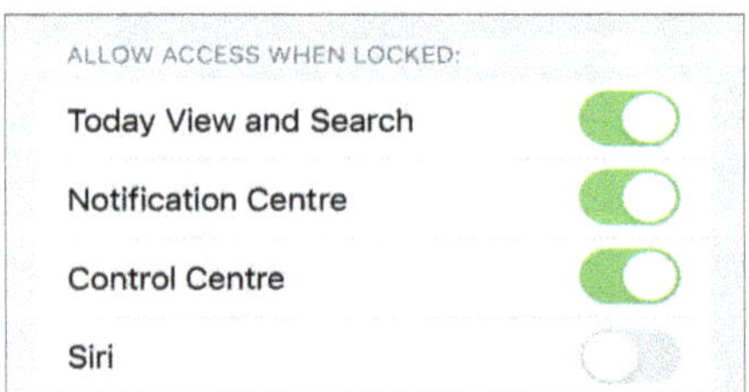


You would be able to access the control center from the lockscreen without unlocking your device, as I've done so above. You can turn these off if you want to lock down your iPhone.

## Alternate Appearance

You can set up an additional face, called an alternate appearance. This is useful if your significant other needs to use your phone, or you use your phone in situations where you need to wear a mask, heavy makeup, or sunglasses.

To set this up, first make sure you're wearing your mask, sunglasses, makeup etc, then in the 'FaceID & passcode' settings, tap 'set up an alternate appearance'.

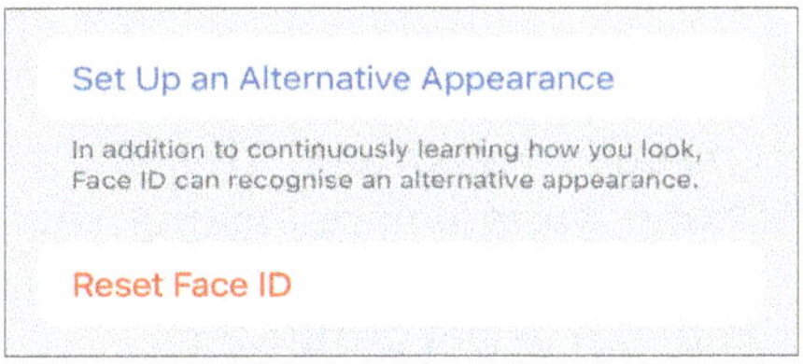


Run through the FaceID setup again.

# Passcode

You can change your passcode using the settings app. To do this, select 'FaceID & Passcode'. Enter your current passcode when prompted to unlock the settings. Scroll down to the passcode settings.

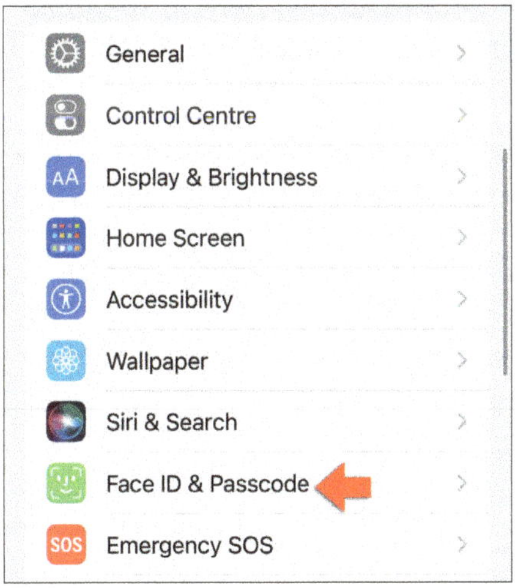


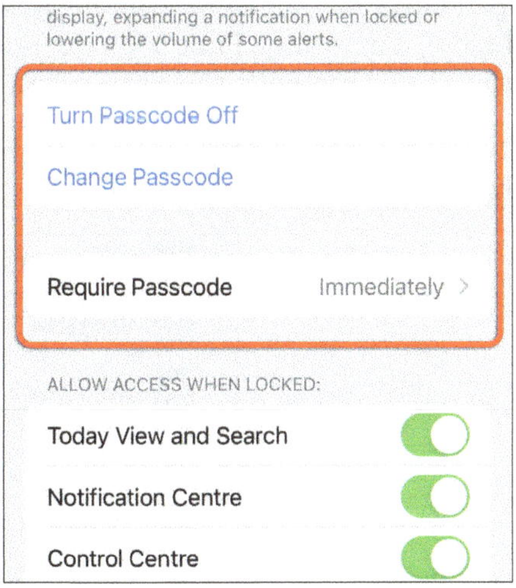


Here, you can turn off passcode. This is not always a good idea, because once unlocked, anyone can access your bank, send emails or texts in your name, or steal sensitive information. However, if you need to turn the passcode off, tap 'turn passcode off'.

To change your passcode, tap 'change passcode'. Enter your current passcode when prompted, then enter your new passcode.

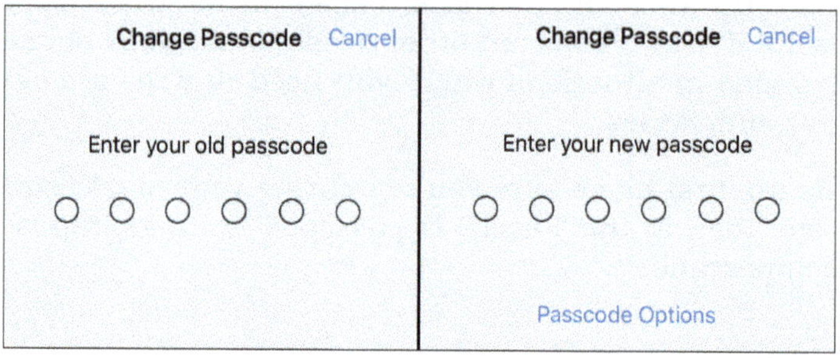


At the bottom, select 'require password'. This allows you to set a timer for how long your iPhone waits before locking your screen when you leave your device. If TouchID or FaceID is enabled, the only option immediately. If not, you can select a duration.

# Privacy

The privacy settings give you control over which apps can access certain resources such as Location Services ie your physical location, contacts, calendar, or reminders, your photos, camera, as well as other hardware devices such as microphone, bluetooth, files and folders. Apps are required to request permission to access these resources. You can grant or deny this permission. For example, here in the image below, I'm using Facebook to take and post a photograph. The first time I do this with the app, it will ask me for permission

To view privacy settings, open the settings app, then select 'privacy' from the list.

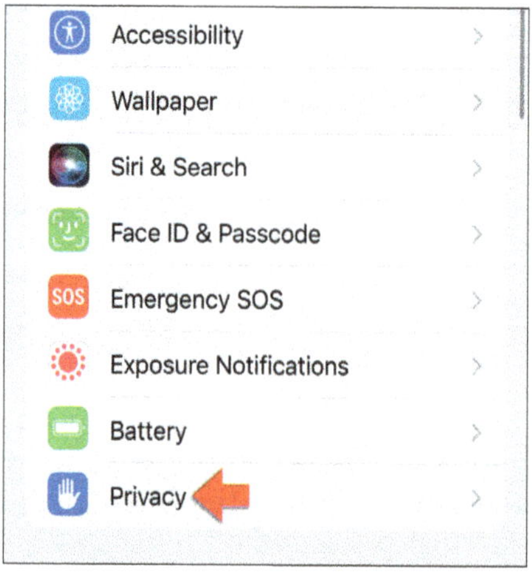

Here, you can see which apps are allowed to access different resources such as location services, tracking, contacts and so on.

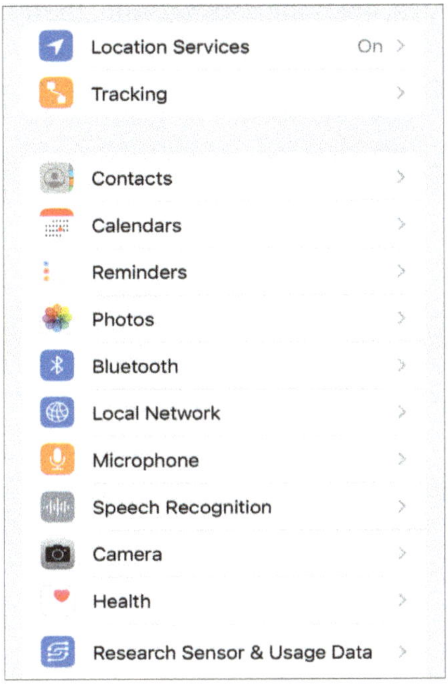


Tap on a resource to view which apps (if any) have requested access to the information. For example, if I tap on camera, I'll see all the apps that have requested permission to use the camera. Tap on the green switches to grant or revoke access.

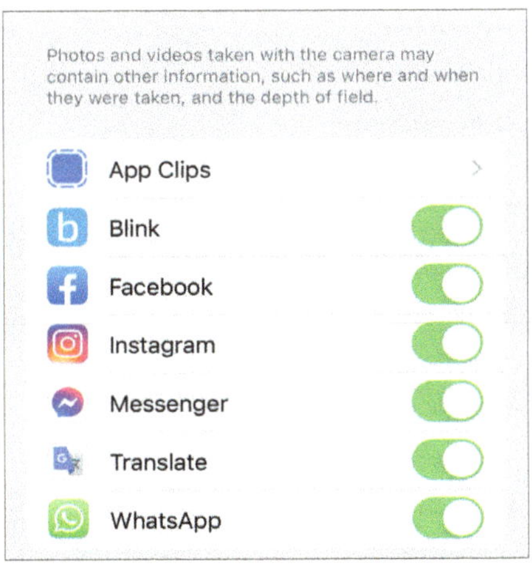


You can see I have granted Facebook access to the camera. To revoke access, tap on the switch to turn it off.

# Siri & Search

To change Siri settings, open the settings app, then select 'siri & search' from the list.

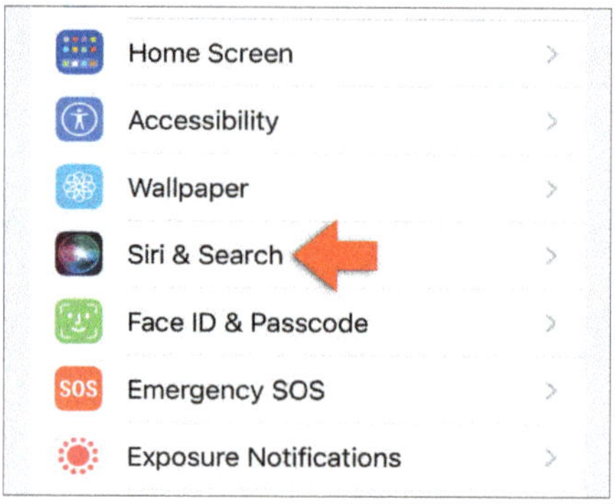


Here, you can customise Siri. Lets take a look at the settings:

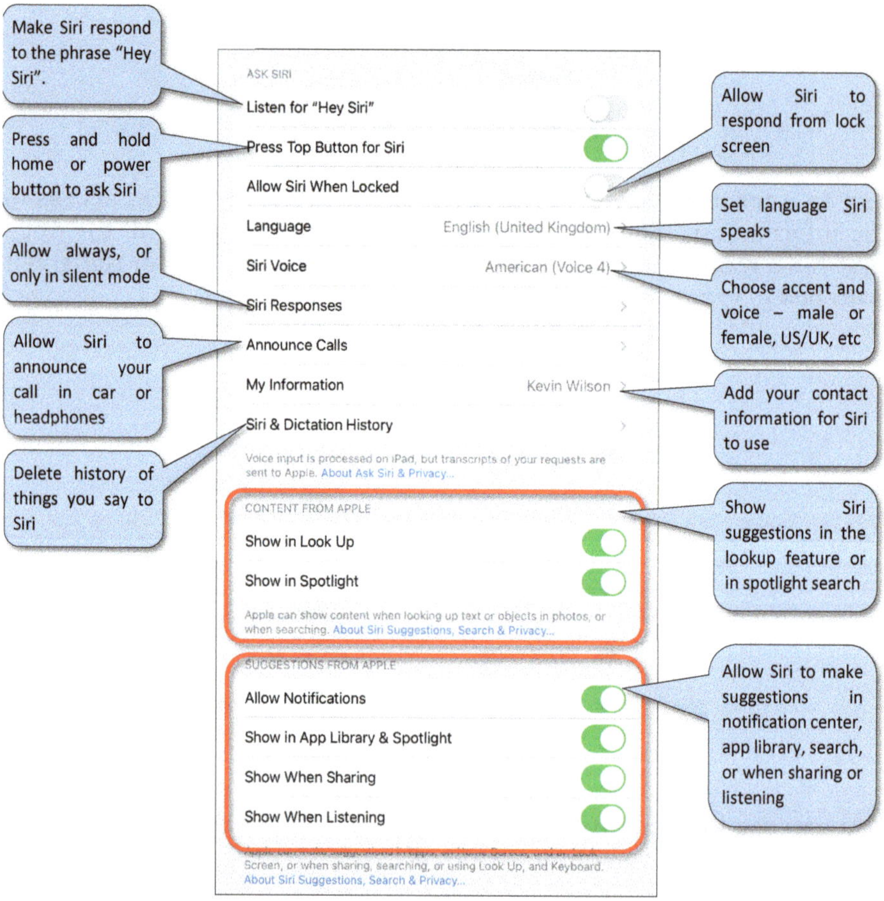

At the bottom, you can select an app. Here, you can allow Siri to learn from how you use the app, as well as allow a particular app to appear in search or Siri's suggestions.

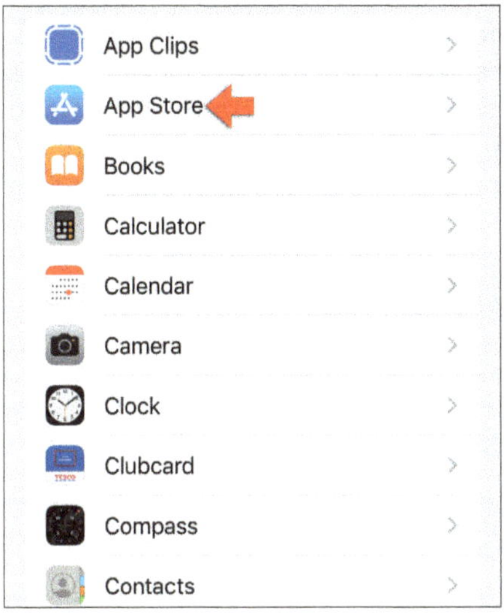


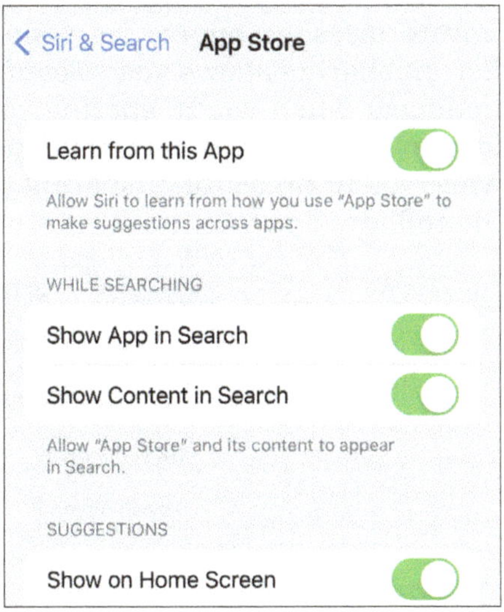


# Notifications

You can customize the Notification Center and select which apps that are allowed to display notifications in Notification Center. You can also customize notifications for individual apps. To do this, open the settings app, select 'notifications' from the list.

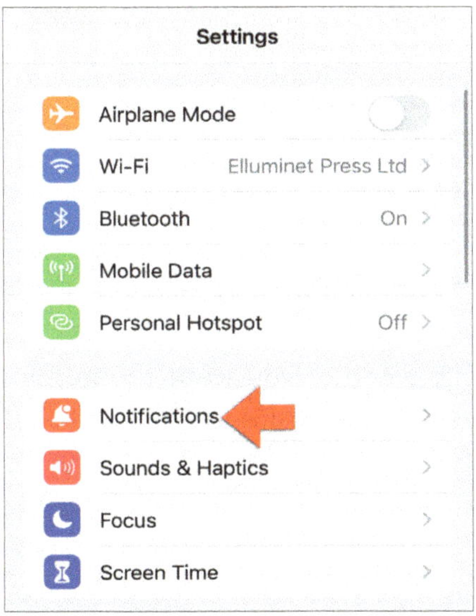

At the top, you'll see three settings. A scheduled summary is a list of notifications for each day. Show previews allows you to show a preview of a notification when the iPhone is locked or unlocked. For sensitive apps, you might want to set this to 'when unlocked', so no private message appear on your iPhone when the screen is locked. Screen sharing allows you to configure whether you want notifications to appear when you're sharing your screen or using SharePlay. Good idea to set this to 'notifications off' to prevent notifications appearing while you're presenting, sharing your screen, or watching together on SharePlay.

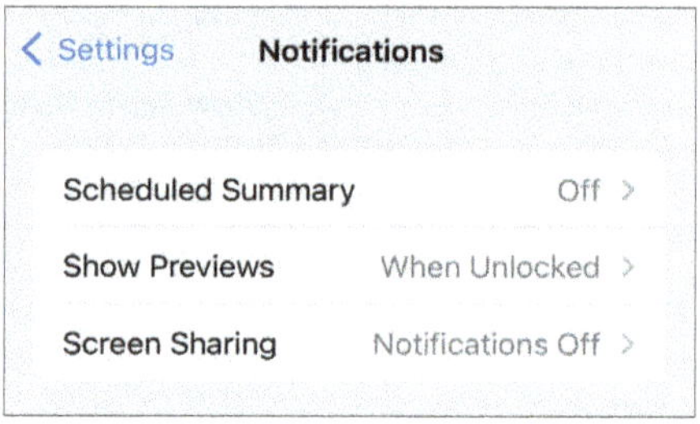


Siri Suggestions allows you to choose which apps Siri is allowed to suggest on the lock screen.

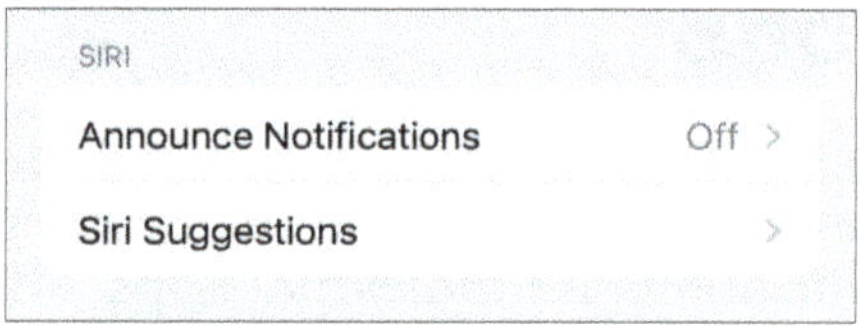


You can change the notification style of a particular app. To do this tap on the app in the 'notification style' section.

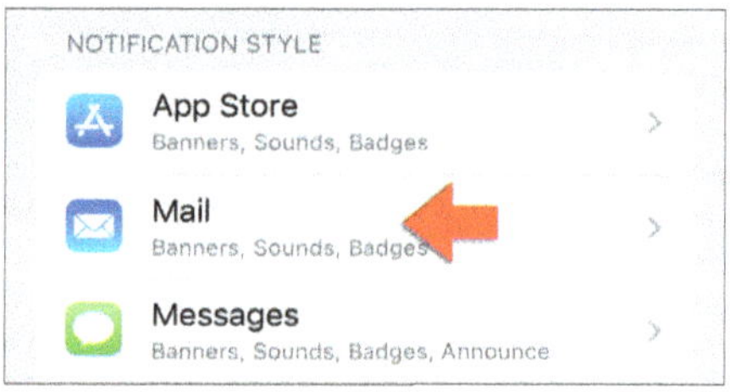


Here, you can specify whether you want the notification to appear for this app or not. To silence this app, turn off 'allow notifications'.

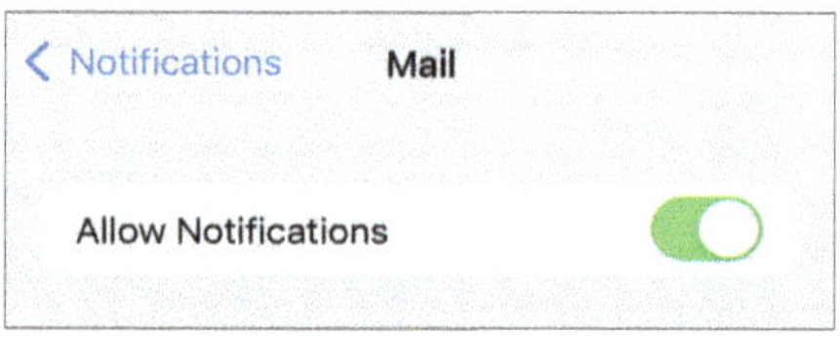

Further down, you can select where you want the alerts for this app to appear: lock screen, notification center, or a banner at the top of the screen.

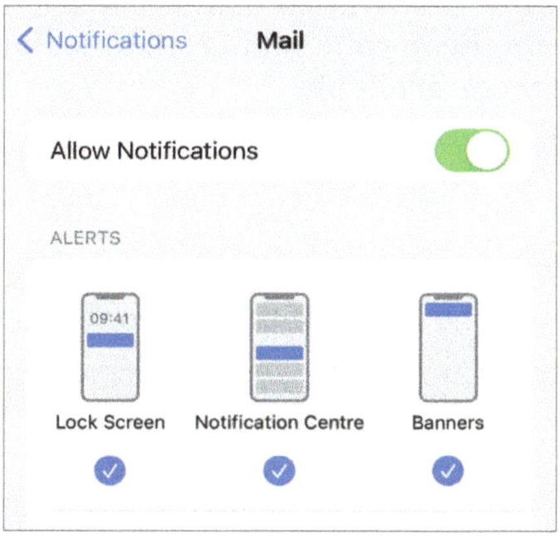


If you want the notifications to stay on your lock screen all the time, change 'banner style' to persistent. If you want the notification to popup, alert you, then disappear, change 'banner style' to temporary

Badges are the little indicators on app icons.

If you want to change the sound, tap sound, then select a sound from the options.

At the bottom, you can allow previews of your message when the phone is locked or unlocked.

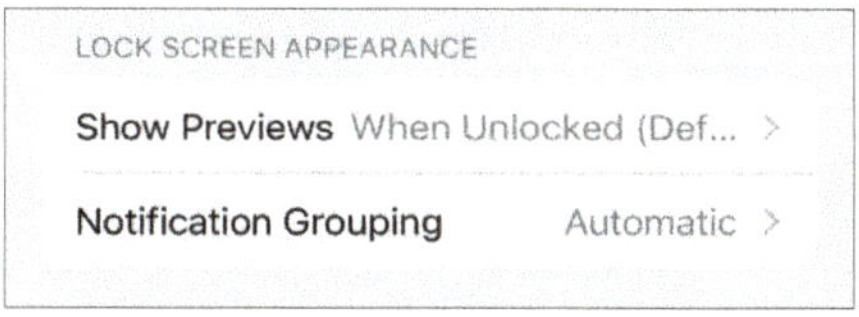


You can also group notifications by app, or allow your phone to automatically group them

# Connecting to the Internet

You can connect your iPhone to the internet using WiFi or Cellular Data. WiFi is often the best way to connect to the internet and won't use your cellular data. Keep your cellular data for when you're out and there is no WiFi network available.

## WiFi

To locate nearby WiFi networks, open the settings app. Select 'WiFi' from the list, then tap the name of the network you want to join.

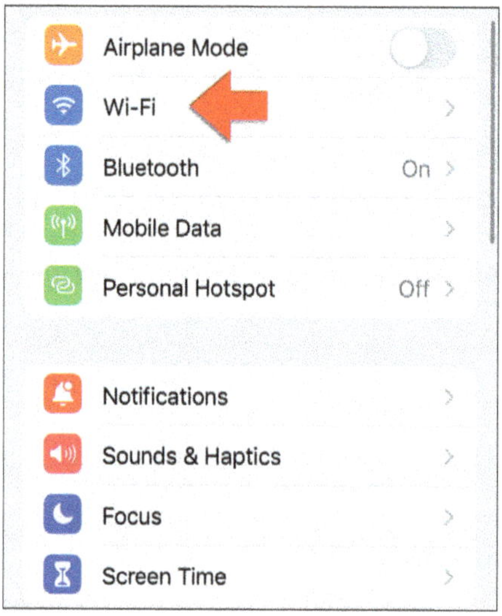


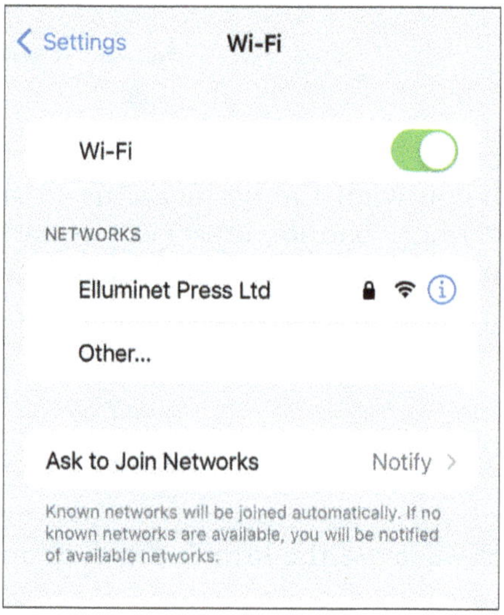


Enter the WiFi password or network key.

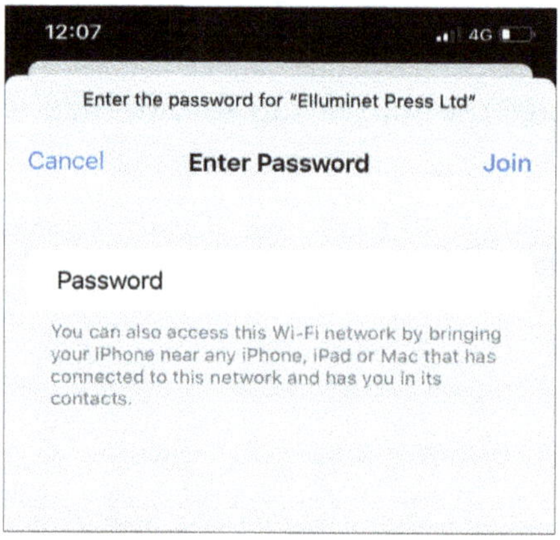


Once you have done that tap 'join'.

For your home WiFi, the network key or password, is usually printed on the back of your router.

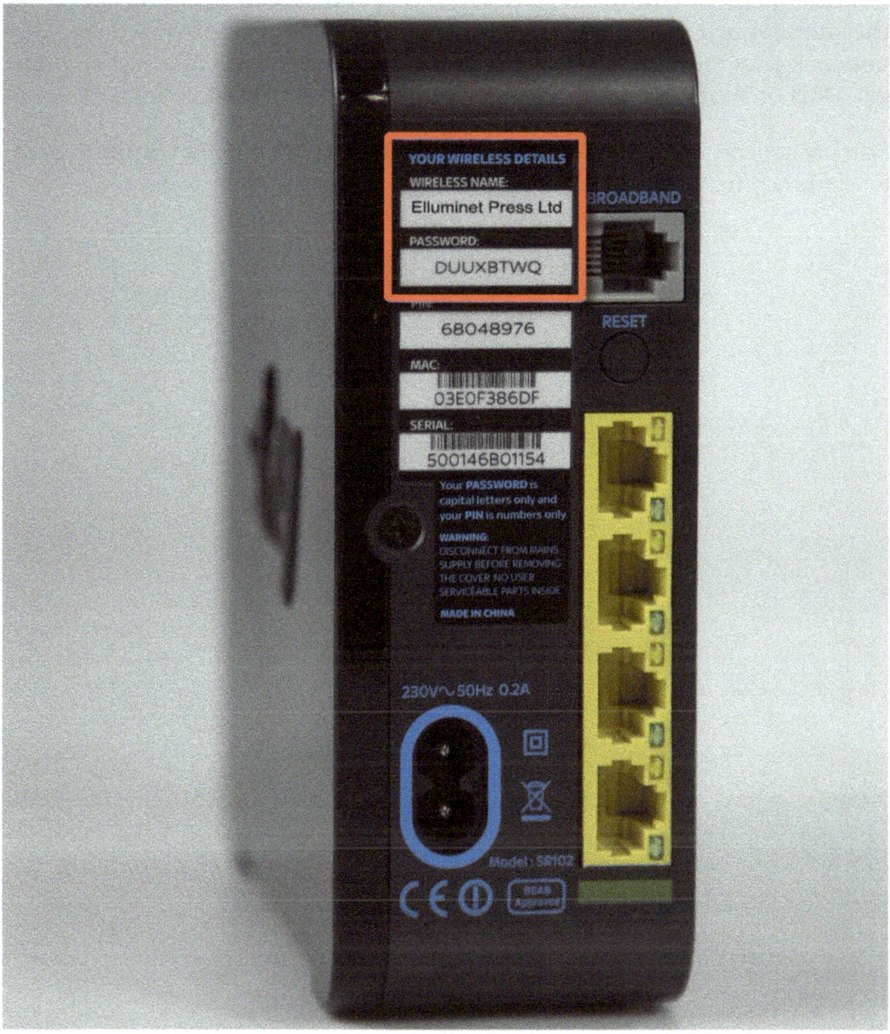


The network name is sometimes called an SSID.

Use the same procedure if you are on a public hotspot such as in a cafe, library, hotel, airport and so on. You'll need to find the network key if they have one. Some are open networks and you can just connect.

When using public hotspots, keep in mind that most of them don't encrypt the data you send over the internet and aren't secure. So don't start checking your online banking account or shop online while using an unsecured connection, as anyone who is on the public WiFi hotspot can potentially gain access to anything you do.

## Cellular Data

Cellular or Mobile data is used when you connect to the internet using the mobile/cell phone network (eg 4G or 5G) and is provided by your network provider. When you take out your phone contract, you'll often get 1GB or more of 'data'. This is your mobile or cellular data.

To change the settings, open the settings app, then select 'mobile data' or 'cellular' from the list.

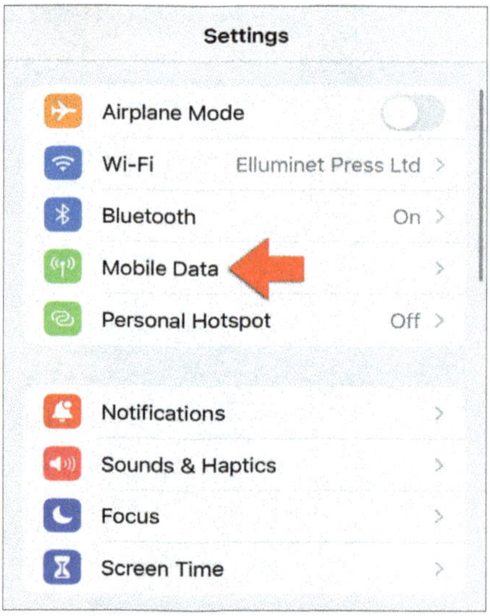


Here, you can turn mobile data on or off, as well as your mobile data options for roaming. Data roaming allows you to use your phone's mobile data while you're overseas. You are said to be roaming the moment your phone connects to an overseas network.

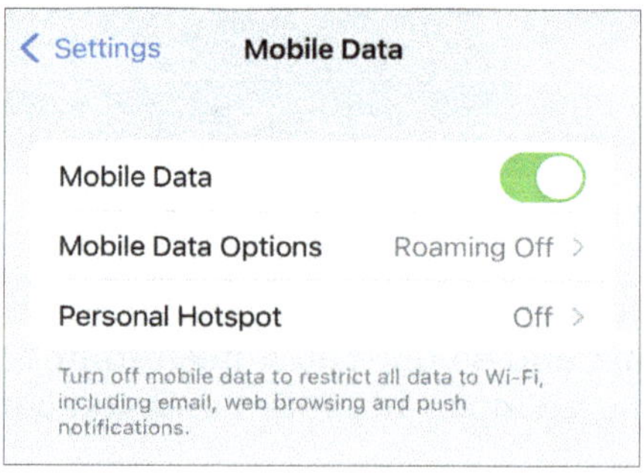


Data roaming can be costly so you are advised to turn this feature off.

A personal hotspot allows you to share your data connection with another device such as your Mac.

Underneath, you'll see your network provider details. WiFi calling allows you make and receive calls using WiFi, if there isn't cellular/ mobile network coverage in a particular area. Some providers don't support this feature. Calls on other devices, allows you to answer a call on your Mac or iPad if they're signed in with the same Apple ID and are close-by. Under 'mobile data network', you can add specific server addresses and passwords to access services such as SMS and mobile data settings provided by your network provider. SIM PIN allows you to lock your SIM card with a PIN number.

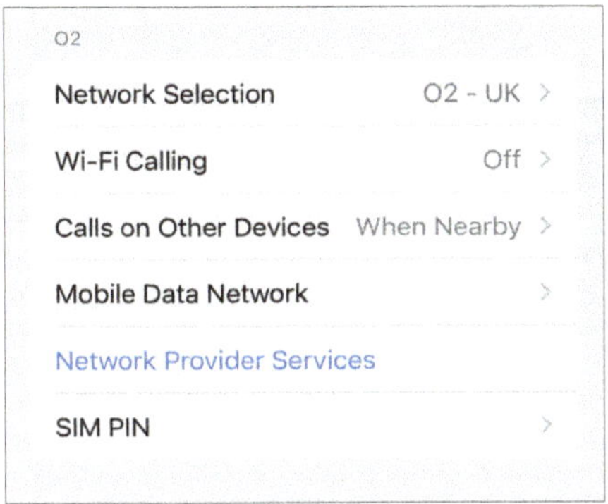


Under the 'mobile data' section, you'll see a list of apps that have used the mobile data connection. You'll also see how much data has been used.

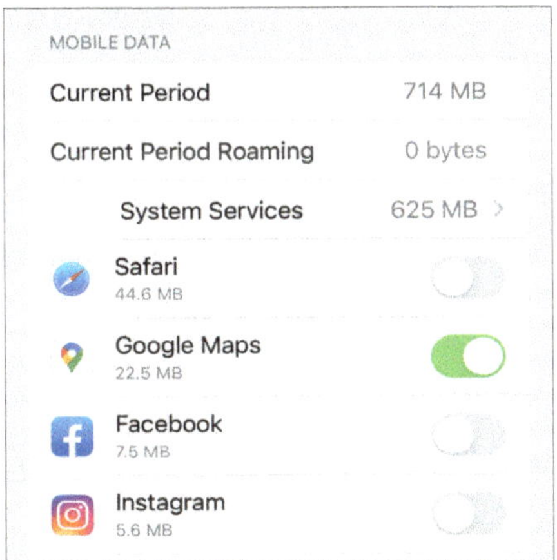


You can stop apps using the data. To do this, just turn off the switch next to the app name. This is useful if you want to limit the amount of mobile data and only allow certain apps such as messages, or email to access your mobile data. If you turn the app off, the app will only use WiFi to connect to the internet.

## VPNs

If you're really concerned about security or use your devices on public hotspots for work, then you should consider a VPN or Virtual Private Network. A VPN encrypts all the data you send and receive over a network. There are a few good ones to choose from, some have a free option with a limited amount of data and others you pay a subscription.

You can download an app from the app store to automatically configure the VPN. Take a look at www.tunnelbear.com, windscribe.com & speedify.com

To set one up manually, open the settings app then select 'general' from the list. Tap 'VPN and device management'.

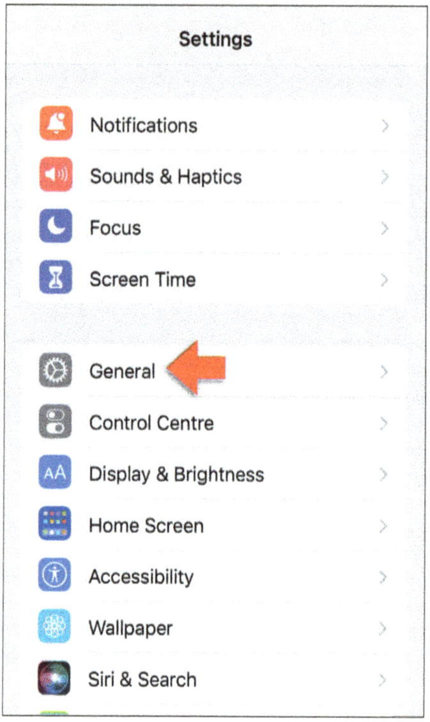


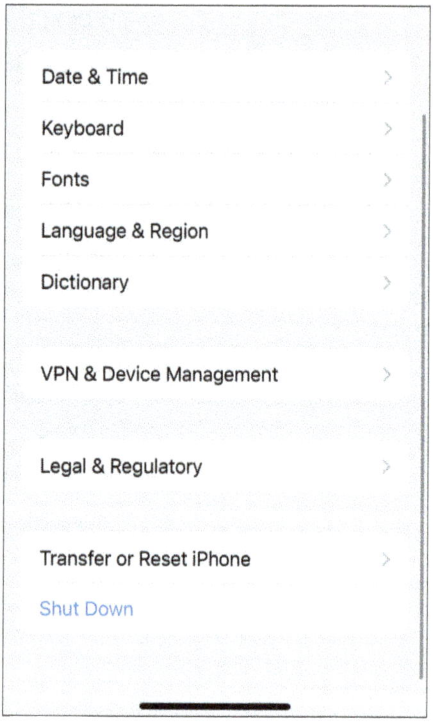


Tap 'VPN'.

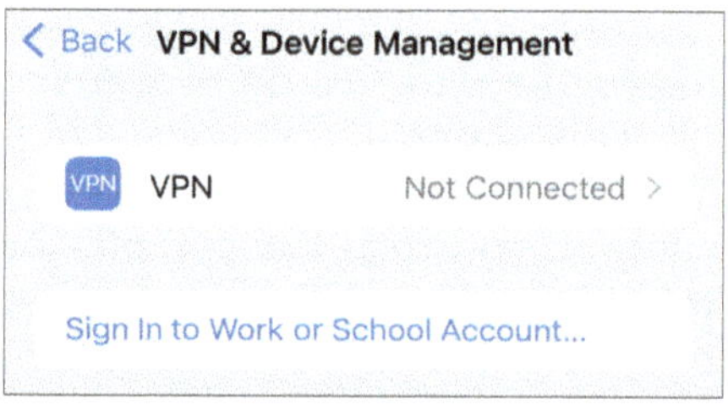

Enter the connection details. You can get these from your VPN provider, school, college or work.

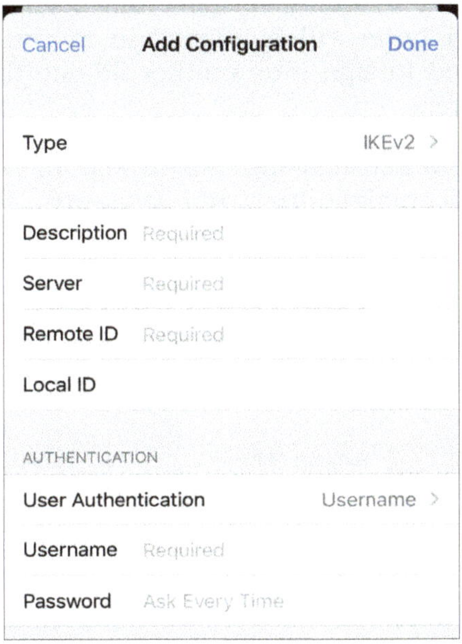


## School/Work Accounts

If your school/college or work provides you with an account, open the settings app, then select 'general' from the list on the left. Tap 'VPN and device management'. Tap 'sign in to work or school account', then enter your account email address and password.

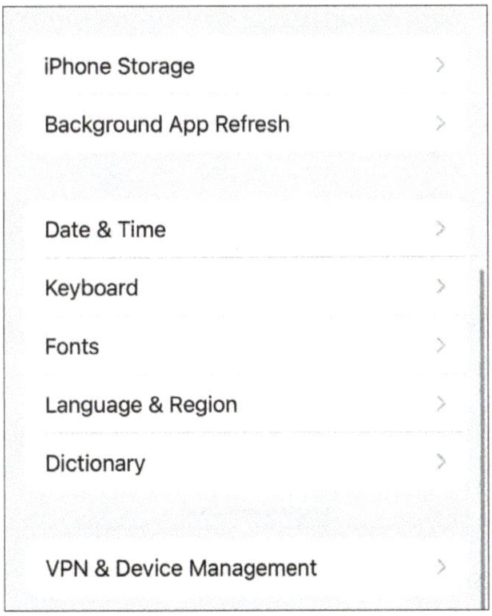


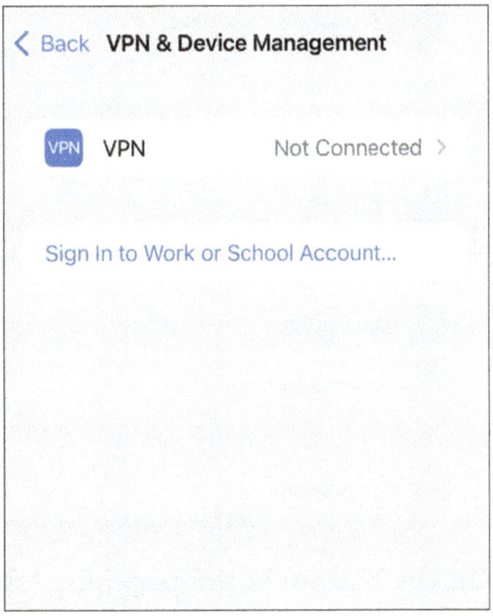

# iCloud

If you've set up your iPhone from new and been through the initial setup, then your iPhone will be signed in to your iCloud account. However if you need to sign into another iPhone then you can do so from the settings app.

To **sign in**, open your settings app, tap on 'sign in to your iPhone' then enter your Apple ID email address and password. Tap 'sign in'.

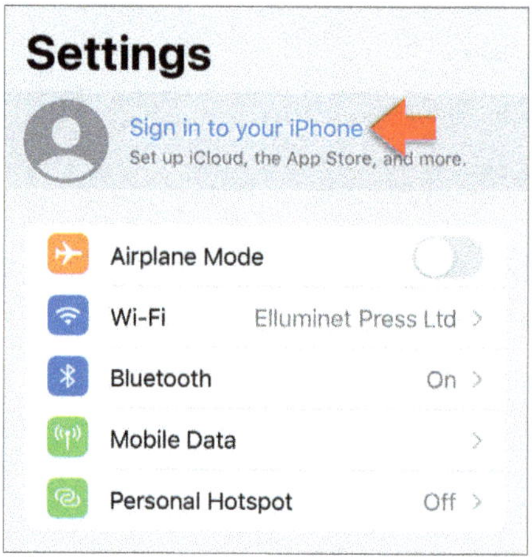


To **sign out**, open your settings app, tap on your Apple ID at the top.

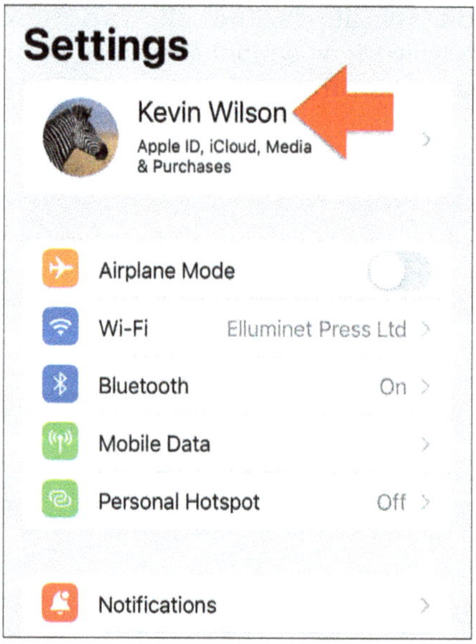


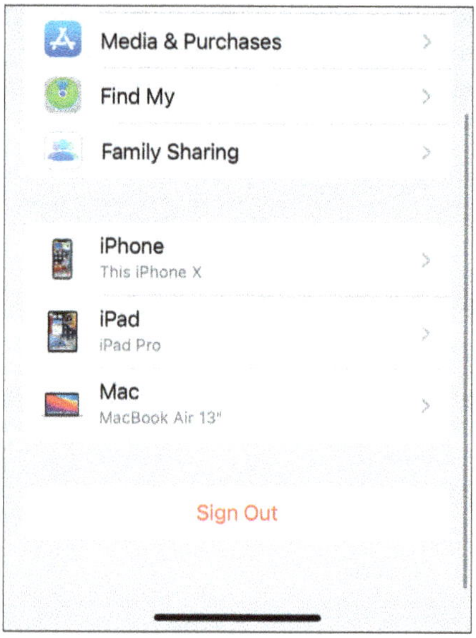


On the bottom of the page, tap 'sign out'.

## Settings

Once you've signed into your iCloud account, you'll see some settings appear.

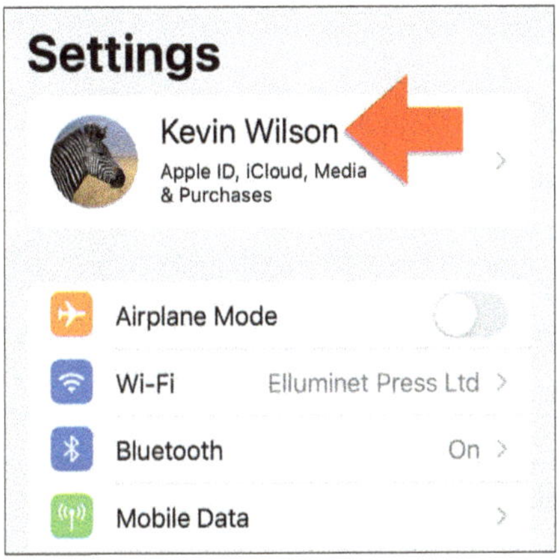


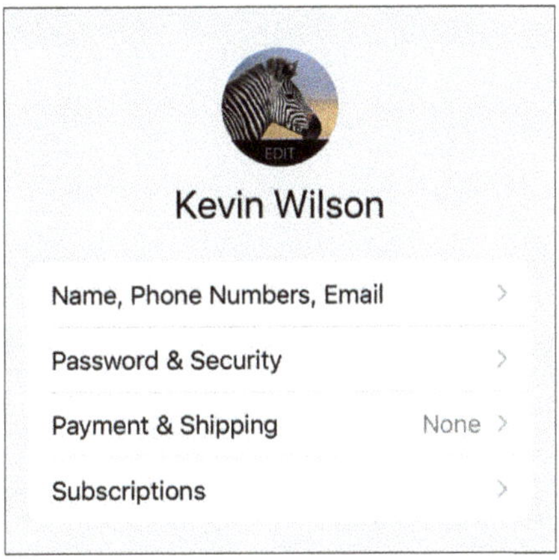


To change your name, tap 'name, phone numbers, email', add phone numbers or email addresses people use to contact you. Just tap 'edit' next to the section you want to change.

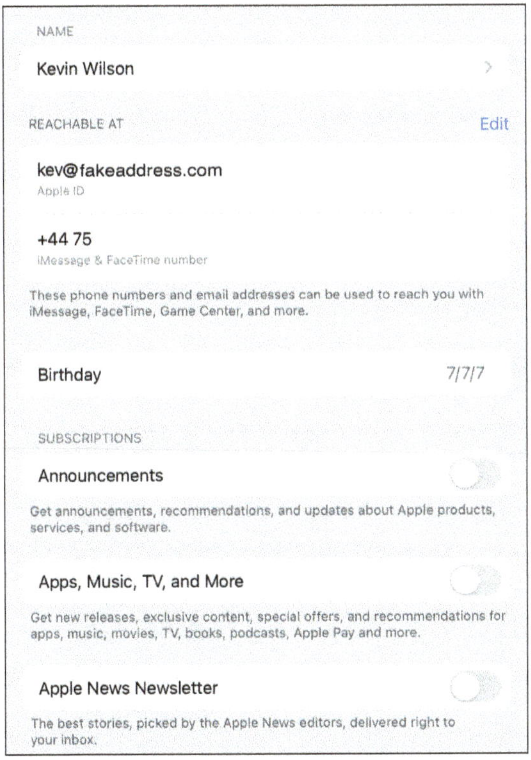

Selecting 'password & security', you can change your iCloud password, as well as enable/disable 2 factor authentication. If you forgot your iCloud password, go to `iforgot.apple.com` then follow the instructions on screen.

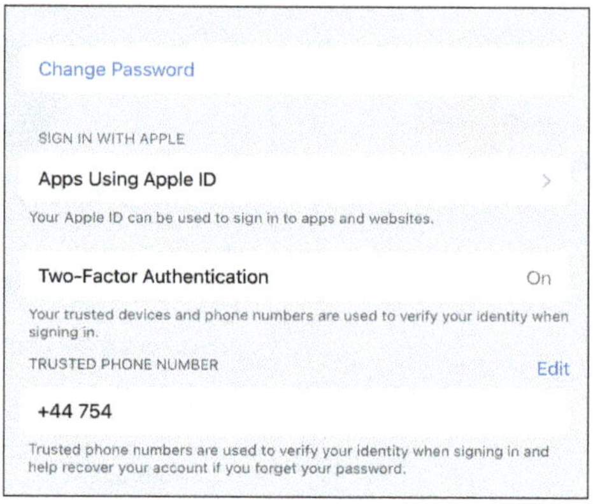


Under 'payment & shipping', you can add apple pay and credit cards to buy things online, in the app store, apple music, apple TV, etc. Tap 'add payment method' to add a new card, or tap 'apple pay' to edit apple pay settings.

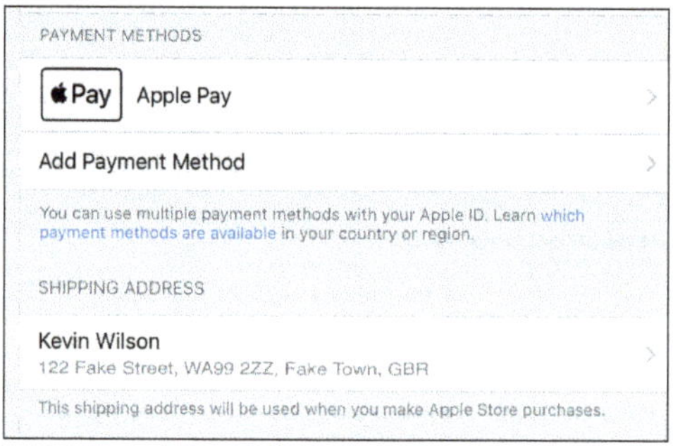


Under subscriptions, you can manage subscriptions to apple music, apple one, iCloud+ and so on.

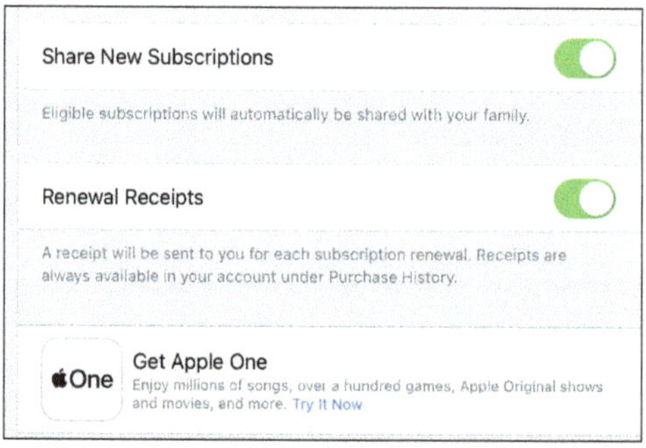

## iCloud Sync

From the settings app, select your Apple ID, then tap 'icloud'.

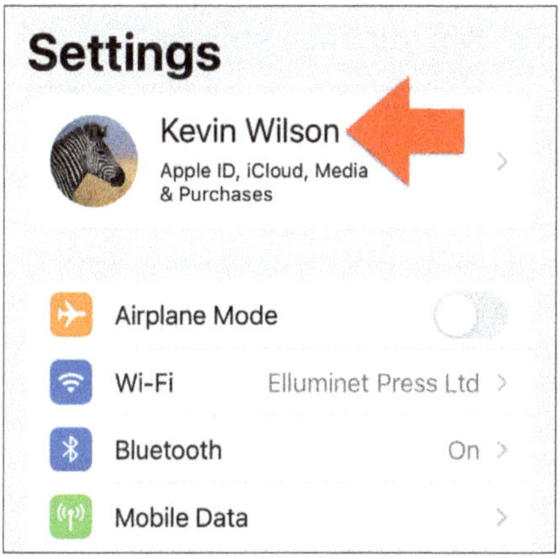


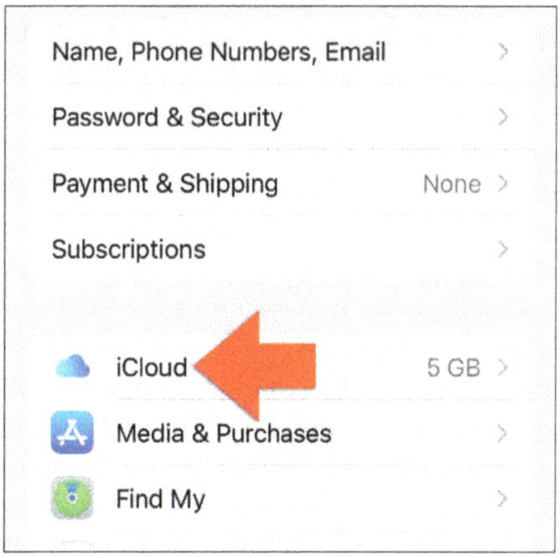


Here, you'll see how much space you've used on your iCloud.

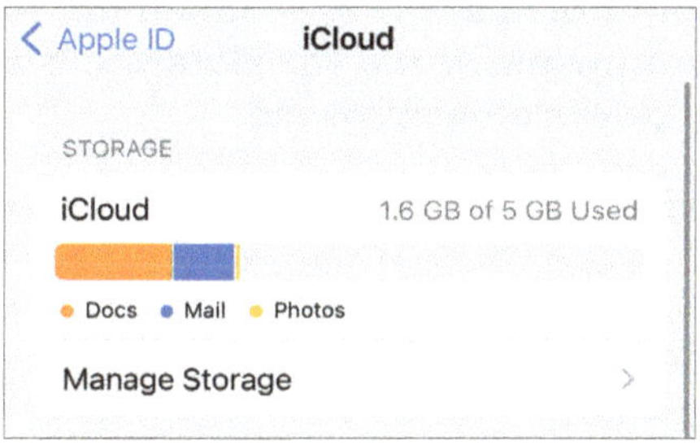


Underneath, you can select which apps you want to synchronise across all your devices.

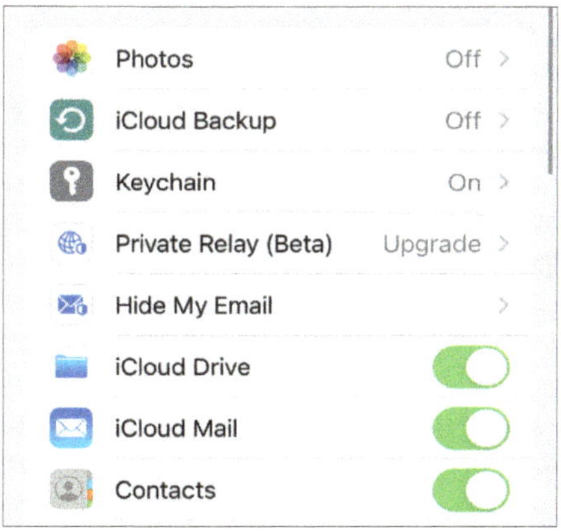


Click the switch on the right to turn on and off.

## Storage Management

From the settings app, select your Apple ID, then click 'icloud'. You'll see a chart at the top of the screen giving you a breakdown of what is taking up space on your iCloud storage. Tap 'manage storage'

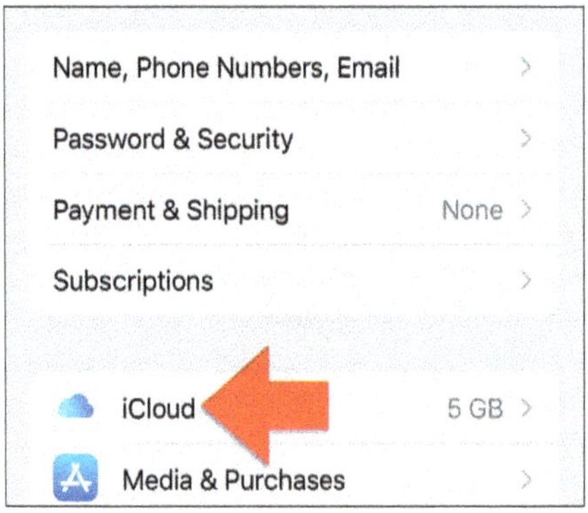


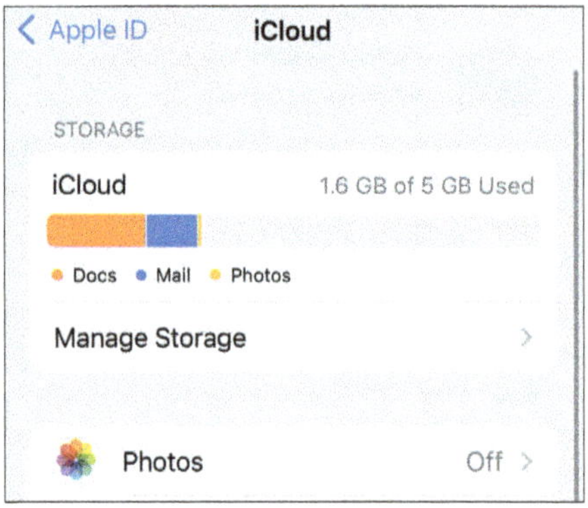


Here, you'll see a more detailed breakdown of the apps using storage on iCloud and the amount of space they've taken up. Now the data stored on iCloud isn't the app itself, it's the data such as your messages, photos you've taken, device backups etc.

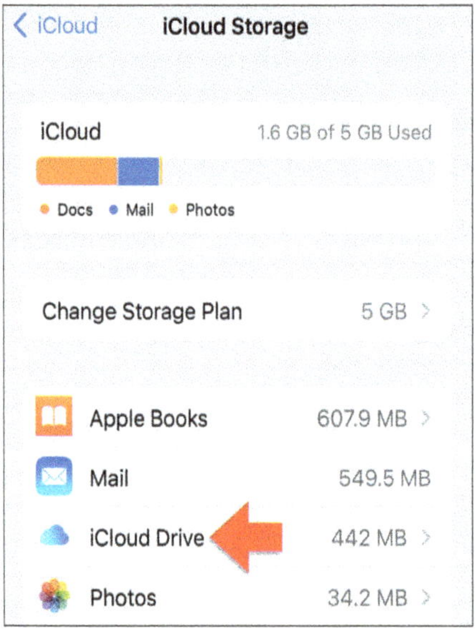


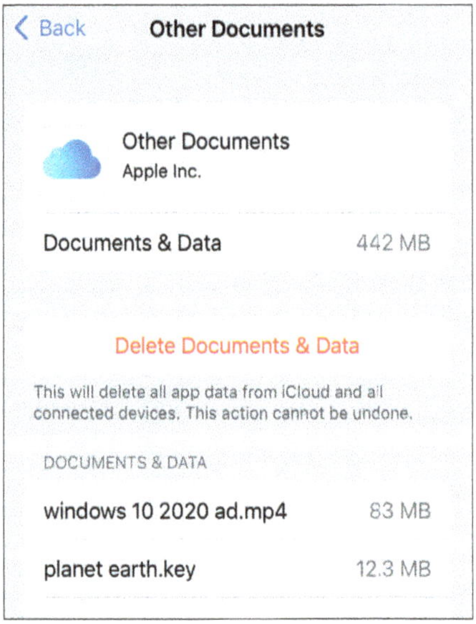


Tap on the app to view details and delete any data. This is useful if your iCloud storage is running low.

Tap 'change storage plan' if you need more than 5GB of iCloud storage. There is a charge for larger storage plans.

## Forgot Password

If you've forgotten your iCloud password, you can attempt to recover it.

On your iPhone or another computer, open your web browser and navigate to

`iforgot.apple.com`

Enter your Apple ID email address, click 'continue'.

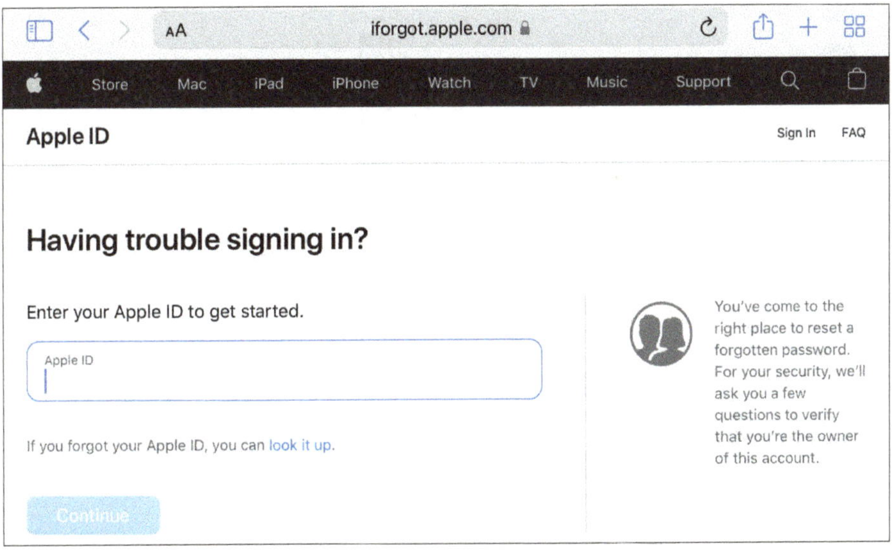


Enter your phone number if prompted, click 'continue'.

You'll receive a 'reset password' prompt on one of your Apple devices, such as your iPhone, iPhone or Mac. In this example, this is on my iPhone. Tap 'allow' on the prompt.

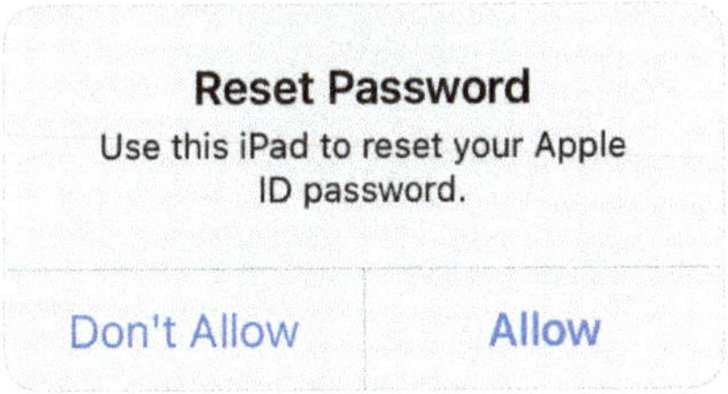

Run through the instructions. Then enter a new password when prompted.

Tap 'next'.

# Adding Email Accounts

If you have multiple email accounts, perhaps one for home, work, school etc, you can add them all to the email app. To do this, tap the settings app icon on your home screen. Scroll down to 'mail', then tap on 'accounts'.

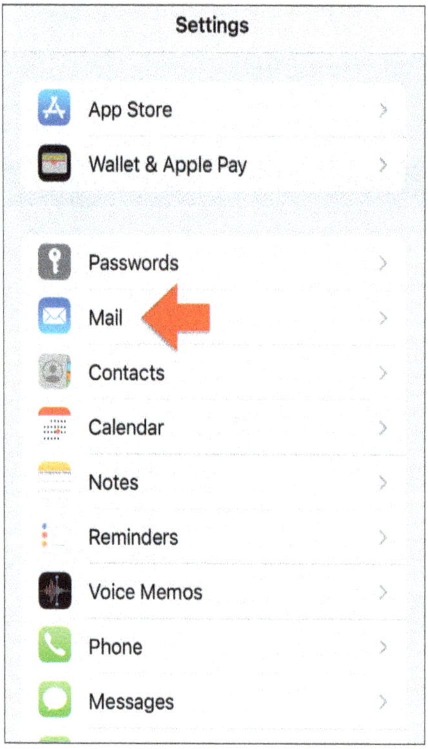


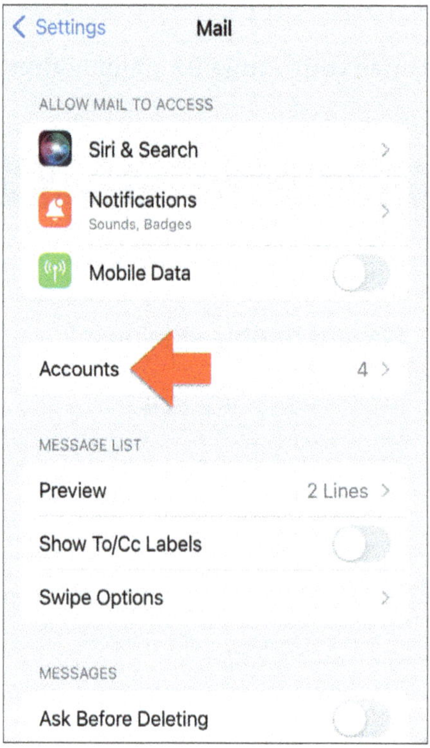


Under the 'accounts' section, tap 'add account'.

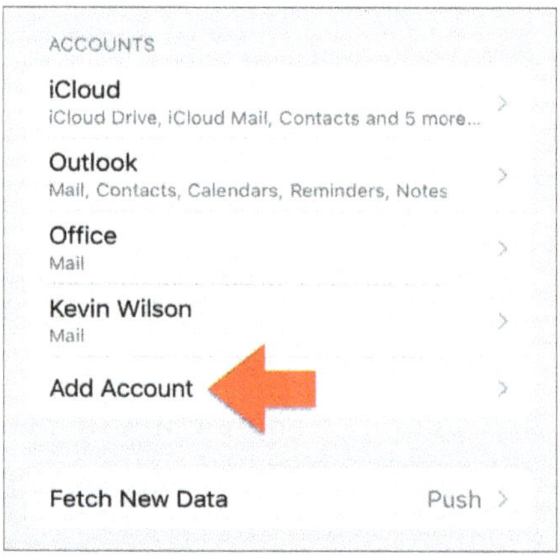

Tap the type of account you want to add. If you have a Yahoo account, tap 'yahoo', if you have a Google/GMail account, tap 'google', or a Hotmail or Microsoft Account, tap 'outlook.com'. In this example I am going to add a Microsoft Account. So I'd tap on 'outlook.com'.

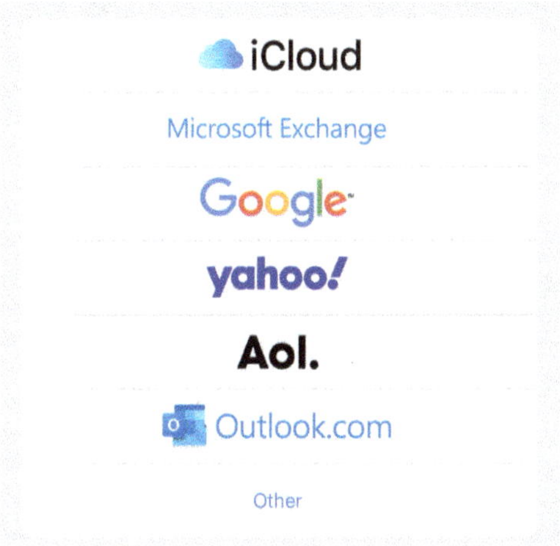


In the box that appears, enter your account email address, tap 'next', then your password. Tap 'next'.

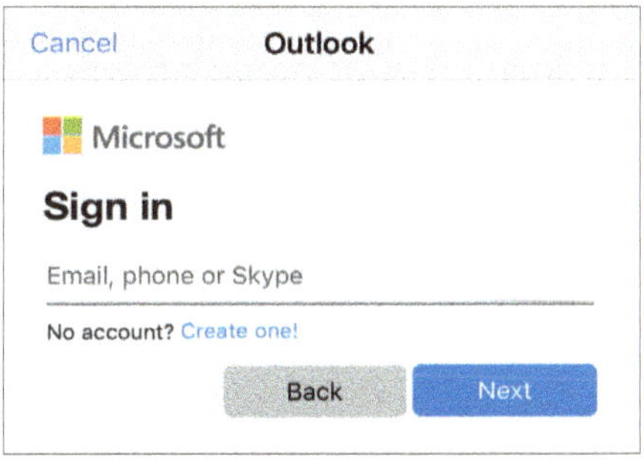


Select 'yes' to the permission confirmation, to allow your iPhone to access your email account.

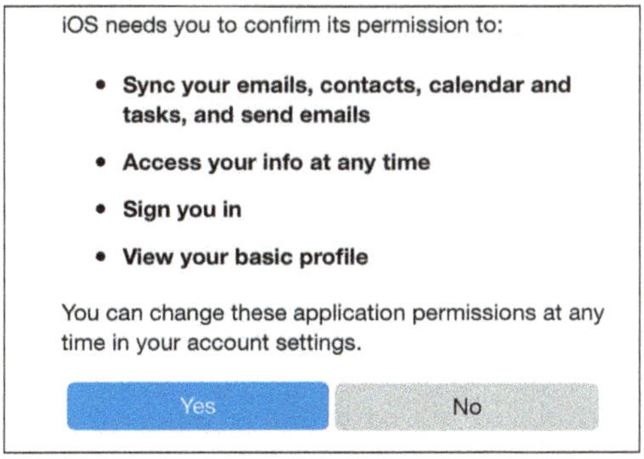

Select what you want your iPhone to sync from the mail server. You can copy email, contacts, your calendar and any reminders onto your iPhone by turning all the toggle switches to green, as shown below.

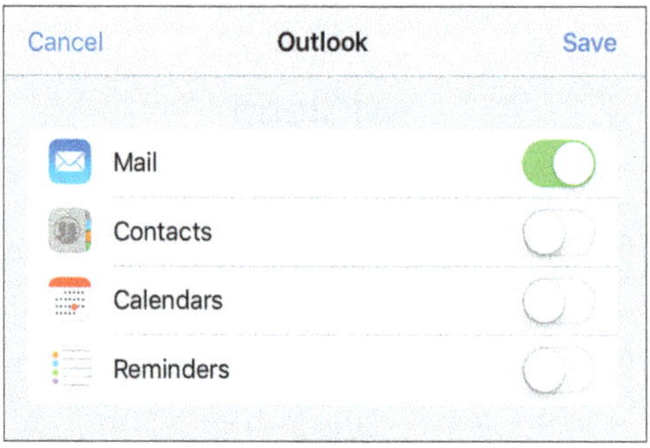


Tap 'Save'.

# Add Social Media Accounts

You can add your Facebook and Twitter accounts to your iPhone. The easiest way to do this is to go to the App Store and download the app for Facebook, Instagram, Twitter, and whatever else you use.

Tap on the 'app store' icon on your home screen.

Tap 'search' on the bottom right. In the search field on the top right type 'facebook'.

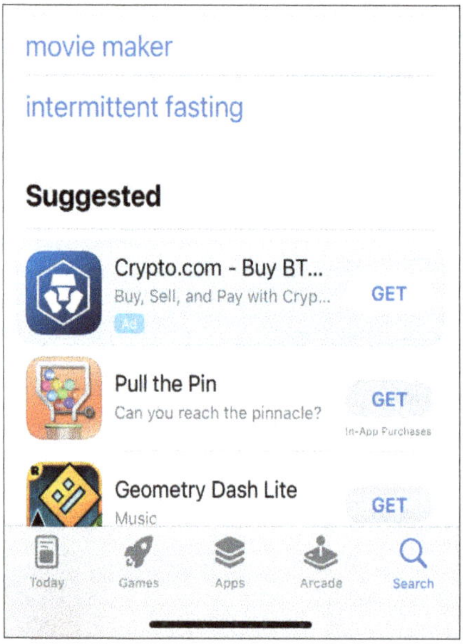


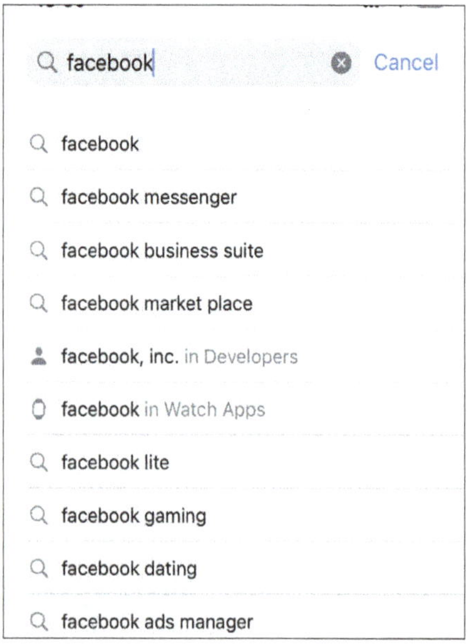

Tap 'get', next to the Facebook icon to download it. This icon might also look like a cloud if you have downloaded it before on another device, such as an iPad or iPhone.

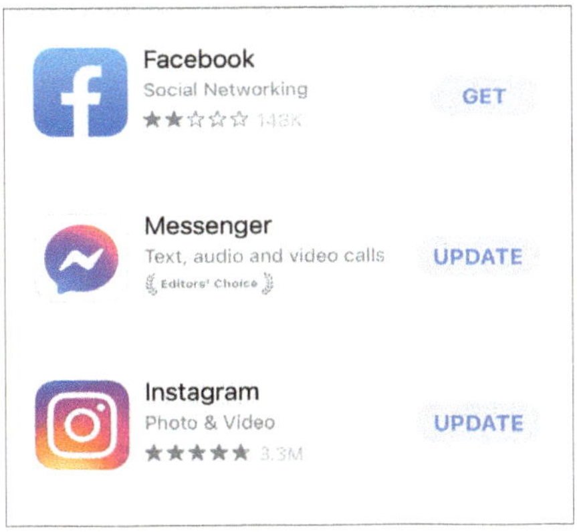


Once the app has downloaded, go back to the home screen, then tap the Facebook icon.

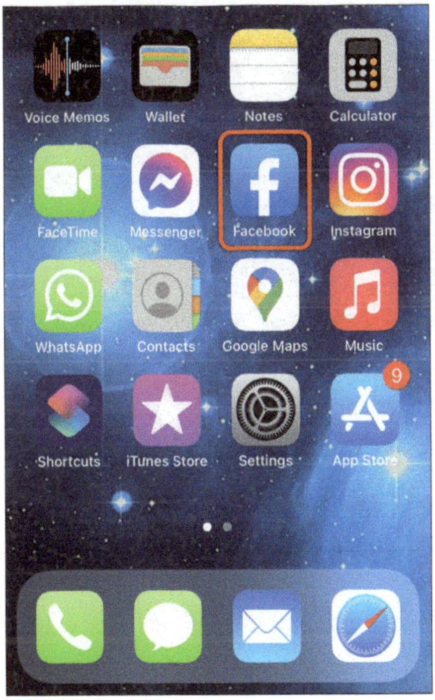

You can now sign in with your Facebook username and password.

Use the same procedure to setup any other social media apps you want to use.

# Connecting Devices

You can connect various devices to your iPhone most of which use bluetooth to connect wirelessly.

## Bluetooth

You can pair bluetooth keyboards, headphones, and bluetooth capable hardware in some cars.

To pair a device, first put the device into pairing mode. You'll need to refer to the device's instructions to find specific details on how to do this. On most devices, press and hold the pairing button until the status light starts flashing. This means the device is ready to be paired with your iPhone.

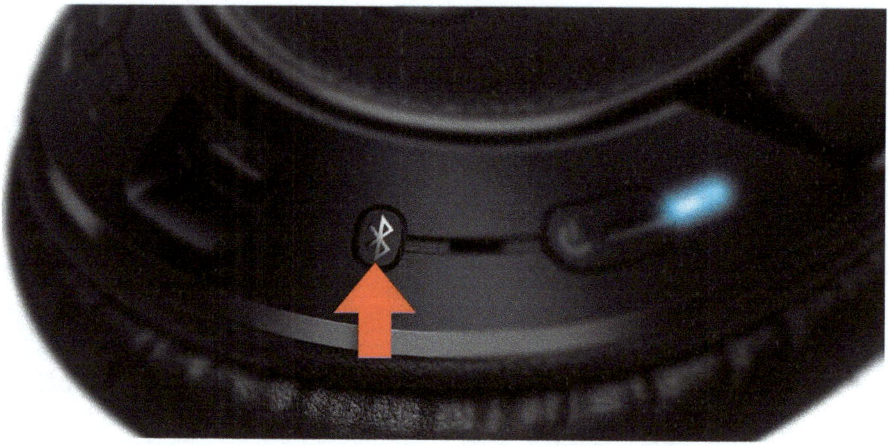

On your iPhone, open the settings app. From the settings app, select 'bluetooth'.

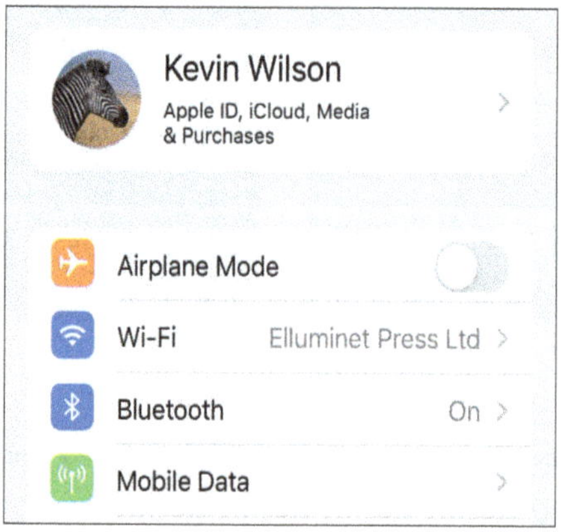

Turn it on, if it isn't already.

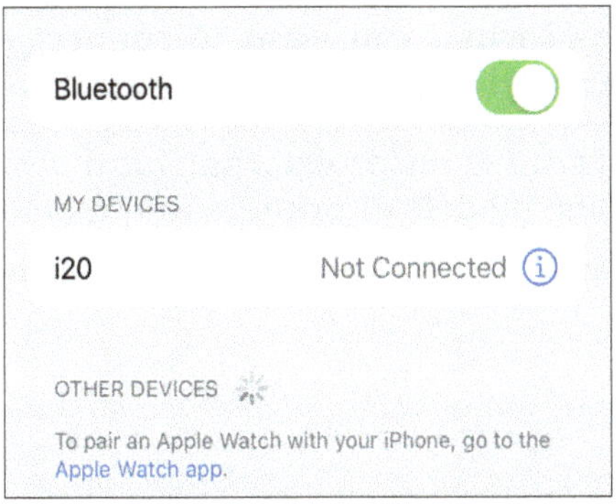


Your iPhone will scan for devices nearby. You'll need to give it a few seconds to work. Any devices found will be listed. Tap on the device in the list to pair it.

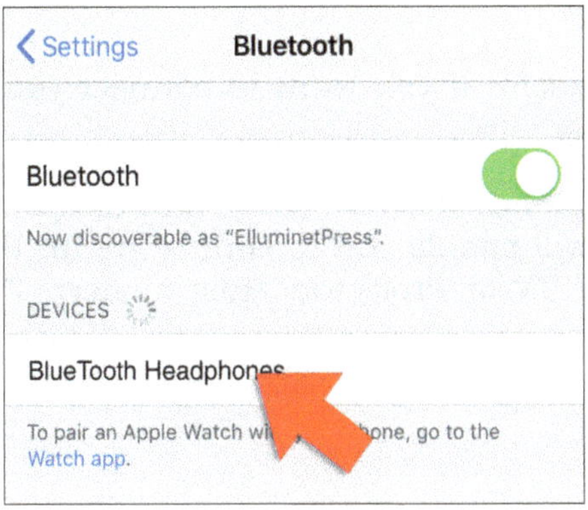


Some devices require a PIN code, enter it if prompted. Refer to the device's instructions to find out what the PIN code is. On most devices the default PIN is 0000, 1111 or 1234, but not always.

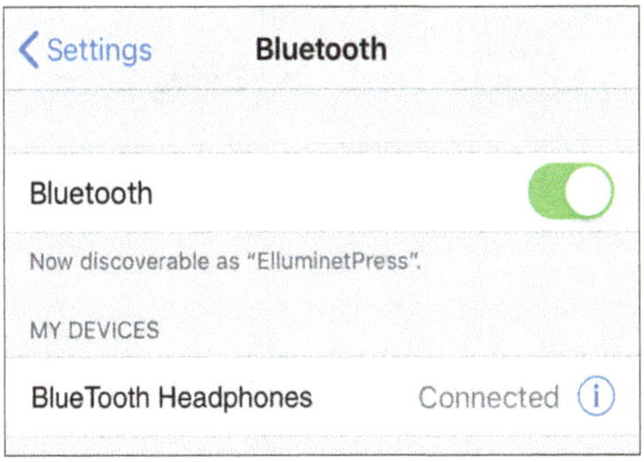


To remove a device, tap the 'i' info icon, then tap 'forget this device'.

## USB

These come in useful when you want to connect something to your iPhone and most peripherals, if they are not wireless, connect via USB.

These can be keyboards, mice, external hard drives, USB memory sticks, cameras, some models of printers and memory card readers.

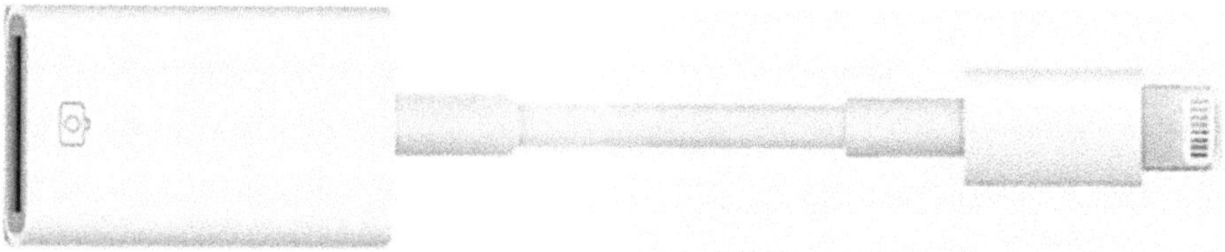

For standard iPhones you'll need one with the lightning plug,

## Video

AV Adapters are useful if you want to connect your iPhone to a TV, Monitor or Projector.

You can buy a small adapter that plugs into the port on the bottom of your iPhone and will enable you to connect to an HDMI or DVI/VGA connector on your TV or Projector. Most modern TVs and Projectors are HDMI.

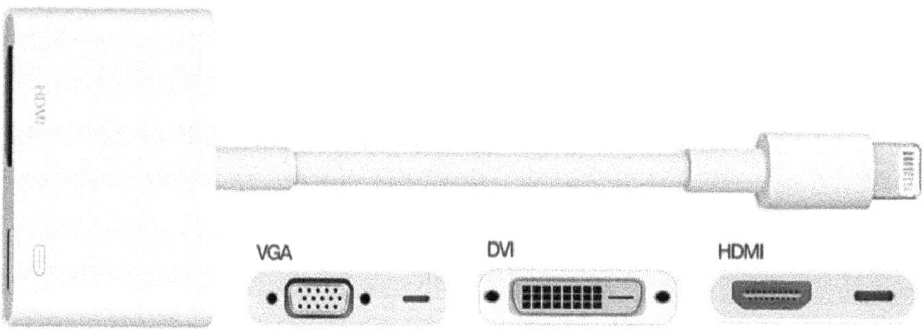


For standard iPhones you'll need one with the lightning plug.

# Connecting to a Computer

Your iPhone lightning cable connects to the port on the bottom of your iPhone.

The other end of the cable can be plugged into a PC or Mac to allow you to load on music, photos, apps etc.

# Apple Pay

Apple Pay allows you to keep digital copies of your bank cards, and lets you pay for things using your iPhone or iPhone. You can use this feature on an iPhone but it is more convenient with an iPhone.

*Apple Pay will run on iPhone SE, iPhone 6, iPhone 6 Plus, and later as well as, iPhone Pro, iPhone Air 2, iPhone mini 3, and later.*

## Setup

Make sure your bank supports Apple Pay. If so, go to your settings app then scroll down the left hand side and tap 'wallet & apple pay'. Then tap 'add credit or debit card' link. Tap 'continue' on the apple pay popup.

Now, in the 'add card' window, if you already have a credit/debit card registered with your Apple ID, then apple pay will ask you to add this one.

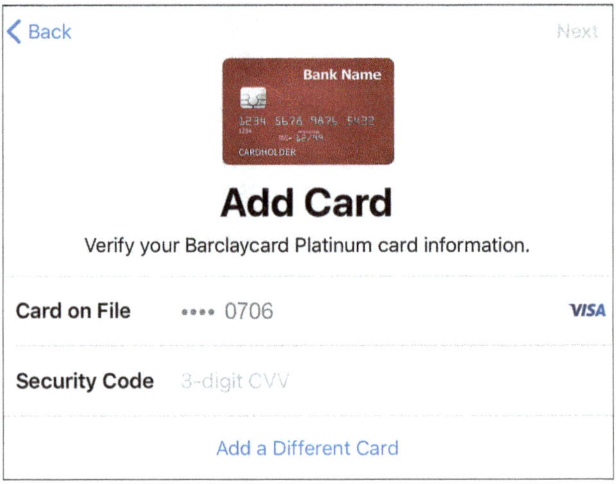


If this is the card you want to use, then enter the 3 digit security code and tap 'next' on the top right. Hit 'agree' on the terms and conditions; your card will be added.

If you want to add a different card, tap 'add a different card', at the bottom of the 'add card' window. You can scan your card with the iPhone's camera.

Position the card so it fills the white rectangle on your screen. Apple Pay will scan your card and automatically enter your details

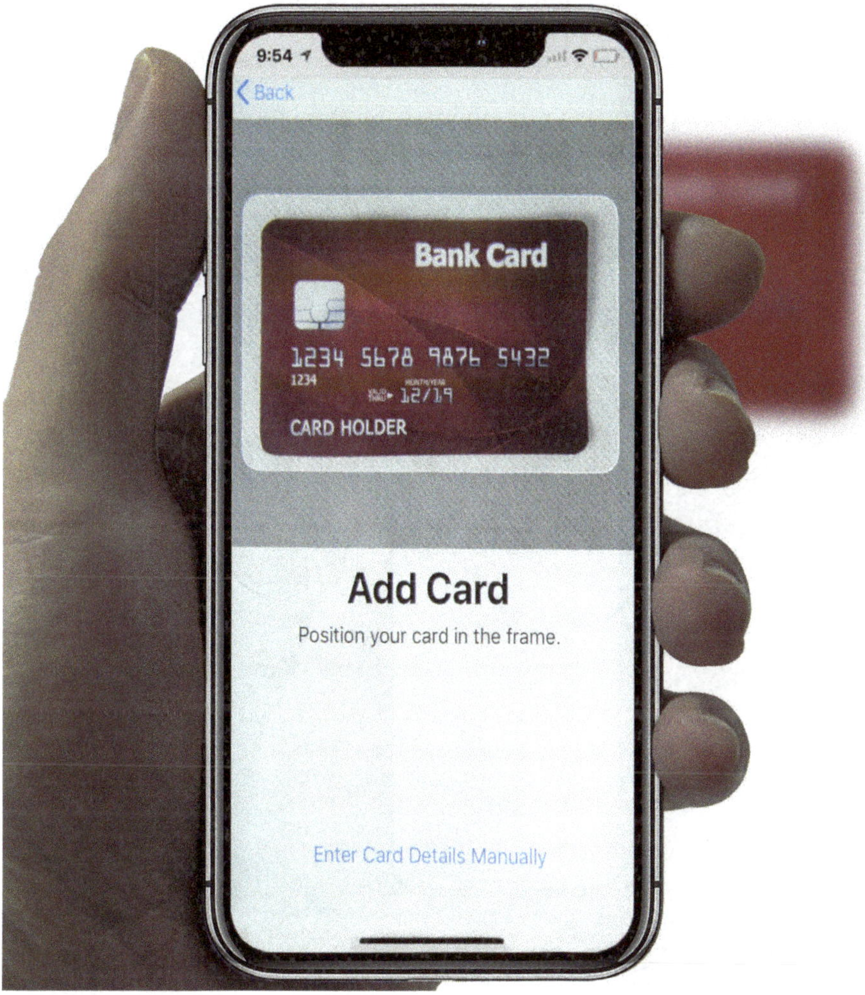


If you can't get the camera to scan the card, tap 'enter card details manually' then key in your card number, exp dates and so on.

Enter the security code from the back of your card. The bank will authorise your card. Accept the terms and conditions.

If you also have an iPhone, these cards will be synced with your iPhone so you can use Apple Pay on there too.

## Using Apple Pay

You can use Apple Pay at any store that supports this feature. You will usually see the logo displayed in store. You can also use Apple Pay on some online stores.

*First, make sure your shipping and contact details are correct for Apple Pay. Open the settings app, select 'Wallet & Apple Pay'. Set a shipping address, email and phone number if you haven't already.*

If you're in a shop, hover your phone over the pay terminal, you'll see your default card appear on your screen.

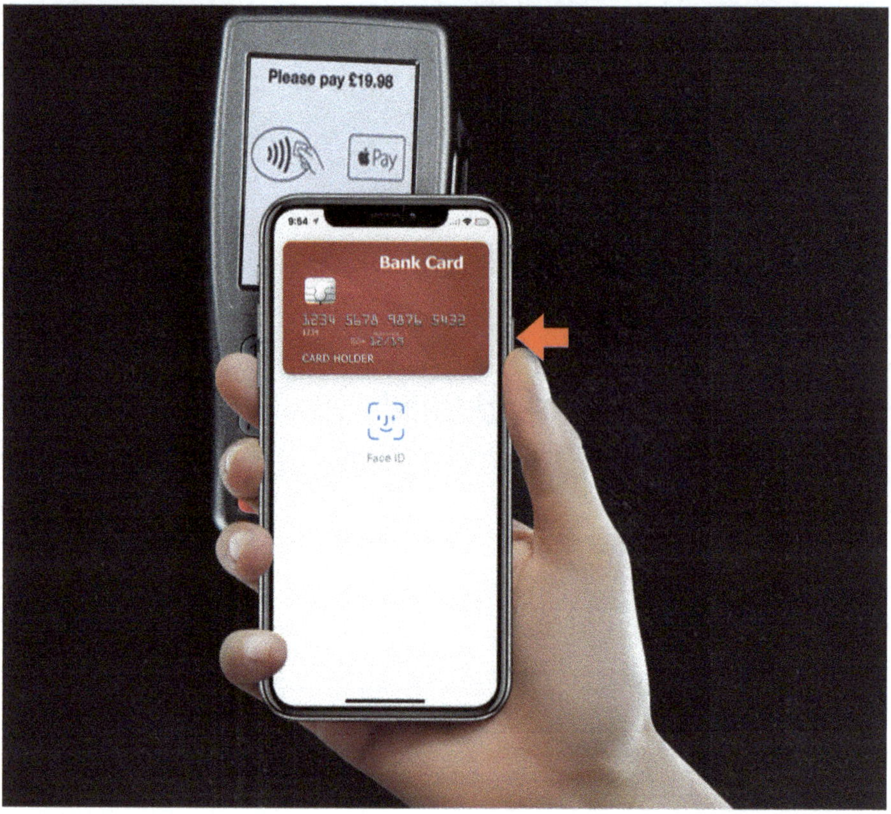


Review the payment information. Then authorise the payment either using your Touch ID or Face ID.

To authorise on the iPhone with Face ID, double-press the side button while looking at the screen.

If you're on an older iPhone, put your finger on the home button to allow TouchID to scan your fingerprint.

If you've purchased something from an online store, you'll see a popup similar to the one below. Double press the side button to authorise with FaceID

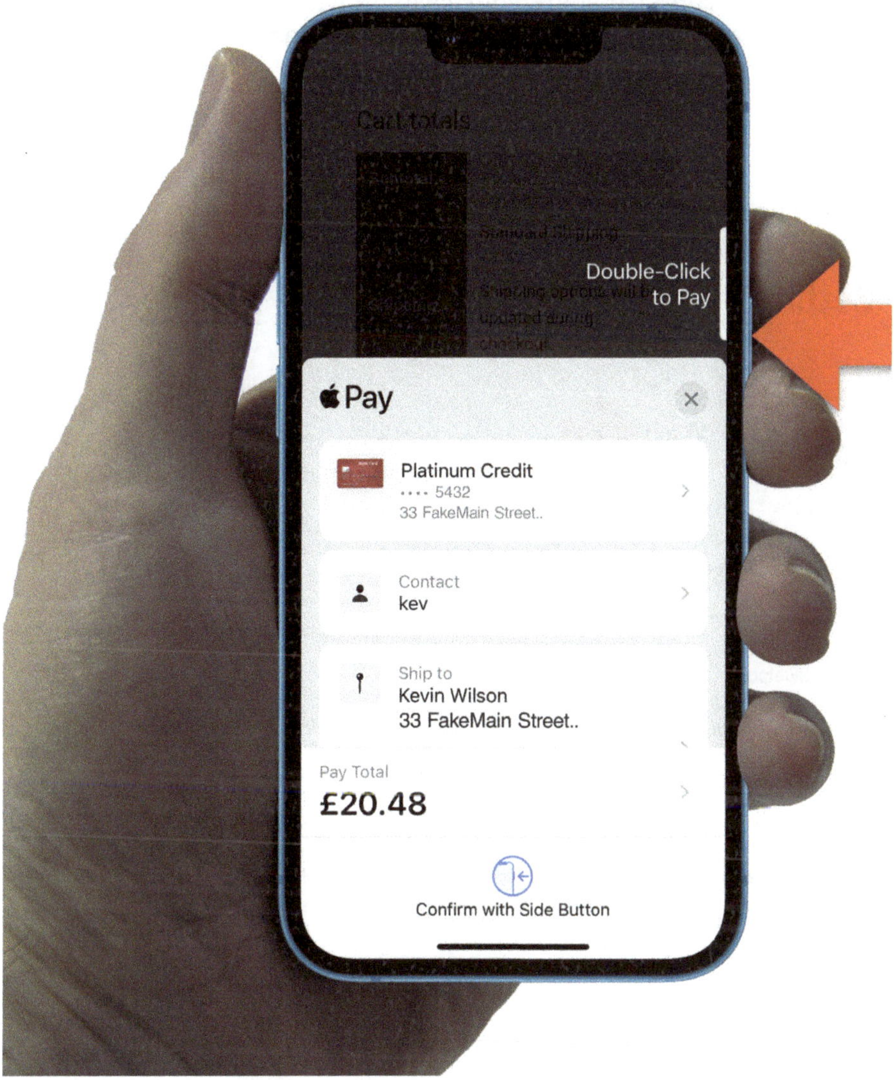


If you're on an older iPhone with Touch ID, authenticate with Touch ID using the home button.

# Find My iPhone

This feature is quite useful if you have misplaced your iPhone or had it stolen. You can also share your location with friends and family - a useful feature to keep track of where your kids are or family members.

## Setup

First you need to activate it on your iPhone. Tap the settings app, select your account, then tap 'find my'.

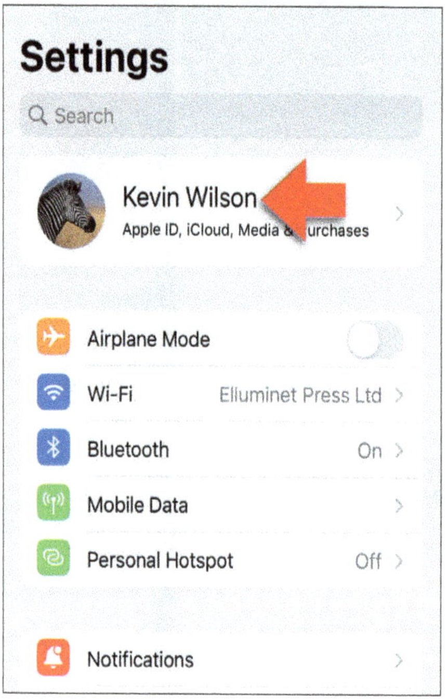


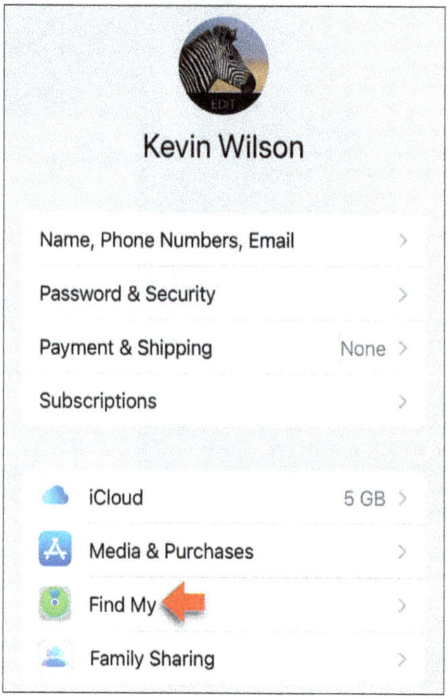


Tap 'find my iPhone.

Switch the 'find my iPhone' slider to 'on'. Turn on the other three switches.

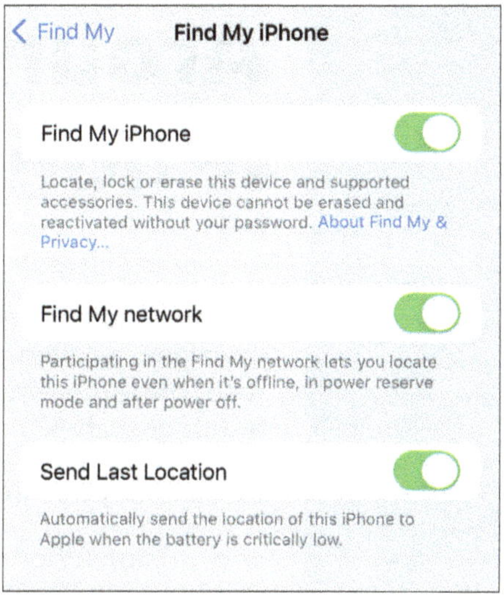


Also make sure location services is turned on. To do this go back to the settings home page and select 'privacy'.

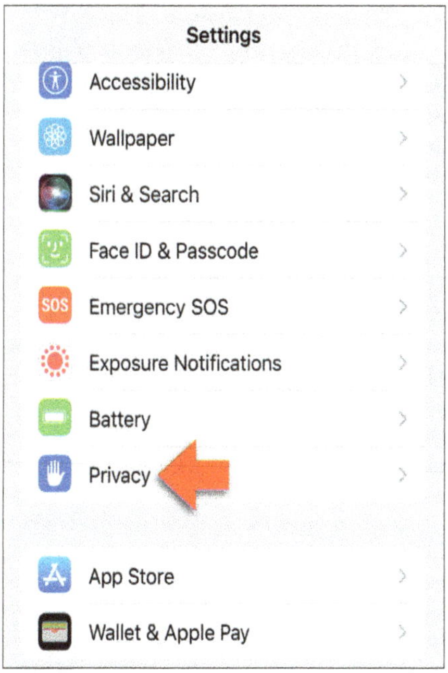


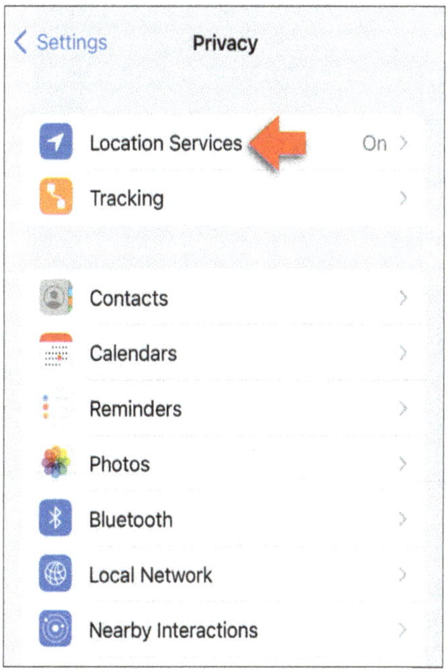


Tap 'location services', and turn the slider to 'on'.

See page 172 for more info on how to use the app.

3

# Getting Around iPhone

iPhones have a touch screen user interface allowing you to interact with the apps on the screen using touch gestures.

In this chapter, we'll take a look at:

- Your iPhone
- Home Screen
- App Library
- Control Center
- Notification Center
- Touch Gestures
- Multitasking
- On-screen Keyboard
- Spotlight Search
- Siri
- Screenshot
- Screen Recording
- Flashlight

Take a look at the video resources, open your web browser and navigate to the following website.

elluminetpress.com/iphone-nav

# Your iPhone

Let's take a look around the iPhone itself. Along the top bezel, you'll see a cut out notch. Here, you'll find the front facing facetime camera, the TrueDepth camera sensors for use with FaceID. The TrueDepth camera consists of a dot projector that projects a grid of infrared dots onto your face, which is then lit up with infrared light by the flood illuminator. An infrared camera takes a picture to generate a 3D facial map. This map is used by FaceID to unlock your phone.

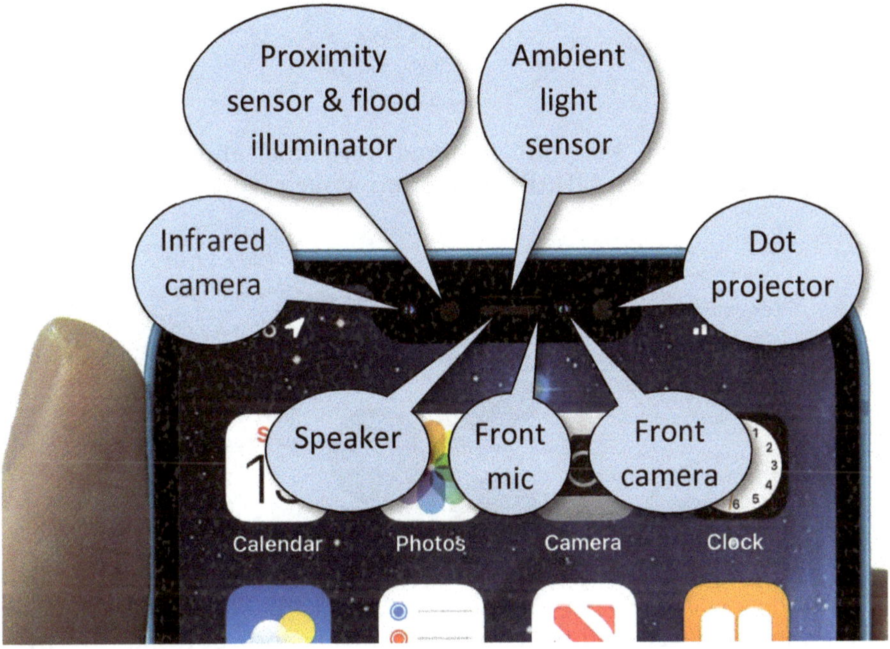


Along the right side edge, you'll find the power button, also known as the side button.

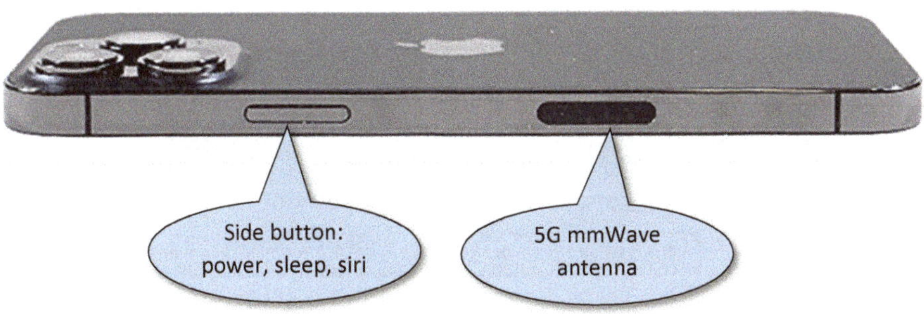


On the iPhone 13, you'll also find a small grey indent. This is a 5G antenna used to connect to the high speed 5G phone network.

Along the bottom edge, you'll find a lightning port. You'll also find two speakers either side.

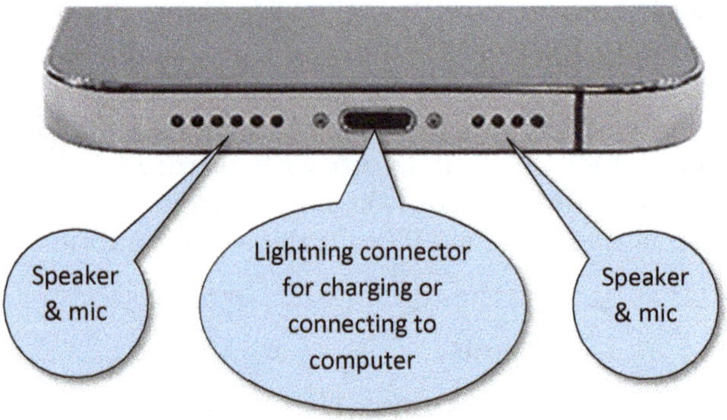


On the back, you'll see your cameras, rear mic, and camera flash/ flashlight, as well as a LIDAR scanner on some models.

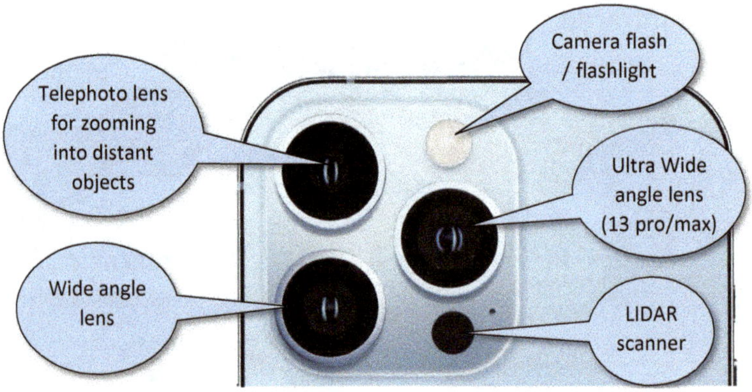


Along the side you'll find your volume controls and your SIM card tray (other side on older models). Here, you can insert a SIM card from your network provider.

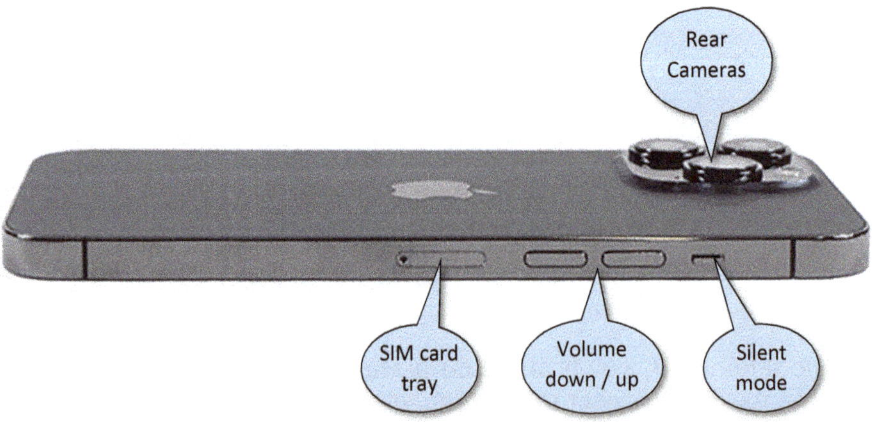

# Home Screen

The home screen is a launch pad where you'll find icons for all your apps.

## Anatomy

Along the top, you'll see the status bar. This shows the time on the top left hand side, with WiFi/Cellular and battery status on the top right hand side.

With iOS 15, you can add widgets to the home screen. These appear along the top, however you can put them anywhere on the home screen.

Underneath you'll see icons for all apps installed on your iPhone. Swipe left or right to move between app pages. The little dots, circled in the illustration above, show you what page you are on and how many pages of icons you have. This will vary depending on what apps you have installed.

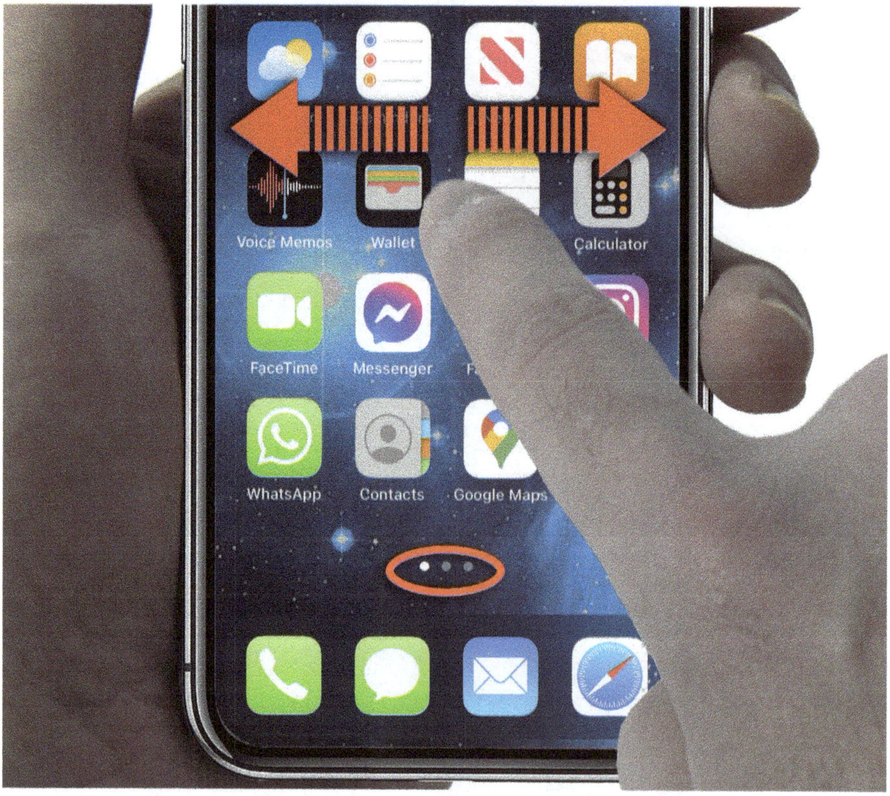


Along the bottom, you'll see the app dock. This allows you to access popular apps such as phone, messages, email and safari.

## Arranging Icons

To move an icon, tap and hold your finger on the icon, then drag your finger across the screen (ignore popup menu).

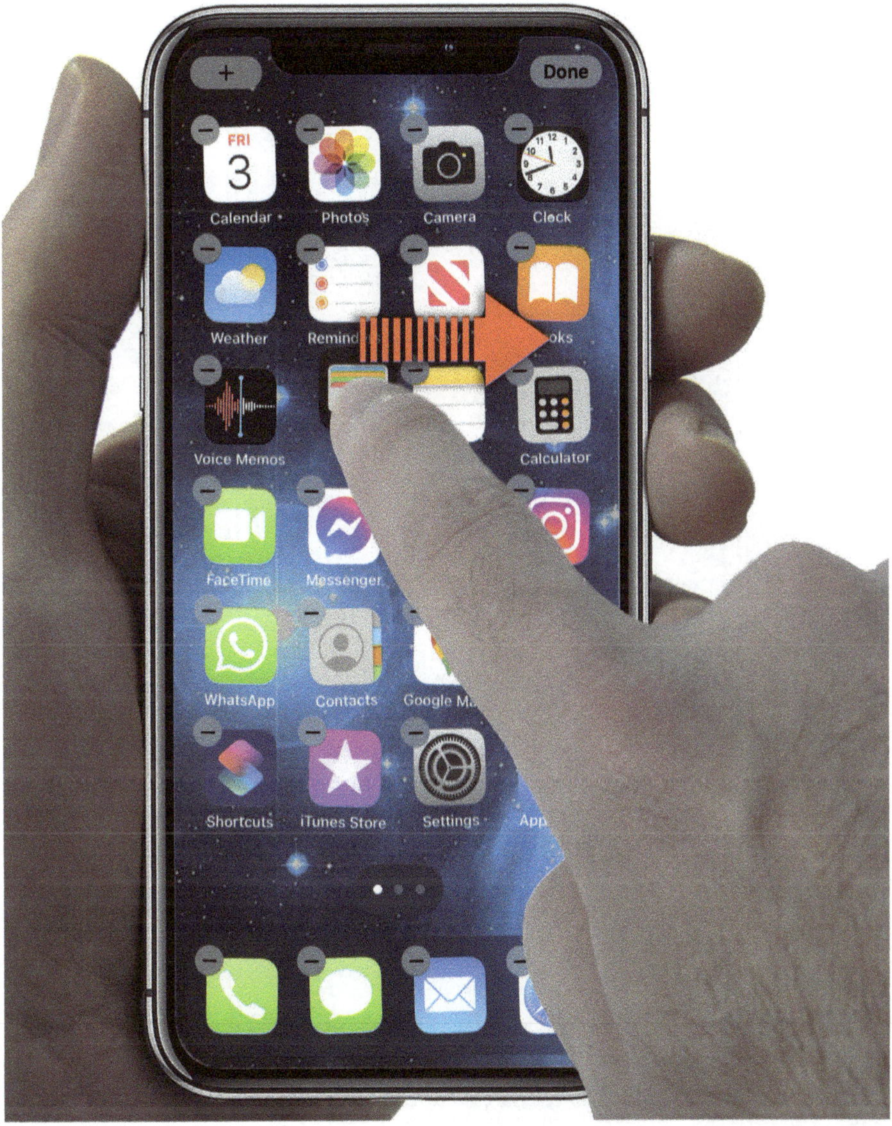


The other icons on the screen will automatically move and rearrange themselves around the icon you're moving. To move the icon onto another page, drag the icon to the right or left edge of the screen. Once the icon page turns, release your finger.

Tap 'done' on the top right when you're finished.

## Removing Icons

To remove an app, tap and hold your finger on the app's icon, until you see the drop down menu.

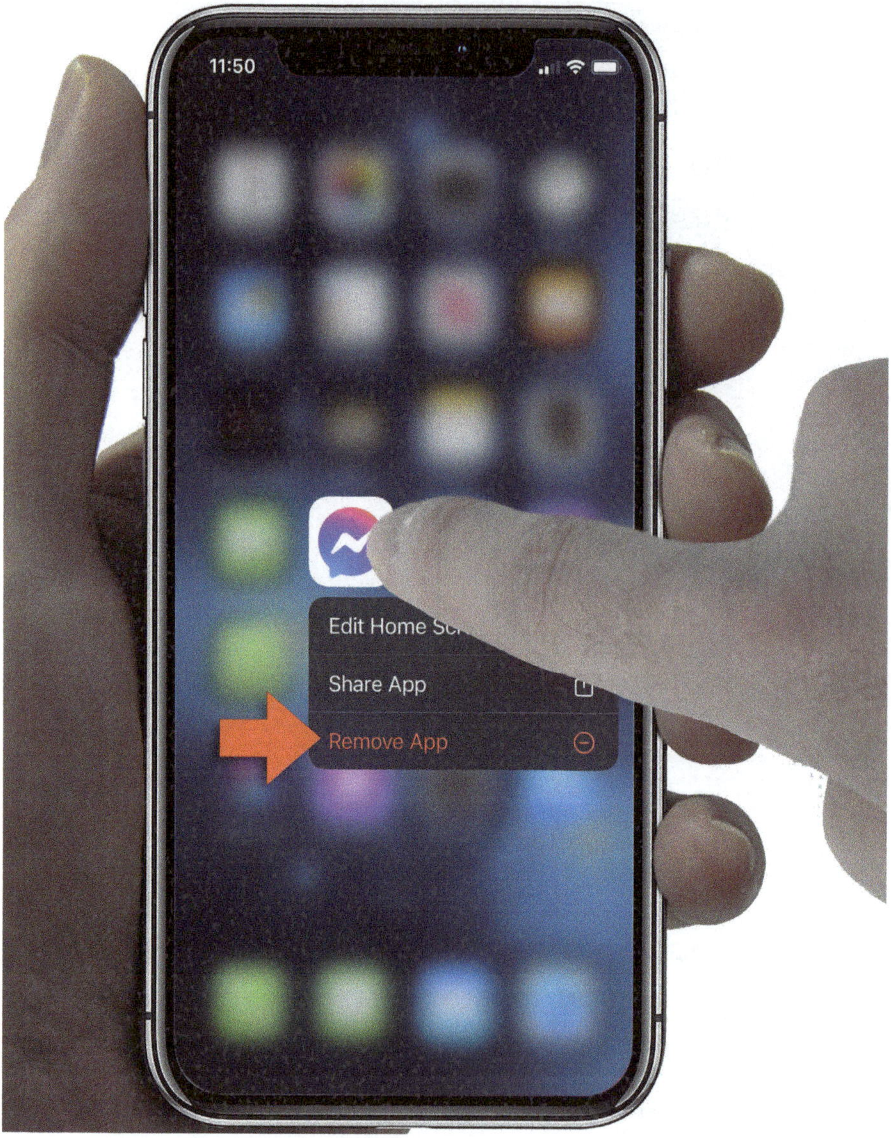


Select 'remove app' from the drop down menu.

This will uninstall the app. To put it back on your home screen, you'll need to download it again from the app store.

## Widgets

Widgets are small applets that give you quick access to information and actions. You can add widgets to your 'today view', or you can add them to your home screen.

### Add to Home Screen

To add widgets, tap and hold your finger on the home screen (ignore popup menu). You'll see a '+' icon appear on the top left of the screen.

Tap the '+' icon on the top left of the screen.

Select the widget you want to add from the list.

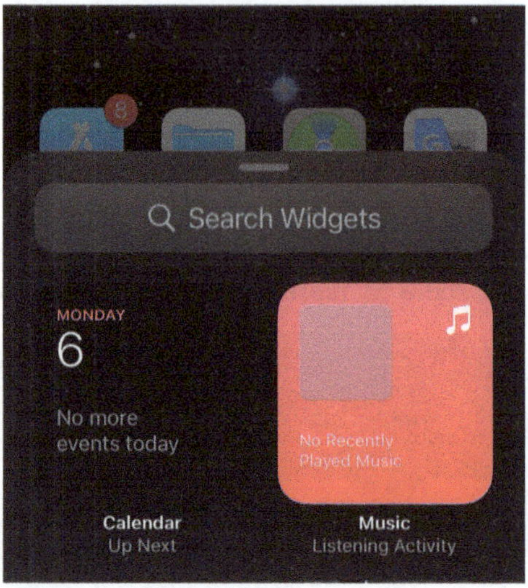


Swipe left/right across the widget to select a size. Tap 'add widget' when you're done.

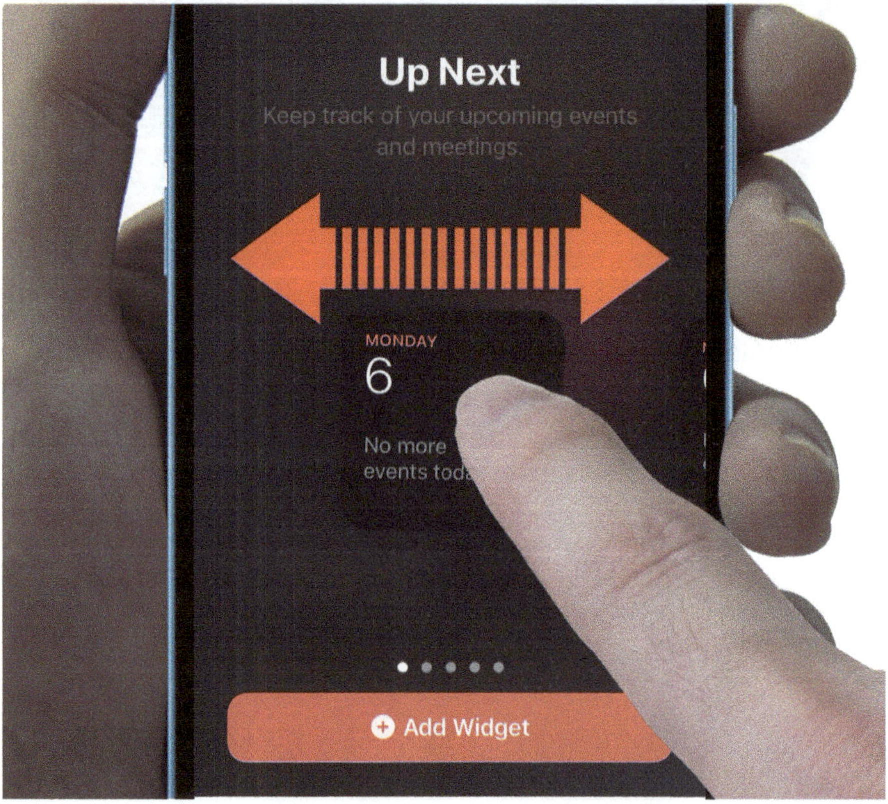

Tap and drag the widget into position, then tap 'done' on the top right when you're finished.

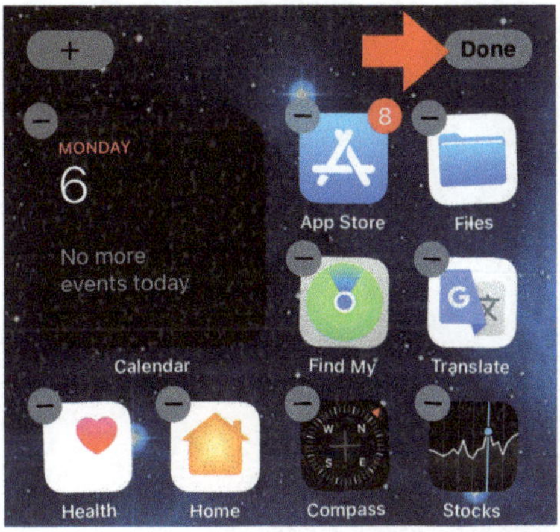


## Add to Today View

To open the 'today view' panel swipe left to right across the home screen until you see the panel open.

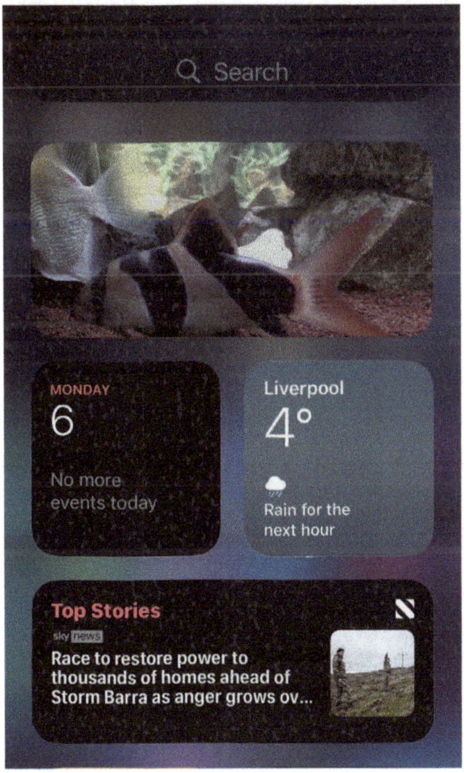

Tap and hold your finger on the screen, then tap the plus sign icon on the top left.

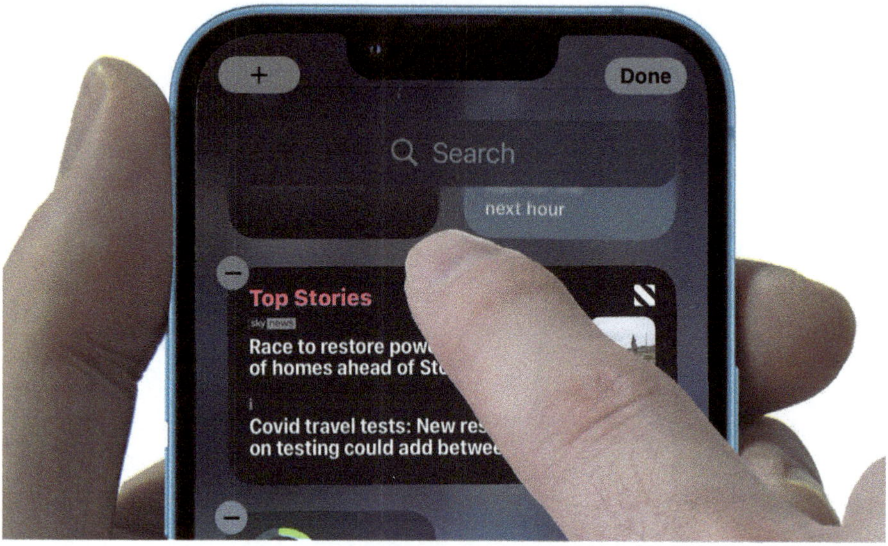


From the popup window, scroll down, tap the widget you want to add. Or type in the name of the widget into the search field at the top.

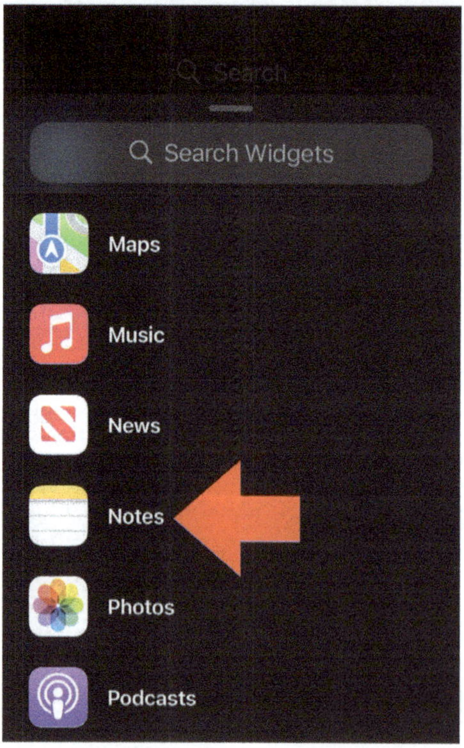

Swipe, left and right to select the size of the widget.. Tap 'add widget'.

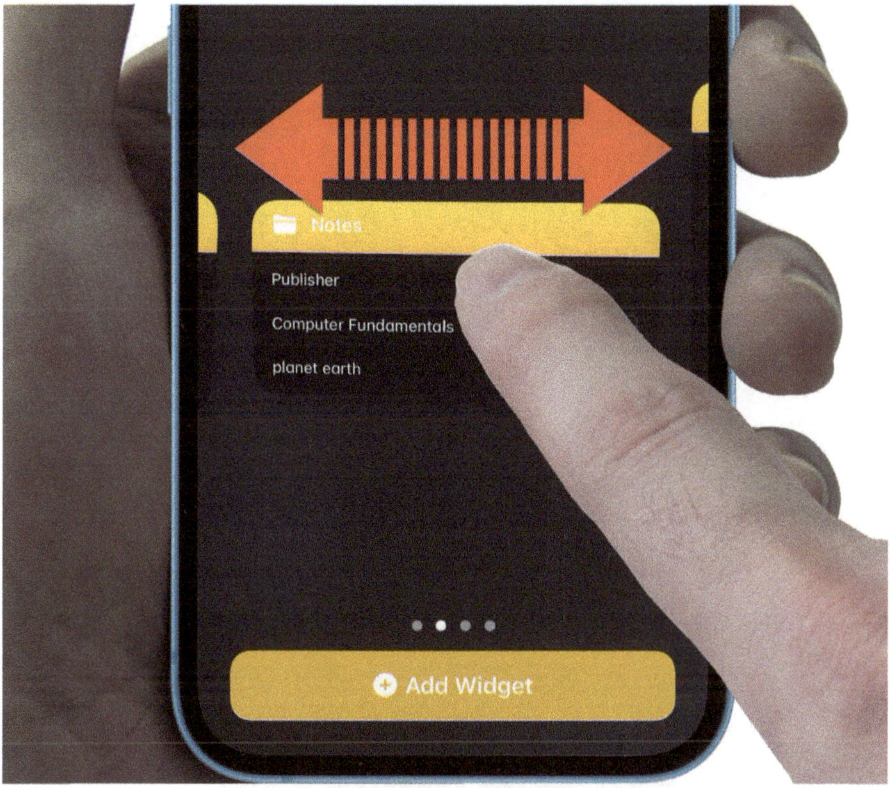


The widget will appear in the 'today view'. To move a widget, tap and drag the widget to a new position on the list.

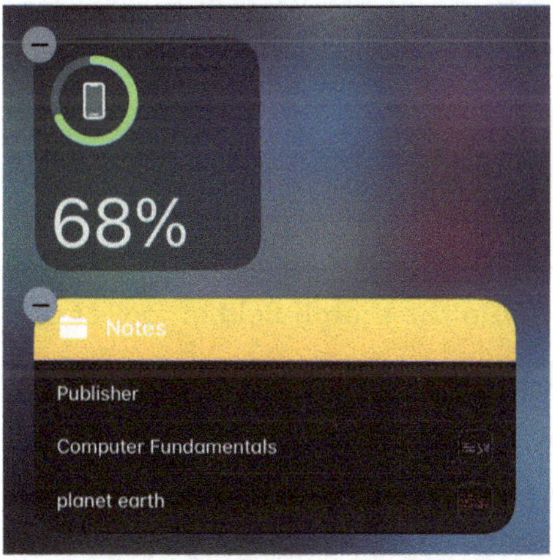


Tap 'done' on the top right of the screen when you're finished.

## Edit Widget

Some widgets you can edit, such as weather, or calendar. To do this, tap and hold your finger on a widget, select 'edit' from the popup menu.

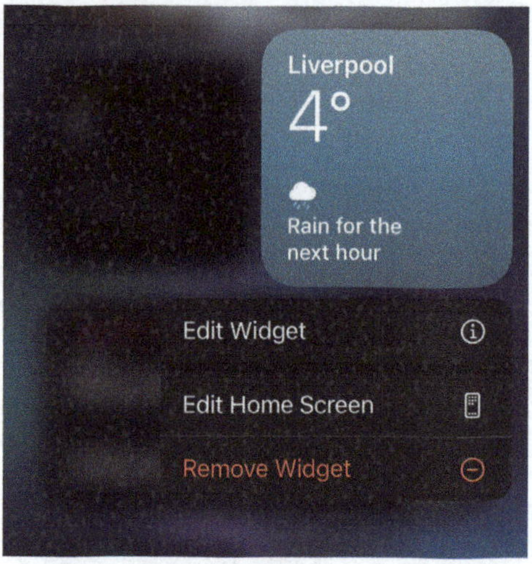


In this particular widget, you can select a location. Tap on the location.

Type your location into the search field or select one from the list.

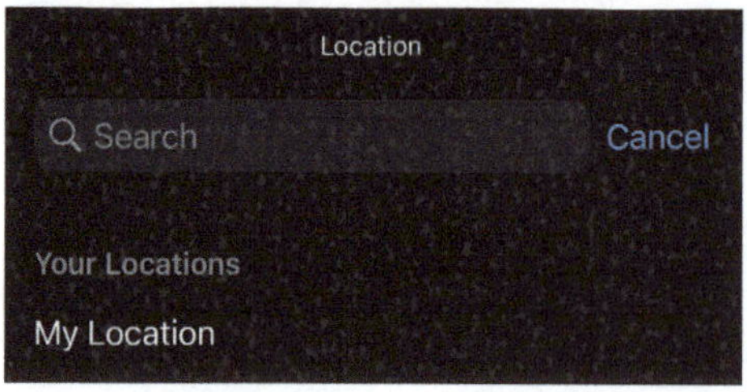

## Remove Widgets

If you want to remove widgets from the home screen, tap and hold your finger on the screen, then tap the '-' icon on the top left of the widget.

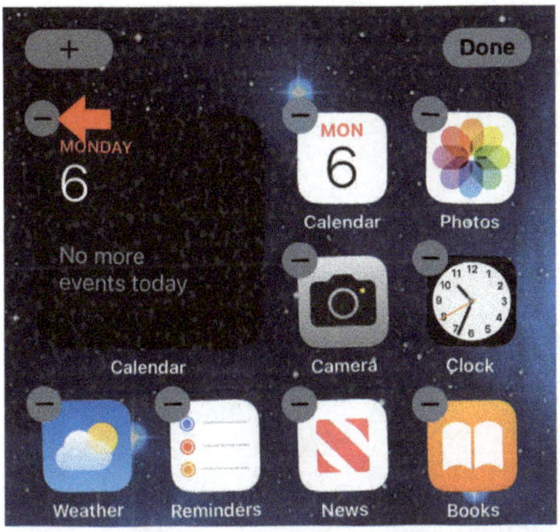


Similarly on 'today view'. Tap and hold, then tap the '-'.

Tap 'done' on the top right when you're finished.

# App Library

The app library a quick access location for all of apps installed on your iPhone. To open the app library, swipe right to left across your home screen until you see the app library.

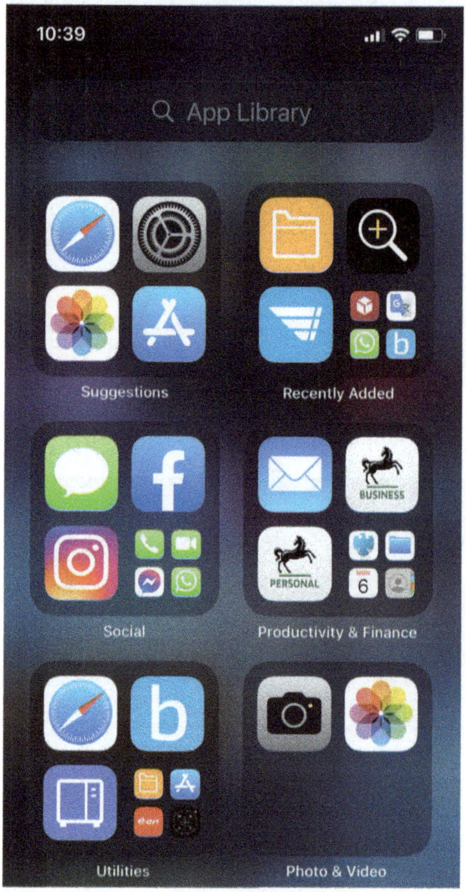


Apps are grouped according to their function, so you'll see groups such as entertainment, productivity, recently added and so on. Frequently used apps appear as larger icons.

You can also search for apps, to do this tap the 'app library' search field at the top.

Underneath, you'll see an alphabetised list of all of your apps. Select and app from the A-Z list.

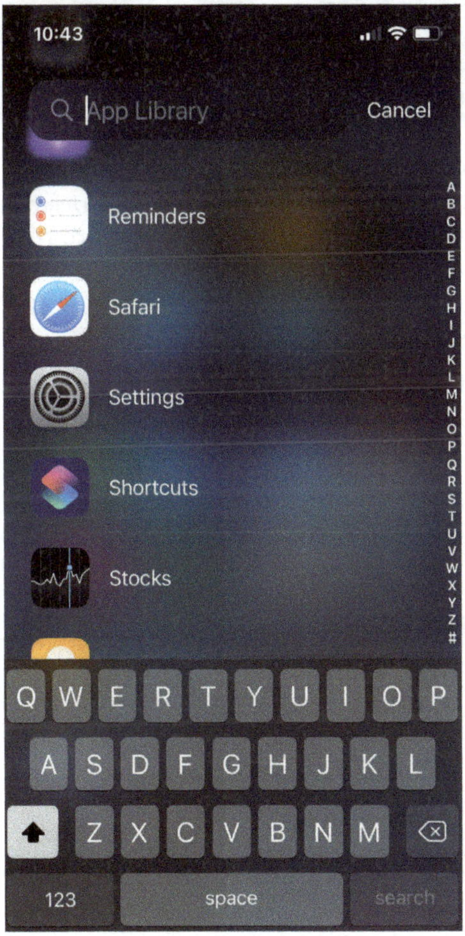

# Control Center

The control center is your control hub where you can adjust screen brightness, volume, access WiFi/bluetooth controls, access your camera, and other controls.

To open control center, swipe downwards from the top right edge of your screen.

Here you can control the volume of playing music, turn on and off WiFi, blue-tooth, access your camera, set the orientation lock to stop the screen shifting - this can be useful if you are reading a book etc.

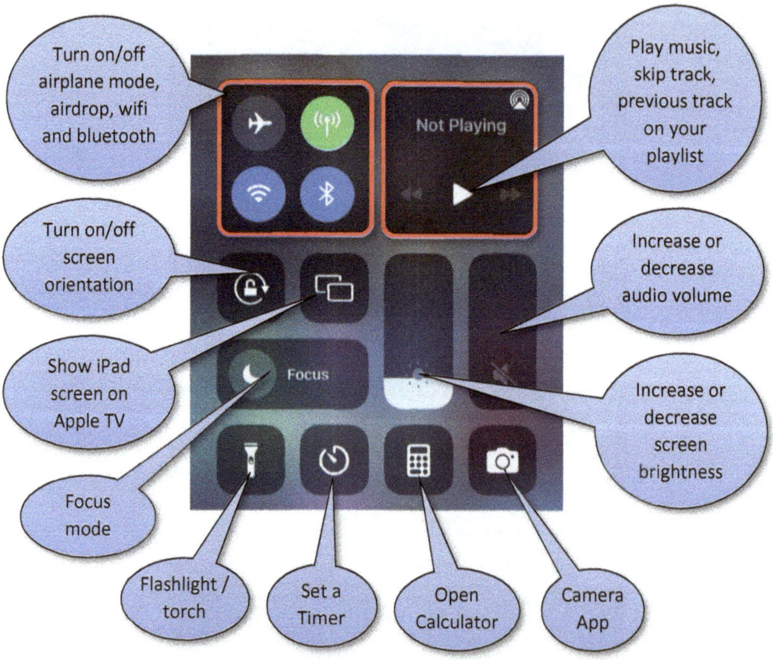

# Notification Center

This is where you'll find notifications from various apps. Notifications will also appear on the lock screen. To open notification center, swipe your finger downwards from the top center edge of the screen.

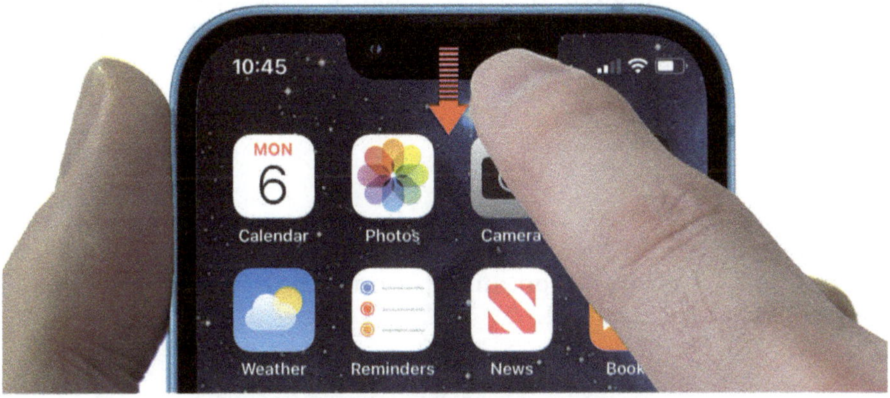


Notifications such as news headlines, new email, sms/text messages, reminders and various others will appear here.

Multiple notifications from the same app are grouped. Tap on one of the groups to open it up.

Swipe right to left over the notification to see additional options such as manage, view and clear notification.

# Touch Gestures

Gestures, sometimes called multi-touch gestures, are what you'll use to interact with the touch screen on iPhone.

While you work through this part, take a look at the 'navigation' section of the accompanying video resources. Scan the code or go to the following website.

elluminetpress.com/iphone-nav

## Tap

Tap your index finger on an icon or to select something on the screen. For example, you can tap on an app icon, a link in safari, or even a song you want to download.

## Drag

Tap on the screen and without lifting your finger off the glass, slide your finger around the screen to drag up and down, left or right, and any other direction on the screen.

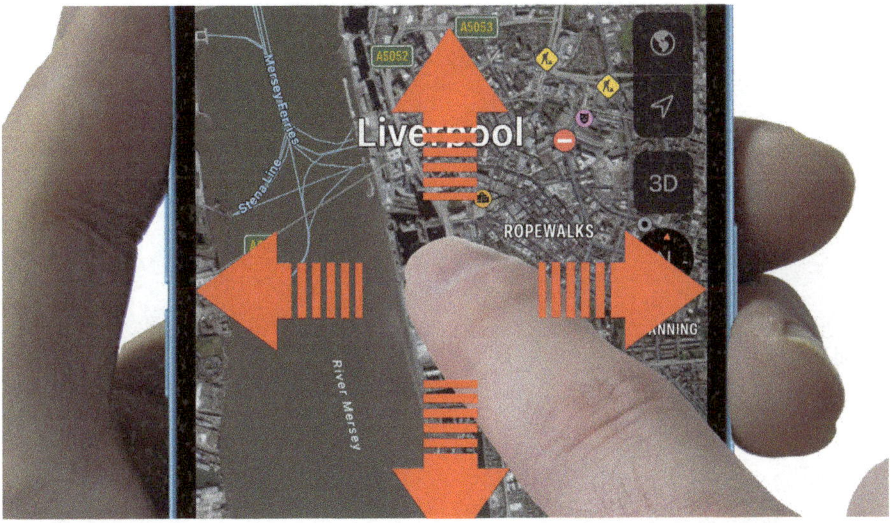


## Zoom

Hold your index finger and thumb on the area you want to zoom in or out of, then pinch the screen to zoom out and spread to zoom in.

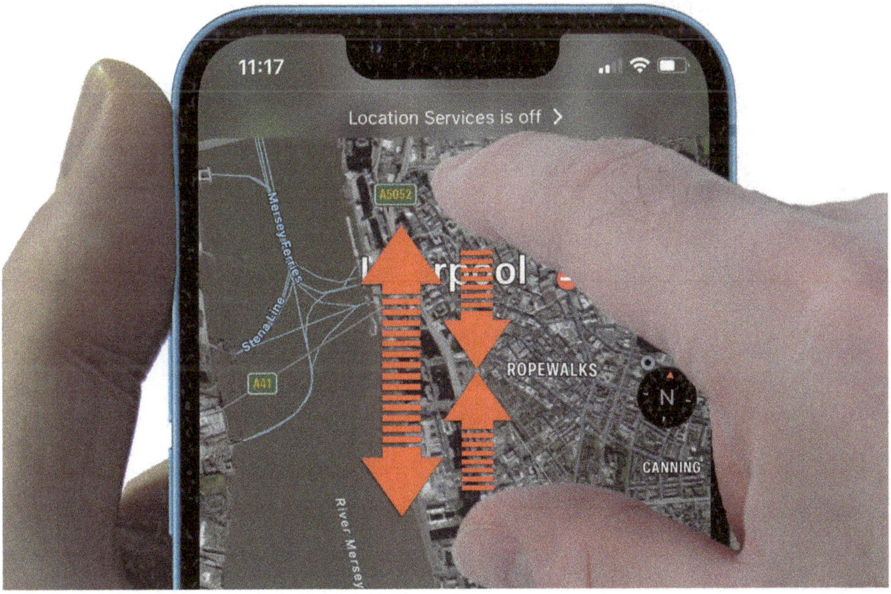

## Swipe

This allows you to flip through photos, pages in an e-book, pages on the home screen. You swipe across the screen almost like striking a match. You can swipe up, down, left, and right.

## Switch Between Open Apps

To switch between open apps, swipe left or right on the bar at the bottom of the screen.

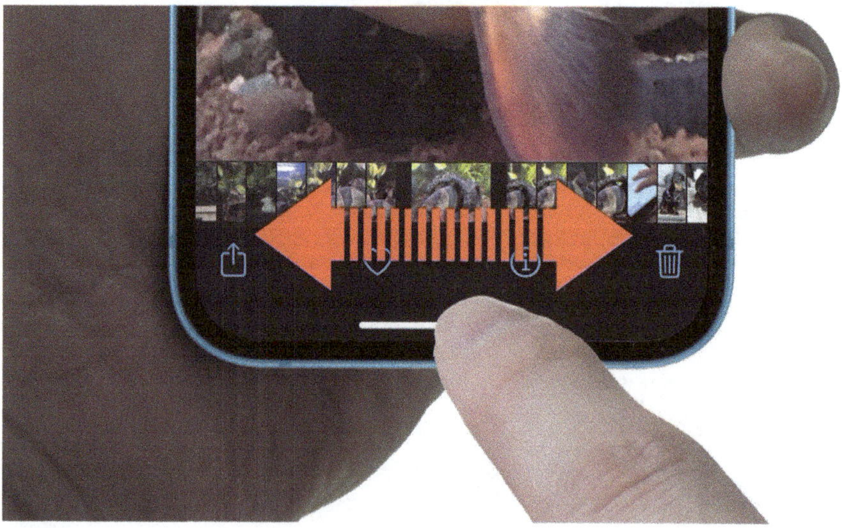

## Return to Home Screen

Flick your finger upward from the bottom of the screen.

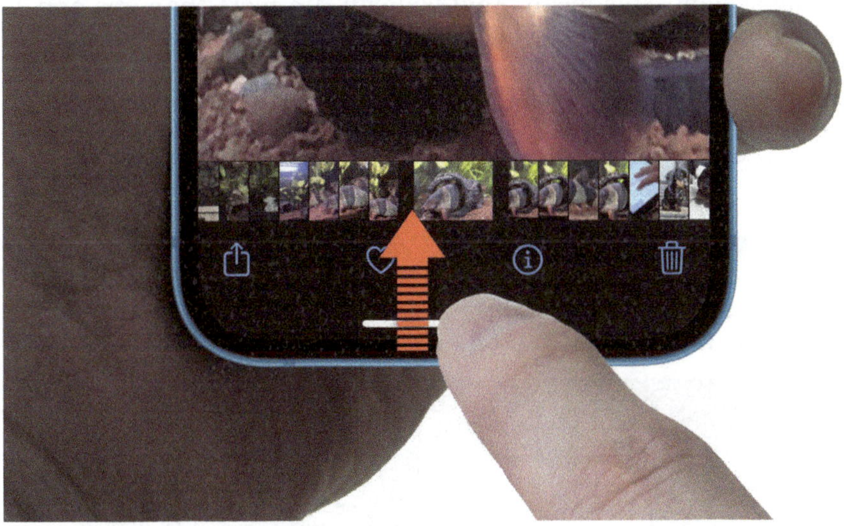

## Open App Switcher

Drag your finger upwards from bottom edge of the screen, until the apps appear.

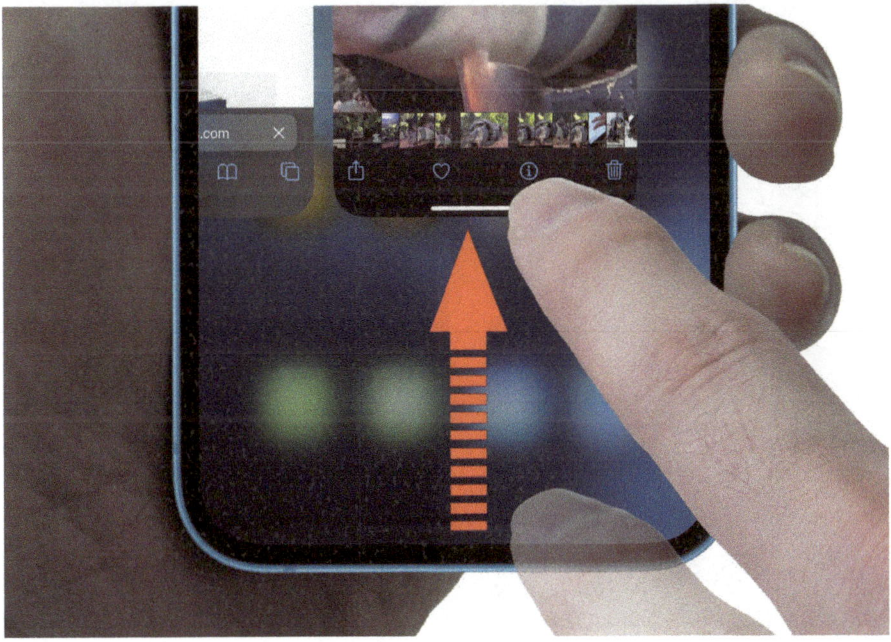

# Multitasking

iPhones run an operating system called iOS. iOS is a multitasking operating system. This means that you can run more than one app at the same time. Open apps that are not currently on your screen will be running in the background. To quickly see what apps are running, press your home button twice, or swipe upwards from the bottom edge to the center of the screen, until the app thumbnail icons appear. "Open App Switcher" on page 103

## See All Running Apps

To switch to another app, open the task switcher. You'll see thumbnail cards of all running apps. Tap on an app to switch to.

## Close a Running App

After using your iPhone, you will find that there are a lot of apps running, this can severely affect the performance of your iPhone and drain your battery more quickly.

To close apps, open the task switcher (see page 103), then swipe your finger upwards on the app you want to close, as illustrated below.

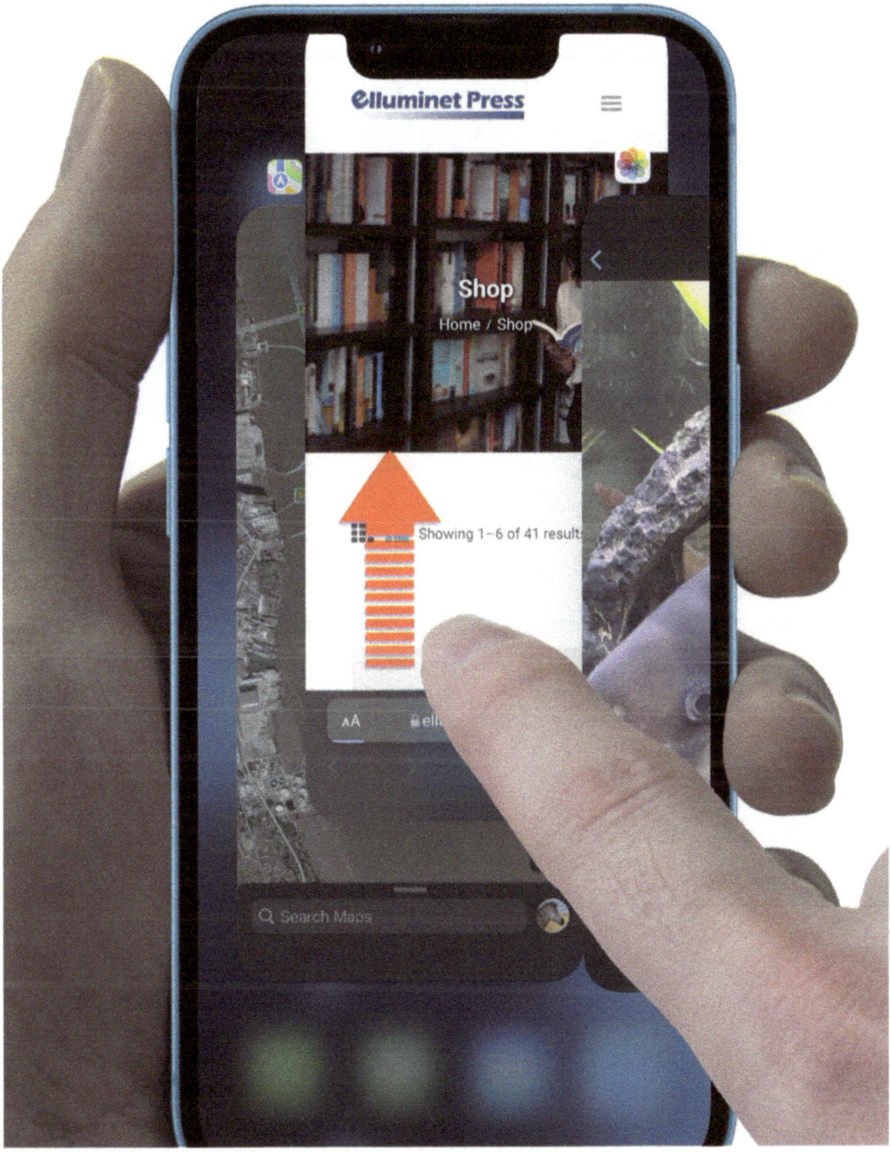


This will close the app. Do this on all the apps you want to close.

# On-screen Keyboard

Typing on an iPhone is easy using the on-screen Multi-Touch keyboard. Tap in any text field, email, document or message, and the on screen keyboard will pop up on the bottom of the screen.

You can tap on the keys to type your message.

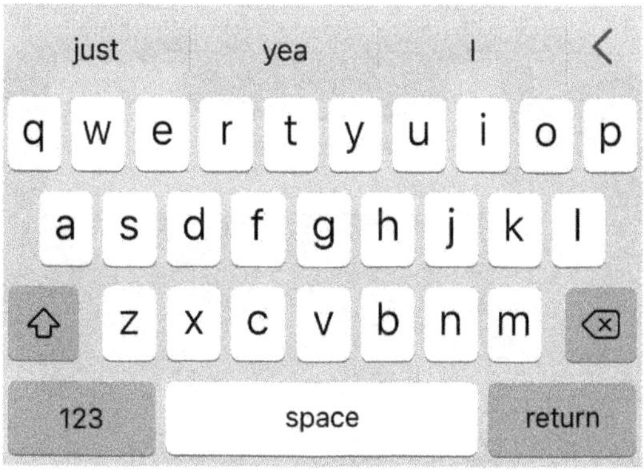


Along the top you will see some predictive text suggestions that appear according to what you're typing in.

If the correct word appears, you can quickly tap on the appropriate suggestion instead of typing in the whole word.

To the right, you'll see an arrow...

Here, you can add a photo, take one with your camera, format your text, add a document, scan a document, or insert a drawing.

At the bottom of the keyboard, you can add an emoticon or memoji, or you can tap the mic icon to dictate text instead of typing it.

# Spotlight Search

Spotlight is integrated with a number of web services so that users can search using Wikipedia, Bing, or Google. Other services include: news, nearby places, suggested websites, movie show times, and content that is not already on the device from the iTunes Store

## Searching for Things

You can activate spotlight search by swiping your finger downwards from the centre of your home screen.

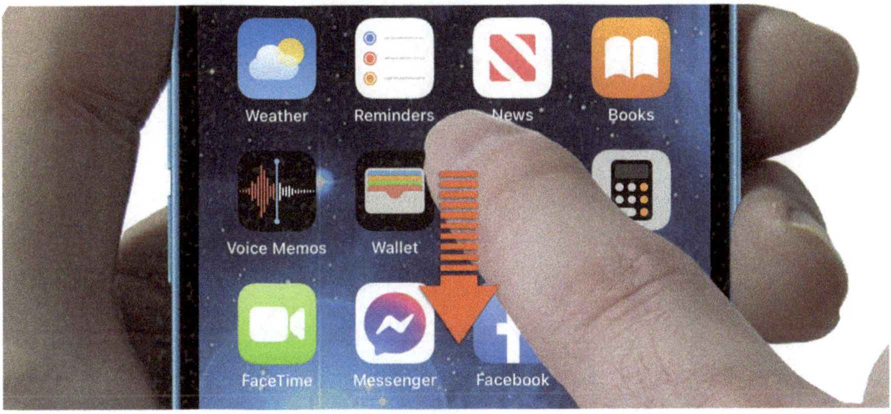


Once you have spotlight's search screen, you can type your search into the search field at the top of the screen.

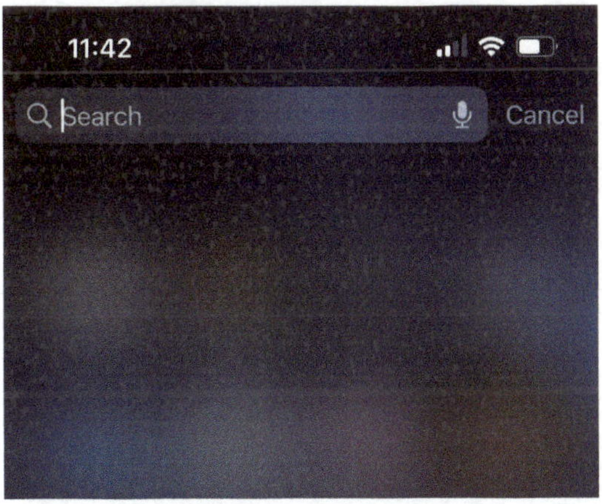


Search also gives you some Siri suggestions. These are taken from your most commonly used apps. Underneath you'll see some shortcuts from some of your most used apps.

In the example below, I am searching for my planet earth notes. Spotlight will search through the web, your apps, documents, books, recently visited sites in safari.

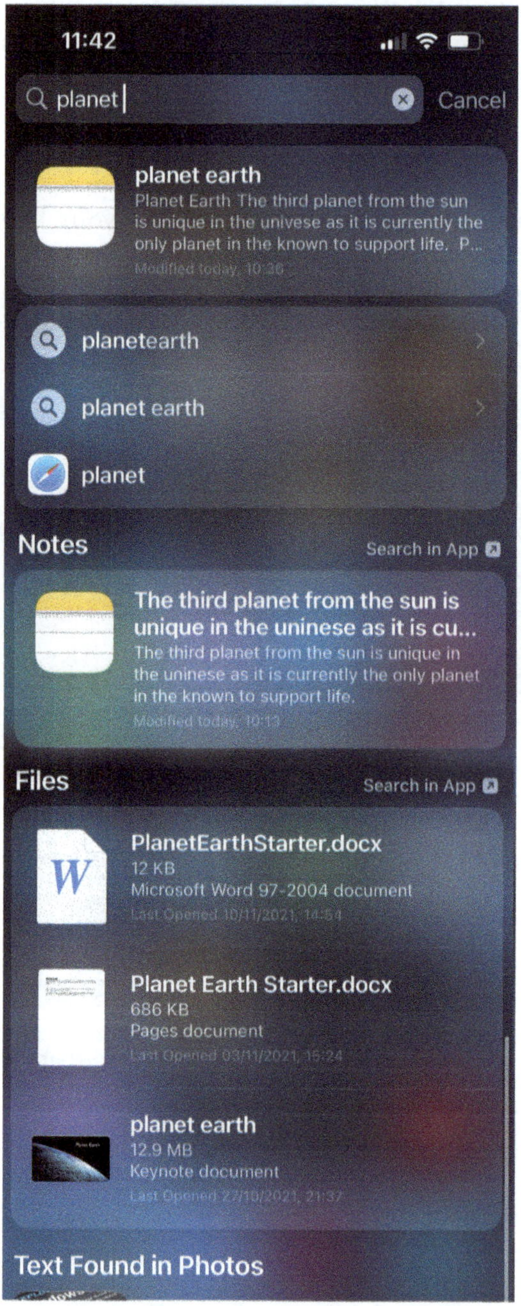


Scroll down the list, select the best match.

# Siri

Siri is an extremely useful feature. She allows you to talk to your iPhone, sometimes referred to as a virtual assistant. She can help you with all kinds of things. You can ask Siri to send messages, schedule meetings, and search for nearby restaurants, all without having to type a single letter.

## Using Siri

To use Siri, press and hold the side button until you see Siri appear on the bottom of your screen.

You can also say "Hey Siri!".

Try some of the following phrases...

- *Try saying: "Hey Siri, schedule appointment for coffee with Claire in Starbucks on Tuesday at 10am"*
- *Try saying: "Send email to..." (pick a name from your contacts list)*
- *Try saying: "What is the weather like tomorrow"*
- *Try saying: "Find me a website on baking a cake"*
- *Try saying: "Remind me to pick up milk on the way home"*
- *Try saying: "Call..." (pick a name from your contacts list).*

## Siri Translate

Here's a good one for those who love to travel but don't speak the local language. At the time of writing, Siri can only translate from US English to French, German, Italian, Mandarin and Spanish.

To use the translator, hold down the side button until Siri appears on the bottom of the screen.

When yo see Siri, say "How do I say where is the train station in Spanish?"

Just replace the underlined bits of the phrase for the phrase and language you want to translate into. Siri will translate the phrase and speak it out aloud.

## Voice Dictation

Another useful feature of Siri is voice dictation, which allows you to enter text without having to use the keyboard. You can search the web, take notes, post an update to Facebook, and more just by speaking.

To use voice dictation, tap the microphone icon on your on screen keyboard. *If the icon isn't there go to your settings app, tap 'general', then 'keyboard'. Go down to 'enable dictation' and switch the slider to on.*

Then start dictating the text you want Siri to type. She listens to what you say, and types it. Here in the photo below, I'm using the notes app to dictate my "planet earth" notes.

You can even add punctuation by saying words like "period", "question mark", "comma", or "new paragraph". Tap the keyboard icon on the bottom right to close dictation mode.

# Voice Control

You can use voice commands to navigate around your device, launch apps and get things done without using your fingers.

## Setup

To enable voice control, open your settings app

Scroll down, select ‘accessibility’, then ‘voice control’.

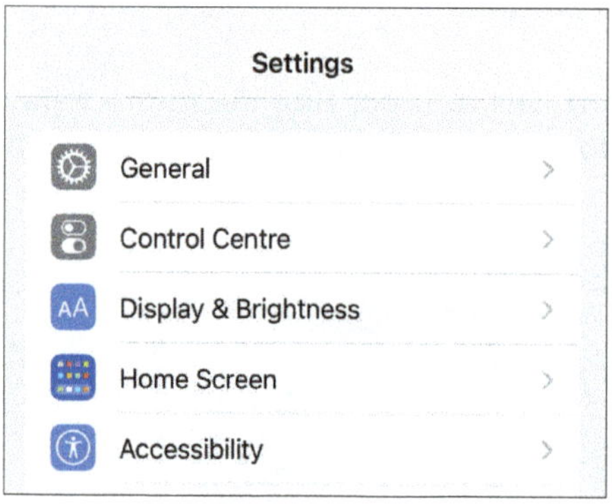


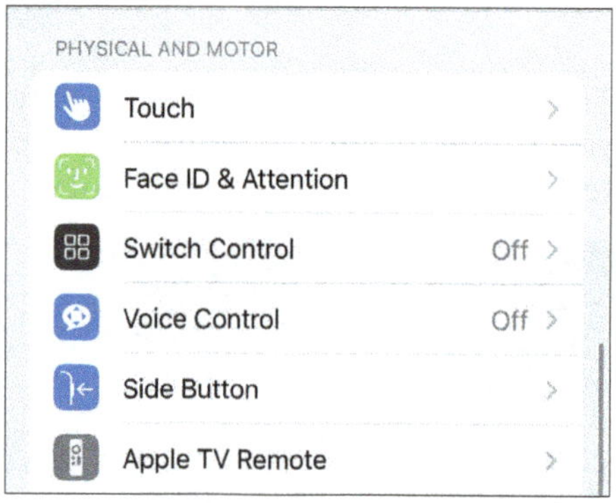


Tap ‘set up voice control’ at the top. Tap ‘continue’.

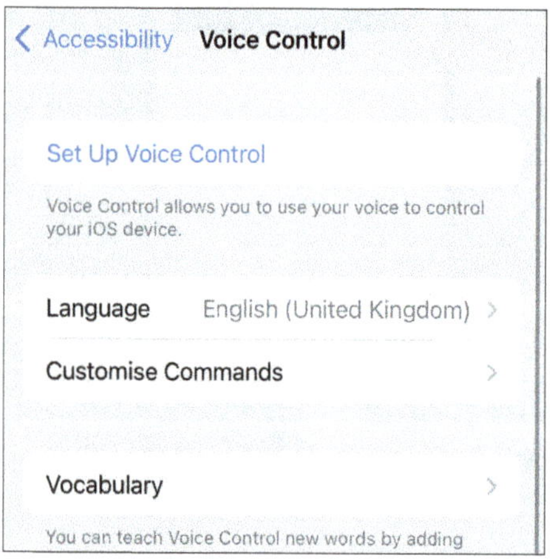


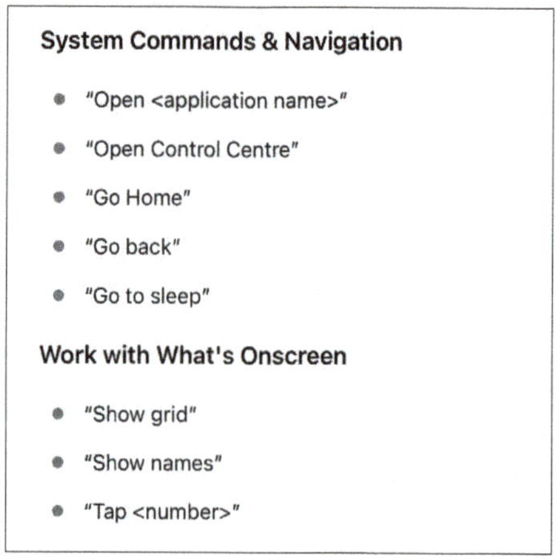


Have a look through all the voice commands you can give. Tap ‘done’ when you’re finished.

Now, try a few voice commands. For example, say “open safari”.

## Customise Commands

You can customise voice control. Here, you can turn on/off voice control, select your language, customise commands, add words to vocabulary if voice control doesn't recognise a particular word or phrase. You can also allow voice control to show confirmation, play a sound when activated or show hints.

To customise commands, open settings app, select 'accessibility', then select 'voice control'. Tap on 'customise commands'. To create a new command tap 'create new command'.

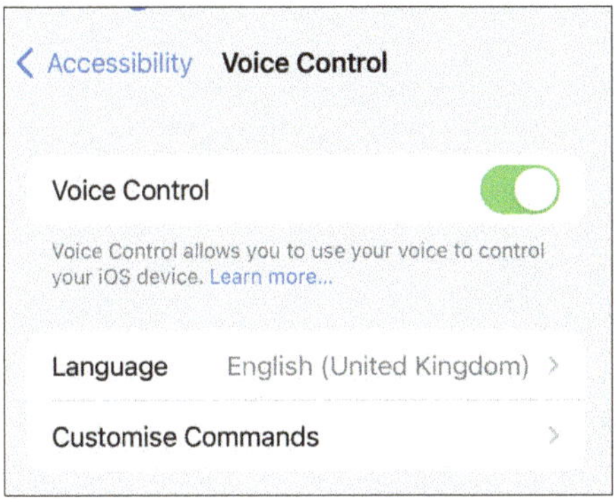


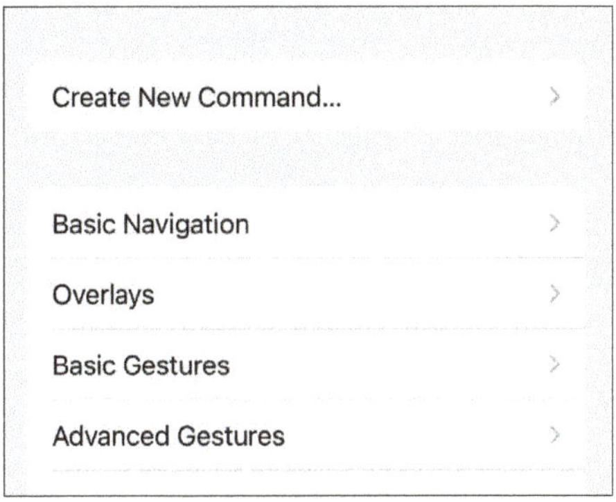


In the 'phrase' field, type in a phrase. This is the phrase you'll say to execute the command. Eg "Insert Claire's address". In the 'action' field, select the action this command is going to carry out. Tap 'insert text', then in the field at the bottom, type in the text to be inserted. Eg an address.

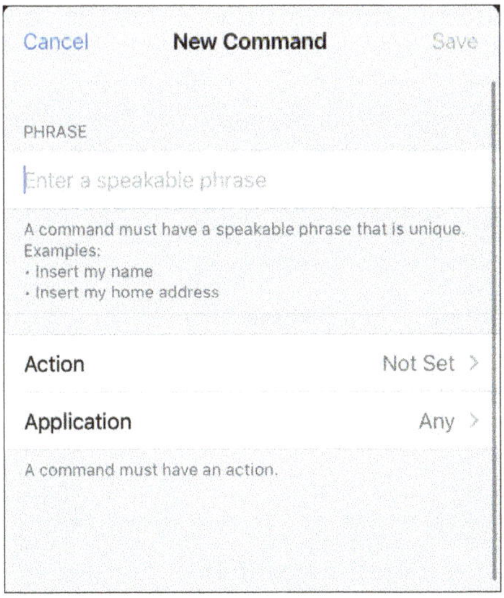


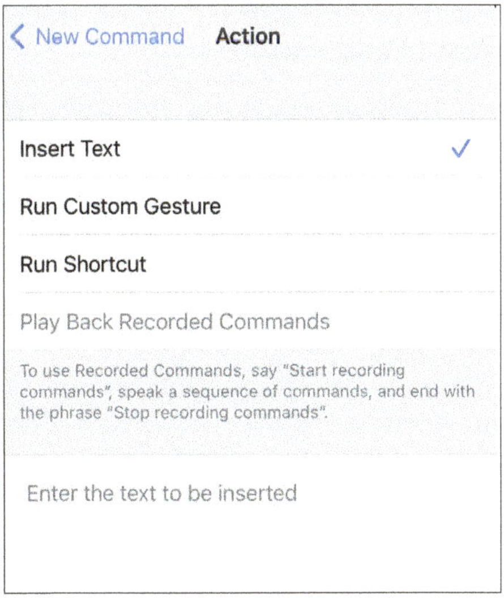


Tap 'new command' on the top left to go back to the previous screen.

In the 'application' field, set this to any app, or tap and select the app you want the command to work in.

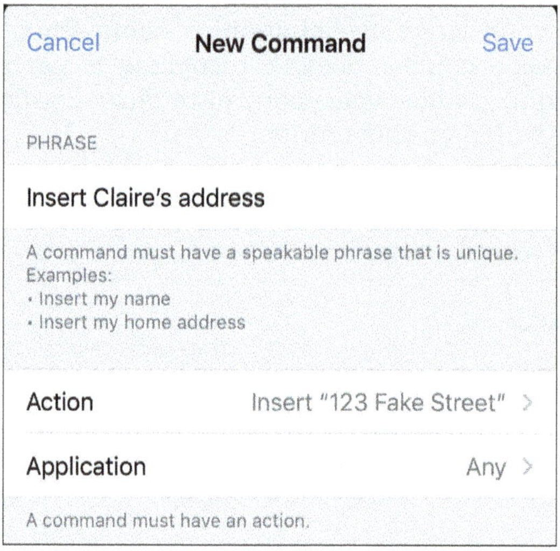


Tap 'save' on the top right when you're done.

## Vocabulary

You can add words you want voice control to recognise. This is useful if you work with specialised apps, documents or you use specific terminology.

To add words or phrases, open settings app, select 'accessibility', then select 'voice control'. Tap on 'vocabulary', then tap the '+' on the top right to add a word.

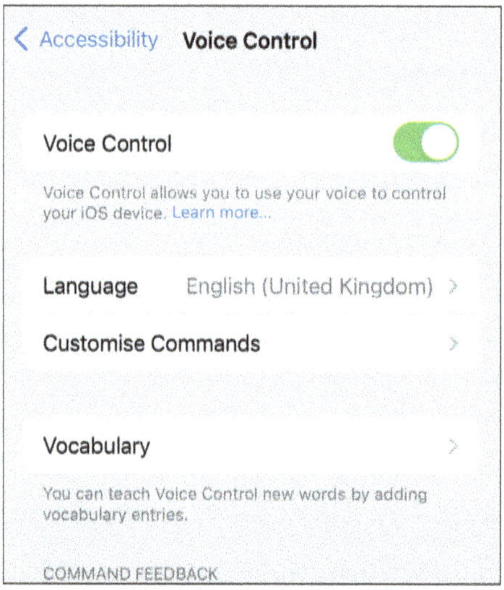


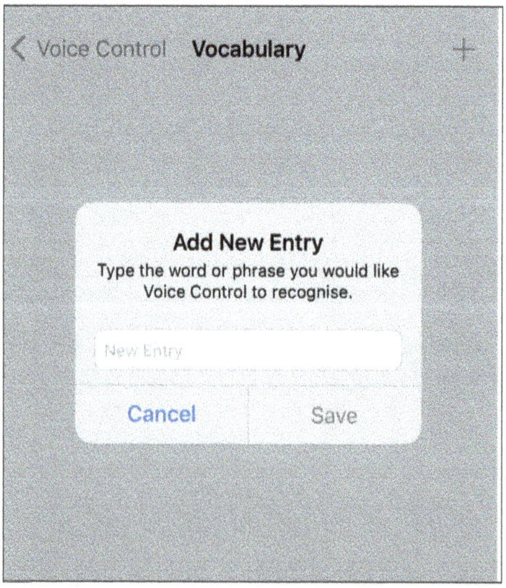

# Screenshot

Press the side button and the volume up button at the same time. You'll hear a camera sound.

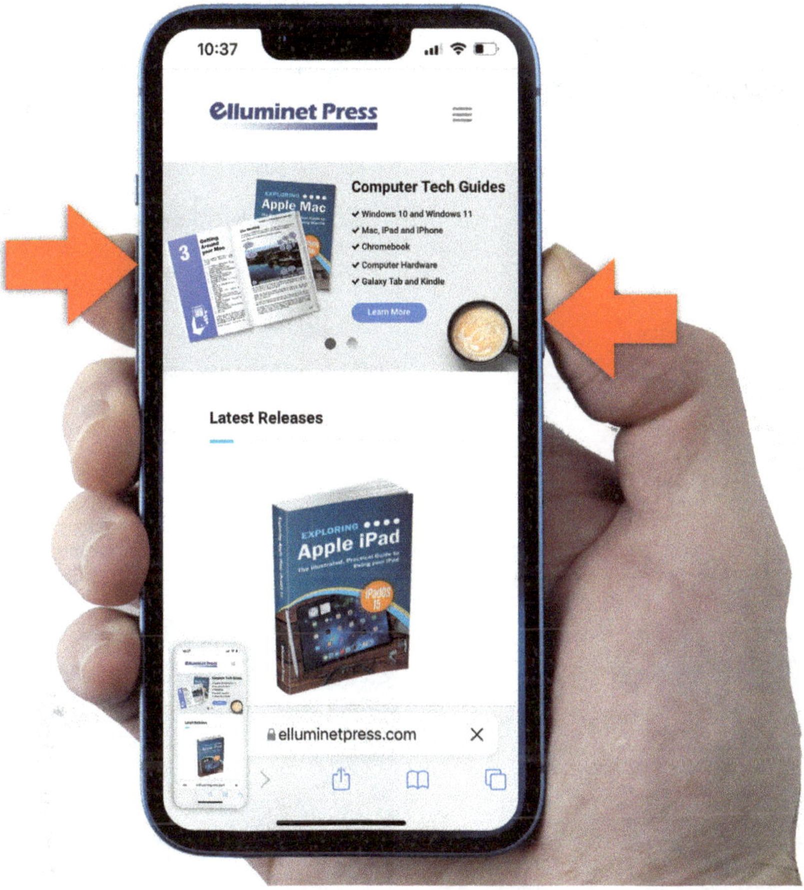


You'll see a small thumbnail of the screenshot appear on the bottom left. Tap on this to edit or share. Screenshots are saved to your photo albums, so you'll be able to see them in the photos app.

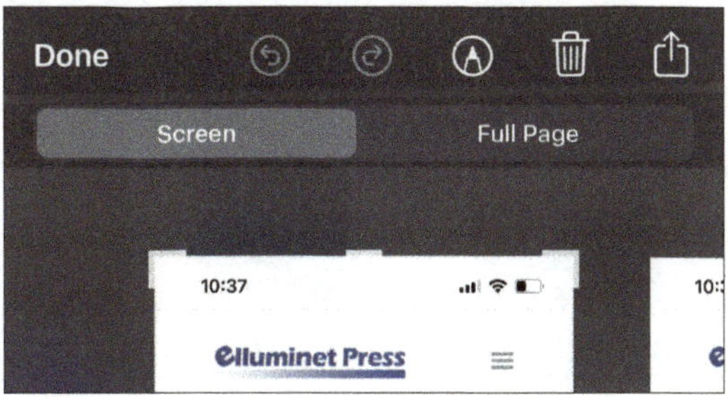

# Screen Recording

To enable the screen recording function, to the settings app, select control center, then scroll down, tap the + next to ‘screen recording’.

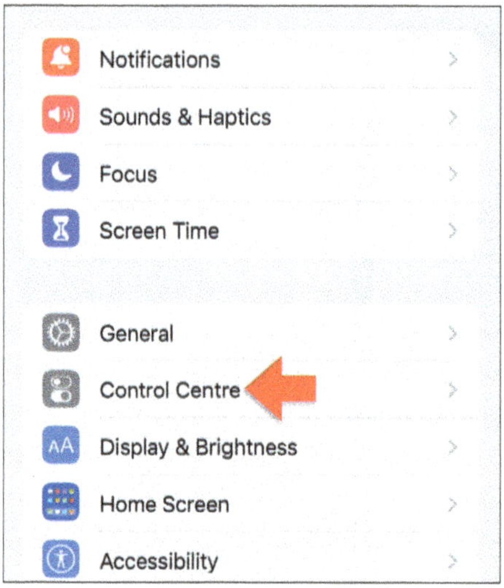


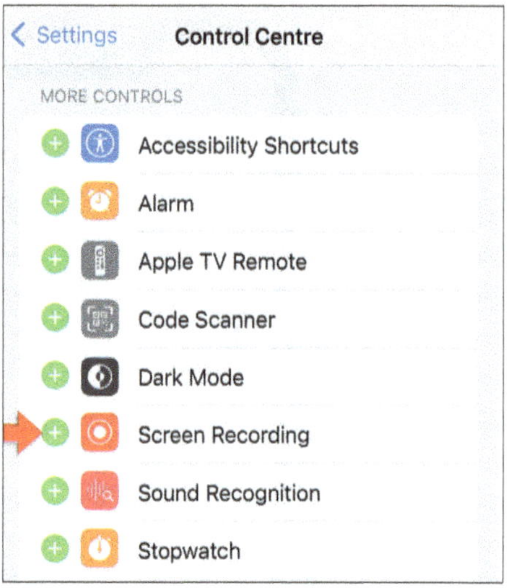


To record your screen, swipe down from the top right of the screen to open control center. Tap the ‘screen recording’ icon.

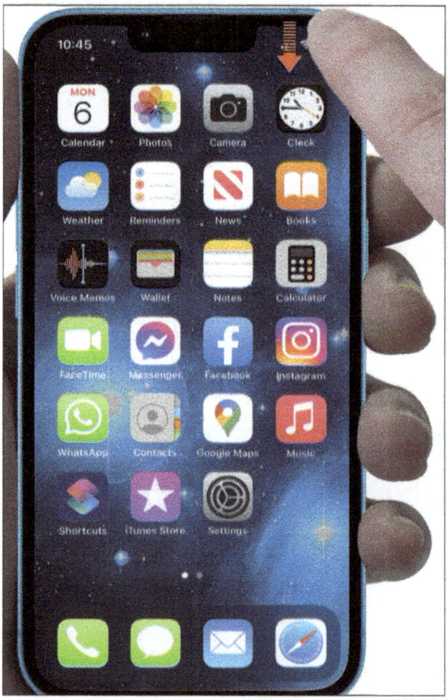

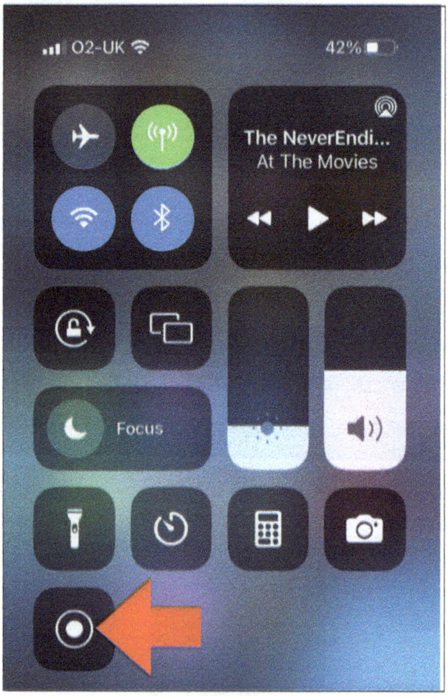

Wait for the three-second countdown.

You'll see the recorder icon highlighted. This is to tell you the screen is being recorded.

Go back to the home screen. You'll see the time highlighted in red on the top left.

To stop recording, tap the time highlighted in red on the top left of the screen.

Your recordings will appear in the photos app.

# Flashlight

On the back of your iPhone you'll find a flashlight. This is useful for finding your way in the dark or looking into something that isn't very well lit. You'll find the flashlight on the back of your iPhone along side the camera lenses.

To turn on the flashlight from the home screen, swipe downwards from the top right edge to open control center.

Tap on the flashlight icon to turn the flashlight on and off.

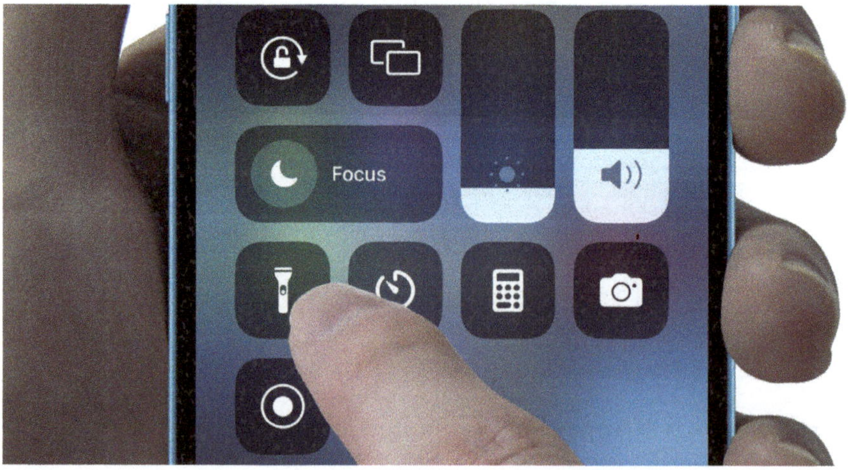

You can also turn use the flashlight from the lock screen. To do this, press the flashlight icon on the bottom left of the screen to turn the light on and off - you'll hear a click when you do this.

You'll see the flashlight light up. Don't look directly at it as the light is very bright.

# 4

# Using Apps

You can pretty much get an app for virtually anything, and these are all available from the app store.

Some are free and others you have to buy. There are games, productivity apps and apps just for fun.

Your iPhone comes with some apps built in. You can also download millions more from the App Store.

In this chapter, we'll take a look at

- App Store
- Taking Notes
- Reminders
- Maps
- News App
- Apple Books App
- Files App
- Find my iPhone
- Voice Memos
- Clock App
- Printing Documents

Take a look at the video resources, open your web browser and navigate to the following website.

elluminetpress.com/iphone-apps

# App Store

The app store has over 1 million apps available for download direct to your iPhone without even going on a computer. To start app store, click App Store app on your main screen.

Once on the app store's main screen, tap the icon on the top right to sign in with your Apple ID if you haven't already done so. If you are already signed in, your Apple ID will be displayed here, you won't need to sign in again.

On the app store, you will find everything from games and entertainment to productivity tools such as word processing, drawing and photo apps. These are split into games and app sections and you'll find these on the bar along the bottom of the screen.

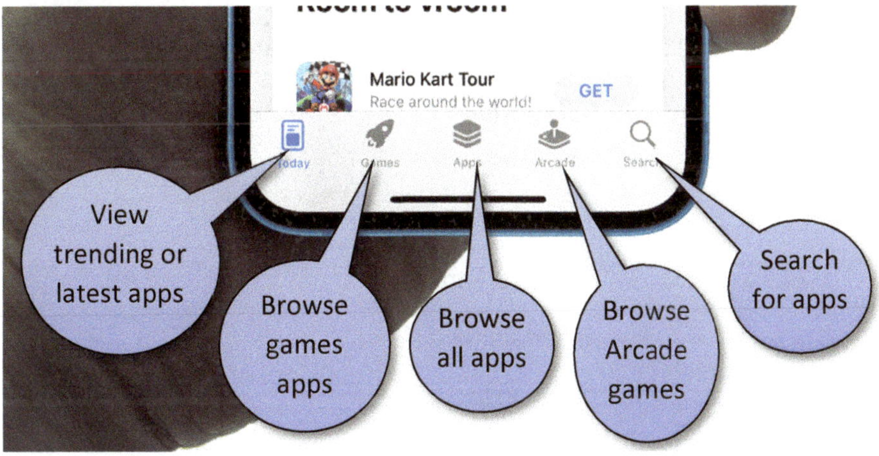


The last icon on the bar along the bottom allows you to search the app store for a specific app name or type/genre of app. You can search for recipes, travel details, maps. There is an app for almost anything you can think of.

## Browsing the Store

If you are more the browsing type, app store has grouped all the apps into categories according to their use. Select 'apps' from the bar on the bottom of the screen. Here you'll see some of the most popular apps, new apps and top selling apps. You can tap on any of these apps to view or download.

Tap on the app's image to view more details, Tap 'see all' at the top of each section to see all the apps in that section. Tap on 'get' or the price to download the app. Scroll down the page to see all the apps in the sections.

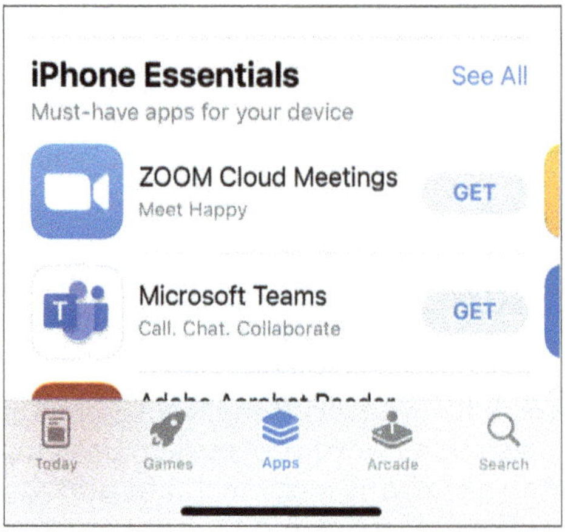


If you scroll down to the bottom of the page, you'll see a section called 'top categories'. Tap 'see all' to see all available categories.

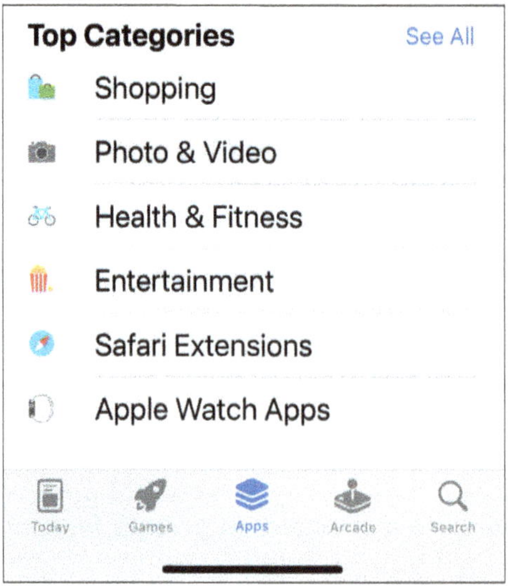

Tap on a category to browse the available apps. In this example, I'm going to explore the 'productivity' category.

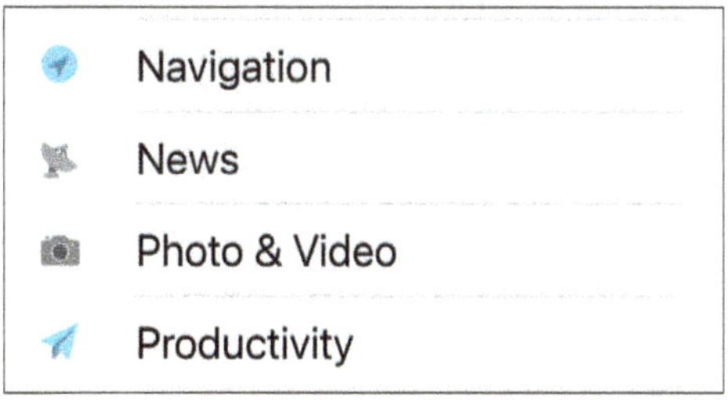


Here, you'll see a list of all the apps available for that category. Again, tap 'see all' on the top right to see the full lists in the different sections.

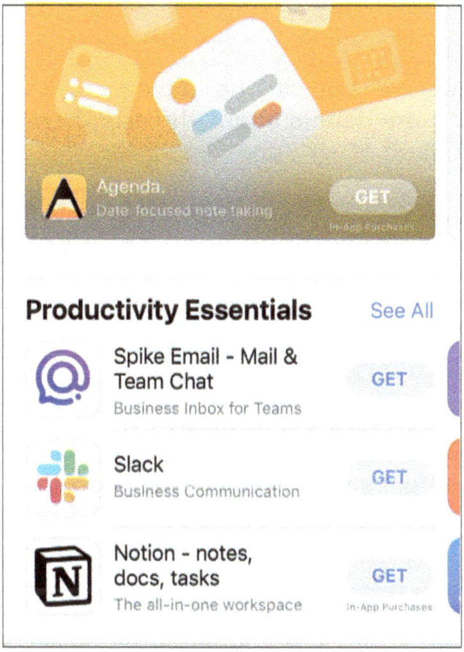


Tap the price tag to download and install the app on your iPhone.

This gives you information about what the app does, what it costs, some screen shots of the app in action and the device requirements in order to run the app.

To download or purchase an app, just tap 'get' or the price tag.

Watch out for 'in app purchases'. In-app purchases unlock additional features for a price. So while an app might be free to download, more often than not, you'll need to pay to unlock features, addons, more levels, or remove ads.

## Search the Store

To find an app, tap on 'search' on the bar at the bottom of your screen.

Type into the search field on the main screen, as shown below.

In this example, I'm going to search for one of my favourite games called 'worms'. From the suggestions, tap on the closest match. Tap on the image to view more details about the app; here you'll see reviews, price, screen shots and other info.

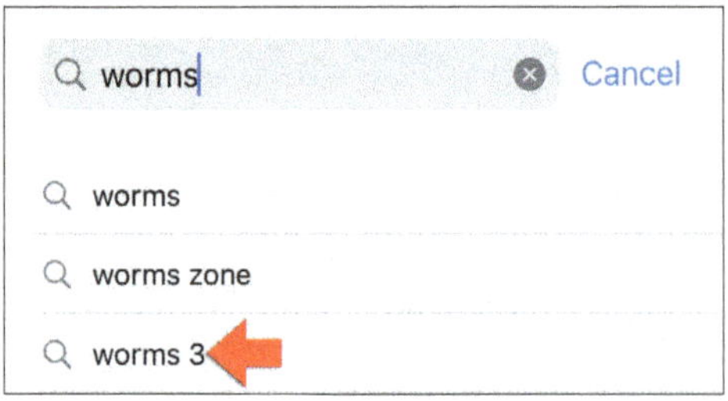


To download the app, tap 'get' next to the app if it's free, or tap the price tag if it's paid.

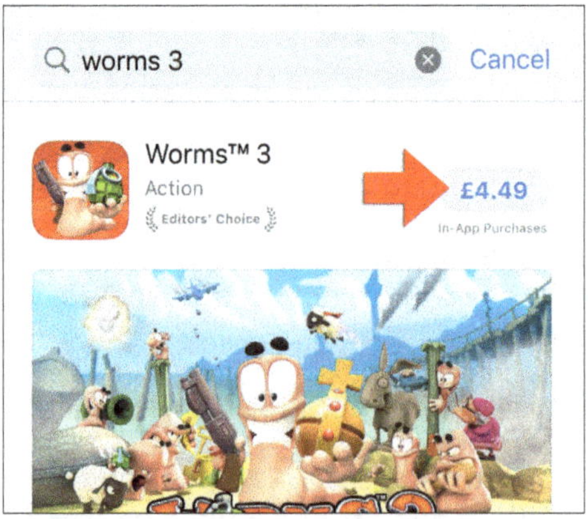


If it's a paid app, tap 'purchase' to confirm.

Authorise the purchase with your Apple ID password, TouchID, or FaceID.

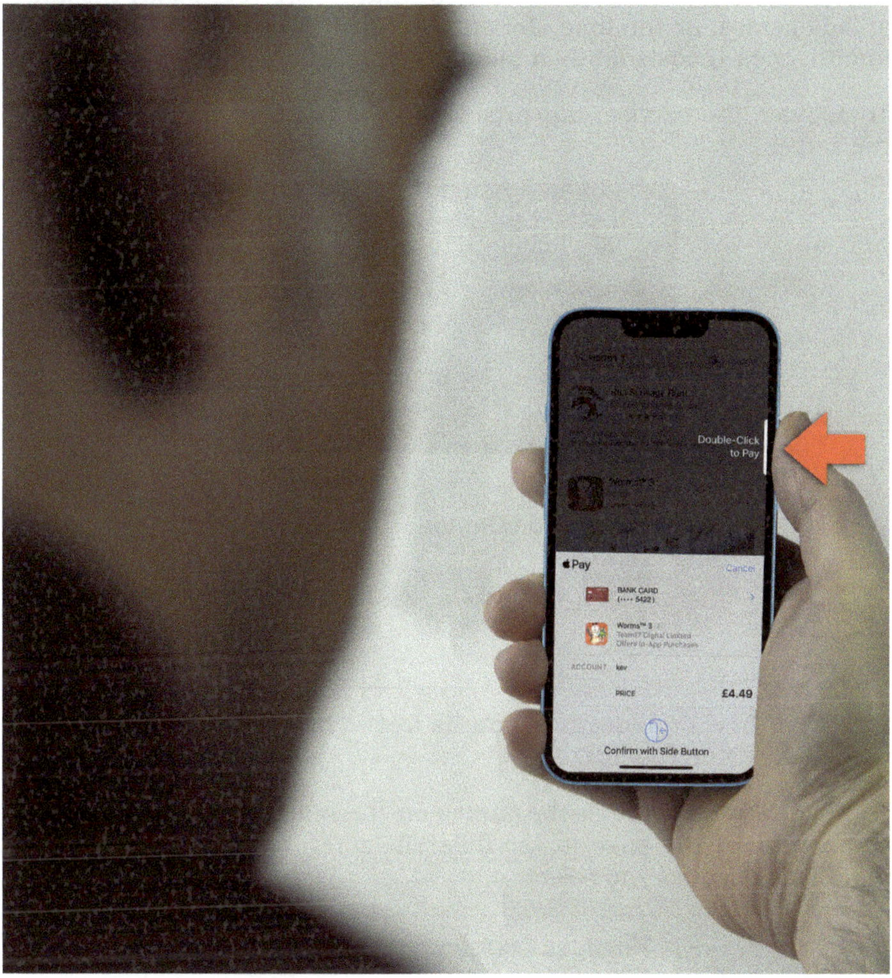


The app will appear on your home screen once it has downloaded and installed itself.

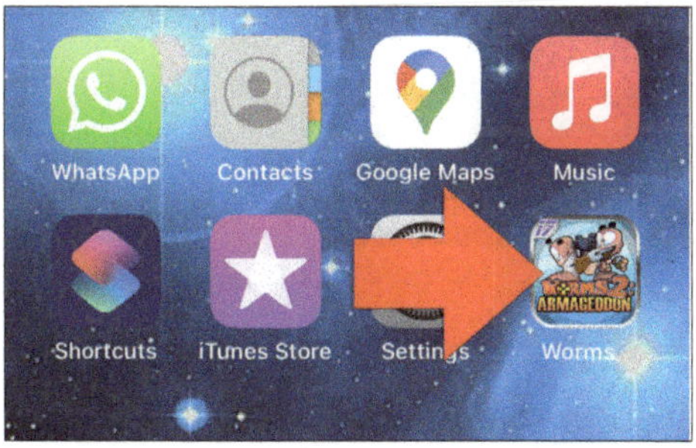

# The Arcade

Apple Arcade is a subscription service that allows you to play the latest arcade games. At the time of writing you can take out a free trial for a month, then it costs £4.99 a month to continue using the service.

To activate the service, tap 'arcade' on the panel along the bottom of the screen,

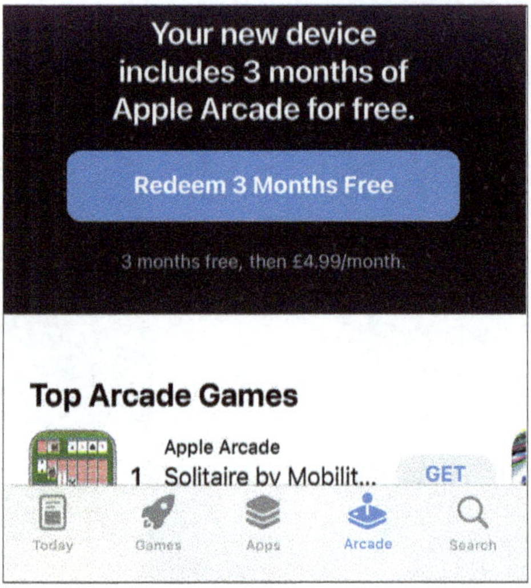


Tap 'try it free' or 'redeem 3 months free'. The confirm your purchase using FaceID or TouchID

You can browse through the games on the main page. Scroll down to the bottom of the page to see different categories of games you can play. Tap a category to select.

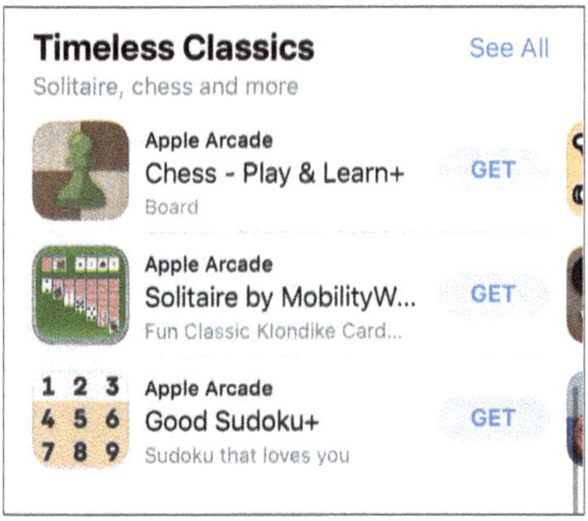


Tap on the game icon to see more information...

Tap 'get' to download the game, tap 'play' to start the game.

You'll find all your downloaded games on your home screen.

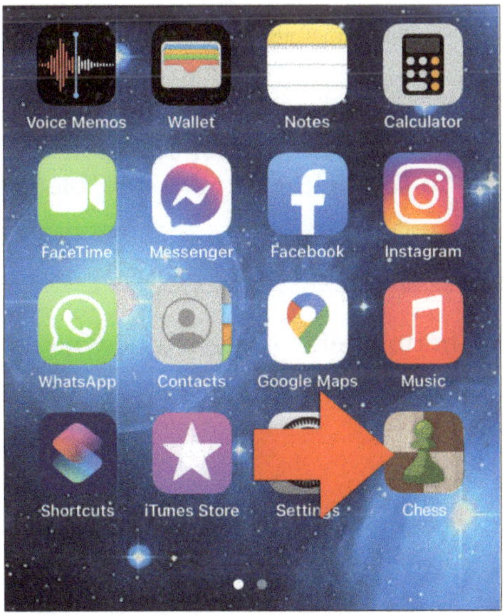

# Taking Notes

The notes app is useful for taking notes, scanning documents, creating check-lists and even taking hand written notes.

To start notes app, tap on the icon on the home screen.

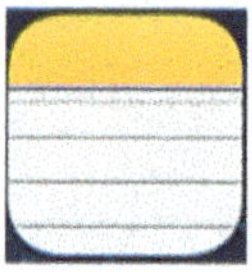

When notes has loaded, you'll land on the folders screen where you can view your saved notes in iCloud. If you've used the notes app before, you'll land on the screen you were using the last time.

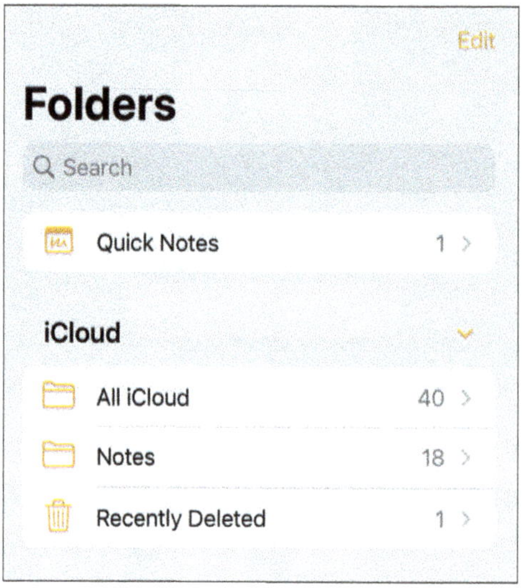


Along the bottom, you'll see two icons. The icon on the left creates a new folder, the icon on the right creates a new blank note.

Tap the icon on the bottom left to create a new note.

## Typing Notes

Along the bottom of a note, the on-screen keyboard will pop up. Along the top of the keyboard, you'll find some icons. You can add a table, tick box, scan documents, take pictures to insert into notes. You can handwrite notes using your finger. You can also add lines and grid lines to help you write.

You can type your notes in as if it were a notepad, using the on screen keyboard.

## Taking & Inserting Photos

You can use the camera on your iPhone to take a photo and video, or you can choose one from your Photos App. To do this, tap the camera icon on the top right of the on-screen keyboard. If you want to take a photo/video with your camera, tap 'take photo or video'.

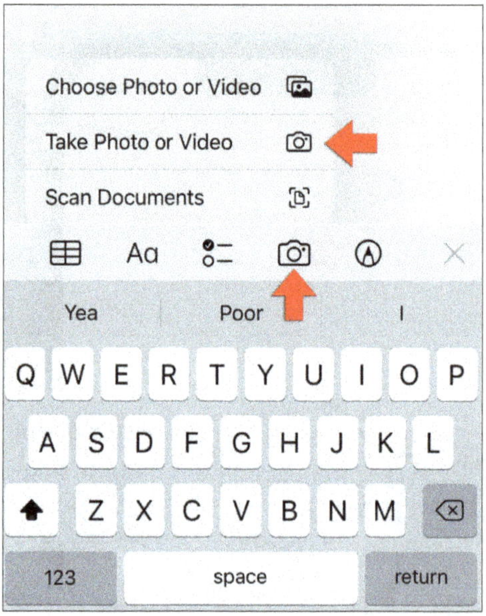


Tap the white circle at the bottom to take a photo of the object you want to add to the note. If you want to take a video, tap 'video', then tap the red circle.

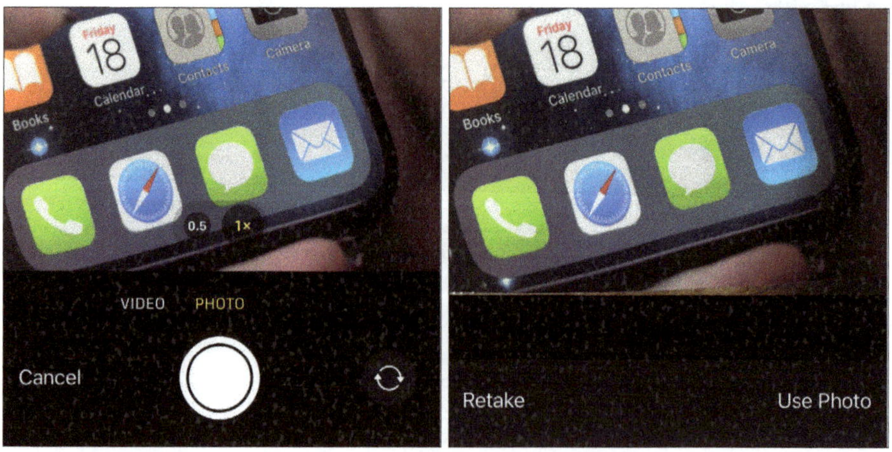


Tap 'use photo' on the bottom right. Tap 'retake' if you want to take the photo again.

Your photo will appear in your notes.

## Inserting Photos from Photos App

Tap the camera icon on the top right of the on-screen keyboard. If you want to insert a photo/video from an album in the photos app, tap 'choose photo or video'.

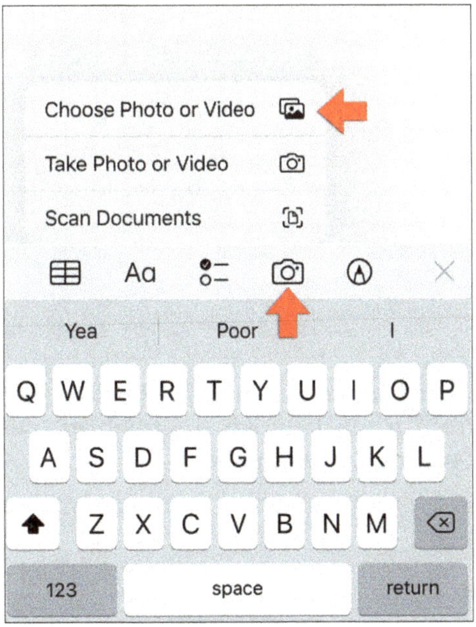

Select a photo/video to add.

## Handwritten Notes

You can use your finger to write notes, draw diagrams, and annotate photos. To do this, open a new note, then tap the small pen icon on the top right of the on-screen keyboard.

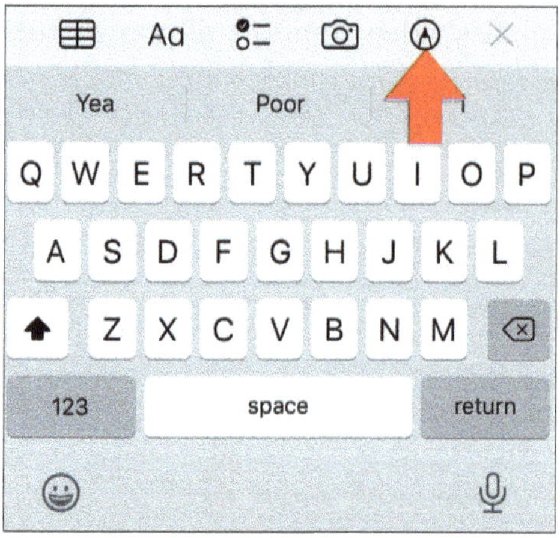


Your drawing tools will appear along the bottom of the screen. Here, you can choose from a marker pen, highlighter, pencil, eraser, or a lasso tool, as well as your colour pallet.

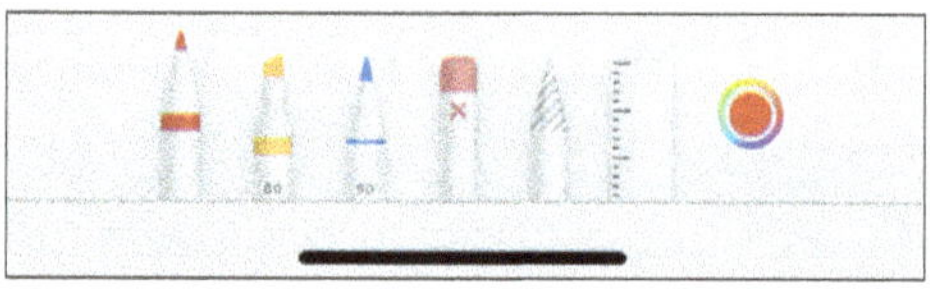

Tap on the pens to select. When you tap on a pen, you'll see a popup menu. Here, you can select pen thickness and opacity. If the pop up menu doesn't show, tap twice on the pen.

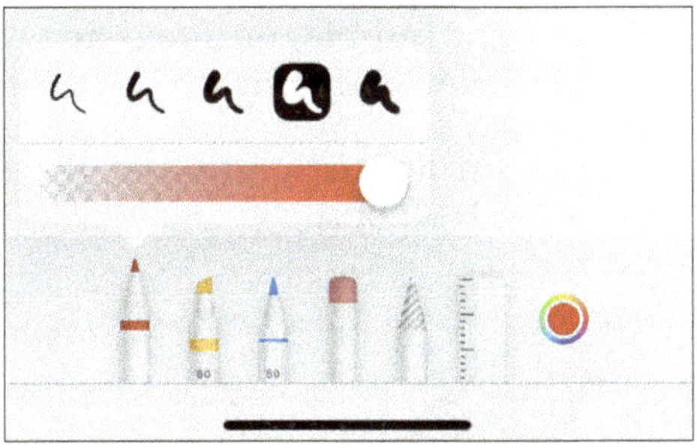

You can also use the selection pen to draw around an object to select it. This helps with copy and paste. There is also an on screen ruler that allows you to draw straight lines with your pen. On the right of the drawing tools you can choose a colour, tap the coloured icon to choose show the colour palette.

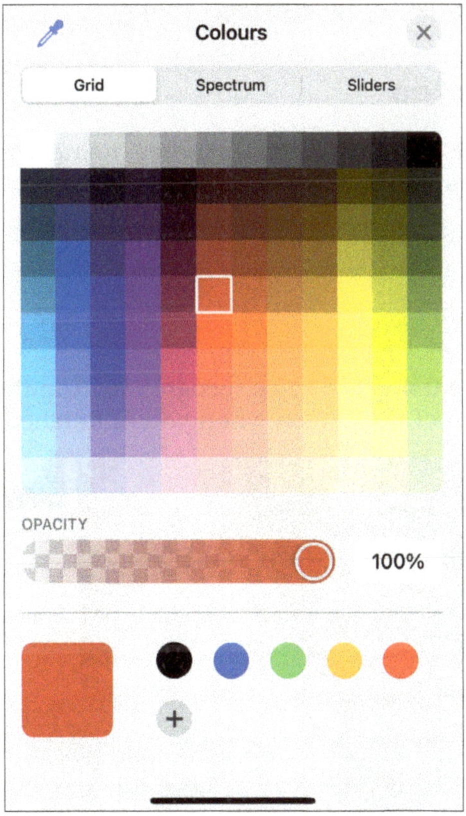


Tap on a colour, then tap the 'x' on the top right to close.

## Shape Recognition

You can create perfect shapes using your pen. Currently, you can draw any of these: line, curve, square, rectangle, circle, oval, heart, triangle, star, cloud, hexagon, thought bubble, outlined arrow, line with arrow endpoint, and curve with arrow endpoint.

To use this feature, draw an approximation of the shape, then hold your pencil on the glass for 1 second.

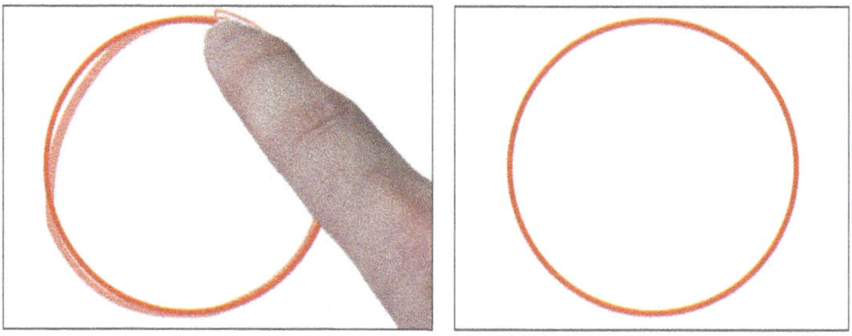

Your shape will convert into a perfect shape.

## Dictating Notes

Instead of typing, you can dictate notes using the voice dictation feature. To do this, tap the mic icon on the keyboard.

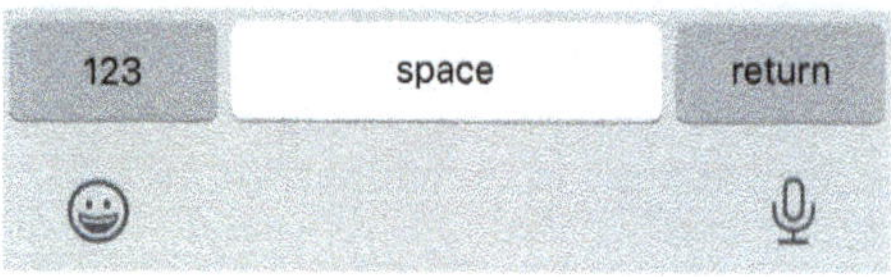


Record your notes using the voice recognition. Tap the small keyboard icon at the bottom of the screen when you're finished.

## Organising your Notes

You can create folders to organise your notes. To put a note into a folder, first open the note, then tap the three dots icon on the top right of the screen.

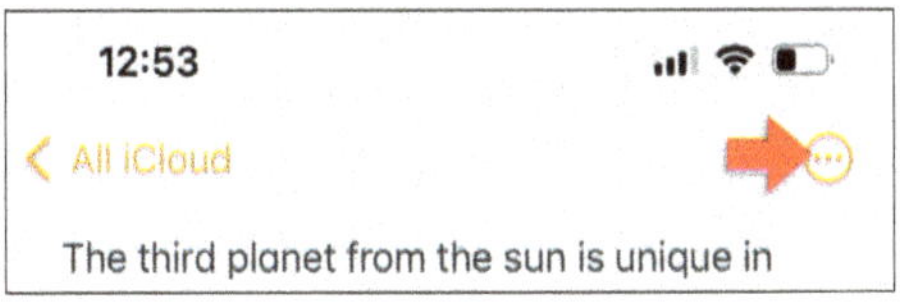


From the menu, select 'move note'

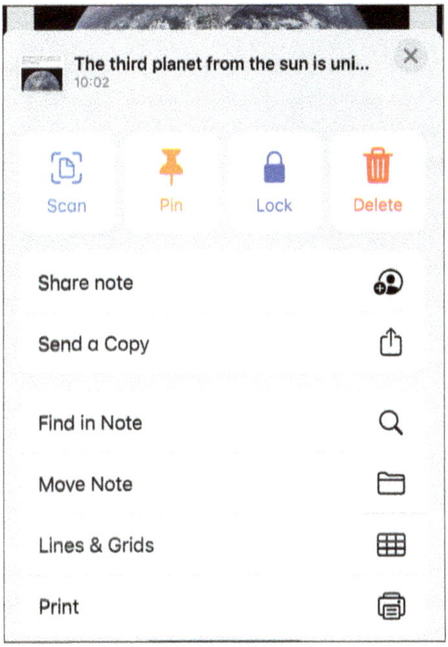


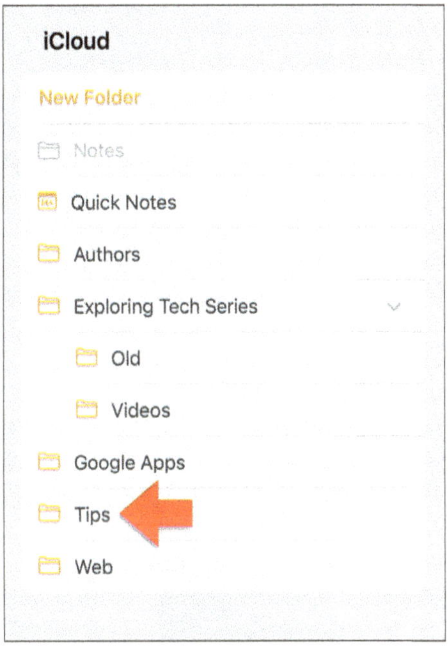


If the folder you want to add the note to exists (eg 'tips'), select it from the list. If the folder doesn't exist, tap 'new folder'.

## Note Folders

Tap the link on the top left until you reach the folders screen.

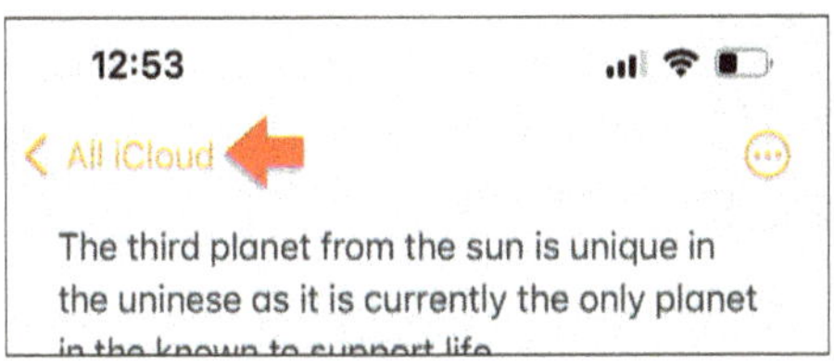

Here you'll see all the folders you've created for your notes. Tap the folder icon on the bottom left to create a new folder. Tap the icon on the bottom right to create a new note.

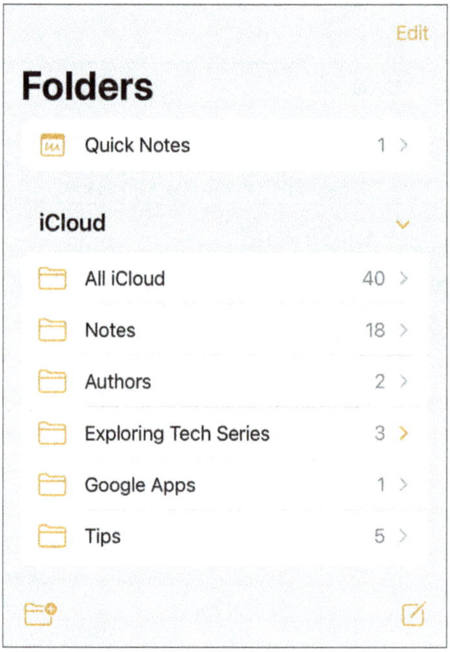


Tap 'edit' on the top right of the screen. Tap and drag the folders using the hamburger icon on the right to organise them or change the order and nesting. Tap the three dots icon next to the folder to share, move or rename folder.

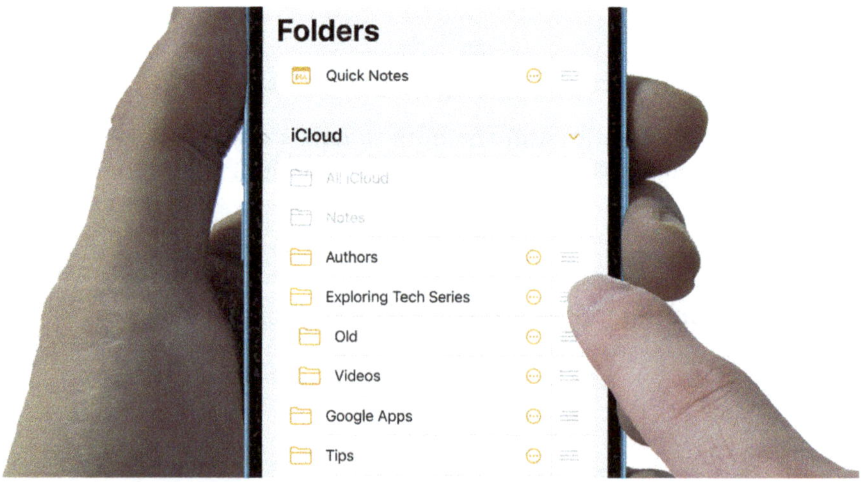


To delete a folder, swipe right to left over the folder.

## Inviting other Users

You can invite other users to view and edit your notes. This can be useful in a meeting where people can add notes from their own iPhone. To share a note, open it, then tap the three dots icon on the top right hand side of the screen.

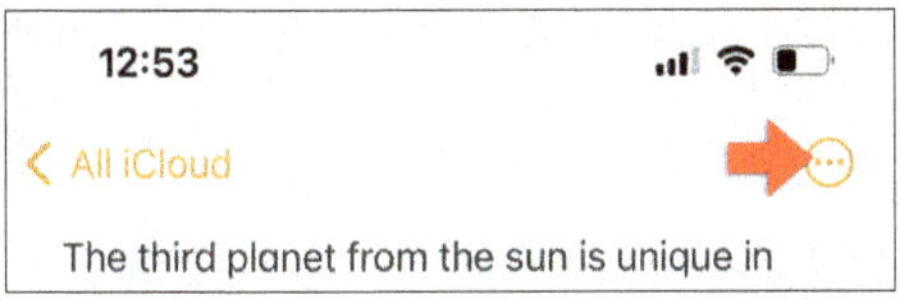


Select 'share note'.

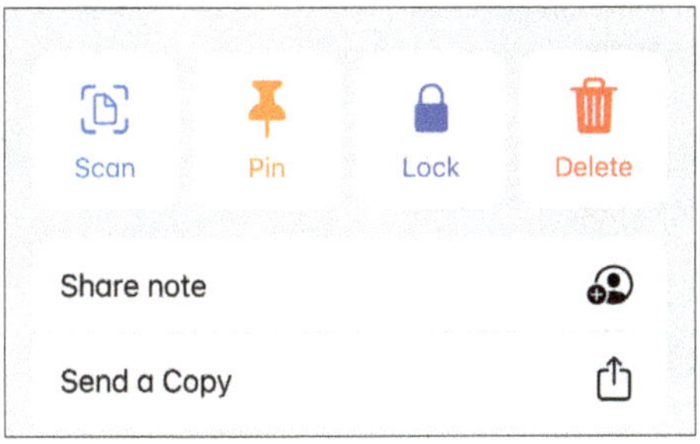


Tap 'share options' at the bottom.

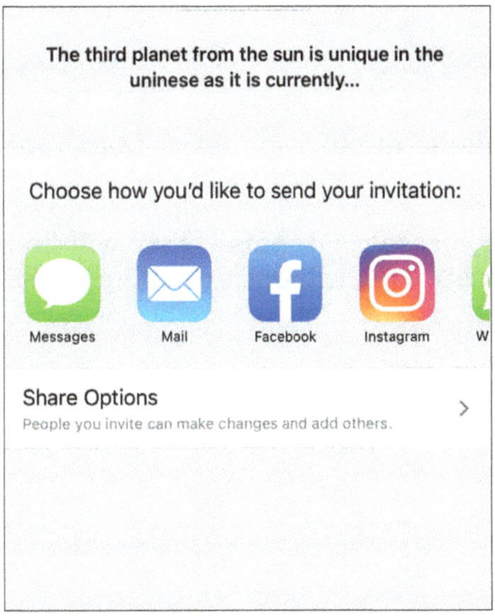


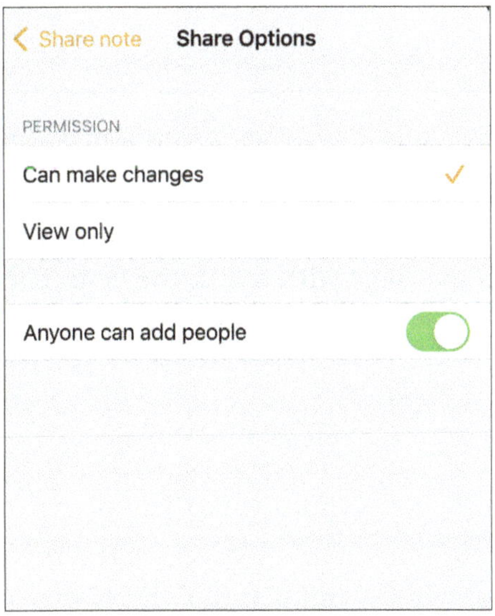


From here, you can select whether you want people to be able to edit your note, or just view it.

Tap the link on the top left to go back.

Tap 'add people' at the top of the drop down to return to the previous screen. Now, select how you want to send the invitation eg email.

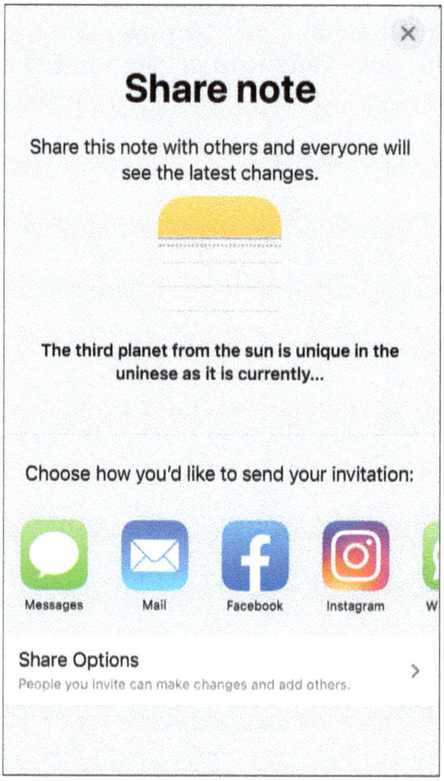


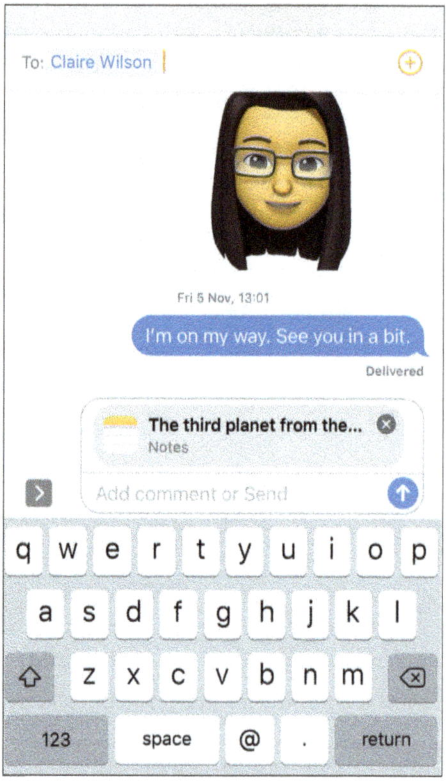


Enter the person's email address/phone number (or select from your contacts). .

When the other person checks their messages or email, they will find a message with a link they can click on. This will open the note in the notes app on their device.

# Reminders

With reminders, you can create to do lists, and set alerts to remind you do to certain things.

To start reminders app, tap the icon on the home screen

## Create a Reminder

Tap the list you want to add the reminder to, then tap 'new reminder' at the bottom of the screen.

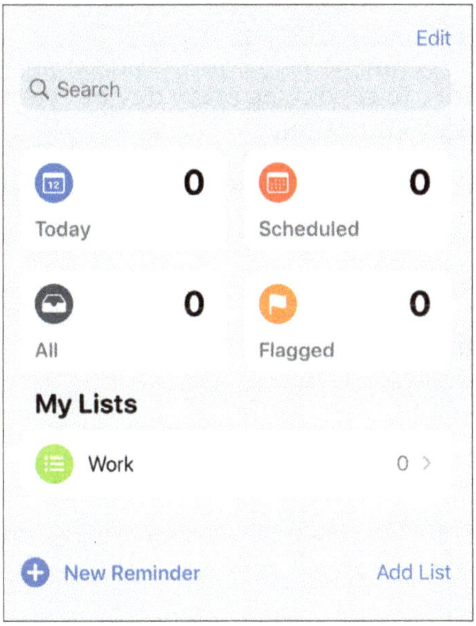


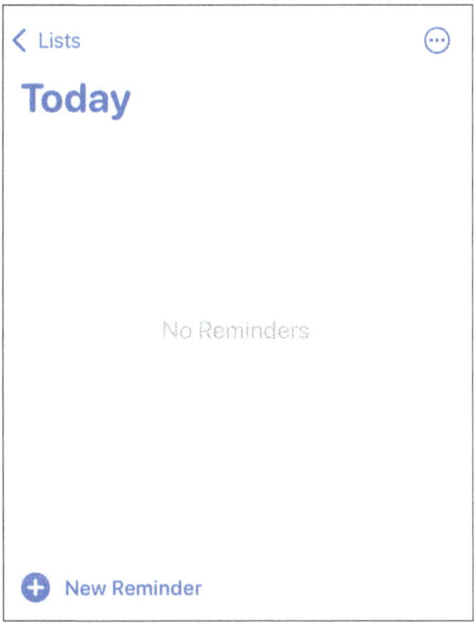


Type in your reminder.

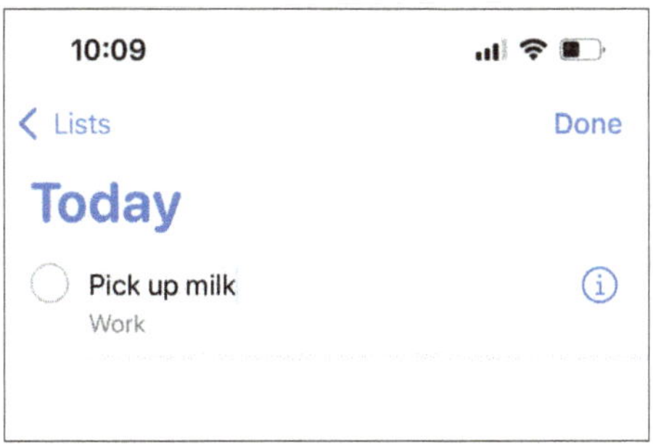

Tap the 'i' icon to edit the details. Here you can add notes if applicable, you can set the date and time you want reminding.

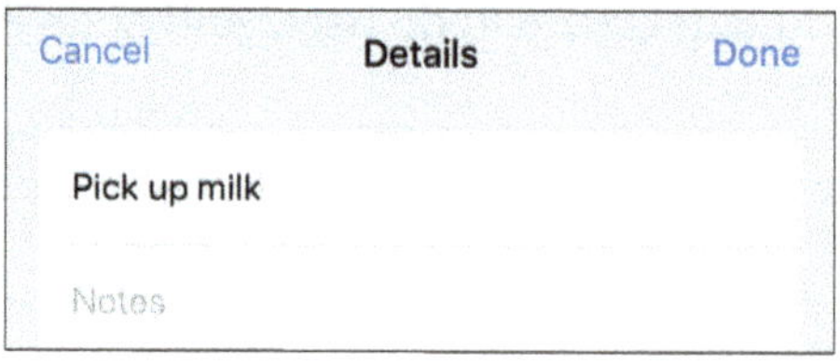


To change the date, tap on 'today' then change the date. To change the time, tap the time switch to turn it on, then select a time.

Further down, you can set the reminder to repeat, eg every day or every week. To do this, tap repeat then select an option.

You can also set the reminder to remind you when you reach a particular location, or when messaging someone.

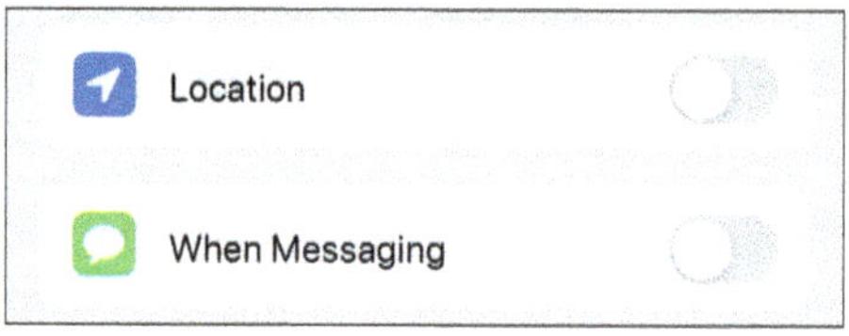


## Reminder at a Location

You can schedule a reminder to remind you of something when you are at a particular location. To do this, tap the list you want to add the reminder to.

Tap 'new reminder' at the bottom of the screen.

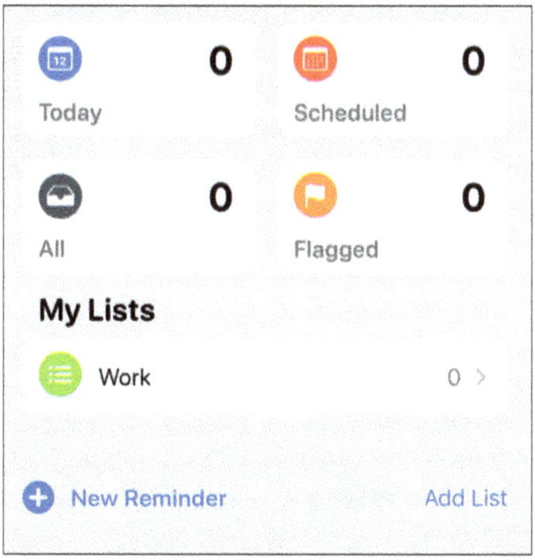


Type in your reminder, then tap the 'i' icon on the right.

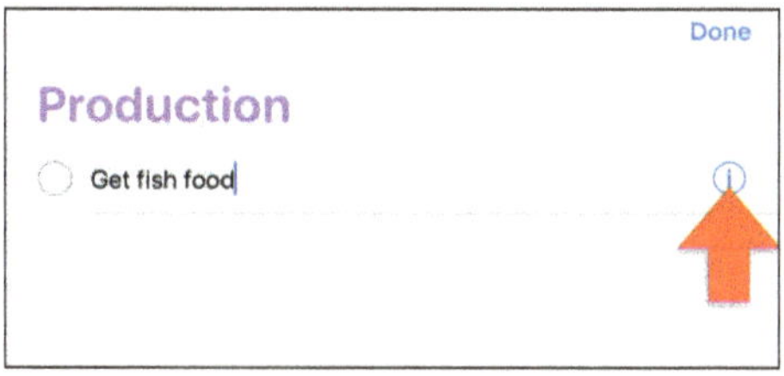


Scroll down to location, turn on the switch, select 'custom'.

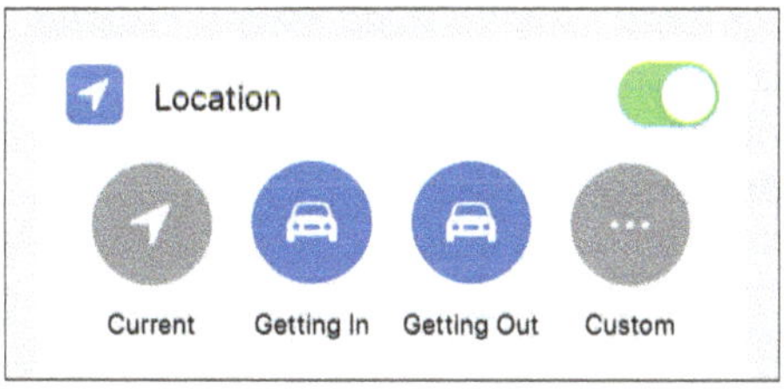


Type in the address, select the closest match from the suggestions.

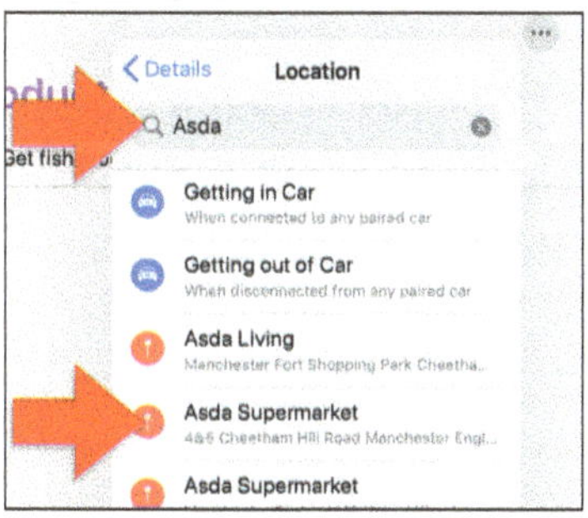

Tap 'arriving' to remind you when you arrive at the destination. Tap 'leaving' if you want to be reminded when you leave the destination. You can also set the distance from the location that triggers the reminder - in the example above, you'll be reminded when you're 524.9ft away. Tap the black circle on the location map and drag it bigger or smaller.

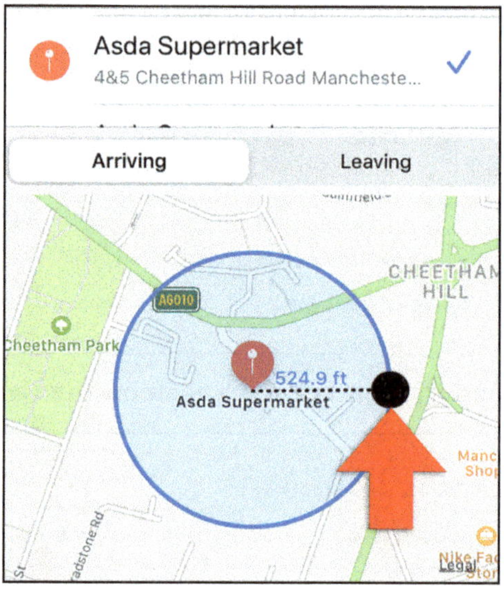


Tap 'details' on the top left to go back, then tap 'done'.

## Reminder When Messaging Someone

You can schedule a reminder to remind you of something when contacting a particular person on your contacts list. To do this, tap the list you want to add the reminder to.

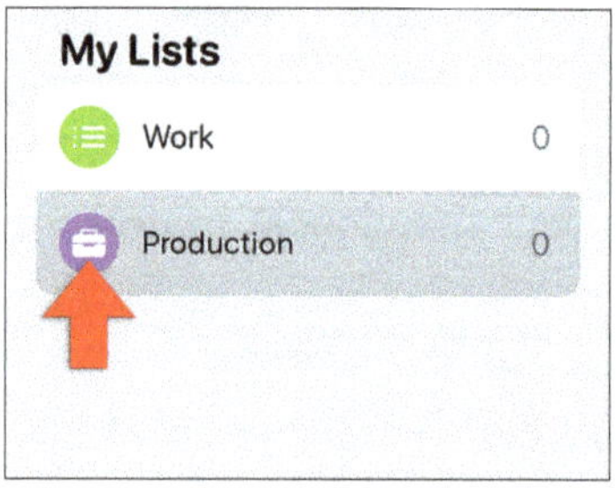


Tap 'new reminder' at the bottom of the screen.

Type in your reminder, then tap the 'i' icon on the right.

From the drop down, turn on 'when messaging', then tap 'choose person'.

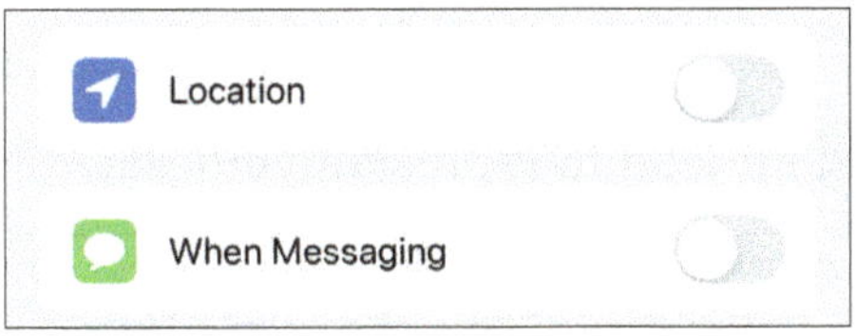


Select the person's name from your contacts list. Now the next time you contact this person, you'll get a reminder.

## Create a New List

Tap 'add list' at the bottom right of the screen if you want to create a new one.

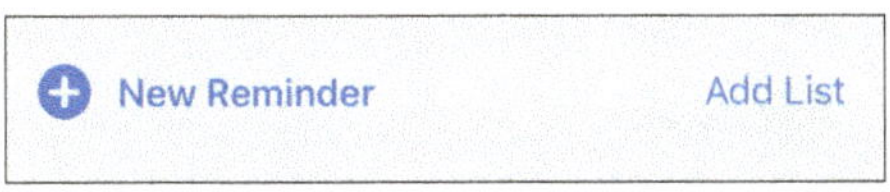

Enter a name for your list at the top.

Select a colour and an icon to represent your list.

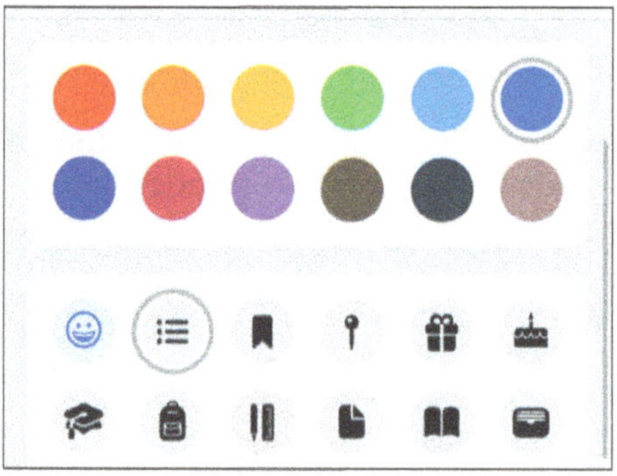

Tap 'done' on the top right when you're finished.

Your lists will appear under the 'my lists' section on the front panel of the reminders app.

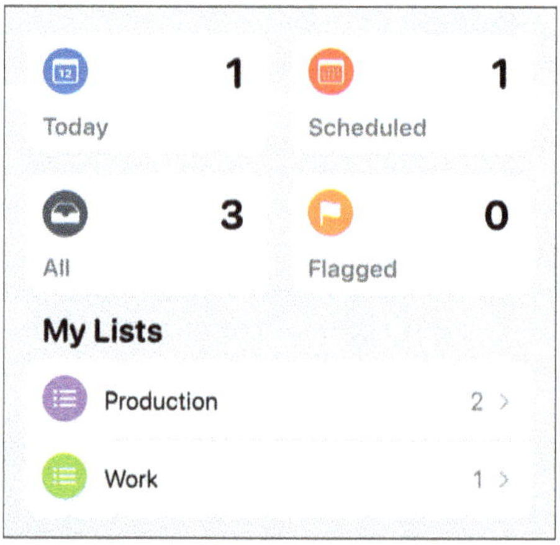

# Maps

Maps is an extremely useful app if you are trying to find out where a particular place is and need to find driving directions. It works like a SatNav/GPS giving you precise directions straight from door to door.

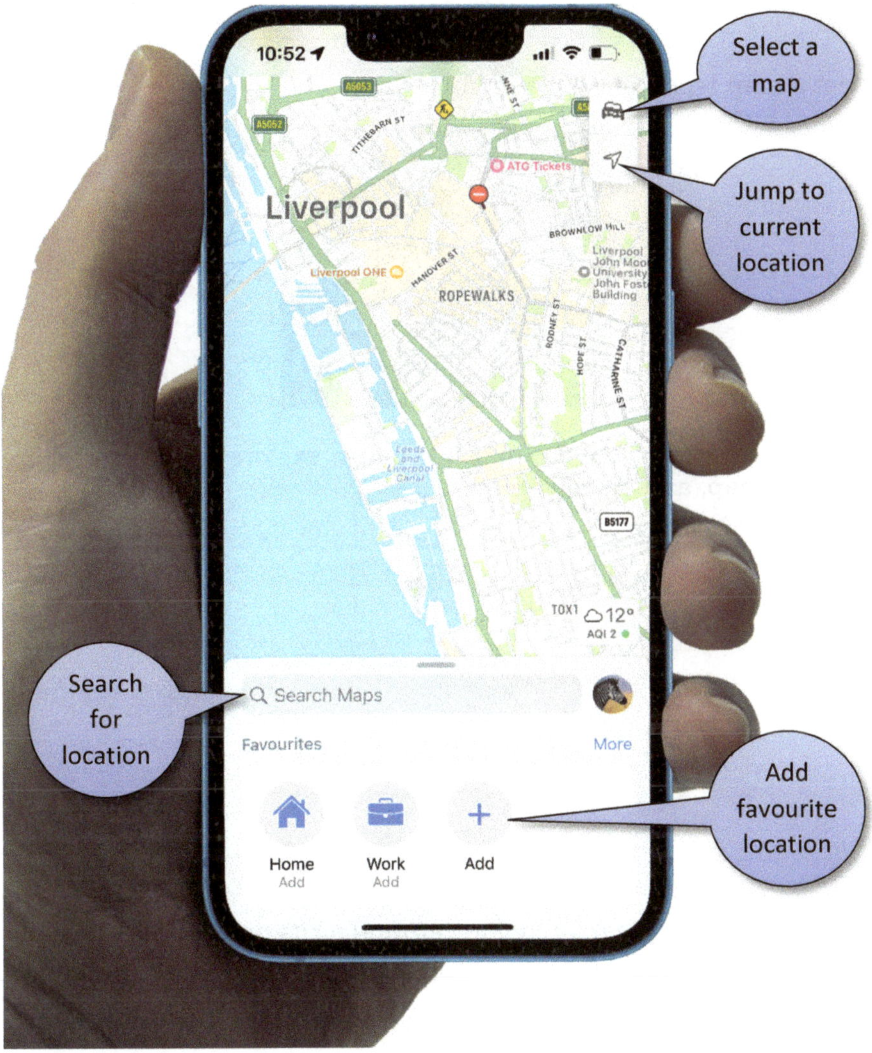


Using the panel at the bottom of the screen, you can search for a location - just type in an address, or place name. Under that, you can add a 'home' location, and a 'work' location. This allows you to tap 'home' or 'work' to find that location and is useful if you want directions to that place, or traffic reports between 'home' and 'work'. You can also add favourite locations, ie locations you travel to regularly.

You can view the map in four different types - tap the map icon on the top right of the screen to change this.

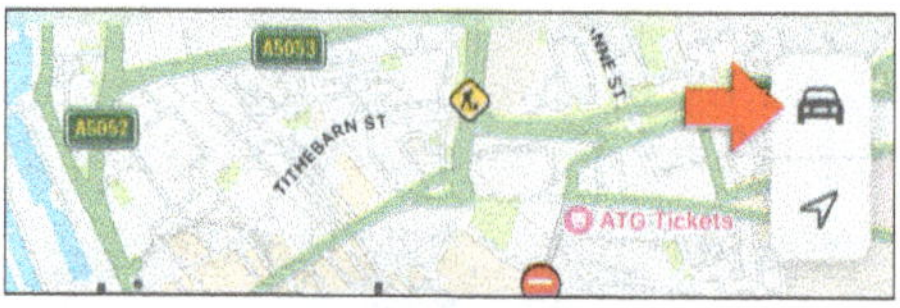


Select a map type from the options.

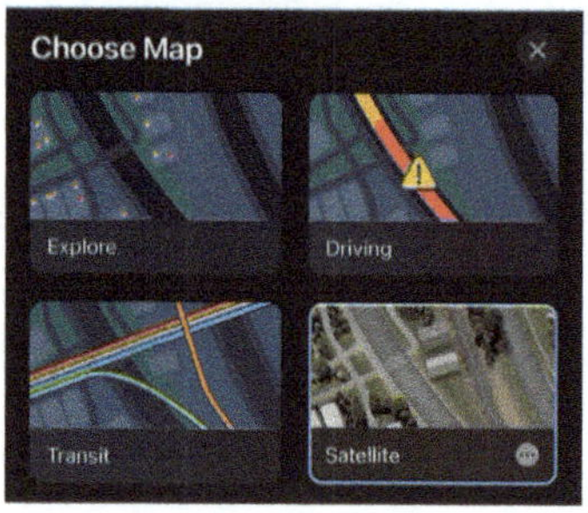


Here below, you can see the different maps: explore map, street map, transport map, and satellite map.

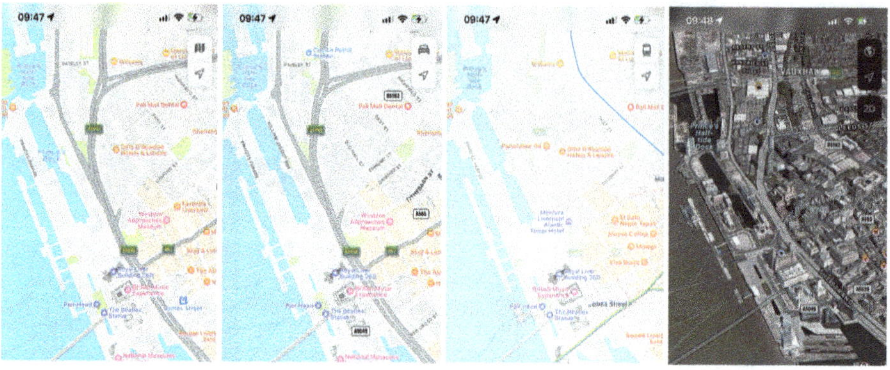

**Explore maps** are great for looking around a city or location. This map renders a location in a detailed 3D landscape.

**Street maps** are great if you are using the maps app as a GPS/Satnav while driving.

**Transport maps** give you public transport routes in a particular location for buses and trains. You'd be wise to check local public transport information for updates and changes.

**Satellite maps** are great if you are exploring a city or area of interest as well as planning a route. You can see these maps in 2D and 3D.

## Guides

The Guides feature is intended to provide expert recommendations for the best places to visit in a city, such as places to eat, shop, and places of interest to explore. Useful if you're visiting a city and want to find out where to eat, shop, or what to do. There are only a few cities such as Los Angeles, San Francisco, New York and Seattle that include this feature at the moment, but more will be added soon.

To view a guide on a city, type the city name into the search at the bottom of the screen. Select the city name from the search results. If the city has guides you'll see them appear in the info card for that city.

Scroll down, tap on any of the guides to view more information and see the location. Select an attraction and you'll see the location appear on the map with an info card.

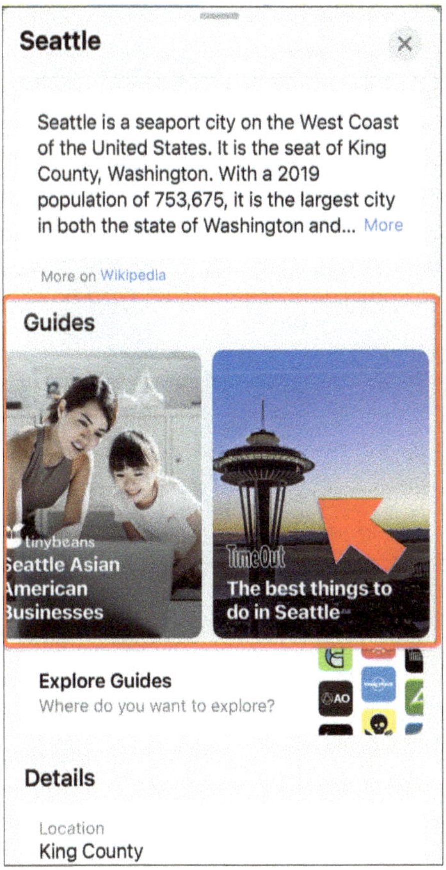

You'll see the location on the map and some details in the info card.

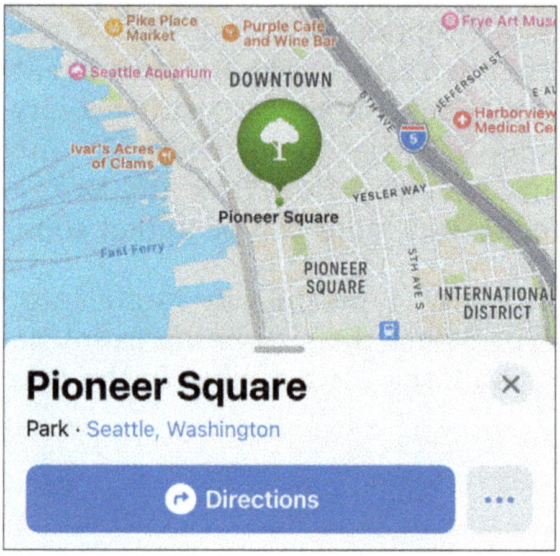


Tap 'directions' to get directions from your location. Tap 'route'.

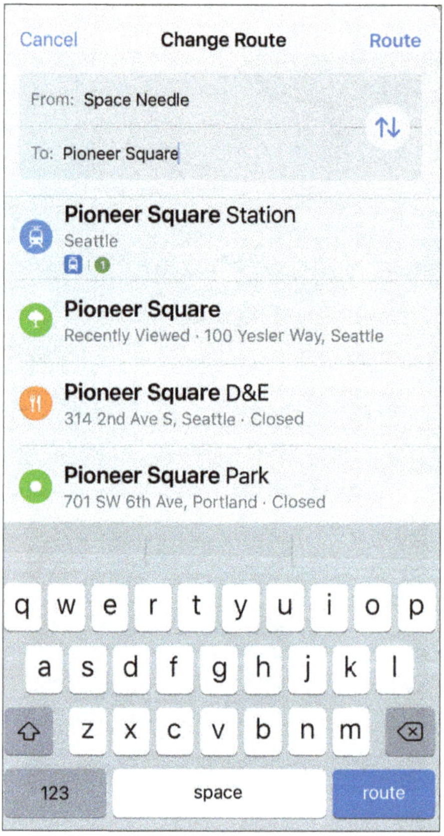


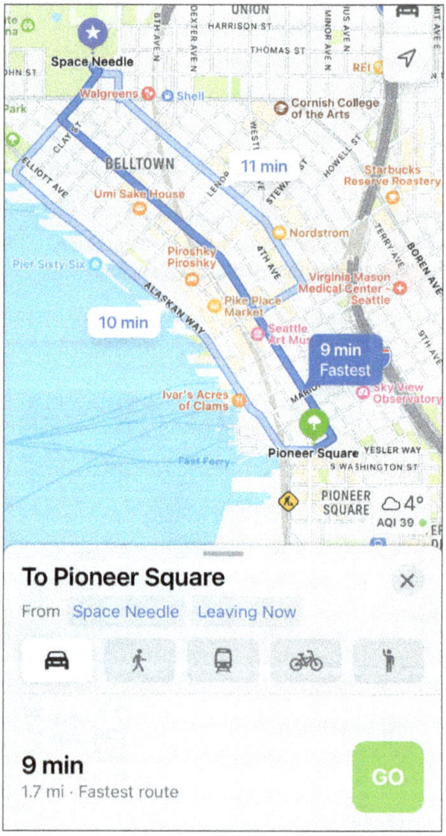


Along the bottom of the map, you'll see multiple routes. Tap 'go' next to the route you want to take.

You can also create your own guides and share them with friends, family and colleagues. To add a location to your own guide, tap the guides icon at the bottom of the info card.

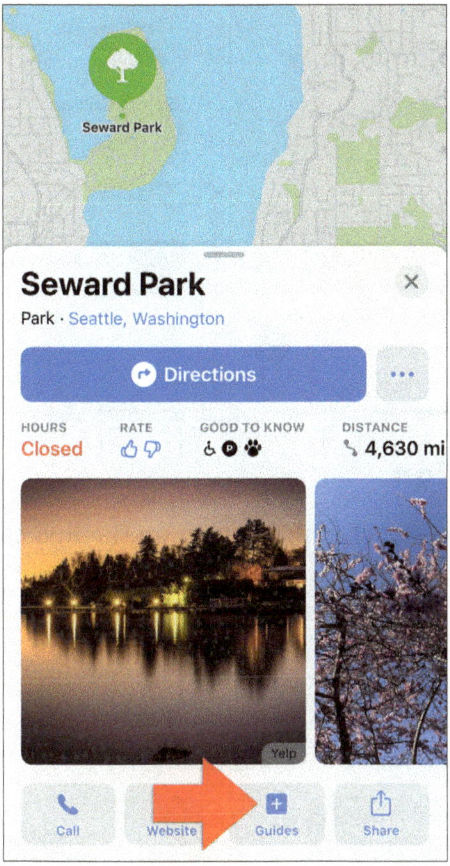


Select the guide you want to add the location to. If you're creating a new guide, tap 'new guide'. Type in a name eg: 'Vacation Day 1'. Tap 'create'.

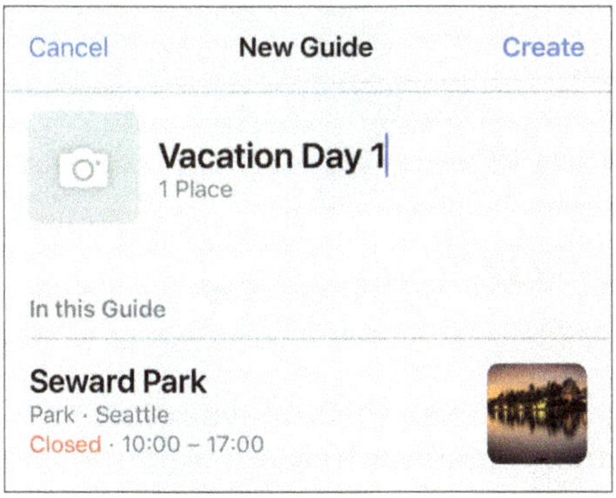

You'll find your guides at the bottom of the info card.

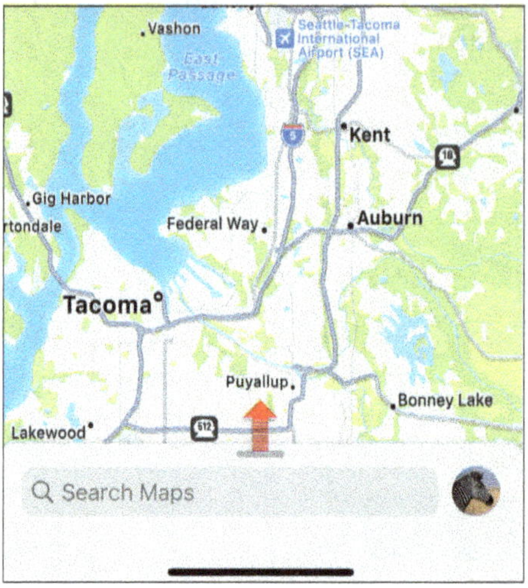


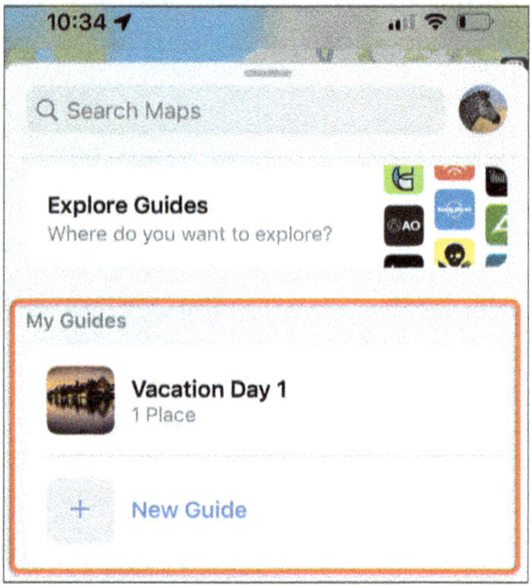


## Share Location

To share a location tap the 'share' icon on the info card.

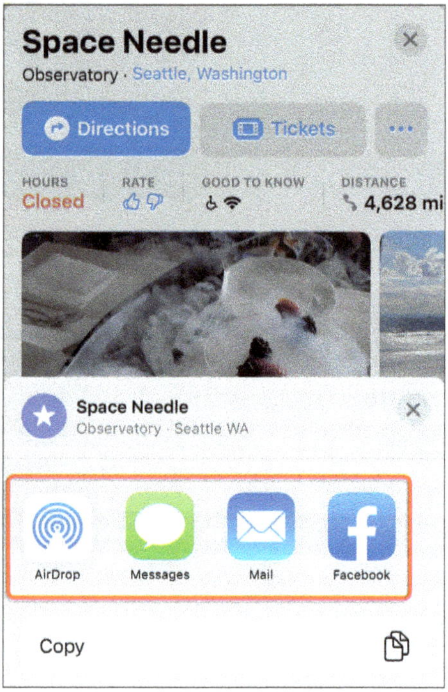


Select the app you want to use to share your location. Select the person or enter their number/email address

## Driving Directions

To find driving directions, type in your destination into the search field on the top left of the screen and select the destination from the list of suggestions.

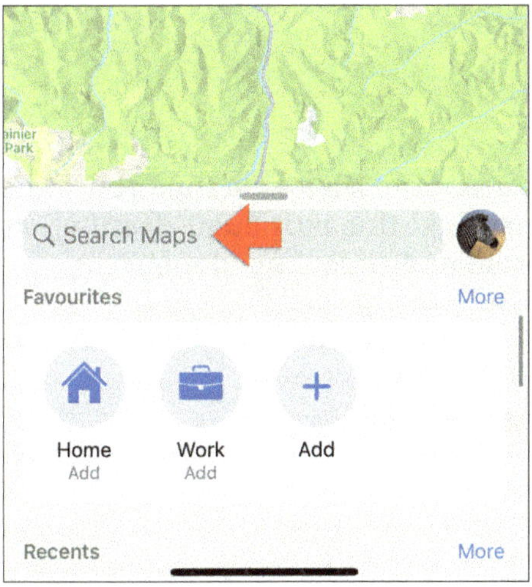


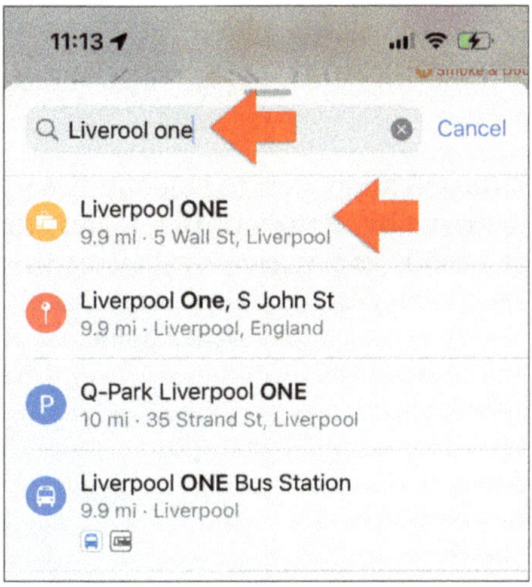


In the info card, you'll see a driving time estimate. This is the time it will take to get to this place from your current location. Tap on this to see the driving directions.

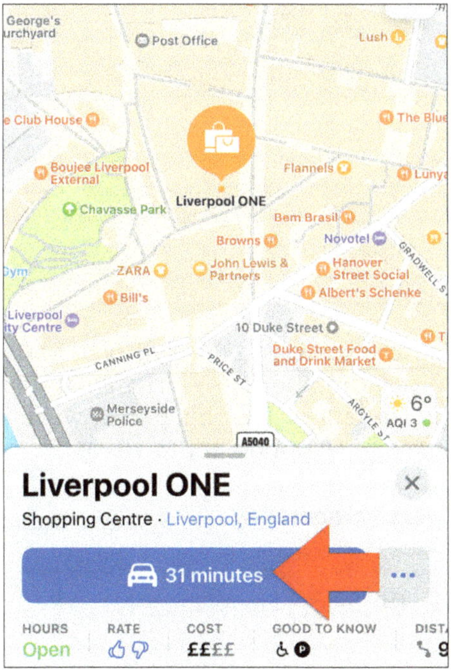

By default, the maps app will start the route from your current location - you can change this, just tap 'my location' then type in another location. If you plan to leave at another time, tap 'leaving now' and select a time.

This will allow you to select a time you want to leave or a time you want to arrive by. For example, I want to arrive at this particular destination at 12:00. Tap 'arrive by', select the date and time. Tap 'done'.

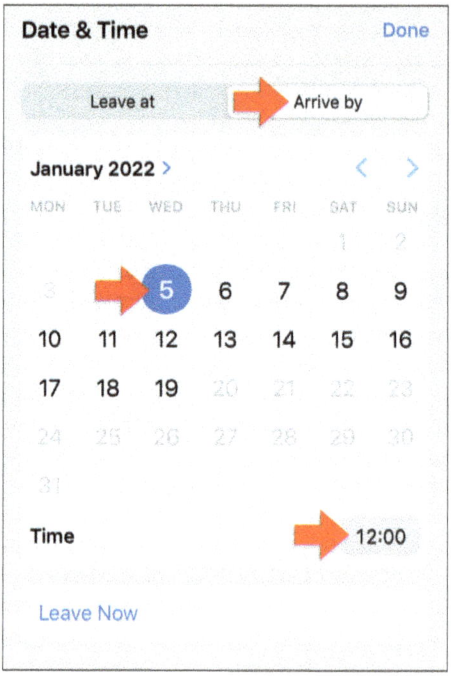


Along the top of the info card, you'll see 'drive', 'walk', and 'transport'. This allows you to get directions for driving, if you're walking, or if you're taking public transport. For this demo, we're looking for driving directions, so we'll keep the option set to 'drive'.

On the screen you'll see an overview of your route. You can zoom in and out or move around the map using your finger to see details or roads.

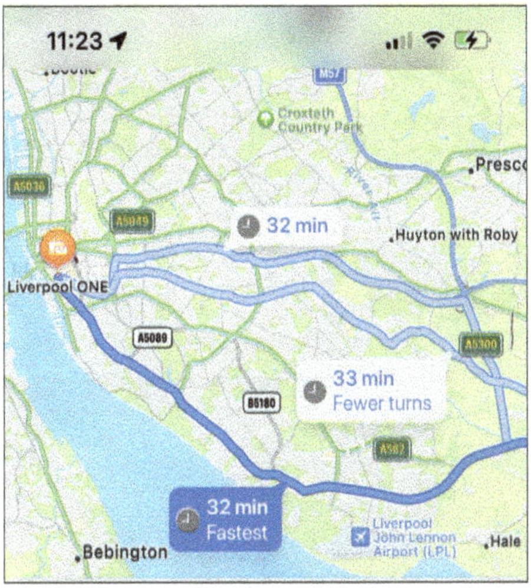


At the bottom, you'll see some estimates. It will tell you when to leave to arrive by the time you set above. Tap on 'go' next to the route you want.

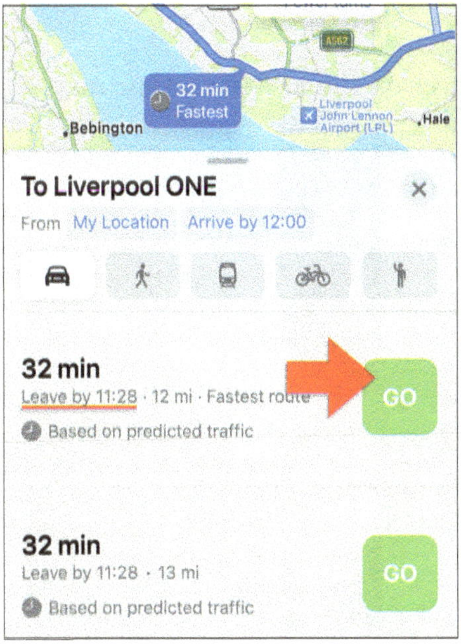


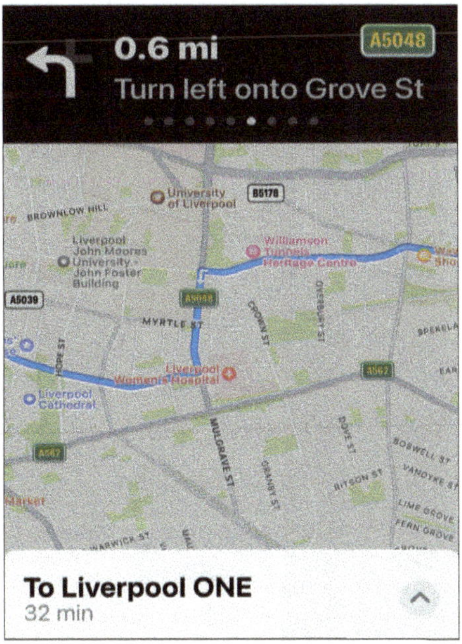


Here you'll see the start of your route, with turn by turn directions that will automatically change as you drive along the route.

You can mount your phone to your windscreen in your car and use it as a GPS SatNav.

Tap 'end' to stop the navigation.

## Drop a Pin

To drop a pin, tap and hold your finger on the location on the map.

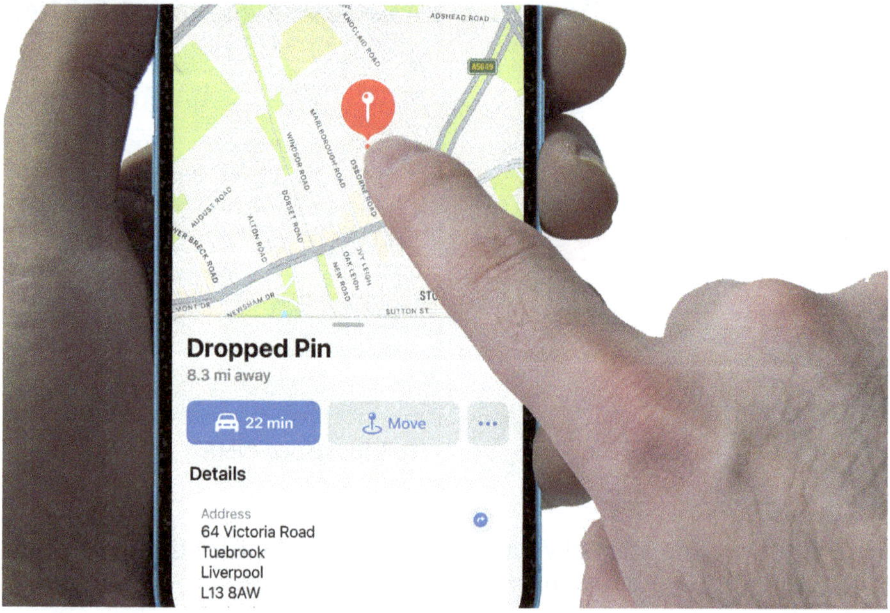

# News App

The news app collects breaking stories from around the world and locally into one app, based on the topics you are interested in.

When you first start the app, you'll see a list of top stories, trending stories, and stories recommended for you. Scroll down the page, tap on a story to read the details.

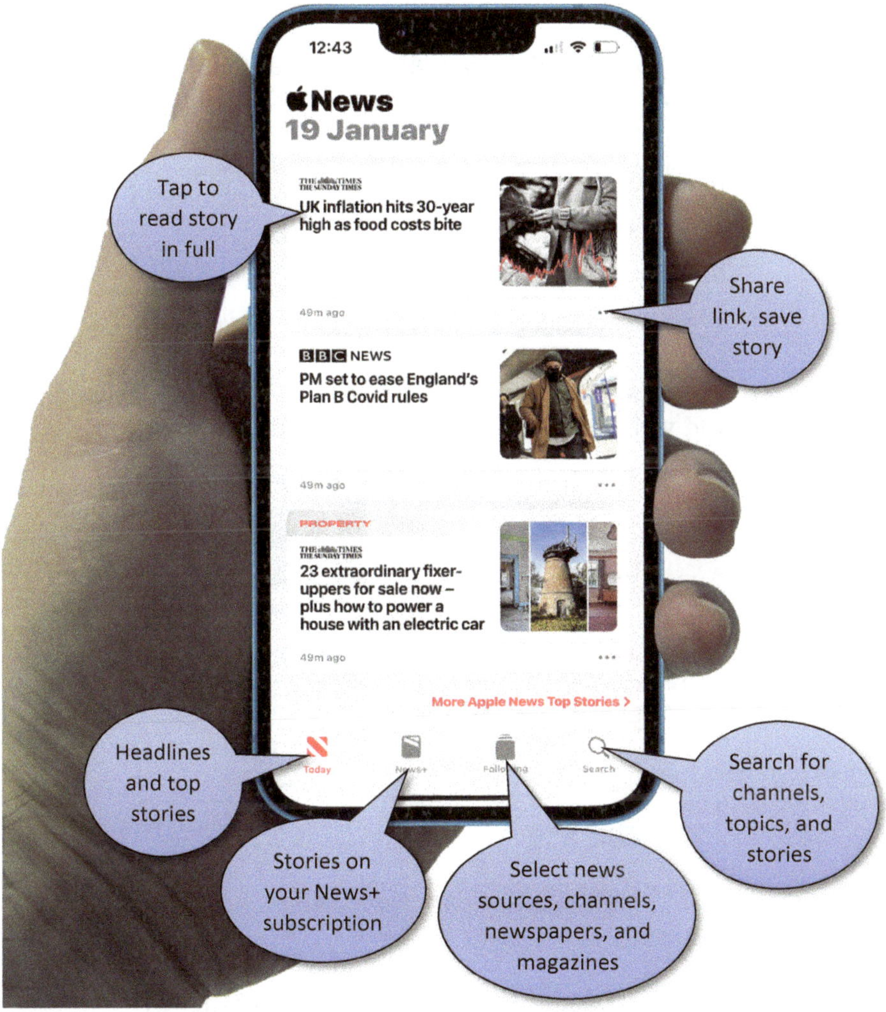

To follow media channels, tap 'following'.

From here you can select different news sources, magazines, newspapers and websites. Scroll down to 'suggested by siri' then tap the '+'icon next to the channels you're interested in.

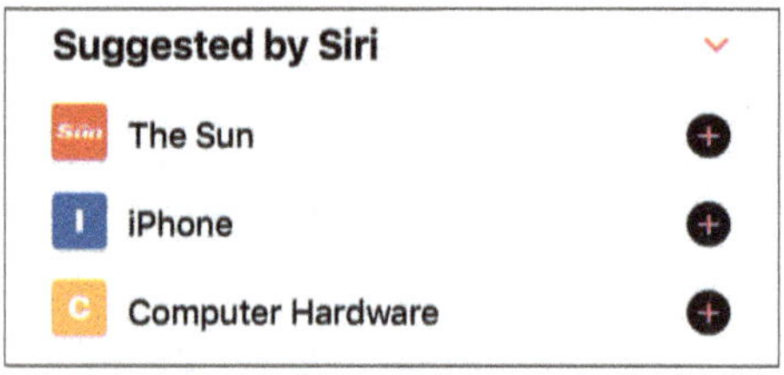


Scroll down to the bottom, then tap 'discover channels'.

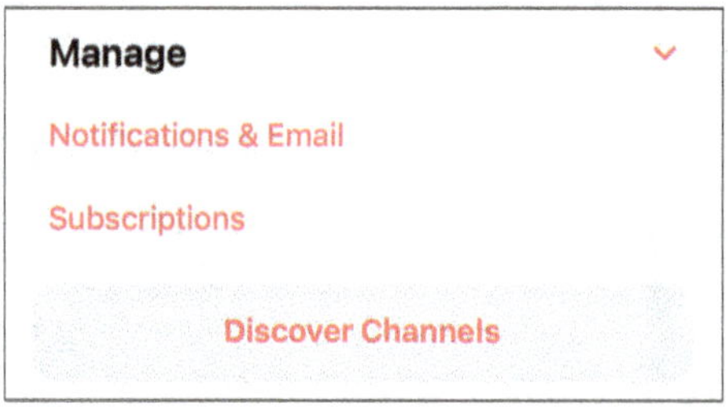


From here you can select different news sources, magazines, newspapers and websites. Tap the '+' icon to add a channel.

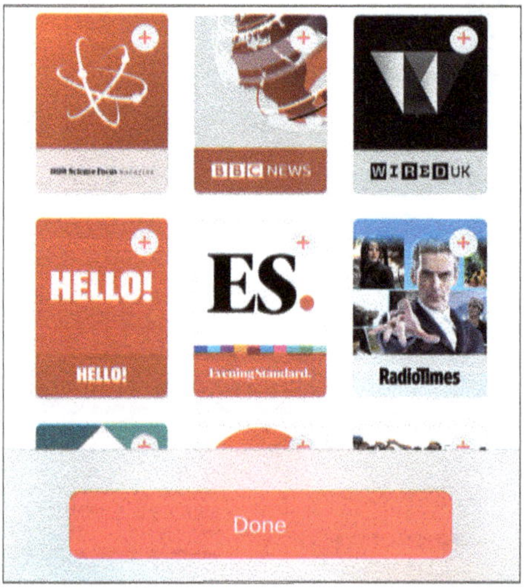


Tap 'done' at the bottom of the screen when you're finished.

You can also search for specific channels. Tap the search on the bottom right.

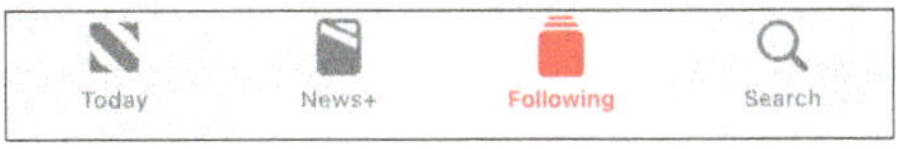


Type your interest into the search field at the top. Tap on any of the stories to open them up.

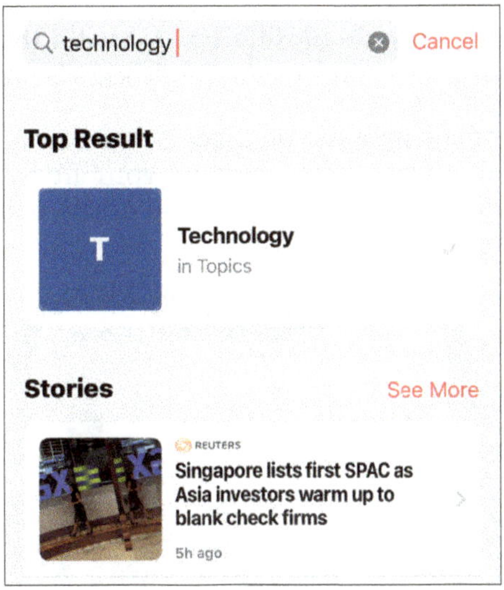


If you scroll down to the bottom of the page, you'll see some channels. Here, you can select the channels you want to follow - that is the channel's stories that will appear in your news feed. Tap 'see more' at the top to show the whole list.

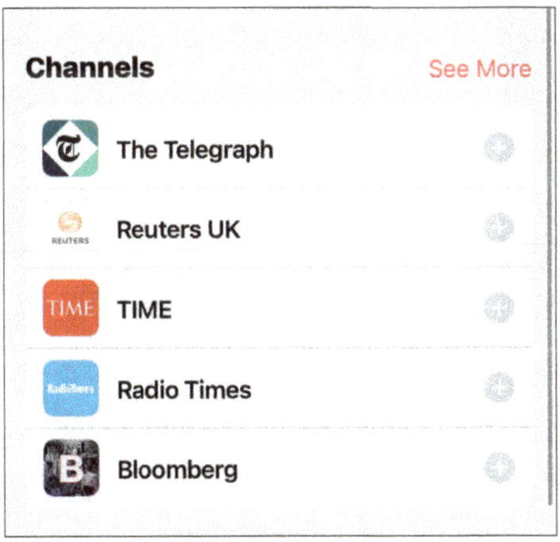


Tap the '+' next to the channel you want to follow.

# Apple Books App

Formerly known as iBooks, Apple Books is your electronic bookshelf and allows you to read ebooks. Tap the icon on your home screen.

You can download hundreds of different e-books that are available in the bookstore; from the latest novels, food, kids books or manuals.

Along the bottom of the screen you'll see some icons. Here you can see the books you are 'reading now', browse your library of books you've downloaded, browse the book store, look at audio books and search for a specific book title or author.

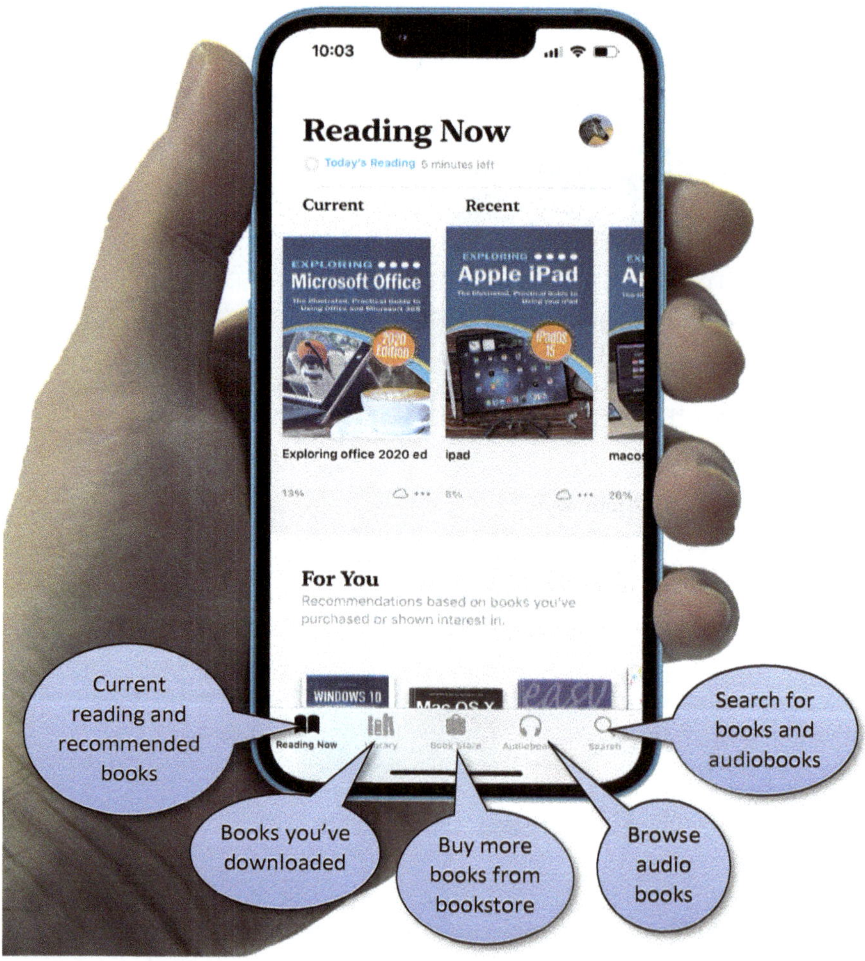

## Browse the Store

You can also browse through the book store. To do this, tap 'bookstore' icon on the panel along the bottom of the screen.

Scroll down the list of books, tap on a book cover to see more details. You can also read reviews and download a sample. To close tap the 'x' on the top right

Scroll down to the bottom of the page, here, you'll see a categories section. Select a category. Perhaps you're into 'crime thrillers', 'fiction', or 'education'. Just tap on a category to view the available books.

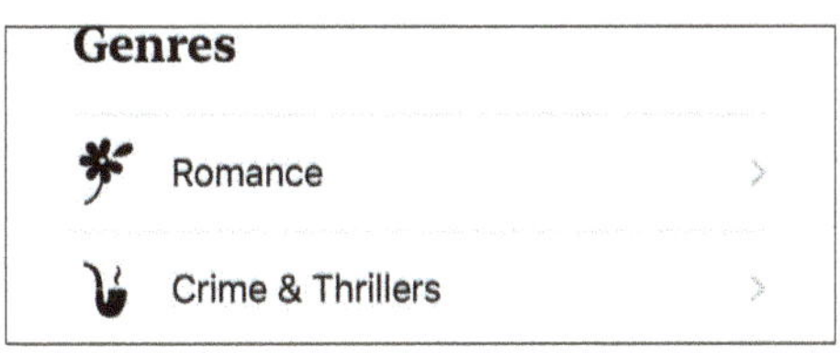

## Search the Store

You can also search for specific authors or titles. To do this tap on the 'search' icon on the panel along the bottom of the screen.

Then type what you're looking for in the search field at the top of the screen. At the bottom, you'll see some suggestions, tap on the closest match.

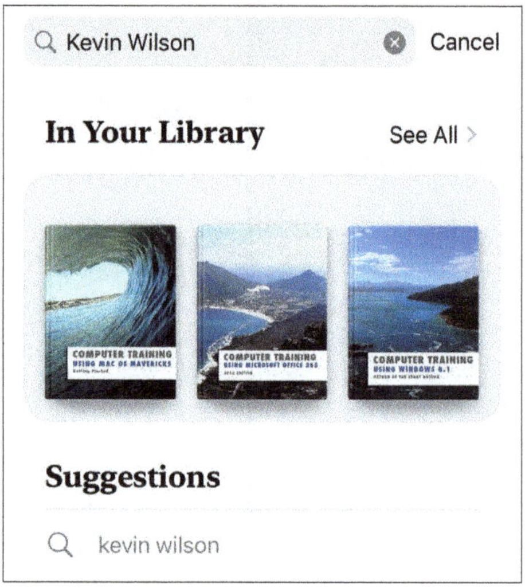


Here, you'll see a list of books that match your search. Tap on a book cover to see more details.

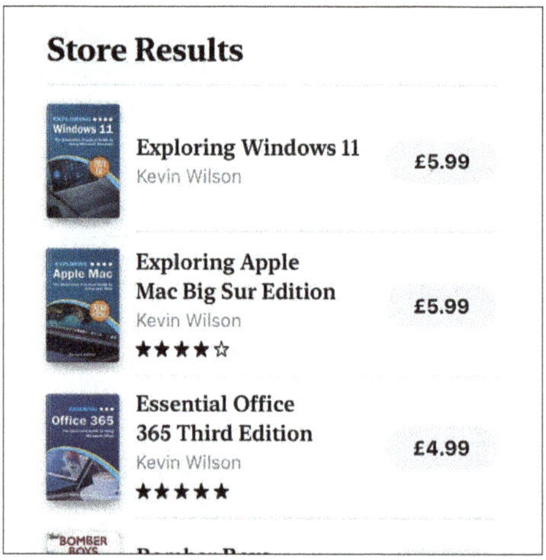

From this page you'll be able to read a sample, the book's description, read any reviews, and buy/download the book.

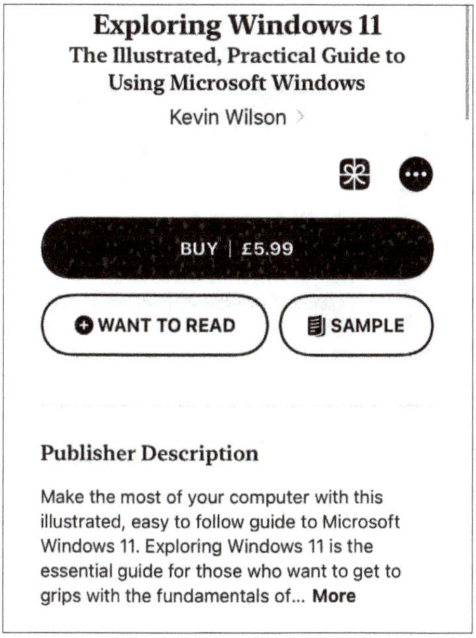


Tap 'get' if the book is free, or tap the price tag to download the book to your library. Once you've downloaded the book, you'll find it in your library. Tap the library icon on the panel along the bottom of the screen.

Tap on the book cover to begin reading.

The book will open up full screen. Swipe left or right across the screen to turn the pages.

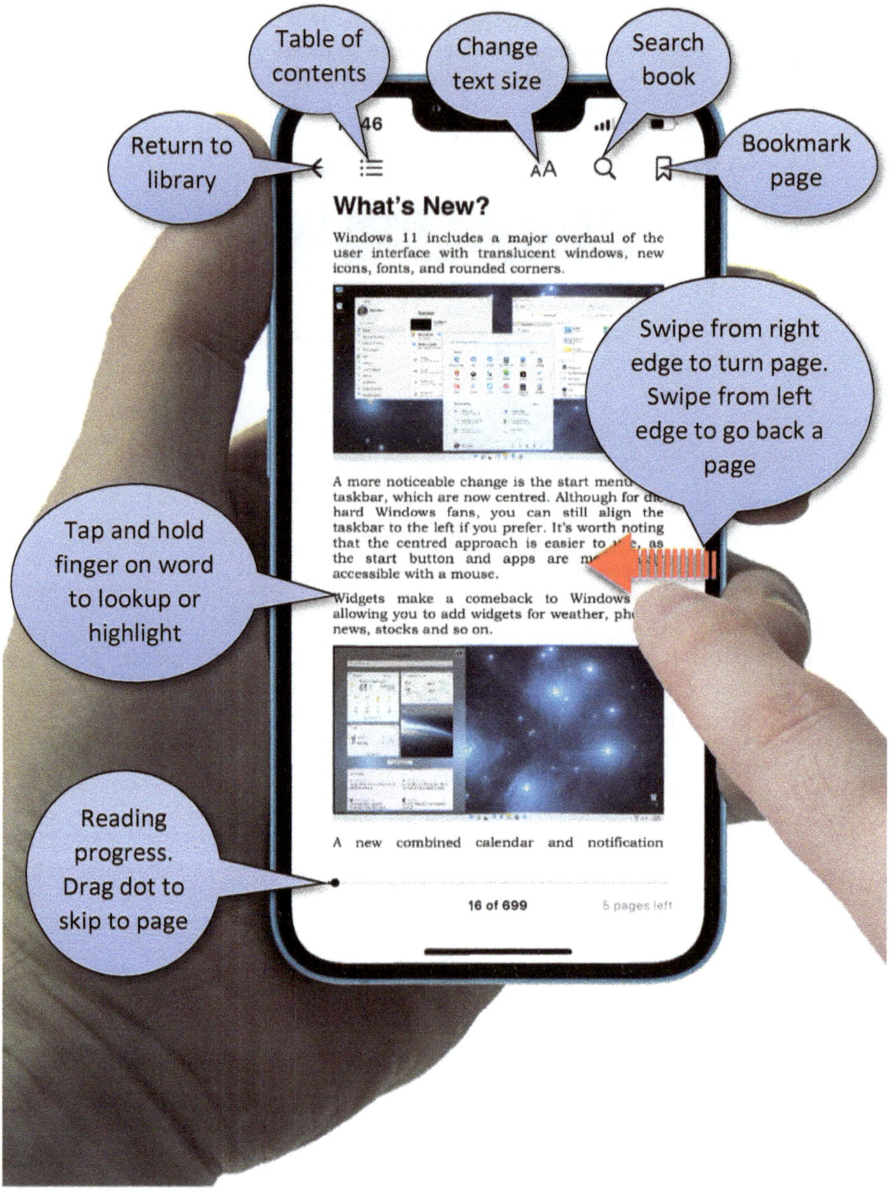

# Files App

The iCloud Drive App has been dropped and replaced with the Files App. You'll find the icon on your dock.

In the Files App, you'll find all your files that are stored on your iPhone and iCloud Drive. When you first open the Files App, you'll see all your files saved onto iCloud.

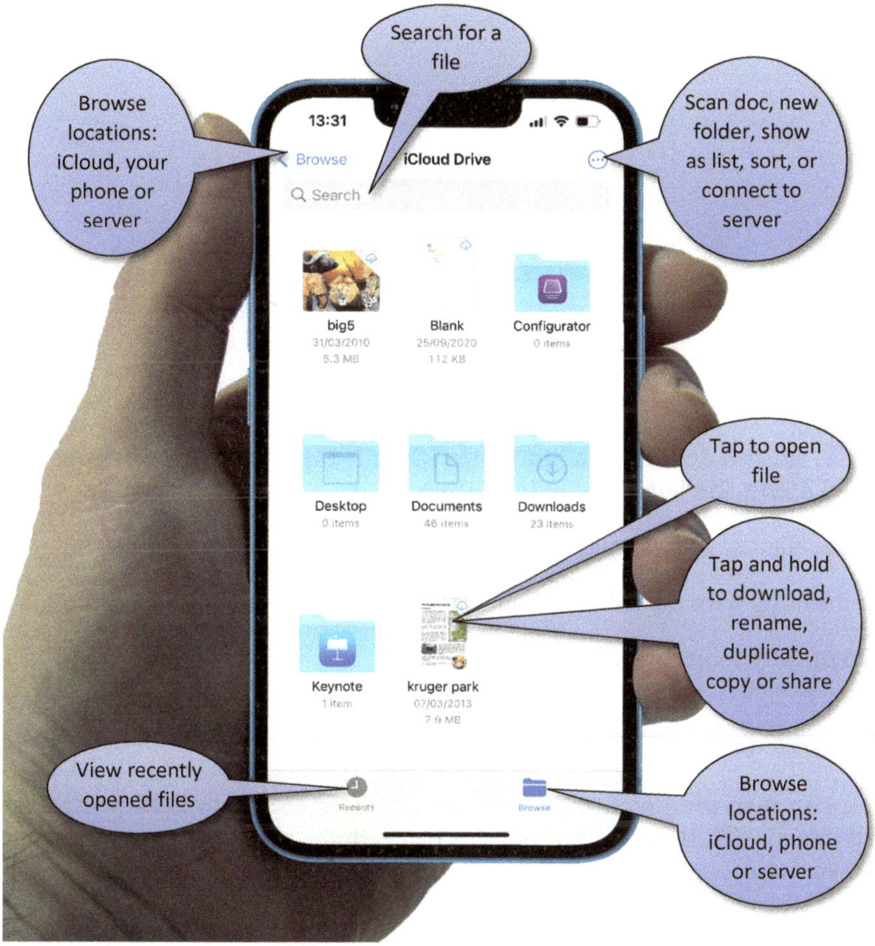


Files can be stored in different locations, most commonly on iCloud, but also physically on your phone, or another server.

To see all your locations tap 'browse' on the panel along the bottom of the screen.

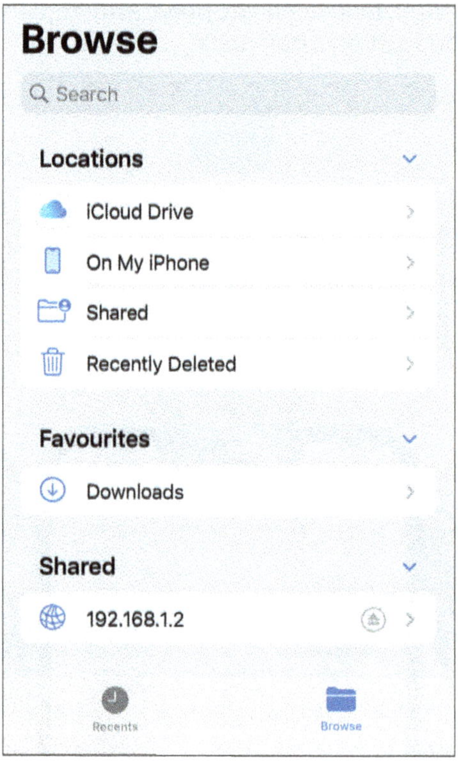


To see all the documents stored on iCloud, tap 'iCloud Drive' from the panel along the left hand side of the screen.

To see files saved physically on your iPhone, tap 'on my iPhone'.

To find any files downloaded with Safari web browser, tap 'downloads'.

Tap on any icon to open the folder or file.

## Create New Folders

You can also create your own folders. This is useful to keep your files organised. To do this, tap on the three dots icon on the top right of the screen.

Select 'new folder' from the menu.

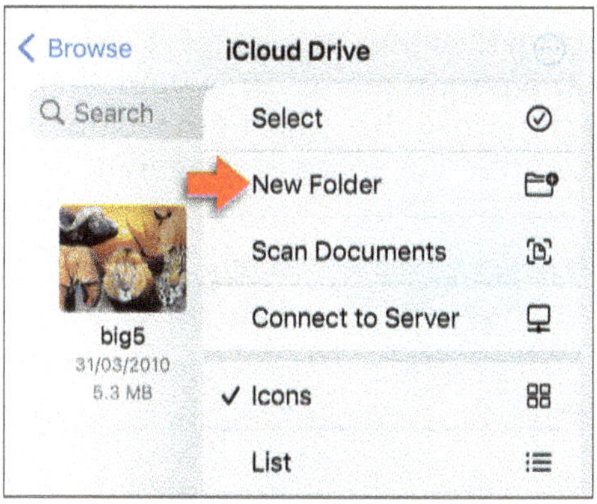


You'll see an 'untitled folder' appear. Enter a meaningful name for your folder.

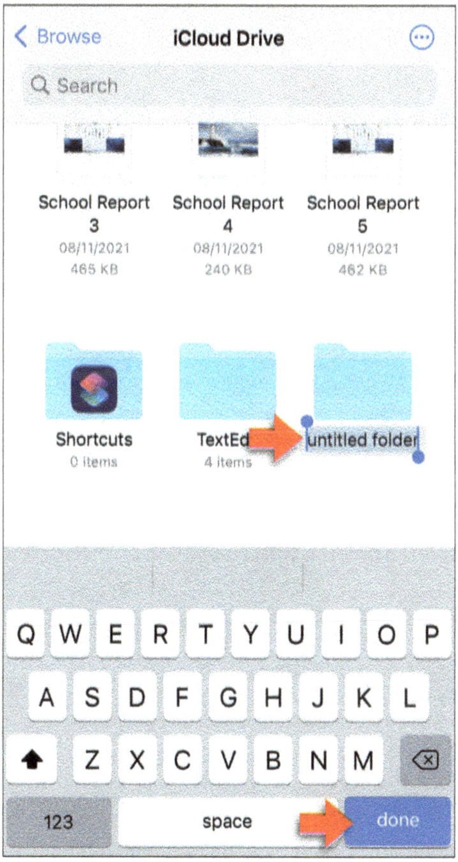


Tap 'done', when you're finished.

## Drag Files into Folders

You can drag and drop files into these folders. Tap and hold your finger on the file, ignore the popup menu. Drag your finger to the side to lift the icon, then drag it across the glass to the folder you want to put the file into. In this example, I'm going to drag and drop a document into the 'Work' folder.

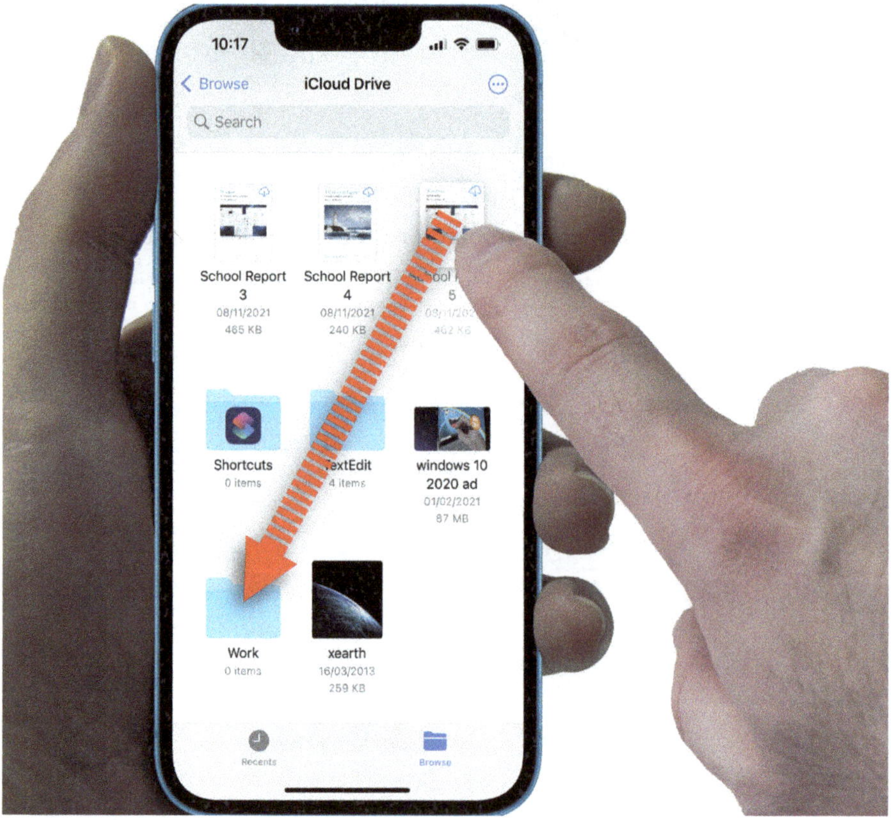


Tap on the folders to open them, tap on the file thumbnails to open the files.

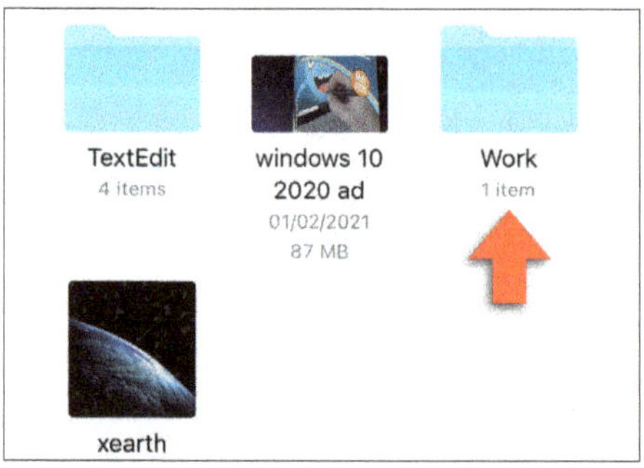


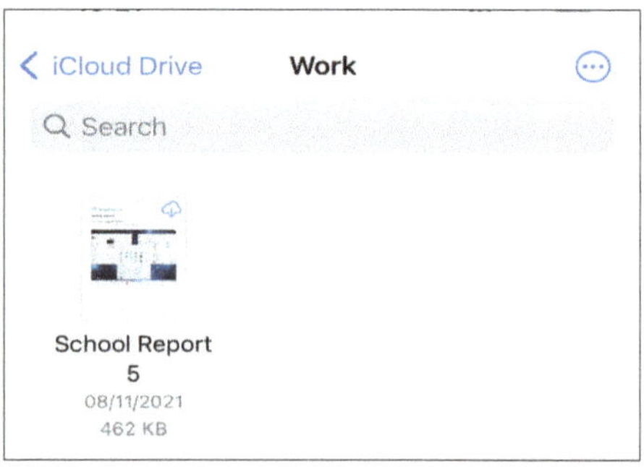

## Delete Files or Folders

To delete a file or folder, tap and hold your finger on the icon. Select 'delete' from the popup menu.

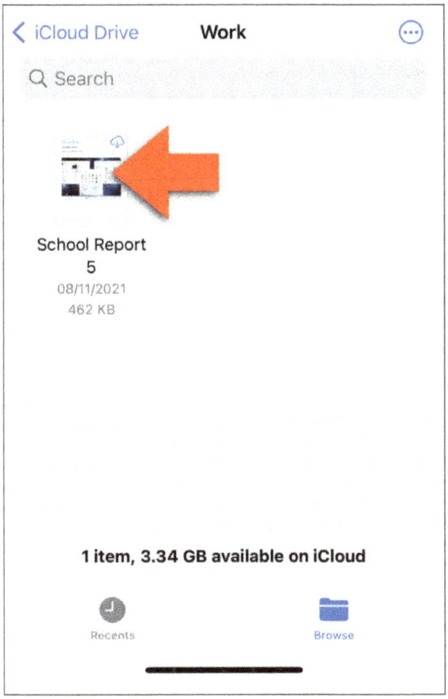


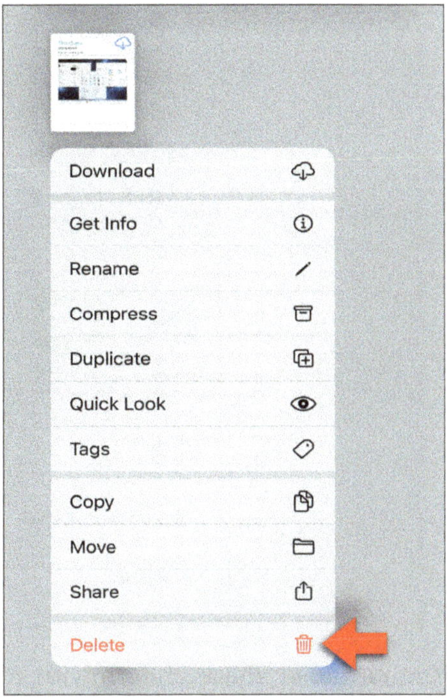


## Share a File

Tap and hold your finger on the file you want to share, then select 'share' from the popup menu.

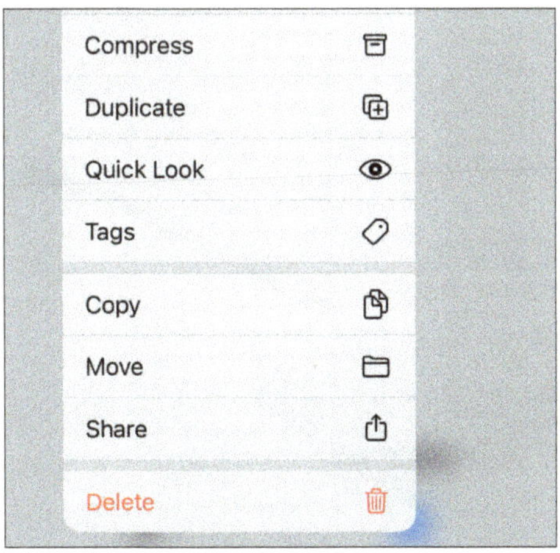

Select your sharing method from the options. You can share with iMessage, email, or AirDrop.

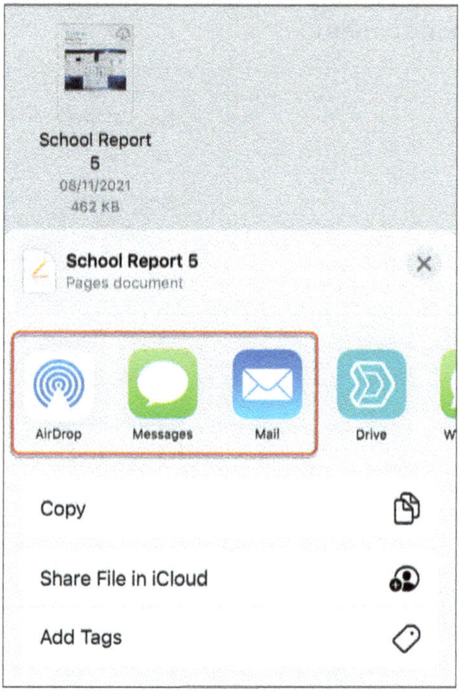


You can also share folders with friends, family and colleagues using iCloud Drive.

## External Drive Support

You can access files on a USB drive, SD card or hard drive. To plug in an external drive into an iPhone, you'll need a Lightning to Micro USB Adapter.

Plug the adapter in the docking port on the bottom of your iPhone. With this, you can plug in a standard USB external drive, SD card reader, or USB drive.

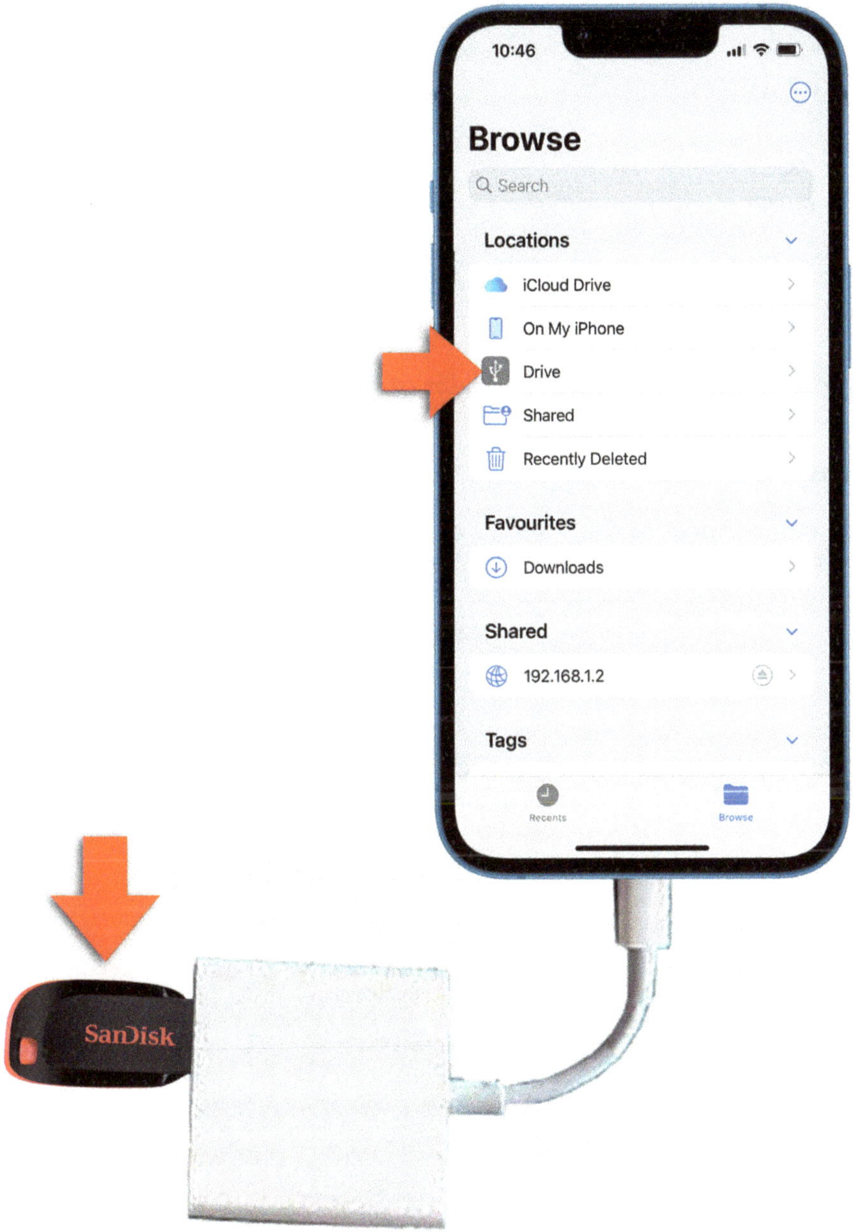


Your drive will appear under 'locations' on the side panel of your files app. Tap on the device to view files and folders stored on the drive.

## Rename Files or Folders

Tap and hold your finger on a file or folder, then select 'rename' from the pop up menu.

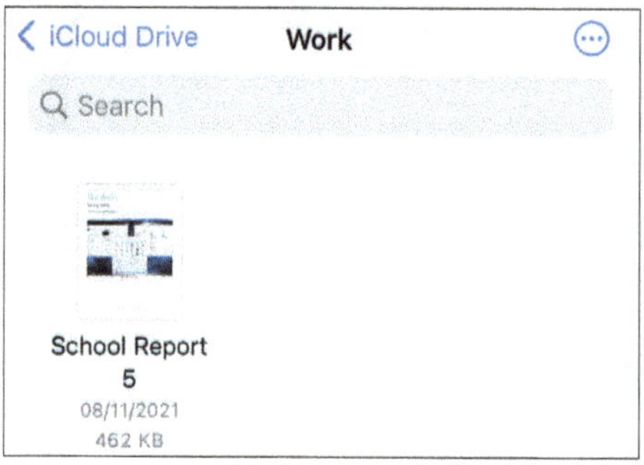


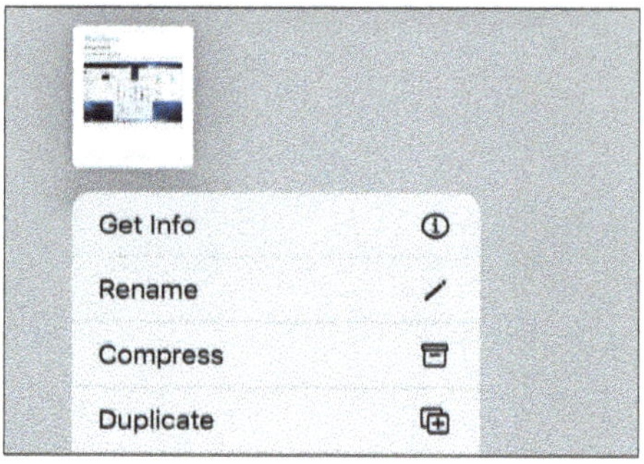


Type in the new name for the folder or file.

## File Servers

You can connect to a file server at work or a home PC using the SMB protocol. To connect to a server, tap the 3 dots icon on the top right.

From the drop down, tap 'connect to server'.

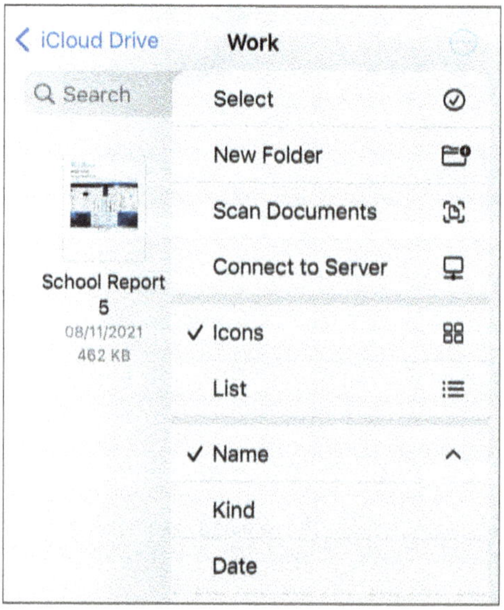

In the 'server' field, enter the server's address.

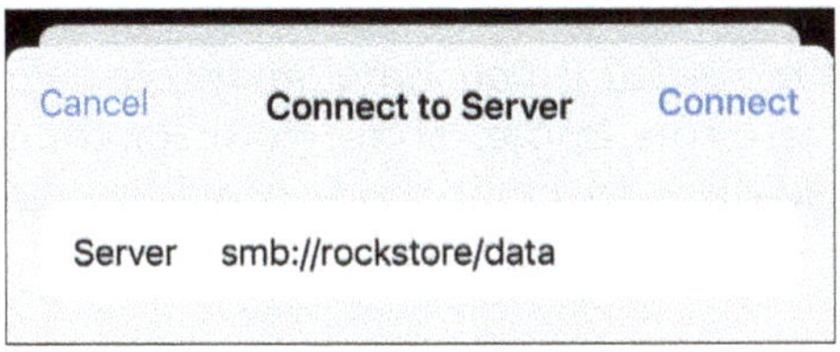


For example, if I wanted to connect to my file server on the network, I'd enter the server name followed by the shared folder name.

`smb://rockstore/data`

Enter the shared folder's username and password when prompted.

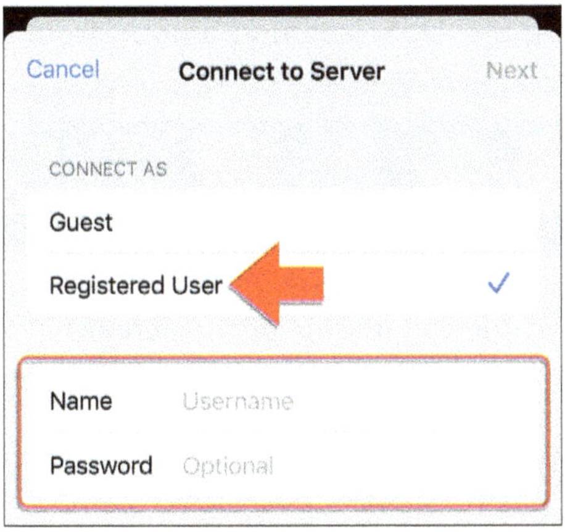


Once connected, your folder will appear on the 'shared' section on the browse panel.

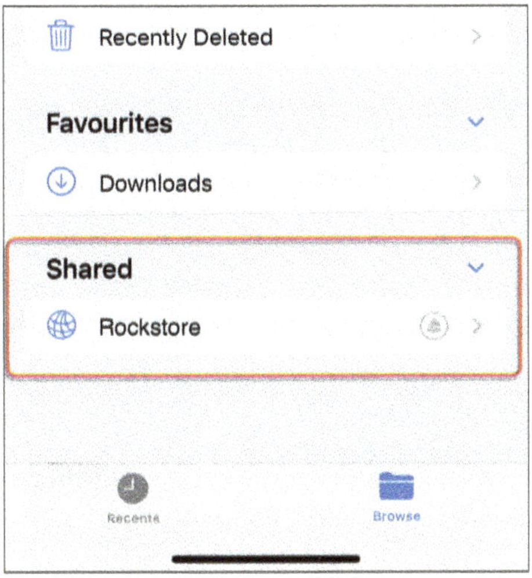

# Find my iPhone

This feature is quite useful if you have misplaced your iPhone or had it stolen. You can use this app to share your location with friends and family - a useful feature to keep track of where your kids or family members are. For setup see page 80.

## Locating your Phone & Taking Action

On any device - iPhone, Mac or PC, open your web browser and navigate to:

```
www.icloud.com
```

Sign in with your Apple ID. Select 'find iPhone' from the iCloud control panel.

You can locate your iPhone. Select the name of your device from the drop down menu in the top middle of the screen.

You'll see a green dot appear on the map. This is the current location of your device.

On the right hand side of the screen, you can take action. Here you can tap 'play sound' to play an annoying sound on your iPhone wherever it might be.

This helps you to locate it, if you've lost it in your house somewhere, or annoy a thief if they have possession of it.

You can also put the iPhone into 'lost mode'. Lost mode allows you to remotely lock your device. You can also enter a message to display on the lock screen of the device.

Finally you can erase your iPhone completely. To remove any personal data that is stored on your iPhone.

## Sharing Locations

You can share your location with friends and family. To share your location, open the 'find my' app.

Select 'people tab'. From the popup panel, select 'start sharing location' (or 'share my location' if you are already sharing your location with someone else).

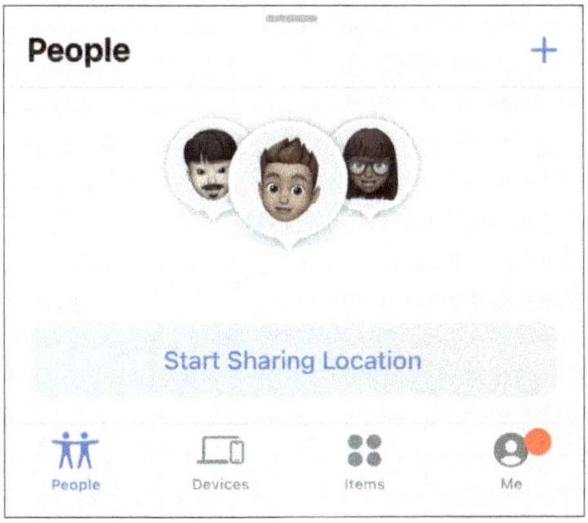


Enter the Apple ID or phone number of the person you want to share your location with. Tap 'send'.

Choose to share your location for One Hour, Until End of Day, or Share Indefinitely. Tap 'ok'.

The other person will get a prompt on their device. This will allow them to share their location with you.

To view the other person's location, tap on the people tab.

You should see the person's location appear on the map on your device.

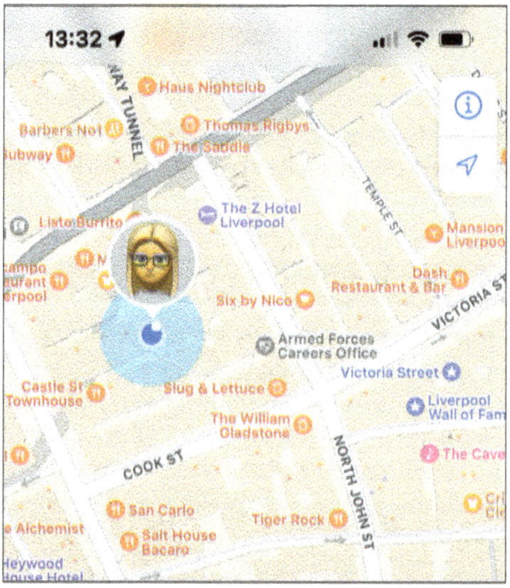

You'll see a panel at the bottom of the screen. If you don't, swipe the small tap upwards.

Tap 'contact' to send the person a message, tap 'directions' to see directions to the person's current location, tap notifications to add a notification when the person arrives at your location, leaves their location or any other location.

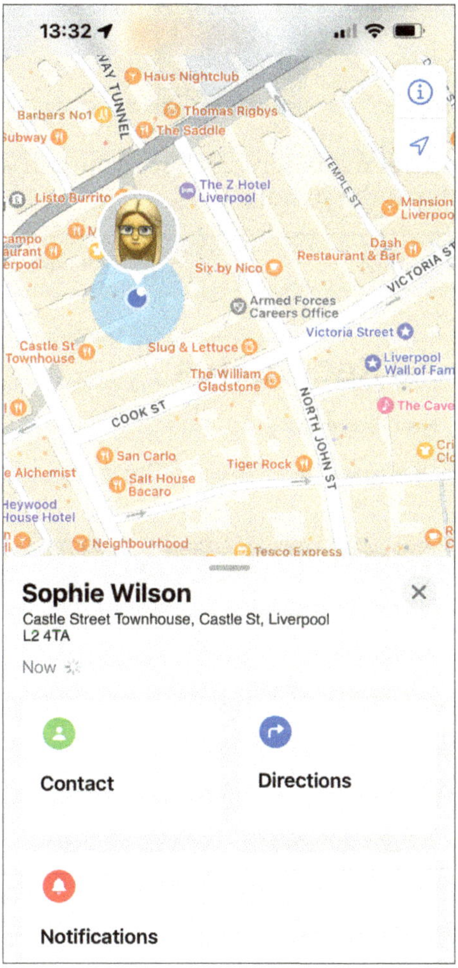

# Voice Memos

You can record audio using your iPhone's built in mic or a bluetooth external mic. You can record voice memos, meetings and lectures.

You'll find the voice memo app on your home screen.

Lets take a look at the main screen. Here you can see your previous recordings listed down the middle.

## Recording a Memo

To record a memo, simply tap the red record button on the bottom left of the screen.

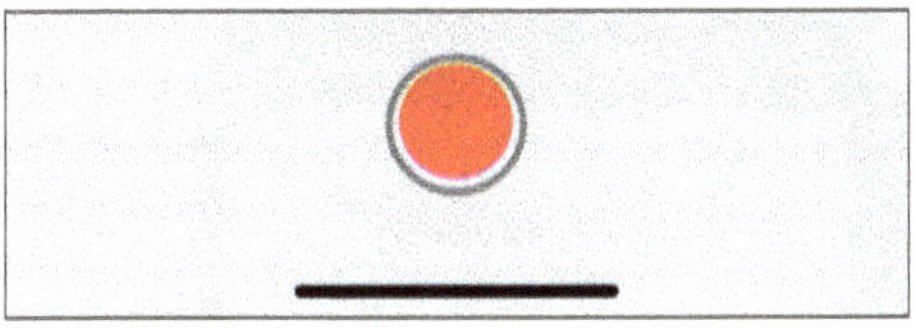

The memo app will start recording. You'll see a wave form appear in the middle of the screen to indicate the app is picking up audio.

Tap on the audio wave to open the controls.

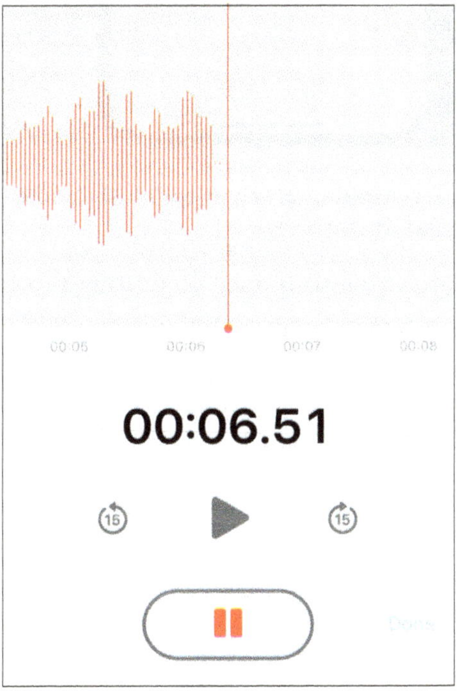


To pause a recording temporarily, tap the pause icon on at the bottom.

When the recording is paused, you can also play back the recording. To do this, tap the play button.

You can drag the audio play head to a new position.

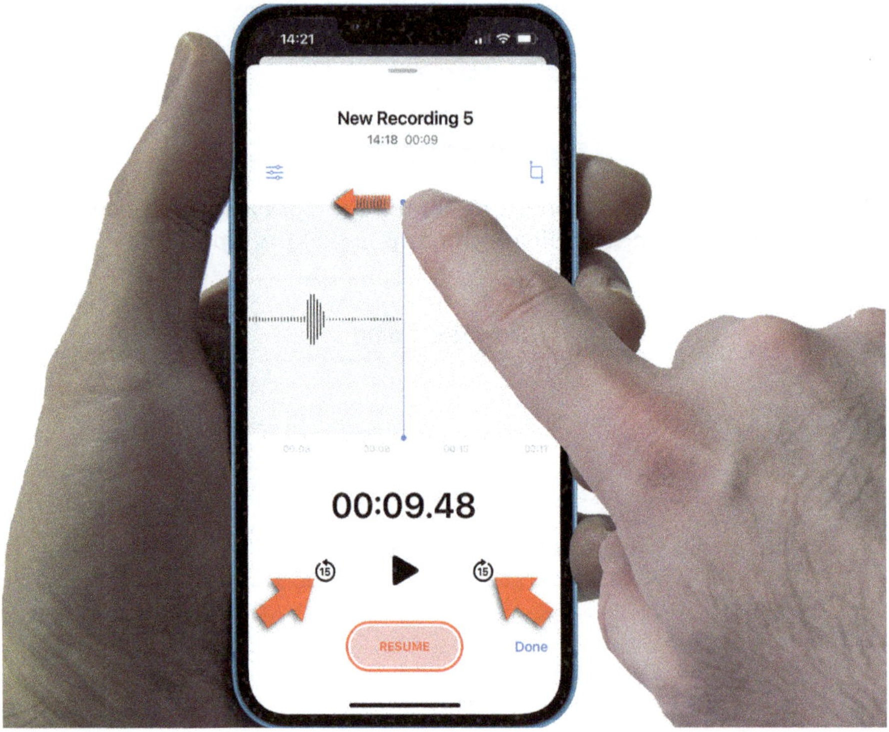


You can go back 15 seconds, or advance 15 seconds. Tap the two icons either side of the play button.

Give the memo a meaningful name. To do this tap on 'new recording' at the top.

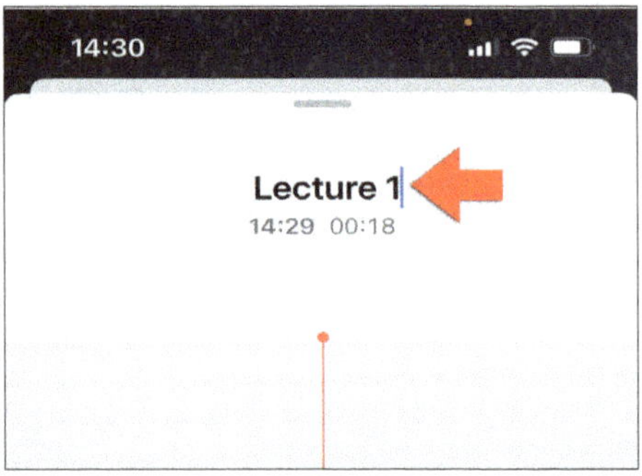


Type in a new name.

To stop the recording, tap 'done'.

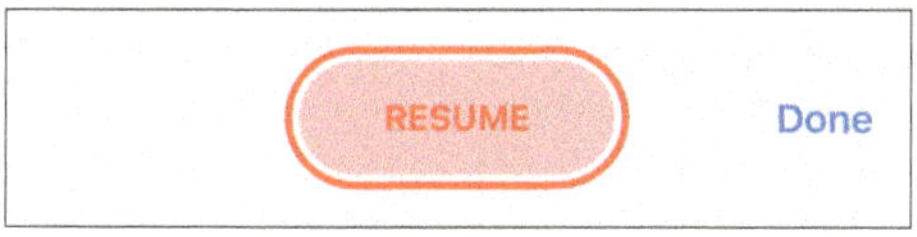


Your memo will appear in the 'all recordings' list on the main screen.

## Play a Recording

On the all recordings screen, tap on the recording in the list.

Tap the play button in the panel that opens up. Tap and drag the play marker to skip ahead.

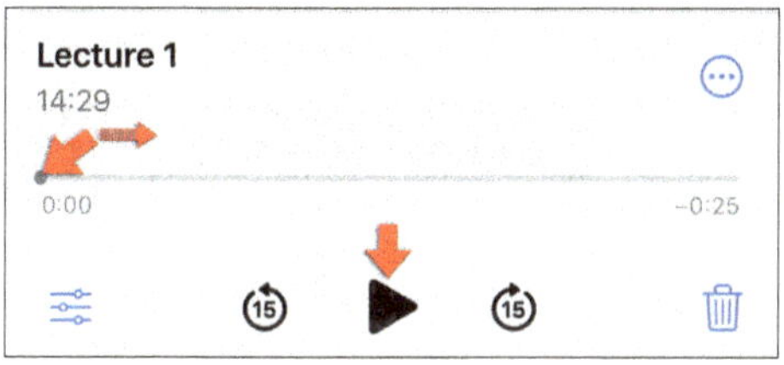


## Trim a Recording

You can trim the beginning and the ends of the memo voice recording. To do this, select the recording you want to trim from the 'all recordings' list.

Tap the three dots icon to the right of the recording you selected.

Select 'edit recording' from the popup panel.

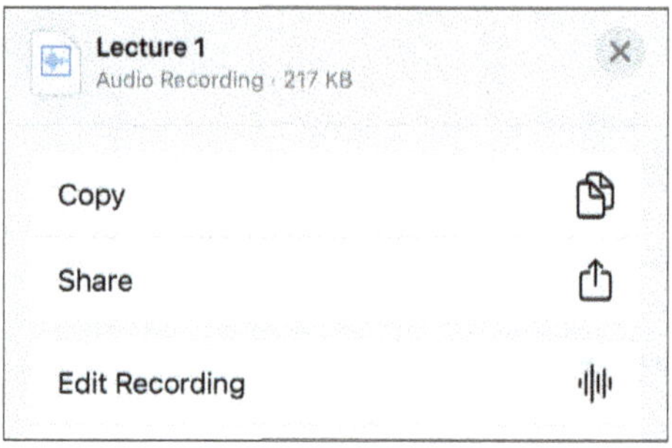


Tap on the trim icon, on the top right of the screen.

Now to trim the beginning and ends of the clip, drag the yellow handles along the track until you get to the start and end points you want.

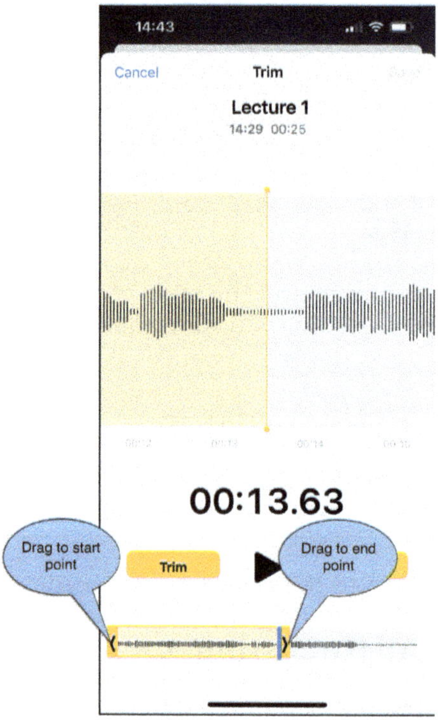


Tap 'trim' when you're done.

# Clock App

You can use the clock app to set alarms, timers, as a stop watch, and create time zone clocks so you can see the time in other countries.

You'll find the clock app on your home screen.

## World Clock

With world clock, you can create clocks for any city or country in the world. This is useful if you have friends or family in another country, so you know what time it is there and don't call them in the middle of the night. It's also useful if you're travelling.

To see the world clock, tap 'world clock' on the panel along the bottom of the screen.

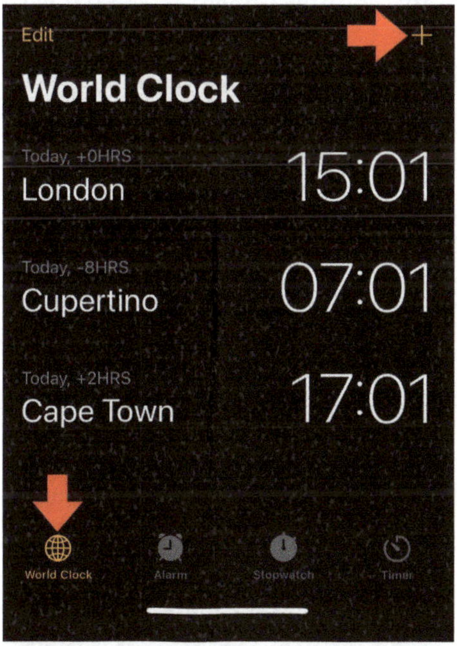


To add a clock, tap the + sign on the top right of the screen.

Type in the name of the city or country you want to add. Select the closest match from the suggestions.

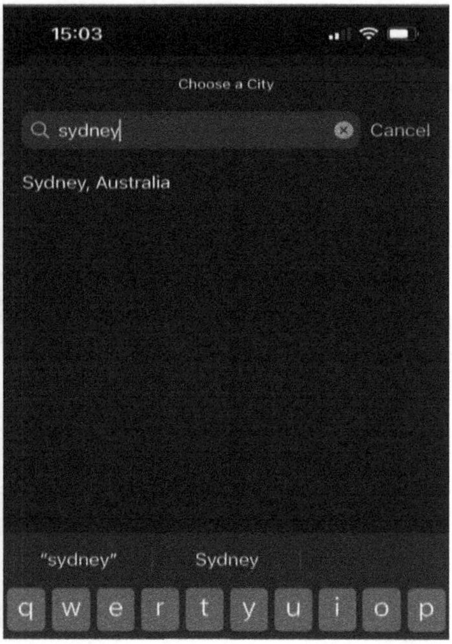


You'll see the new city/country appear in the list with the current local time.

## Alarm

You can also set multiple alarms. Eg one for wake up. To do this, select 'alarm' from the panel along the bottom of the screen.

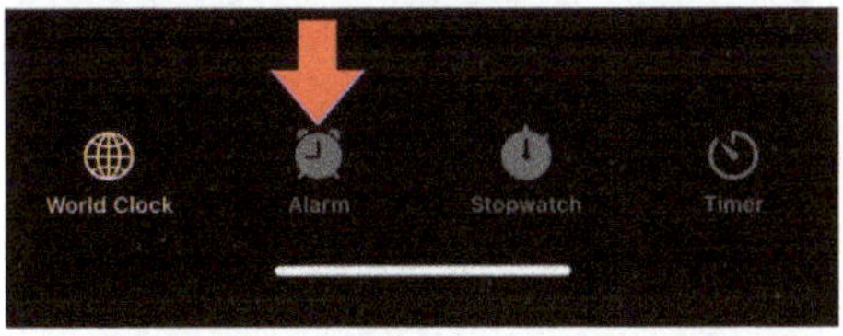


This will display all the alarms you have set. To set a new alarm, tap the + sign on the top right.

Set the alarm to the time you want the alarm to go off.

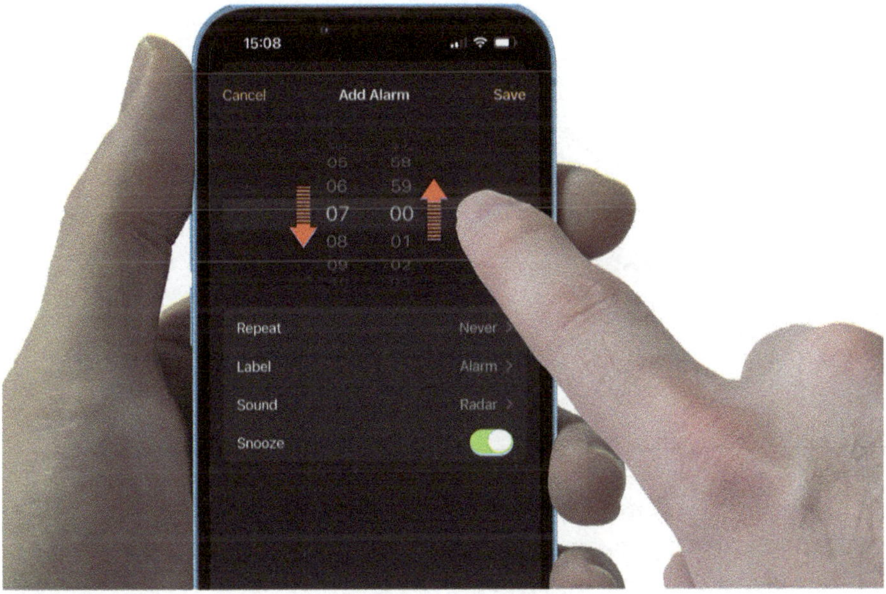


Tap 'repeat' to set what days you want the alarm, eg 'weekdays'. Tap 'label' to name the alarm, eg 'wakeup'. Tap 'sound' to choose what your alarm sounds like - you can select a sound or a song from your music library. Tap 'save' on the top right when you're done.

You'll see the alarms you've added. Tap the green slider on the alarm to turn it on and off.

## Stop Watch

Use the stopwatch to time events. Eg an athletics event. Select 'stopwatch' from the panel along the bottom of the screen.

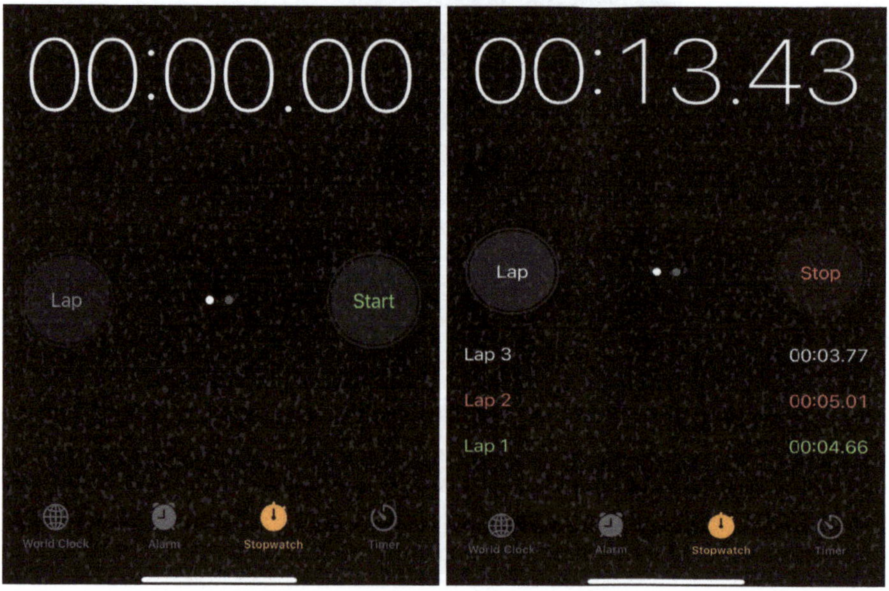


Tap 'start/stop' to start and stop the timer.

Tap 'lap' to count the number of laps if you are timing a sporting event such as athletics or racing.

## Timer

Use the timer to set a count down timer. Select 'timer' from the panel along the bottom of the screen. Use the sliders to select the length of time in hours, minutes and seconds. For example, if you're playing a game or timing an egg, just set the amount of time allowed.

Tap 'when timer ends' to change the sound the timer makes when the time runs out.

Tap 'start' to start the count down.

You'll see the countdown start. Tap cancel to stop.

# Printing Documents

To print documents from an iPhone you'll need a printer that is compatible with Air Print. Most modern printers will have this feature included.

## Air Print

If your printer is Air Print enabled, then your printer will show up in the print dialog box automatically.

To print a document, select the share icon, then tap 'print'. For example, here in Safari, select the share icon.

From the share sheet, select print.

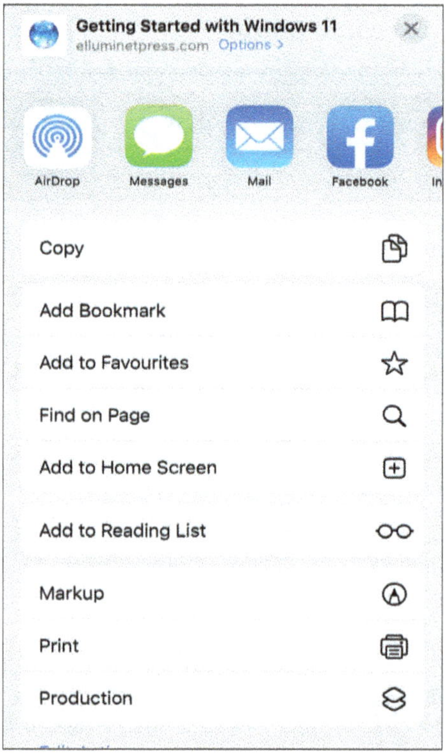

Select your printer from the printer field.

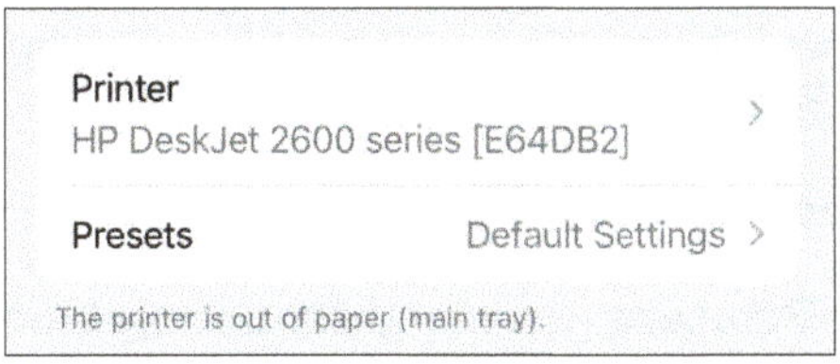


Enter the number of copies you want, what pages you want to include (leave blank for all pages), and whether you want to print in black and white or color.

Select the page size, then the page orientation (landscape or portrait)

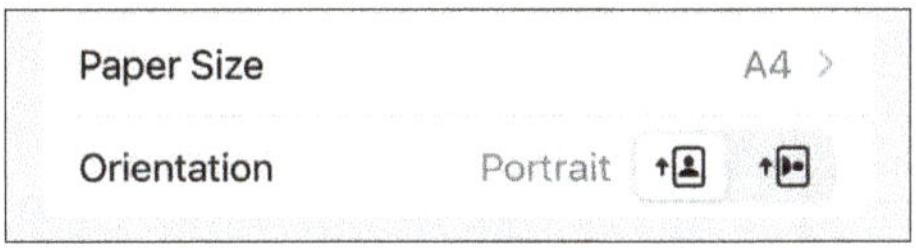


At the bottom, you might see media quality options. Here, you can select the media type (plain paper, or card), and select the print quality.

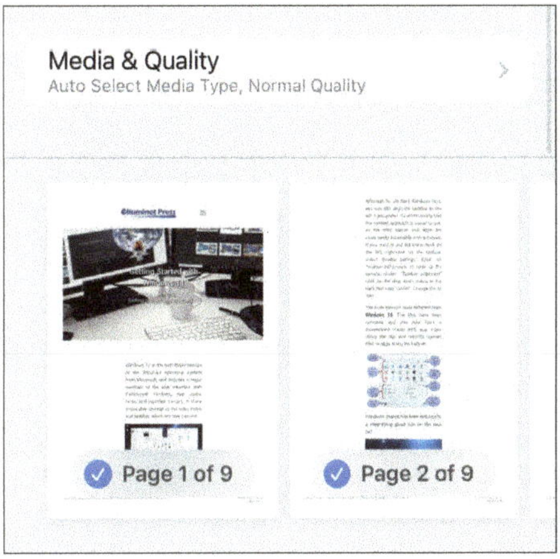


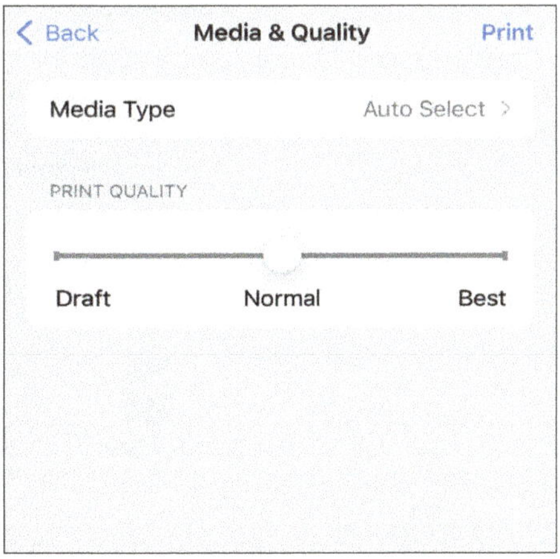


For everyday prints, select 'normal'. For high quality final prints slect 'best'. For test prints select 'draft'.

Tap 'print' on the top right when you're done.

## Older Printers

If your printer doesn't have the Air Print feature, you can download an app from the App Store for your printer.

- **HP Printers** download **HP Smart**
- **Samsung Printers** download **Samsung Mobile Print**
- **Epson Printers** download **Epson iPrint**
- **Canon Printers** download **Canon Print**

Open the app on your iPhone, then select the document you want to print. This is usually in 'documents'.

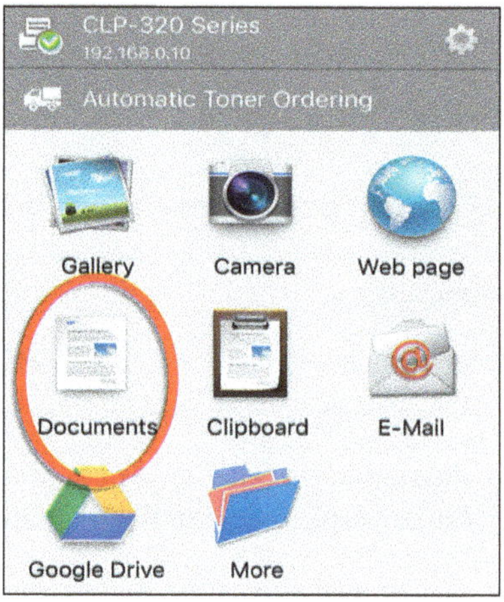


You might need to browse through the documents on your phone.

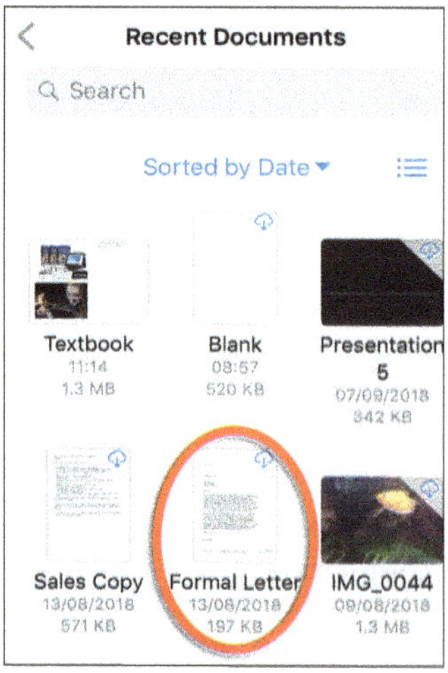

Once you've selected a document, tap print.

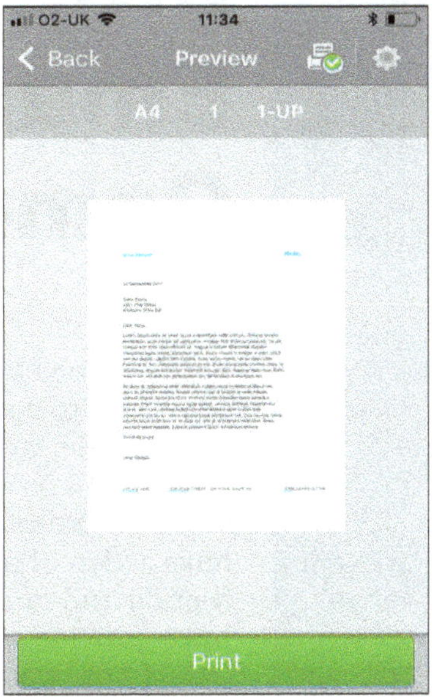


Follow the instructions on screen.

5

# Internet, Email and Comms

Your iPhone has a lot of features that allow you to connect to the internet, browse the web, send and receive emails, share pictures with friends, store addresses and contacts, or have video chat conversations with friends and family. To do this, Apple have provided some built in apps: Safari for web browsing, Mail for email and Face Time for video chat.

In this chapter, we'll take a look at

- Using Safari
- Using Email
- Contacts
- Calendar App
- FaceTime
- Group Chat
- SharePlay
- Phone App
- Messages App
- Animojis and Memojis
- AirDrop

Lets start by taking a look at Safari web browser. Take a look at the video resources.

elluminetpress.com/iphone-comms

# Using Safari

To launch safari, tap on the safari icon located on your dock.

## Start Page

The start page appears whenever you open a new tab. Along the top you'll see your favourite websites. Underneath you'll see a privacy report, reading list, Siri suggestions, iCloud tabs from your other Apple devices and so on.

To customise the start page, scroll down to the bottom, tap on 'edit'. Here, you can sync your start page across all your devices. This means you'll get the same start page on your Mac, iPhone as well as your iPad, depending on what Apple Devices you have.

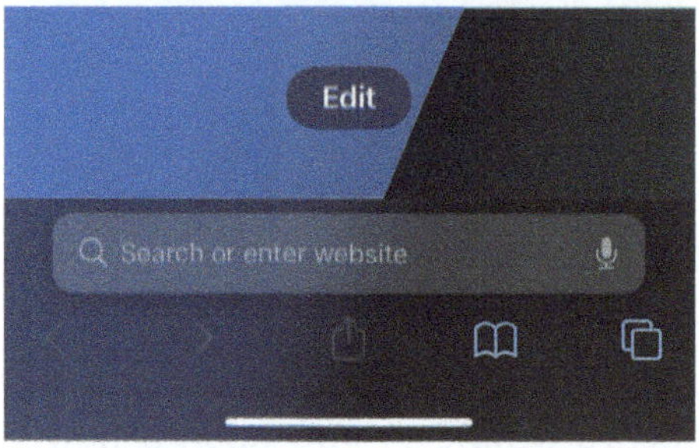


Further down you can add sections to your start page such as favourites, frequently visited websites, privacy reports, siri suggested content, your reading list and iCloud tabs that sync open tabs in Safari across all your devices. Just turn on/off the switch next to the options.

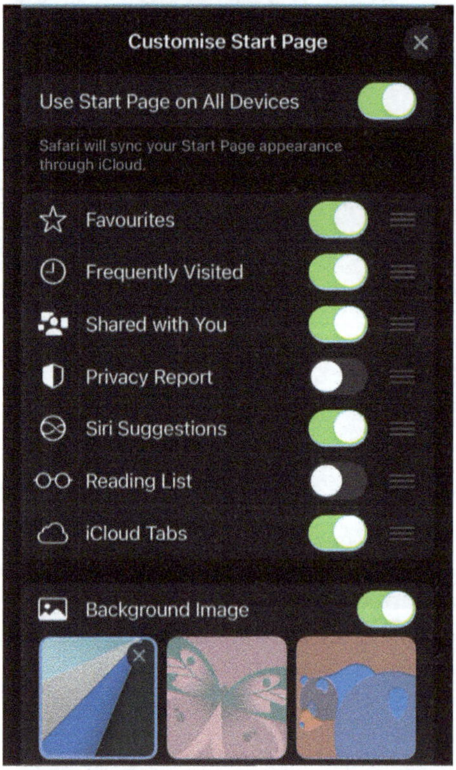


You can also select a background, just click on an image from the selections.

## The Toolbar

Lets take a look at the toolbar along the bottom of the main screen.

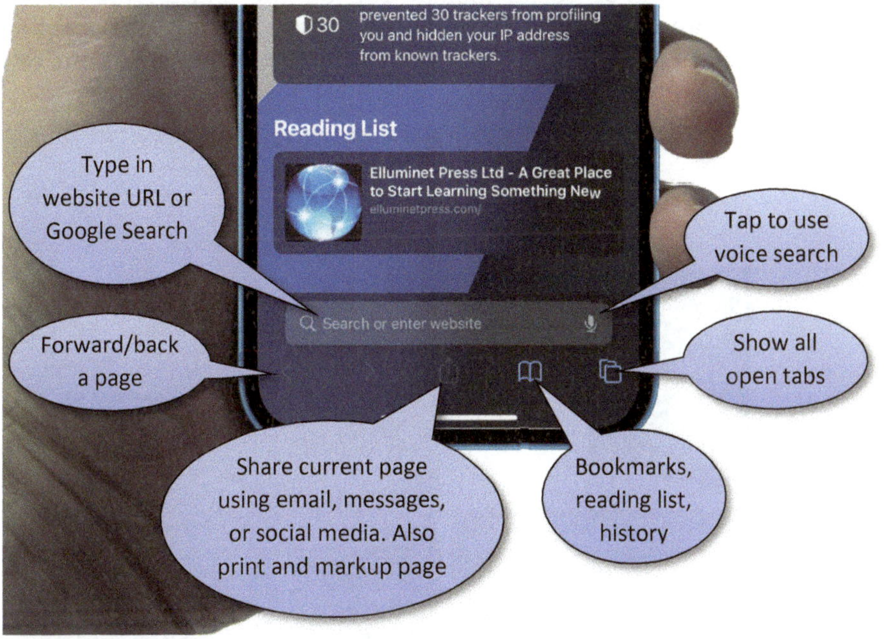


Tap in the website address field, to enter the website's address, or Google search keyword.

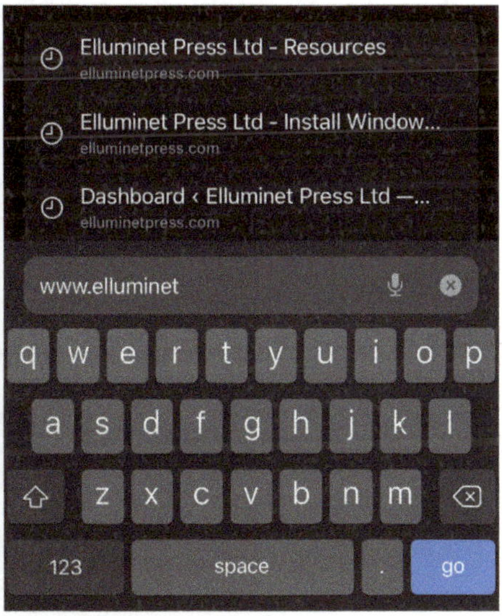


As you type, you'll also see a list of suggestions or previously visited sites. Tap on these if you want to visit the site.

## Share Menu

The share menu  allows you to share the current website link via text message, email or social media. Tap on the share icon on the toolbar. Then tap on the icon to share the site on Twitter Instagram or Facebook. You can also email the link, send it via messages or airdrop it to someone nearby.

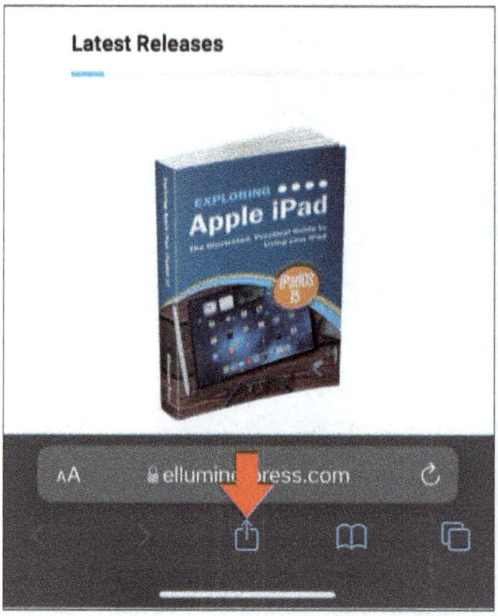


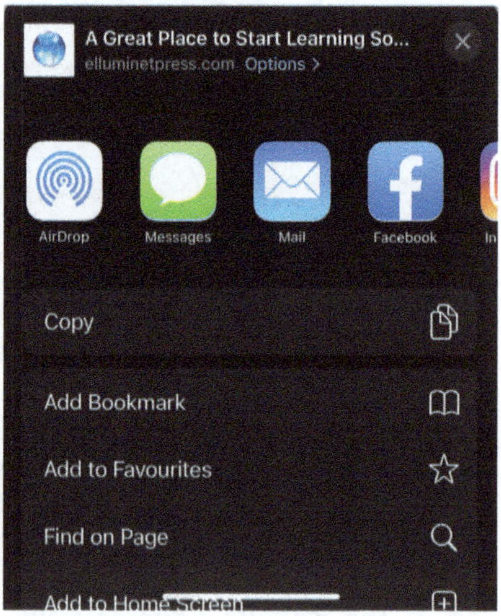


Along the bottom of that menu, you can add the current site to bookmarks. To do this tap ‘add bookmark’. You can also add the site to the favourites section on the safari start page.

## Browsing Tabs

You can open sites in multiple tabs, this helps to keep track of open sites.

### Tab Bar

The tab bar appears along the bottom of the screen.

To switch between tabs, swipe your finger left or right over the tab. If you have more than one tab open, you'll see the tabs move as you drag your finger.

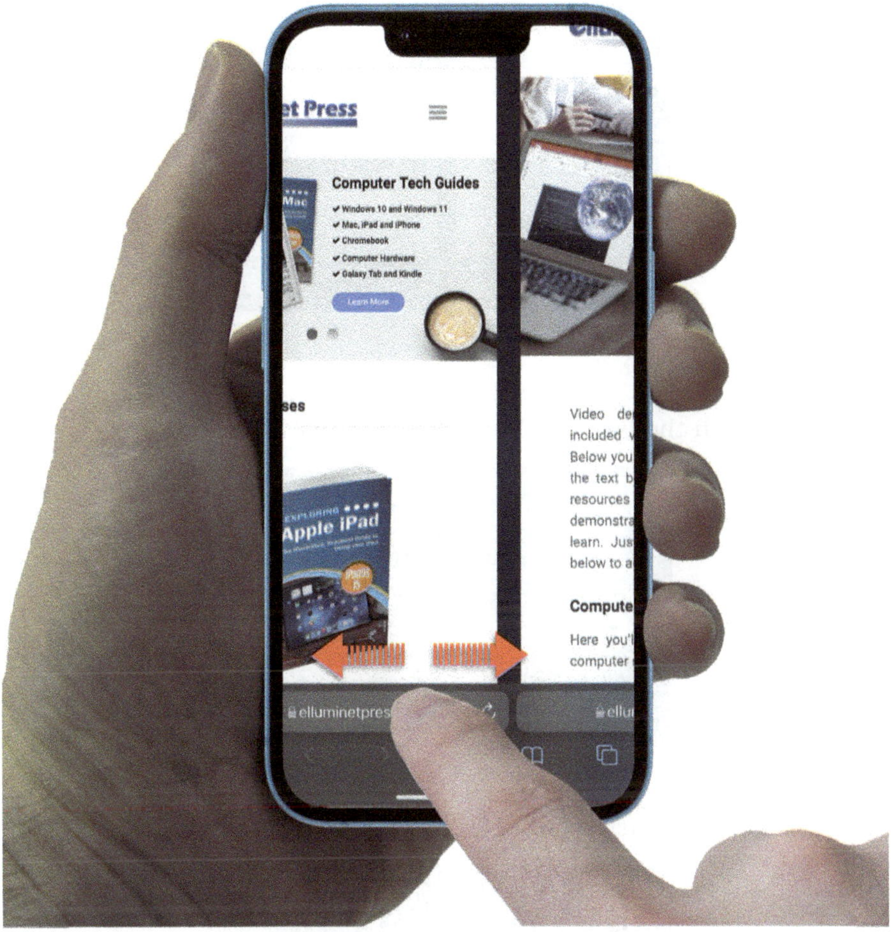


## Show All Tabs

To show all tabs, tap the icon on the far right hand side.

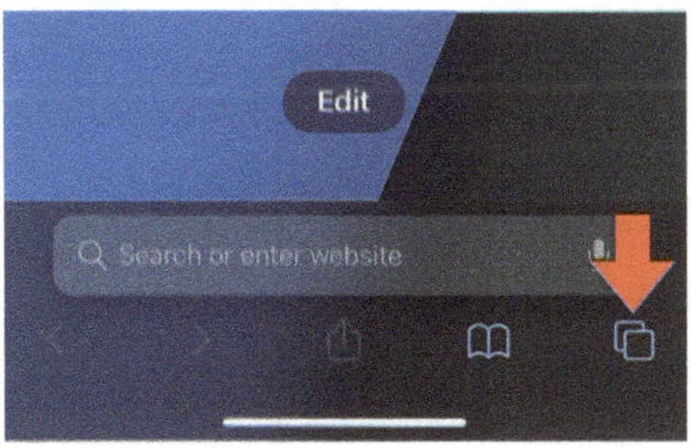

Safari will display your open tabs/websites as thumbnail previews, you can tap on to open up.

## New Tab

Tap the icon on the far right hand side to show all tabs.

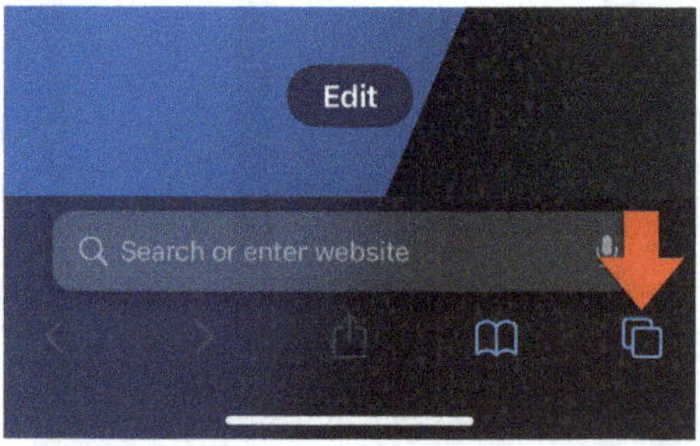


Tap the + sign to add a new tab where you can open another website, Google search, favourite and so on.

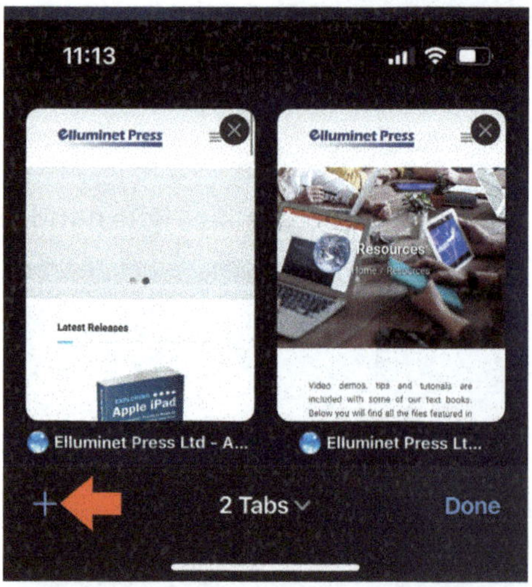

## Close a Tab

Tap the icon on the far right hand side to show all open tabs.

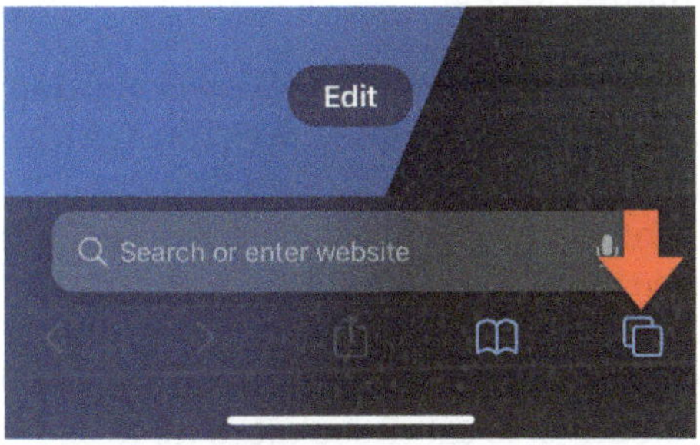


Swipe left over the tab thumbnail preview to close.

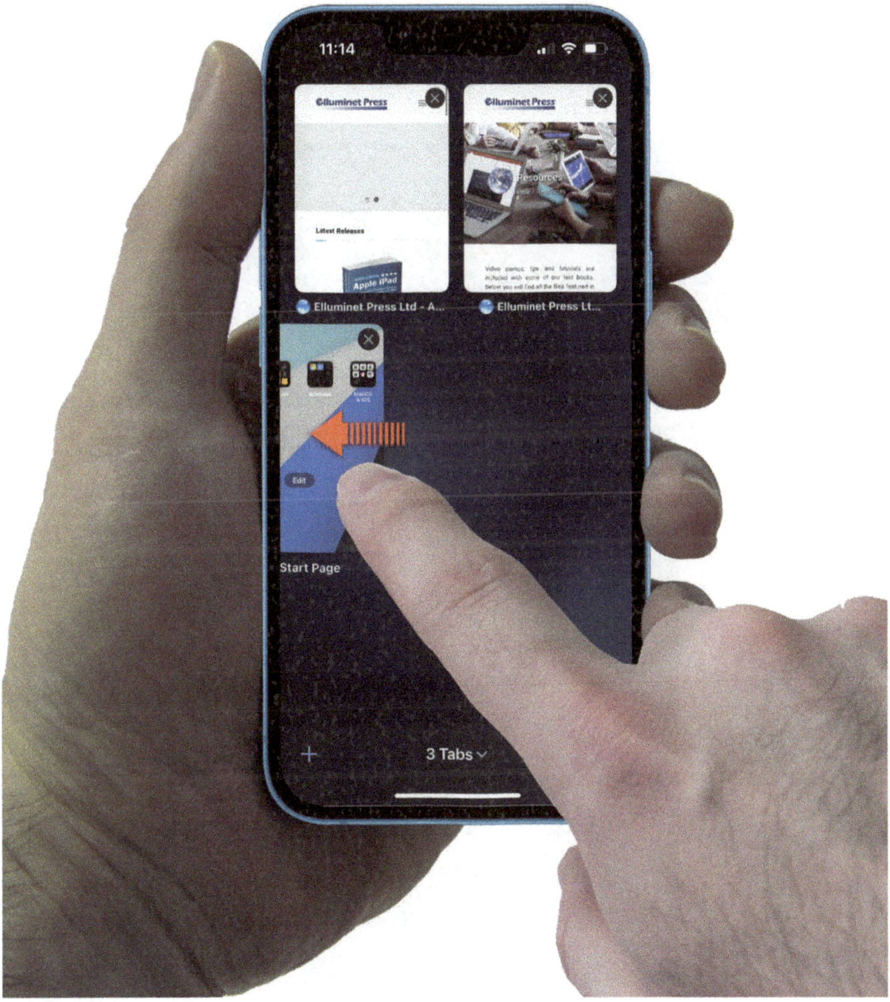

## Tab Groups

With tab groups, you can organize your tabs and keep them together in groups according to interest.

If you're doing web research, it can involve visiting several websites meaning you can have multiple sites open in tabs at the same time If you're researching multiple things, this can quickly become difficult to track. This is where group tabs come in. Tab groups allow you to save groups of these tabs together. For example, if you are planning a holiday (or vacation), you could be visiting multiple sites to compare prices for flights and hotels, as well as checking weather forecasts and local activities. You can save all these sites as tabs into a tab group, so you can return to the sites later.

### New Tab Group

To save your open tabs into a new tab group, tap the show all tabs icon on the bottom right. Then select 'tabs'.

If you currently have tabs open and want to add those tabs to a group tap 'new group from tabs'. To create an empty group, select 'new empty tab group.

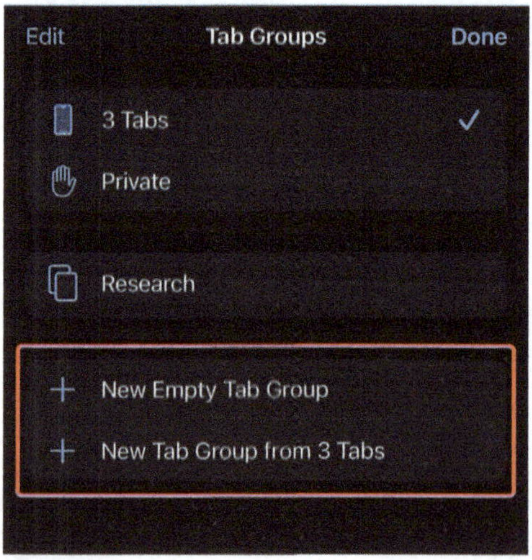

Give the tab group a meaningful name...

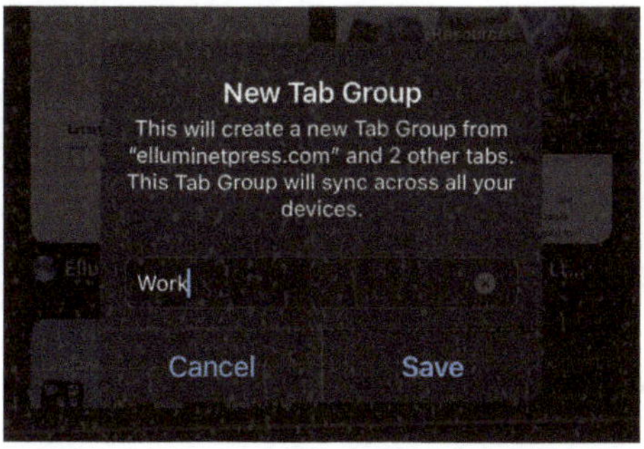


To see all your tab groups, tap the show all tabs icon on the bottom right. Then select 'tabs'.

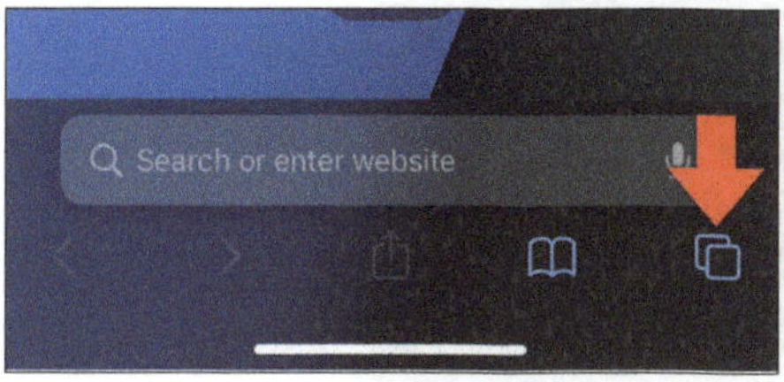

You'll see the tab name appear in the tab groups.

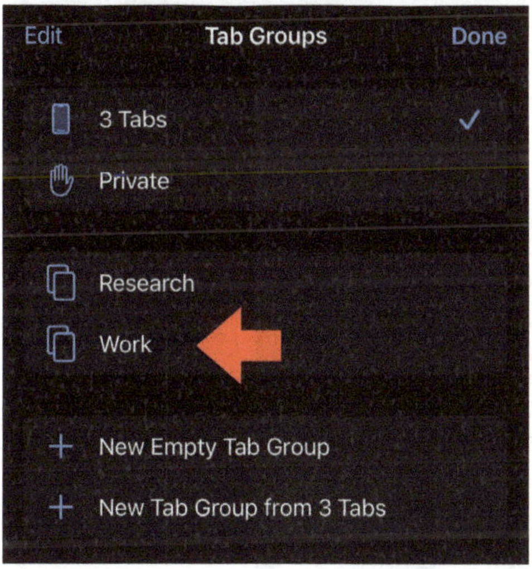


Now, when you open more tabs, they will be added to this tab group.

Use this group for one task. Create more tab groups for other tasks such as research, vacation/holiday, and so on. Then open the tabs to do with this task. This helps to keep your website tabs organised.

## Reopen Tab Group

Tap the show all tabs icon on the bottom right. Then select ‘tabs’.

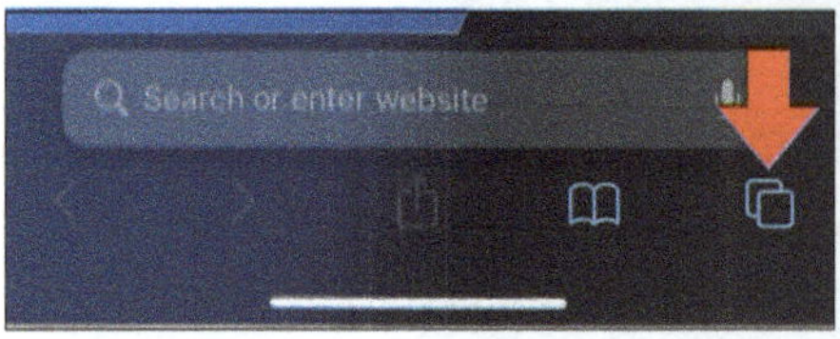

Halfway down the panel, you’ll see your tab groups. Tap on the group to reopen.

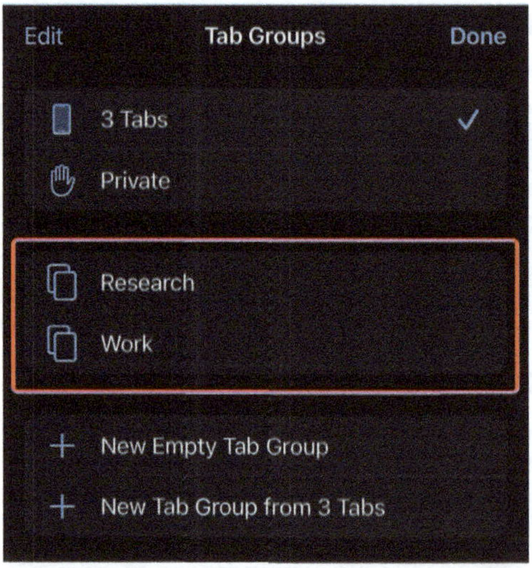


You’ll see the group name appear on the bottom, with all your tabs open in the tab bar above.

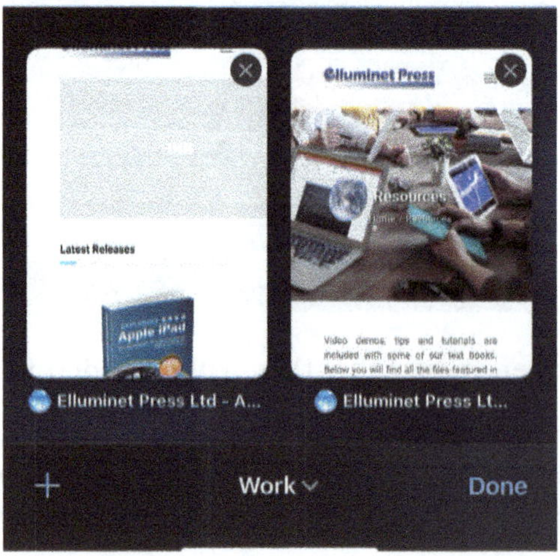

## Delete a Tab Group

Tap the show all tabs icon on the bottom right. Then select 'tabs'.

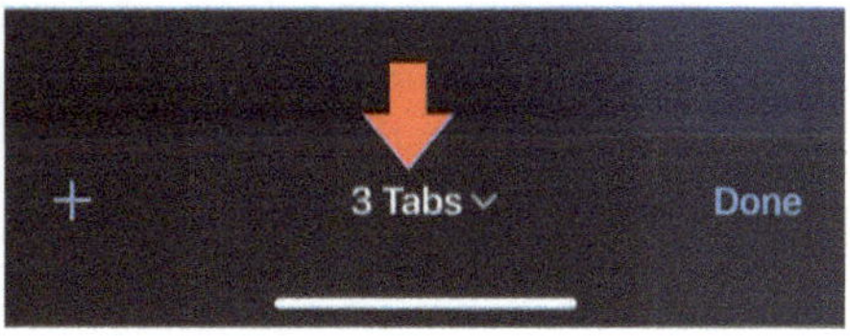


Swipe your finger to the left over the tab group in the list.

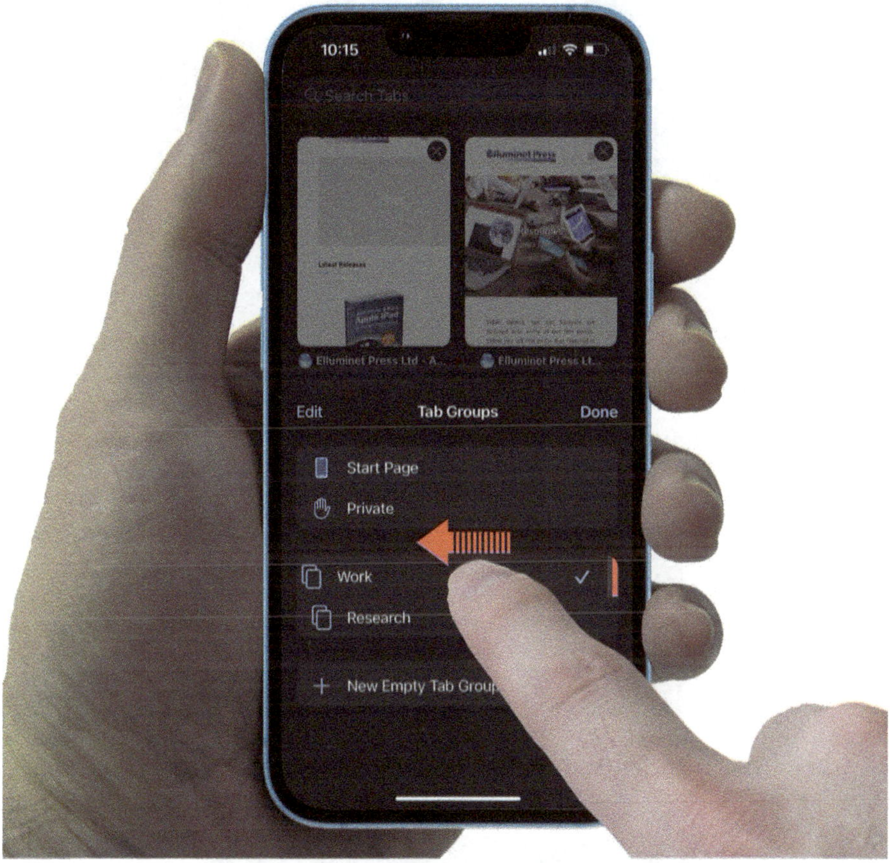


Tap the delete icon.

## Bookmarking a Site

Bookmarking sites makes it easier to find websites that you visit most often, without having to search for them or remember the web address. To bookmark the site you're on, tap the sharing icon on the bottom of the toolbar. From the popup menu, tap 'add bookmark'.

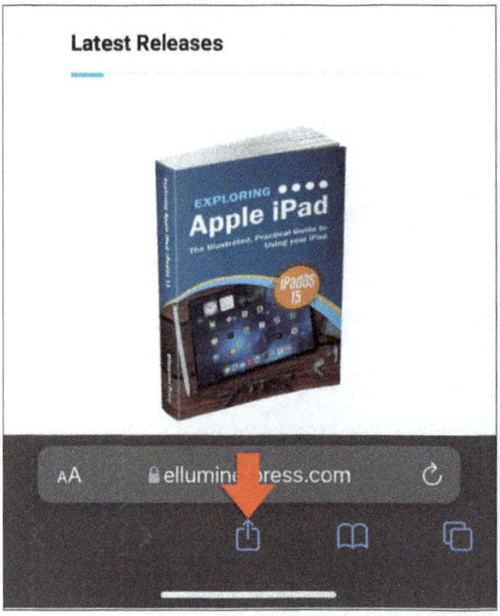


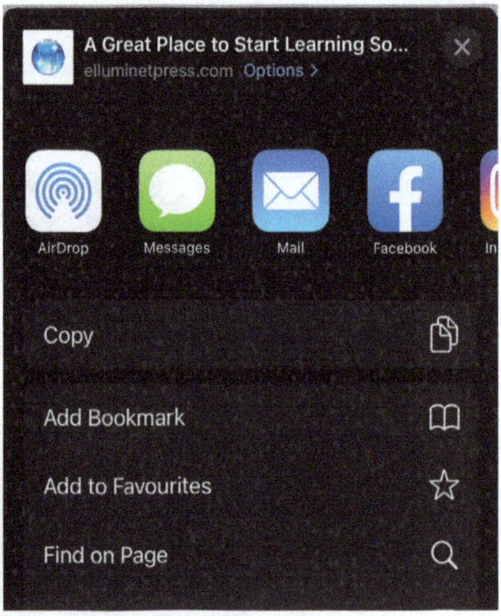


Enter a meaningful name if required as indicated below.

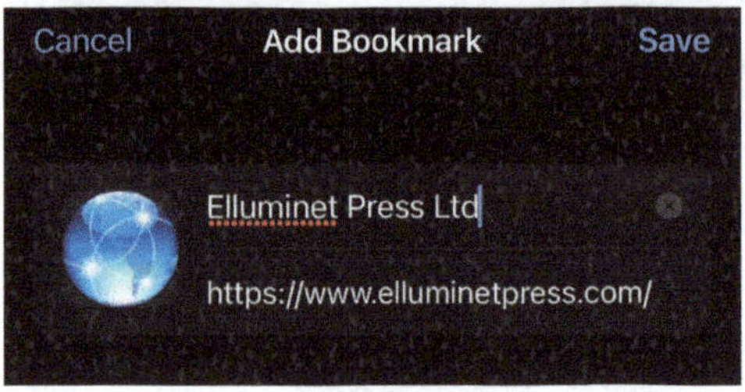


Tap 'favourites' under 'location' to select a folder to save your bookmark into.

Select 'bookmarks'. This will save the website into the bookmarks folder.

## Revisiting a Bookmarked Site

You'll find all your bookmarked sites on the sidebar. To access this menu, tap the icon on the toolbar along the bottom of the screen. Select the bookmarks link along the top of the popup panel.

You'll see a list of sites you have bookmarked. Tap bookmark to revisit site.

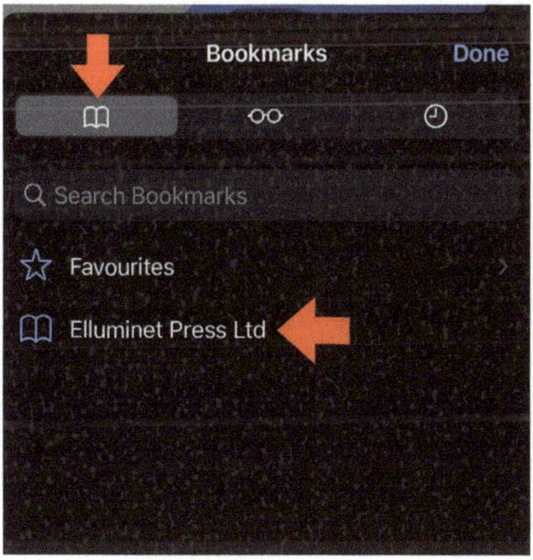


**To Delete:** Swipe right to left across the bookmark, and tap delete, to remove a bookmark.

**To edit a bookmark**, tap and hold your finger on the bookmark in the list.

Select 'edit' from the popup menu at the bottom. You can enter a new name, or change the web address.

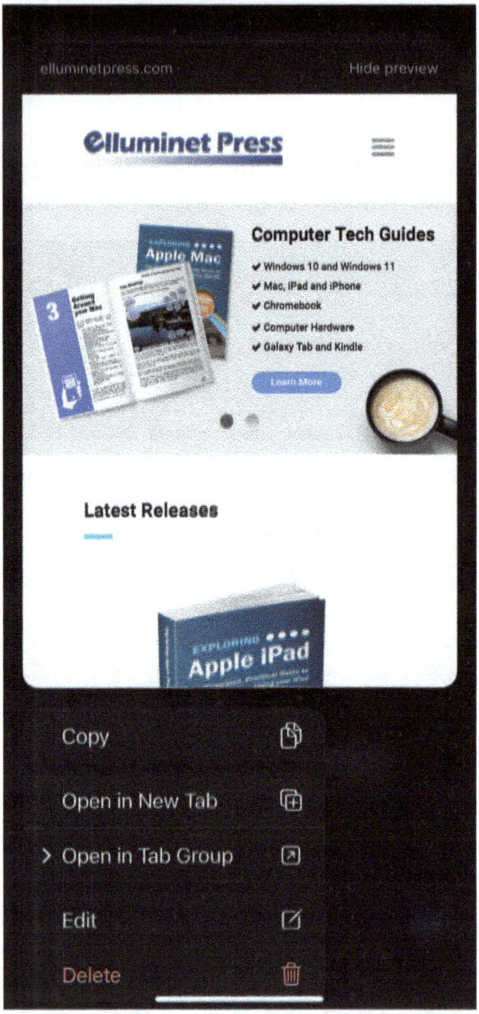


You can also open the bookmarked site in an existing tab group or open it in a new tab group

## Browsing History

Safari keeps a list of all the websites you have visited in the browser history. To view the history, tap the icon on the toolbar at the bottom, then select the 'history' link from the list.

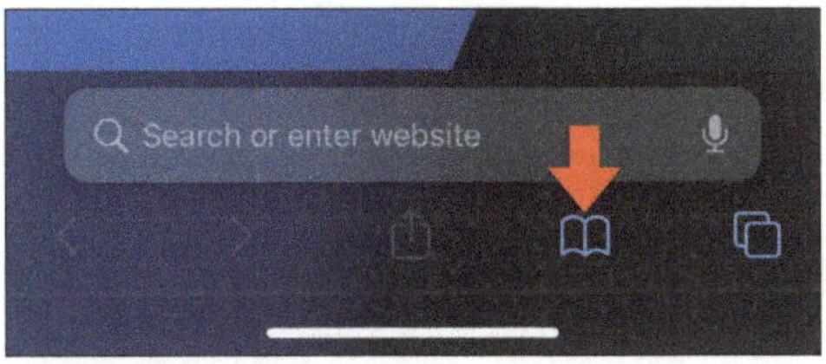


Scroll down the list, tap on a site to revisit.

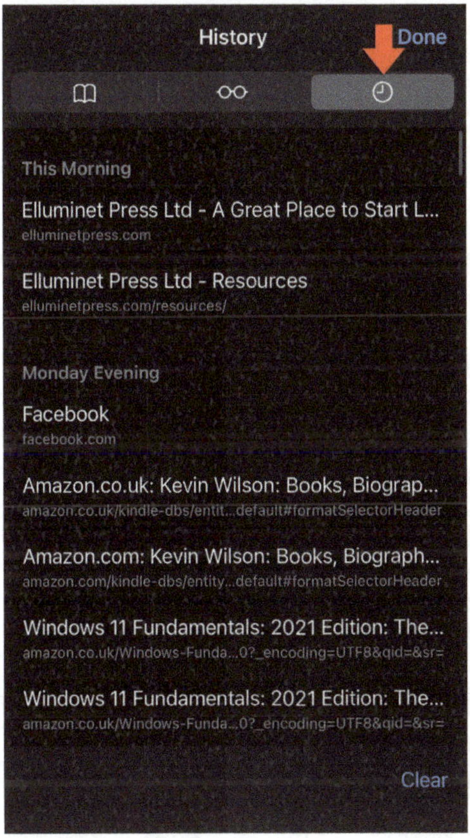


Swipe right to left over the site in the list and tap delete, to remove the site from the history.

Tap 'clear all' on the bottom right to clear the entire history.

## Reader View

Reader view makes it easier to read web pages without all the unnecessary background clutter that usually comes with a website.

Reader view is not available on all web pages but is on most. To enable reader view, tap the 'AA' icon on the left hand side of the web address search field. From the menu, select 'show reader view'.

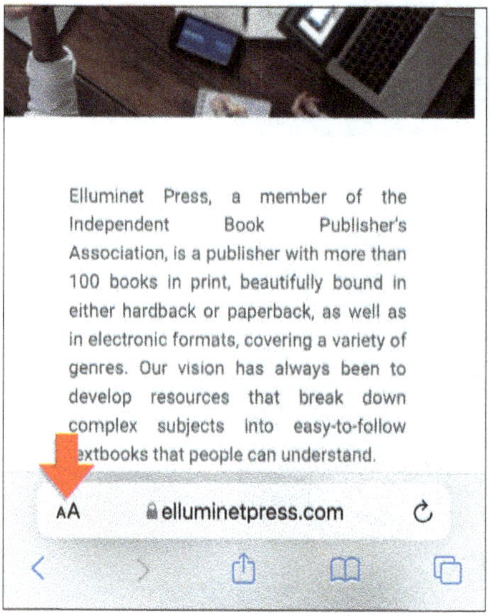


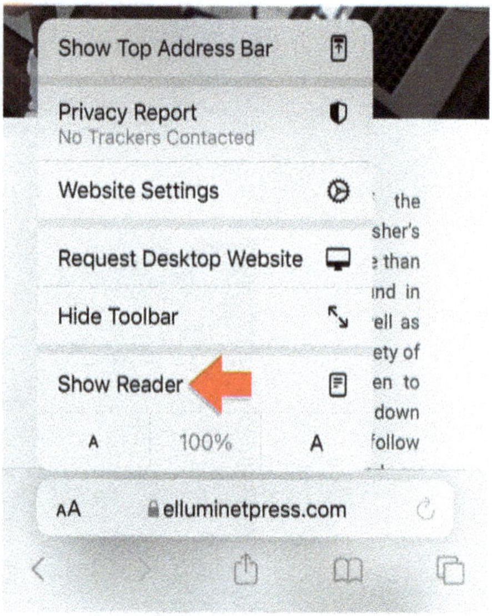


When you're in reader view, tap the AA icon again. Here you can change the font size of the text, the type face, and the background colour.

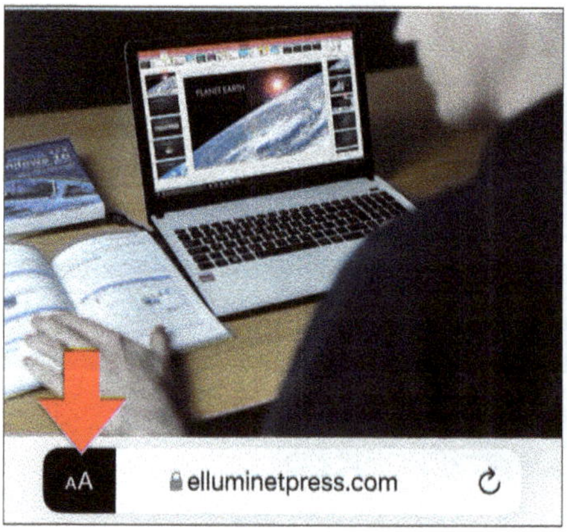


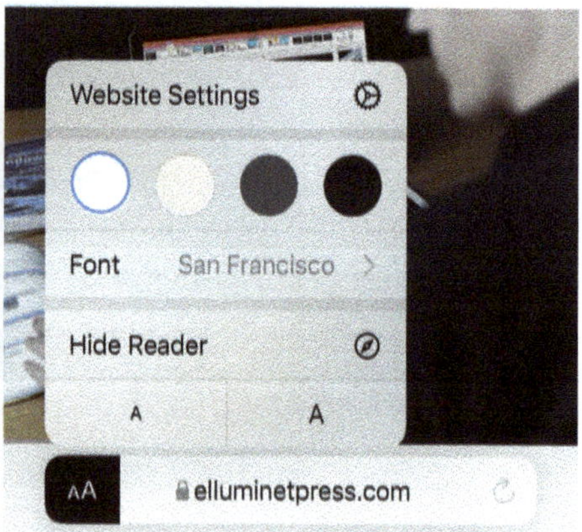


Tap the 'A' icons at the bottom to make the text smaller, or larger. Tap 'font' to change the reader font, tap a colour to change the reader background. To go back to normal view, tap the 'hide reader'.

## Page Zoom

You can quickly zoom in and out on a website's text. To zoom in, spread your thumb and forefinger apart across the glass. To zoom out, pinch your thumb and forefinger together.

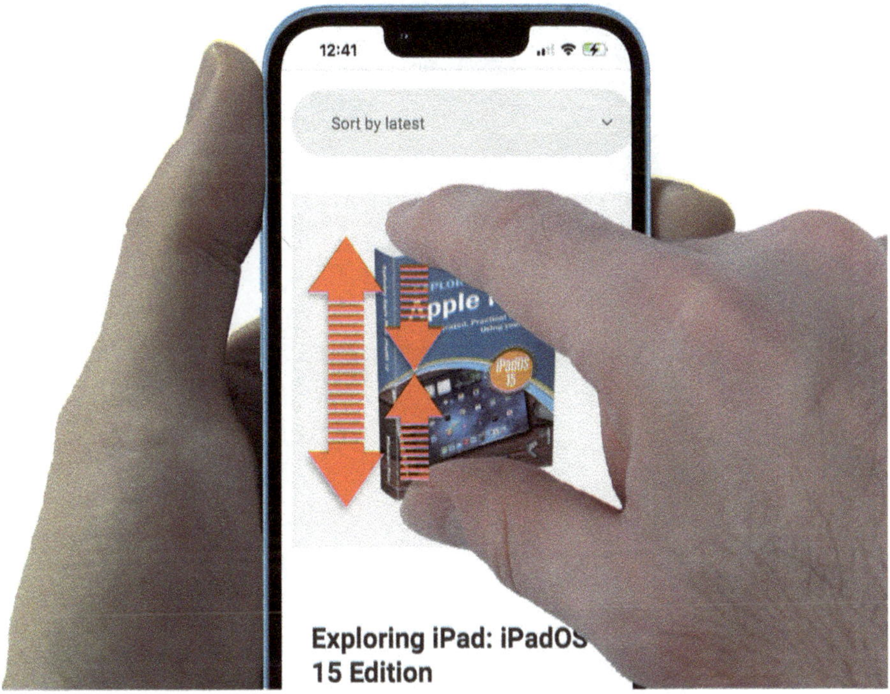


## Clicking Links

If you tap on a link, Safari will take you to that page.

However, if you tap and hold your finger on a link, you'll see a preview of the linked page.

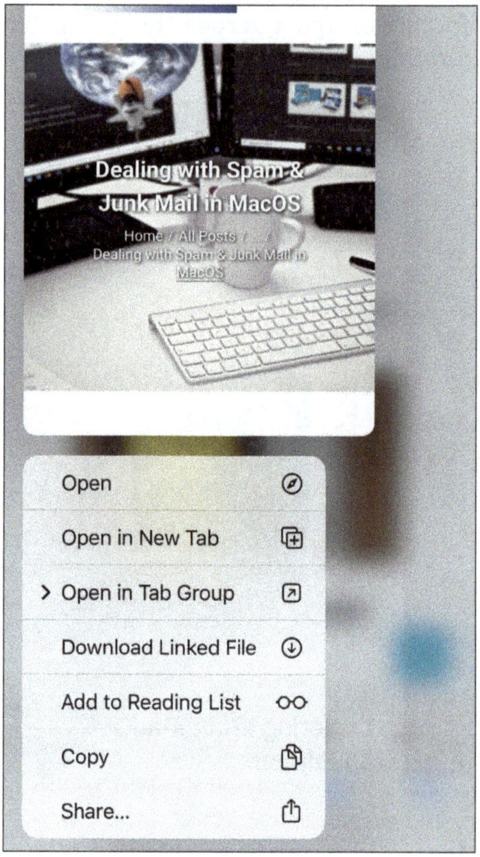


Here, at the bottom of the preview, you can open the website as normal, open the site in a new tap, open the site in a tab group, download the linked file, add the site to your reading list, copy the site to the clipboard, or share the site with someone using email, messages, or social media.

## Go Back a Page

You can go back a page using the navigation icons on the bottom left of the screen.

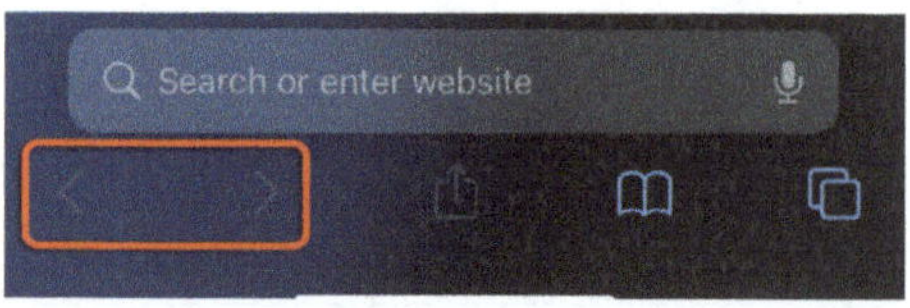

Or you can swipe from the left edge of the screen.

## Saving and Sharing Images

To save an image to your Photos, or share an image with someone, tap and hold your finger on the image.

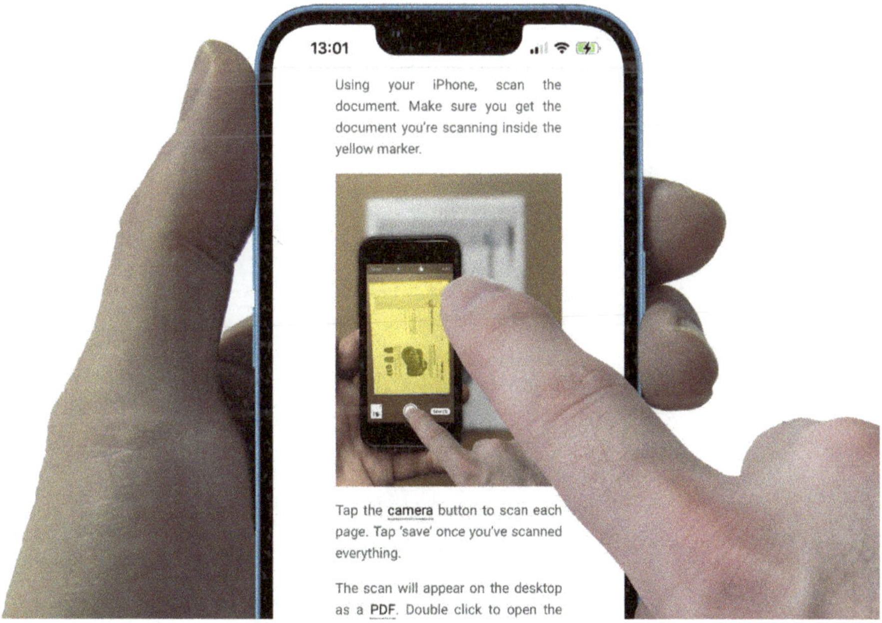

From the popup menu at the bottom, select 'add to photos' to save the photos to your Photos app.

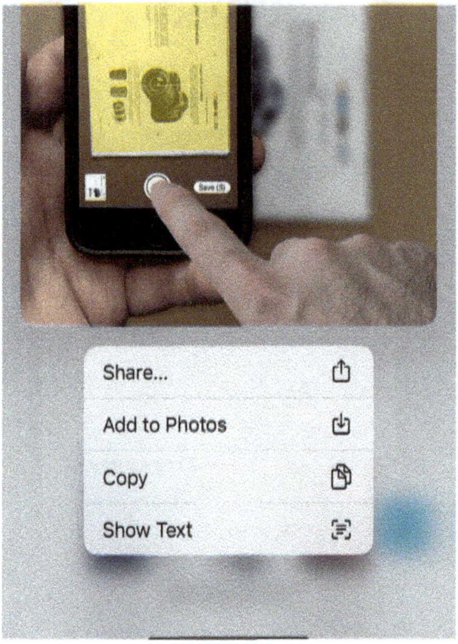


Tap 'copy' to copy the photo to the clipboard, or tap 'share' to share the photo using email, messages, or social media.

## Download Manager

When you download a file in Safari, you'll see a prompt. Tap 'download' to download the file.

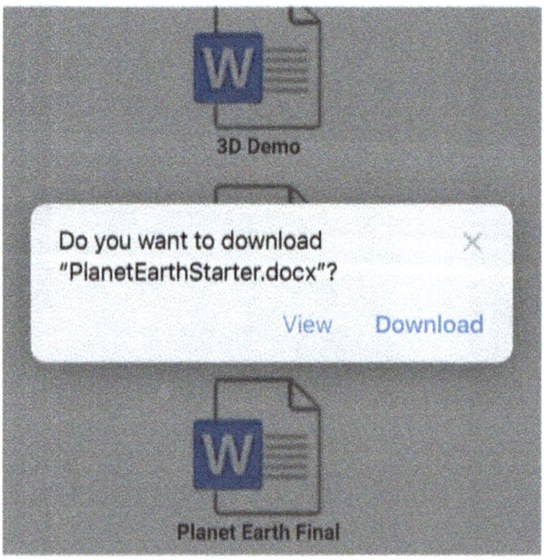

Once you've downloaded the file, you'll see a small icon appear on the bottom left. To see your downloads, tap on the 'AA' icon, then select 'downloads' from the menu.

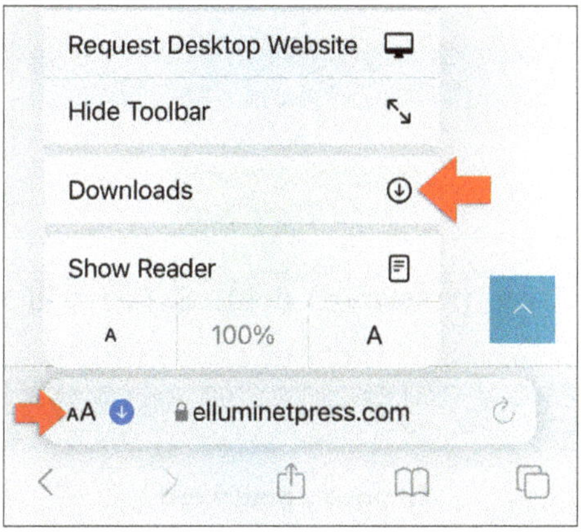


You'll see the status of files you're downloading, as well as files you've downloaded. You can tap on the filename to open the file, or tap the magnifying glass icon to open your downloads folder.

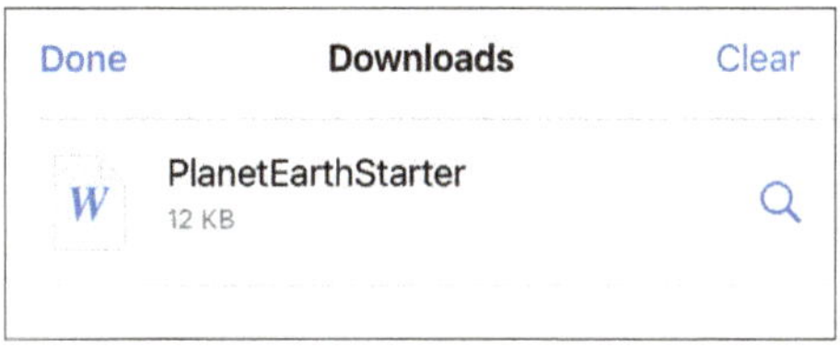


You'll also find your downloads folder in the files app. Here you'll find all the files you've downloaded.

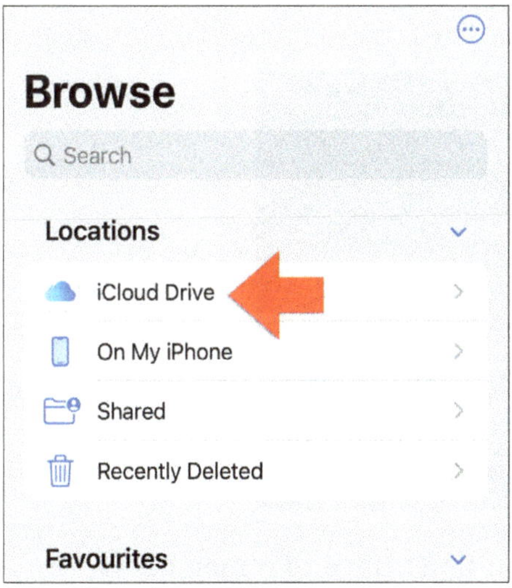


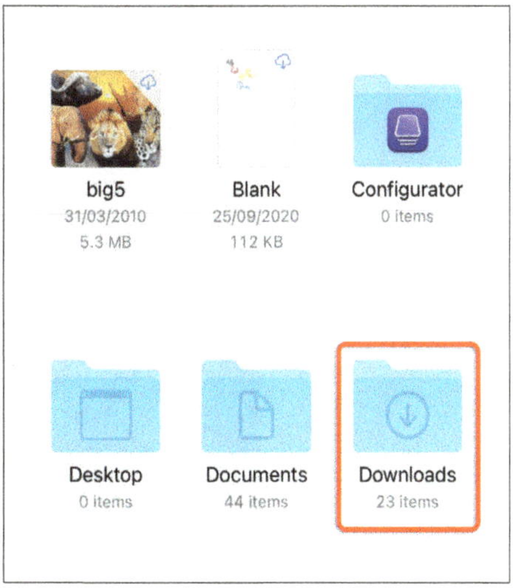

## Generate Automatic Strong Passwords

Tap Safari and go to a website where you need to sign up for an account. In this example I'm creating a new Facebook account.

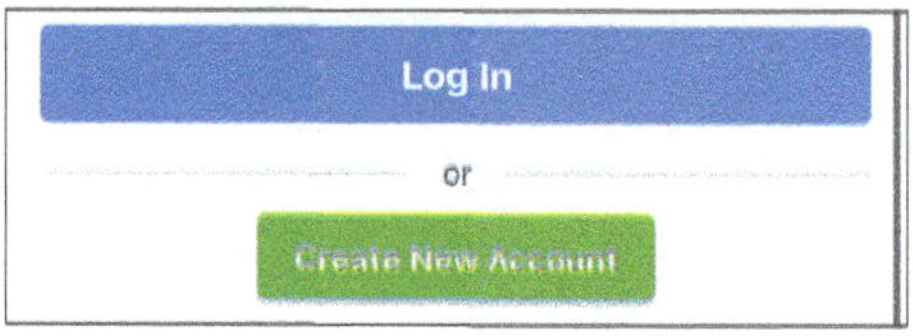


When you tap in the 'password' field, Safari will suggest a strong password.

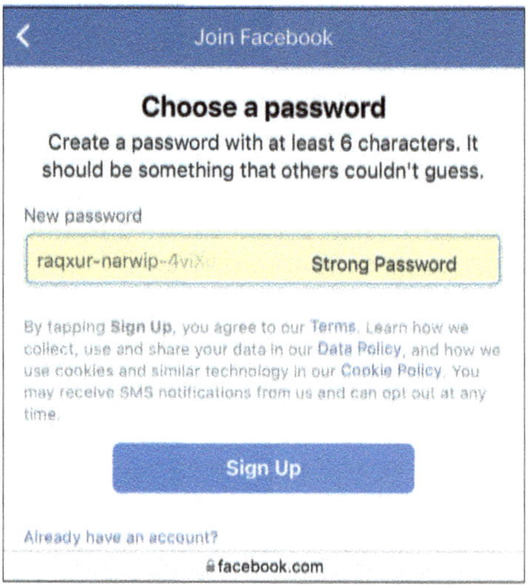


In the panel that appears at the bottom, tap 'Use Strong Password' to store it in your keychain.

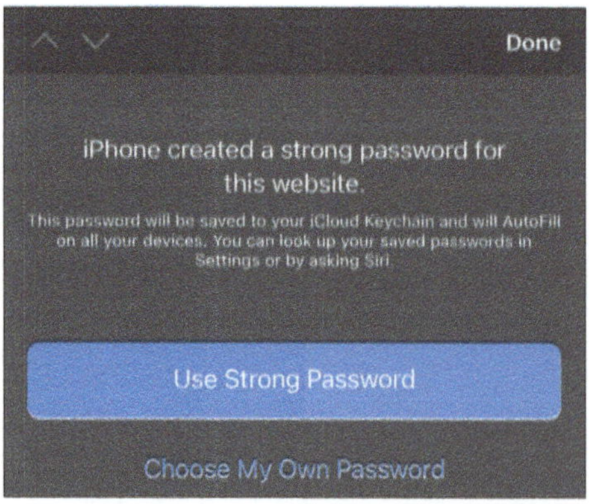


This will store your password, so you don't have to remember it

## Autofill Passwords on Websites

Tap Safari and go to a site that you already have an account with. Eg the Facebook account we created earlier. Select the text input field for the username or email address associated with the account.

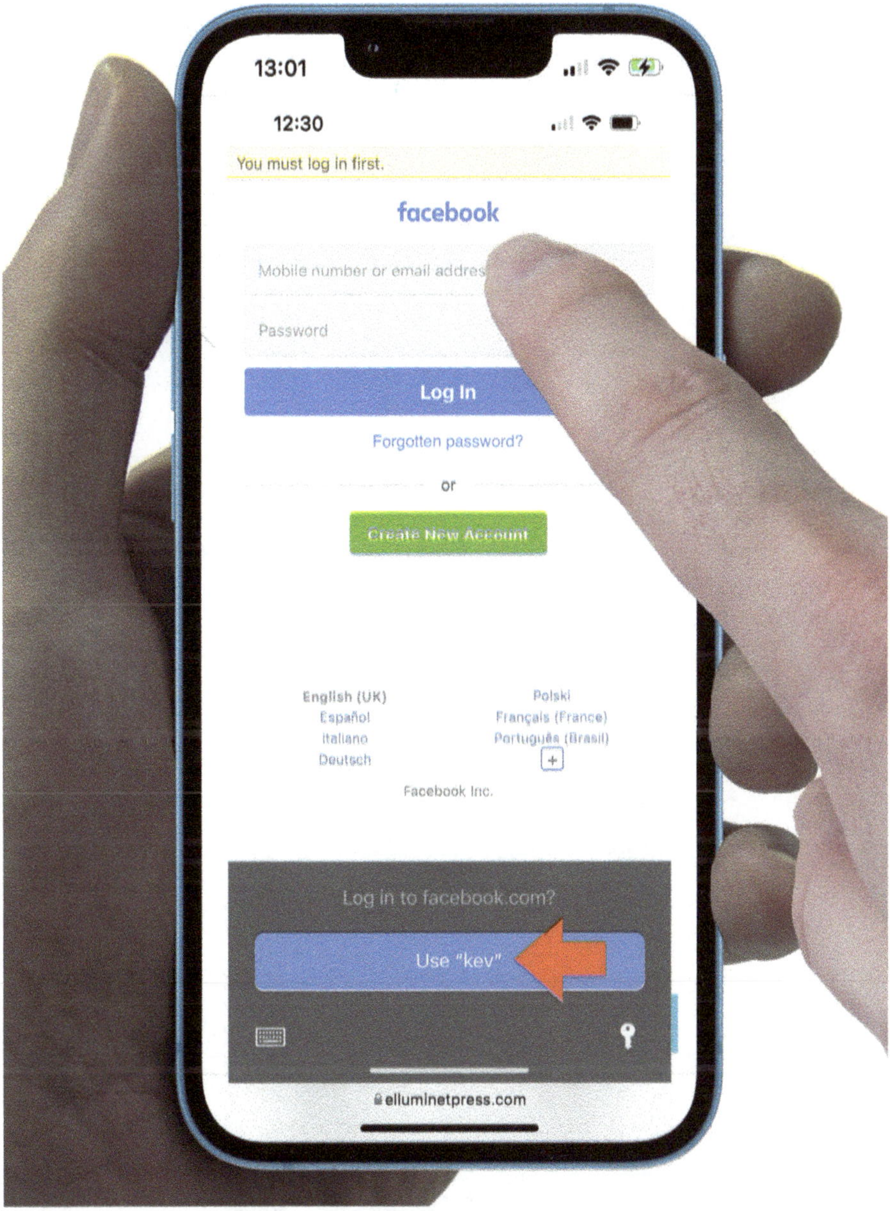


In the suggestions on the keyboard below, select "use...". Authenticate the action with your Touch ID, Face ID, or passcode when prompted.

## Automatically add Password to Keychain

When you sign into a website or for the first time, you will receive a prompt asking you whether you want to save your login details to keychain.

Tap Safari and navigate to the website you want to sign into. In this example, I'm signing into an Outlook account.

Sign in with your username and password, in the normal way .

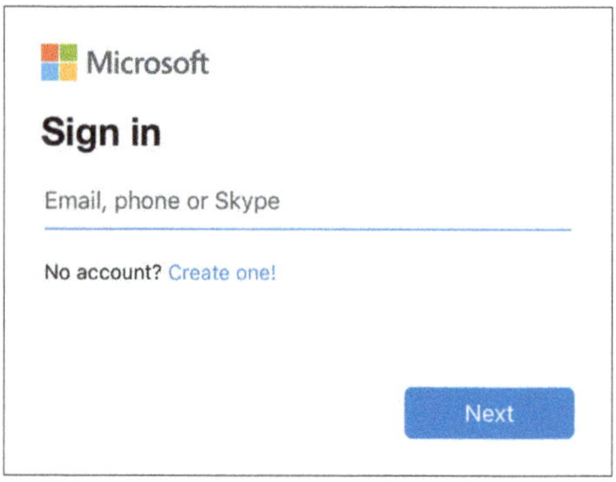


Once you sign in successfully, Safari will prompt you to save the password to your keychain. Tap 'save password'.

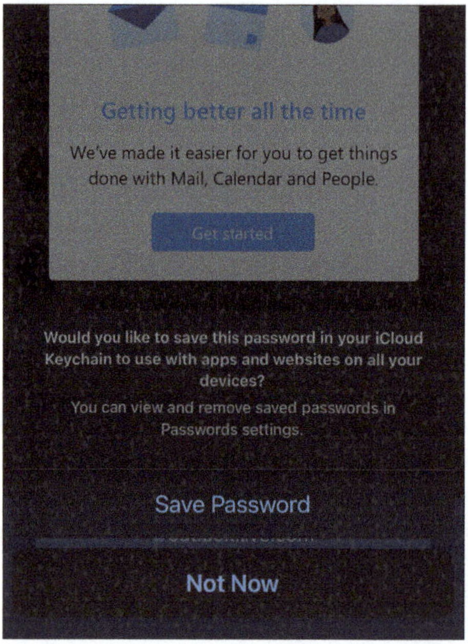


This will save your password so you don't have to type it in each time.

To sign in the next time, just click in the username or password field.

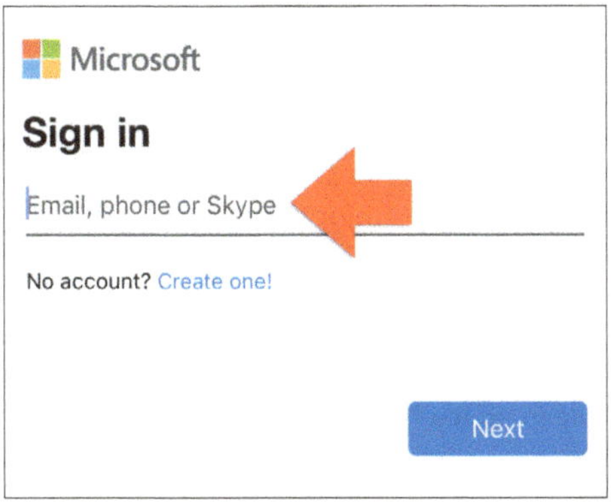


Select the password from the suggestions along the top of your keyboard

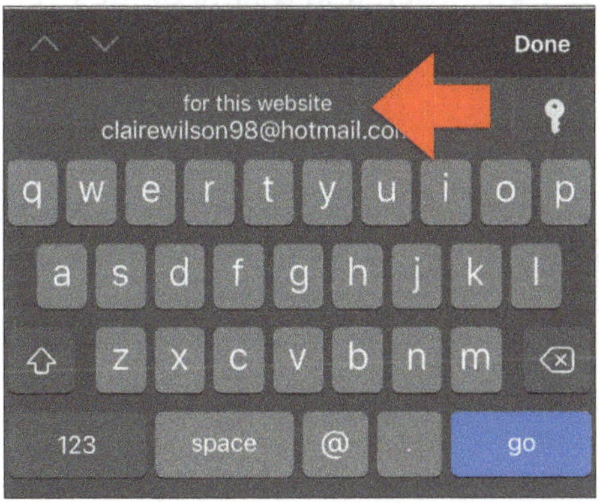


Tap the password suggestion from the options on the top of your keyboard. If your password isn't there, tap the key icon then select the password from the list.

## Forms Autofill

You can get safari to automatically fill in a form for you using your contact information.

### Add Contact Info

To set it up make sure you have filled in your contact information correctly in the contacts app. Open the contacts app.

Select the contact card with your name on it (it will have 'me' written next to it). Enter your contact details.

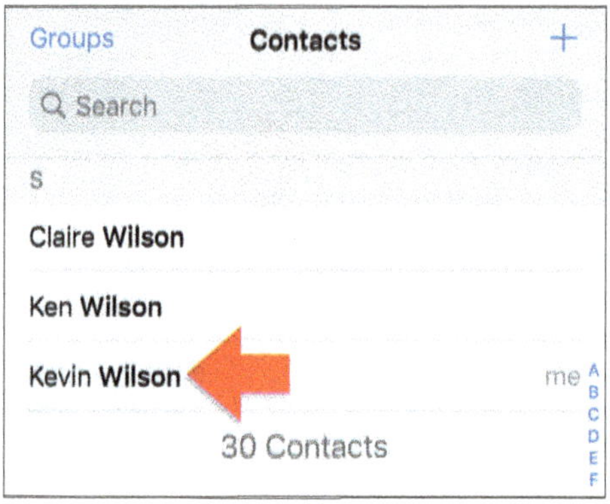


Tap 'edit' on the top right, then add all the details you want to show up in the forms you fill in online. Name, phone number, email address, street address, and so on. Click 'done' on the top right when you're finished.

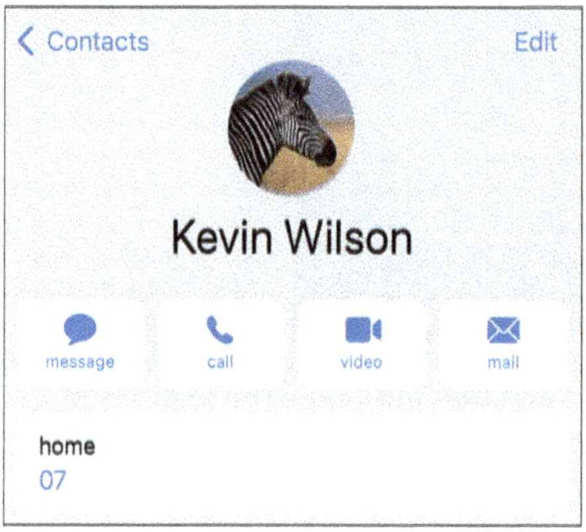


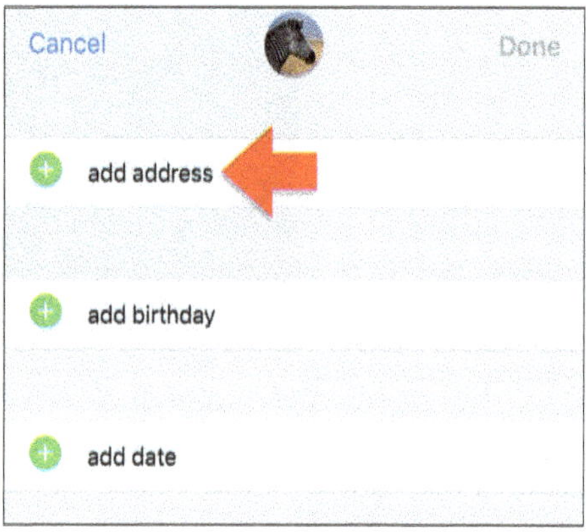


Now, open the settings app, scroll down, select 'safari' from the list.

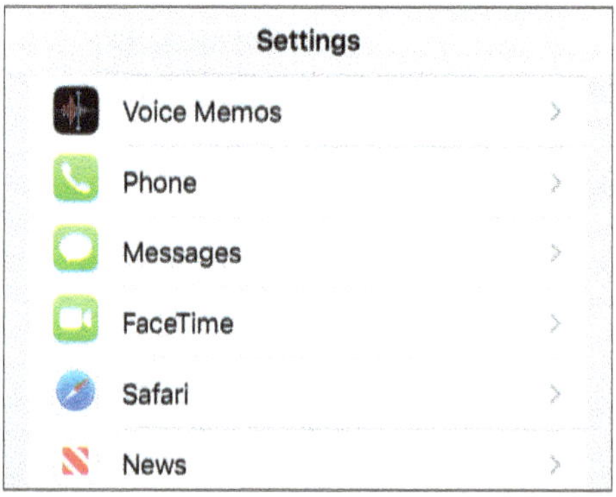

Select 'autofill'. Turn on 'use contact info', then tap 'my info'.

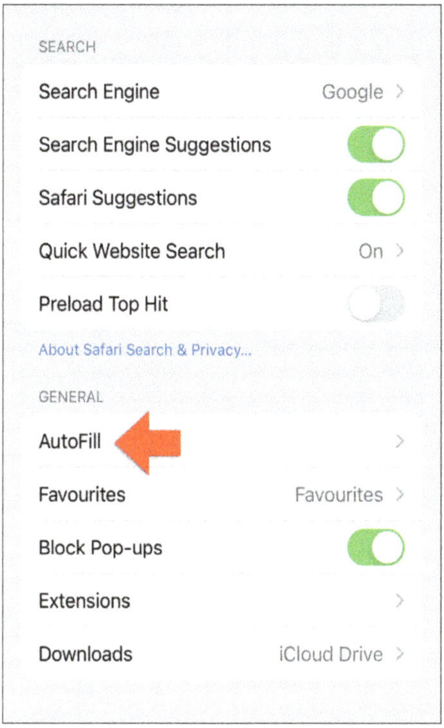


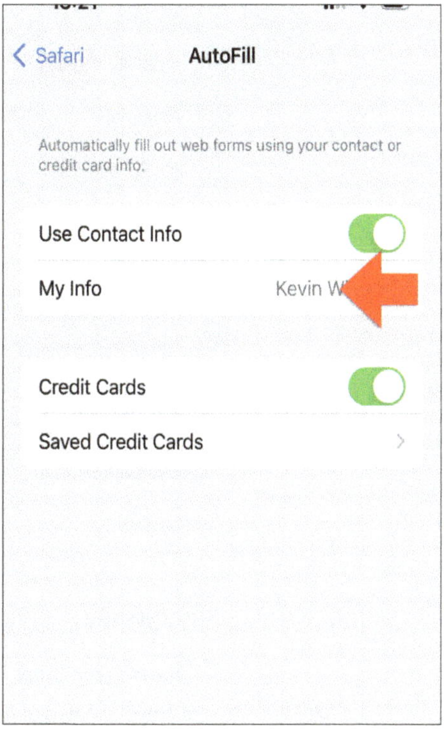


Select the contact card you edited earlier.

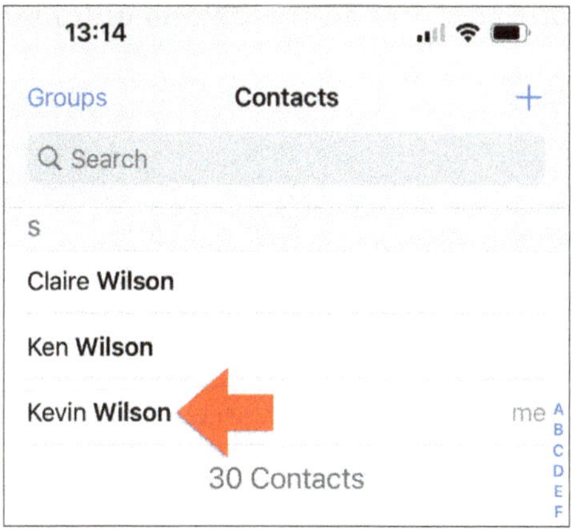


Close the settings app.

## Adding Credit Cards

Open the settings app, select 'safari' from the list on the left hand side.

Select 'autofill'.

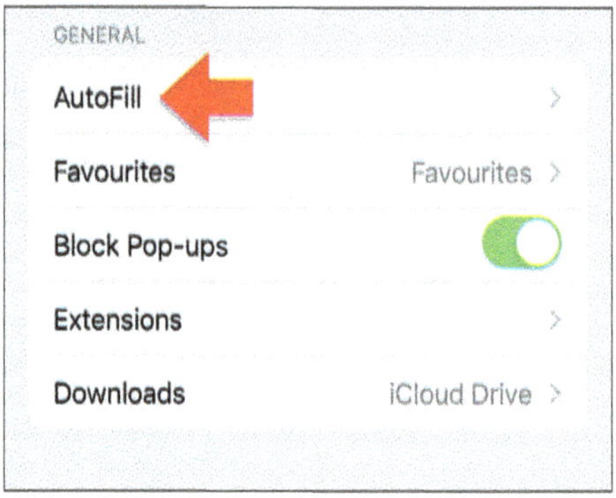


Select 'saved credit cards'.

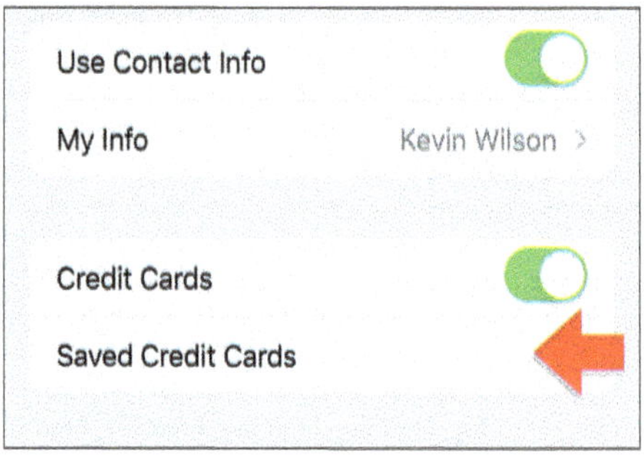


Tap 'add credit card', then enter your credit card info. Or tap 'use camera' to scan your card to add the details automatically.

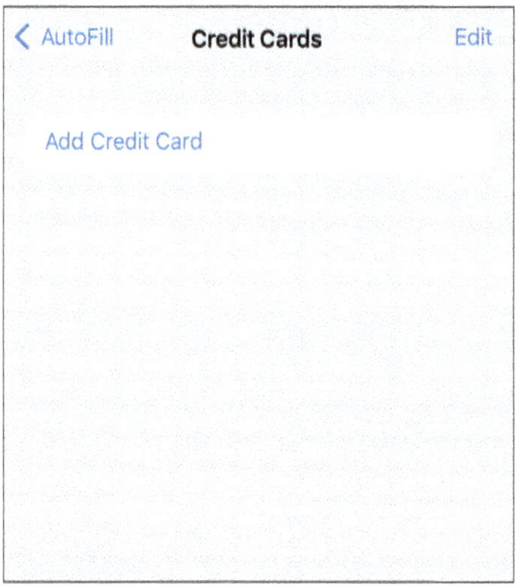


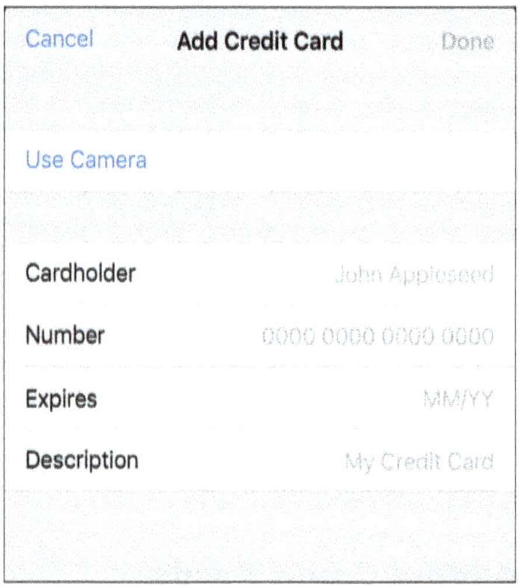


Tap 'done' on the top right when you're finished.

## Using Autofill to Fill in a Form in Safari

In safari, tap in a field on the form. For example, here I'm filling in my contact details on an online store.

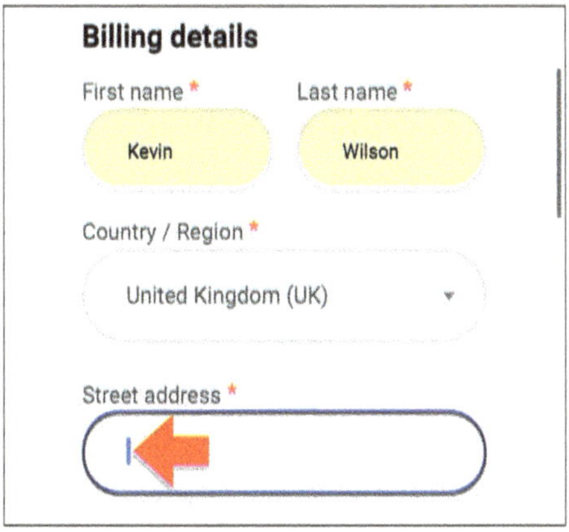


Select the contact info from the popup.

## Using Autofill to Fill in Payment Details in Safari

Here in Safari, I'm filling in my contact details on an online store. Tap in the credit card field on the form.

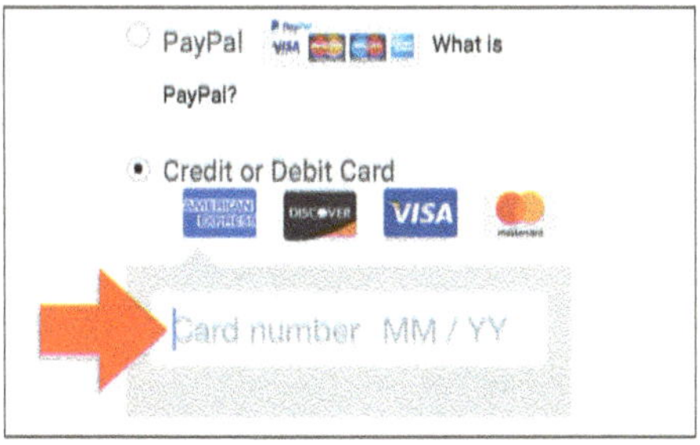

Select the card from the options along the top of the popup.

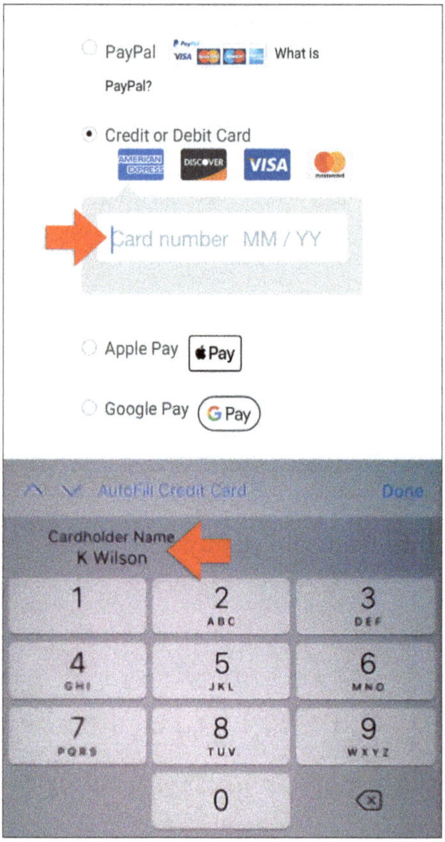


Use your Face ID or Touch ID to authorise the payment. You'll see the card details appear in the fields. Enter the CVC code on your card.

## Password Monitoring

Safari monitors passwords you've saved to your keychain, keeping an eye out for passwords that may have been involved in a data breach or passwords that have been repeated or are considered easy to guess. If Safari discovers a breach, it will alert you and help you generate a new secure password. You can see any password alerts in the settings app. Open the settings app and select 'passwords'.

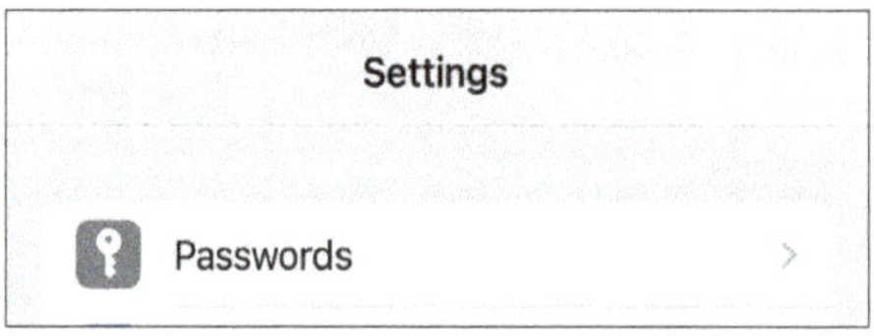

You'll a 'security recommendations' section where you can see passwords that have been compromised or are weak.

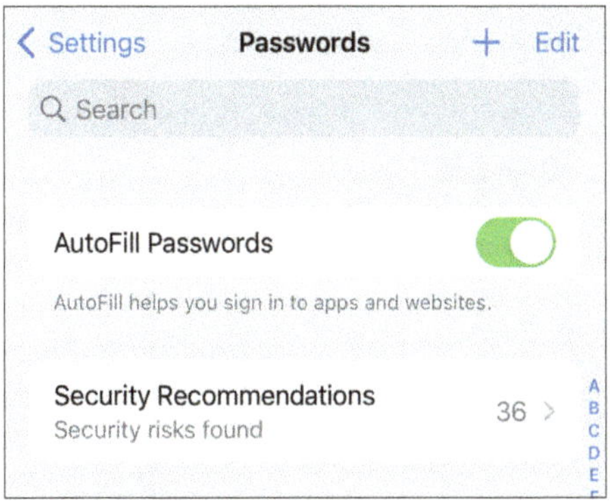


Underneath, you'll see a list of sites Safari has saved a password for. Tap on one of these to view details.

Tap 'change password on website'. To delete the site from your passwords list, tap 'delete password'.

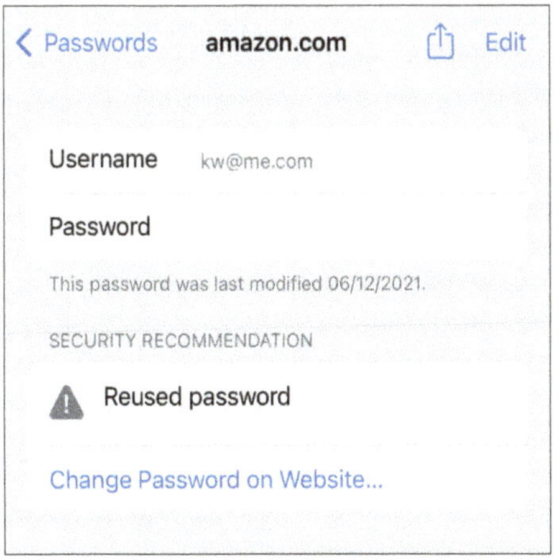


This will take you to the website and allow you to log in. Then you'll need to go to the 'change password' section in your account with that website and follow the 'change password' steps.

You can also airdrop the password to someone or another device. To do this, tap the share icon on the top right of the screen.

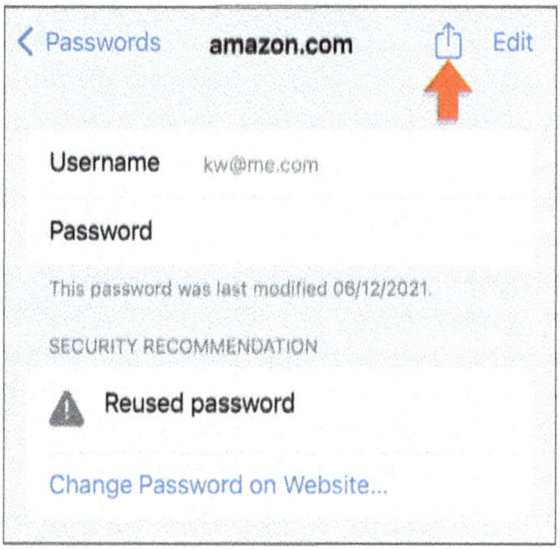


If you want to edit the password, or delete it, tap 'edit' on the top right of the screen.

Here, you can edit the username/password, remove the website, or delete the password.

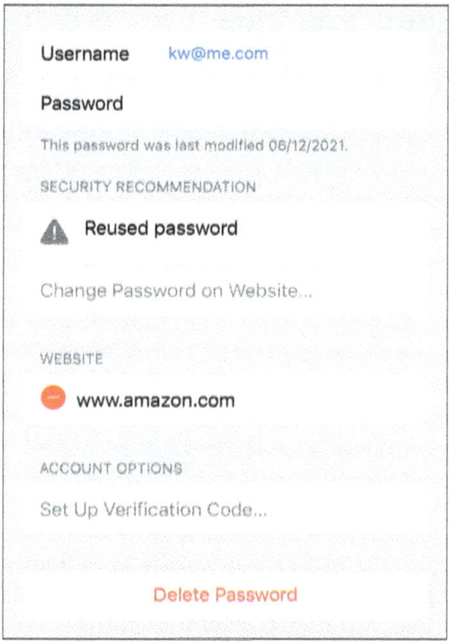

## Website Privacy Report

Safari uses it's Intelligent Tracking Prevention to identify and block trackers advertisers use to track your web activity. On the toolbar tap the 'AA' icon. Select 'privacy report'.

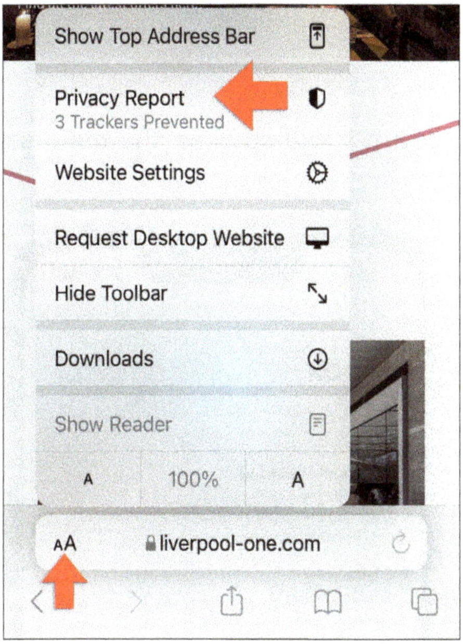


You'll see some stats. Tap the 'websites' tab to see all the websites where trackers have been blocked. Select the 'trackers' tab to see a list of all the trackers that have been blocked and who they belong to.

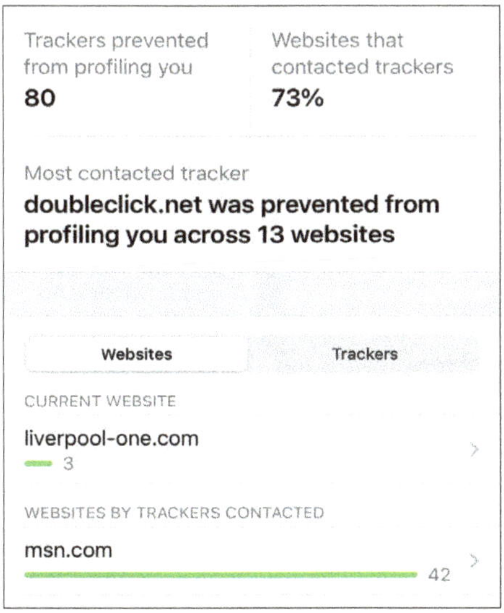


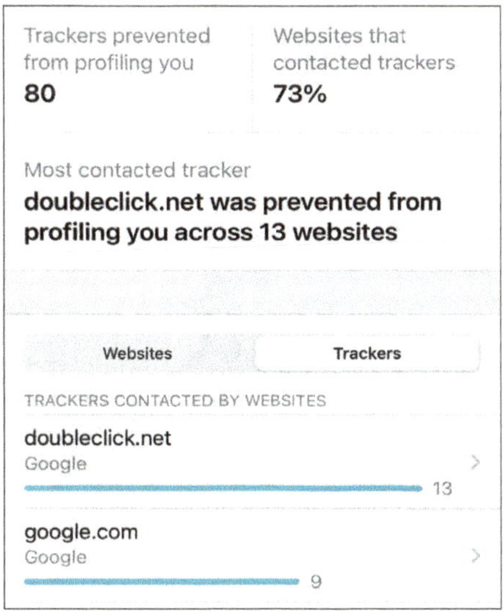

# Using Email

To start the mail app, tap 'mail' on the dock at the bottom of the screen.

Once your email is setup it will open on the main screen. Let's take a look around...

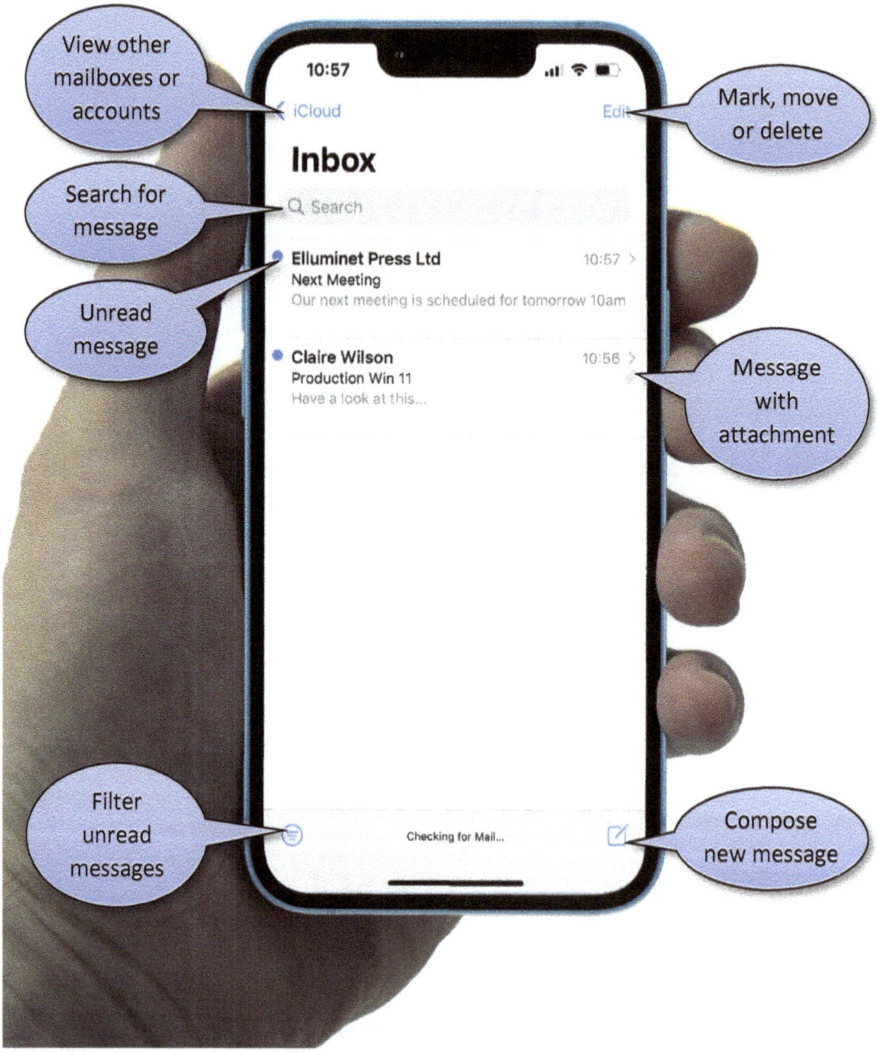


You'll see a list of all your emails. Just tap on one to view.

## Reply to or Forward a Message

To reply to an email, select the email you want from your inbox, then tap the 'reply to sender' icon on the bottom right.

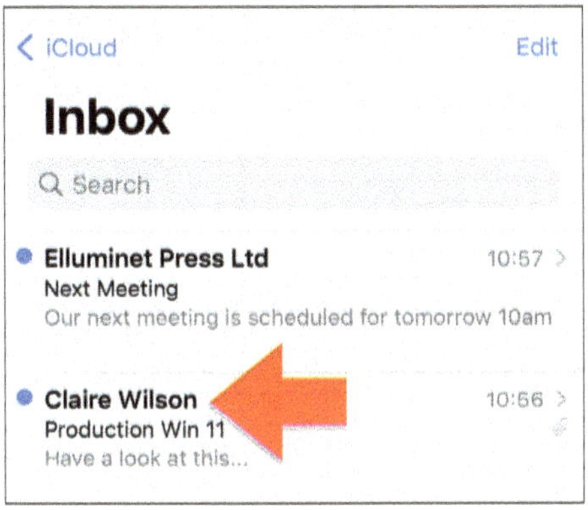


Tap on the 'reply' icon on the bottom of the screen.

From the popup, tap 'reply' to reply to the sender, tap 'reply all' to reply to sender plus any other recipients who were copied in, tap 'forward' to send the message to someone else. Or tap the bin to delete the email.

Type in your reply at the top of the message, then tap the send icon on the top right.

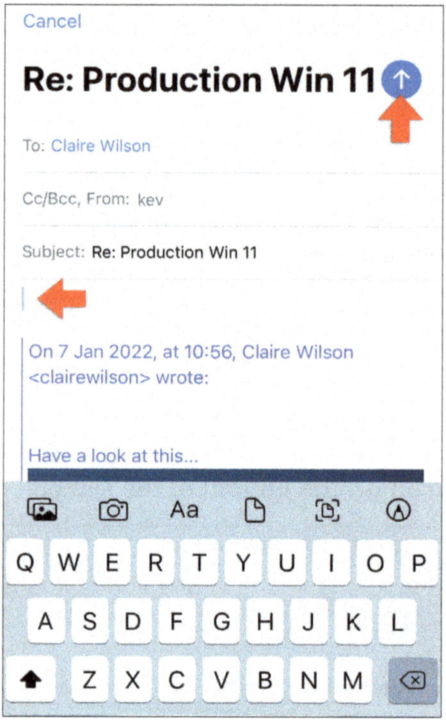


## Email Threads

An email conversation that spreads across dozens of messages in your inbox is called a thread. Apple Mail organises your email messages by thread. Here in the demo below is an email conversation between Claire and me. Tap the small blue arrow to the right of the email to open the thread.

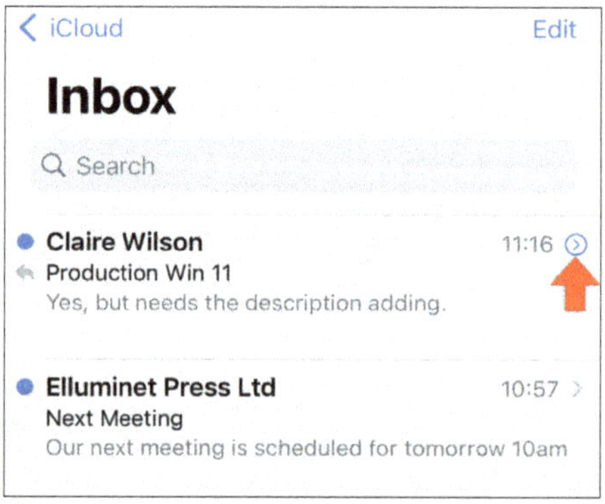

You can see in my inbox below, my email conversation with Claire. The messages in the thread are highlighted. Notice the latest email is at the top of the thread.

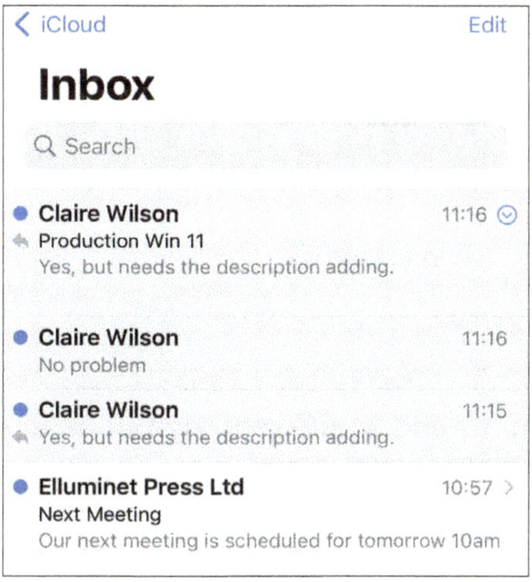


When you select the email conversation in the inbox, you'll automatically see the latest message appear, just scroll down to see the history. To reply to the message, select it from the conversation, then tap the reply icon on the bottom right of the thread.

Select 'reply' from the popup menu.

## Add a Signature

An email signature is text that is added to the end of each email message you send. This text is usually your name and contact information.

To create a signature, open your settings app. Select 'mail' from the list. Scroll down to the bottom, tap 'signature'

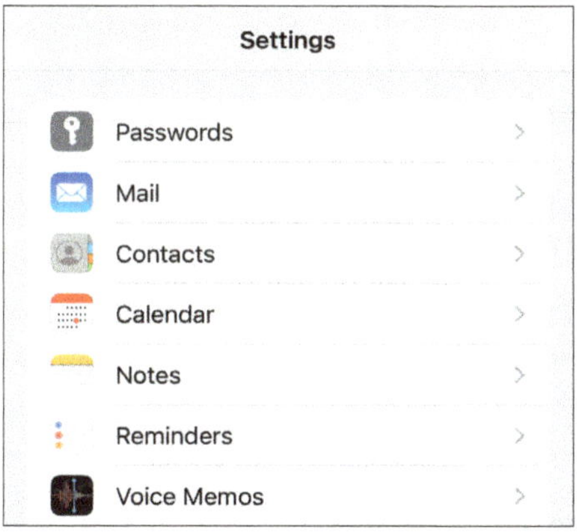


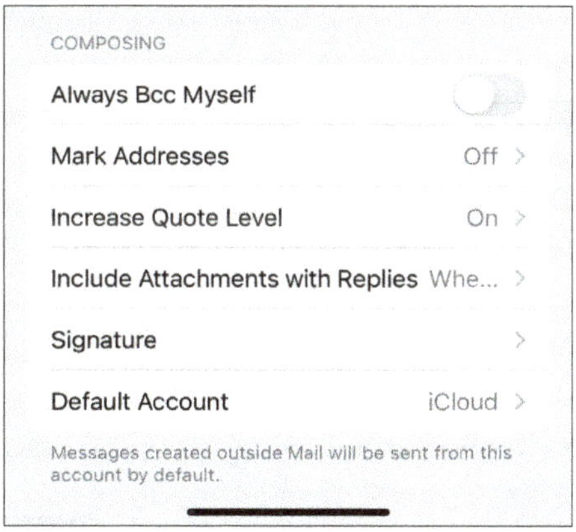

Select 'all accounts' to add signature to all your email accounts.

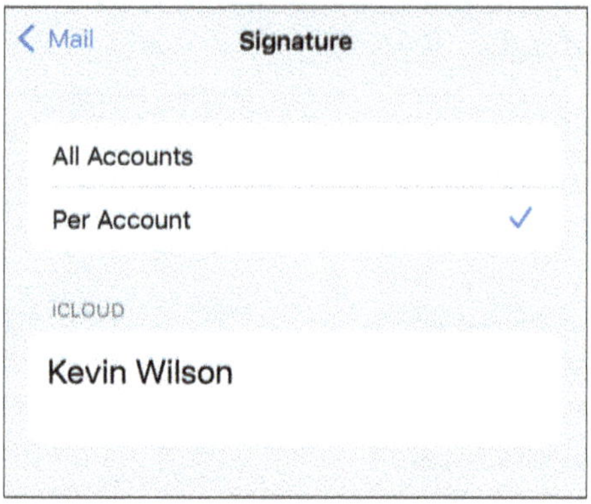


Select 'per account' to add a different signature to each account you have. Enter the signature you want.

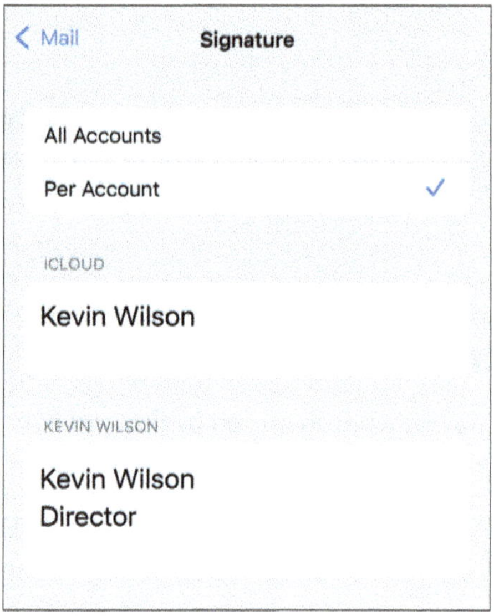


## New Message

To send a new message, click the 'compose new email' icon on the bottom right. This will bring up a new email.

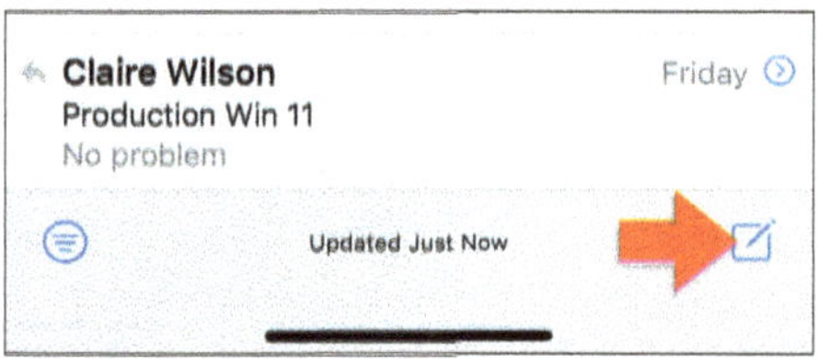

Tap in the 'To:' field to enter an email address. If you are replying to a message, the email address of the person that sent you the message will appear here automatically. Tap in the subject field and add some text.

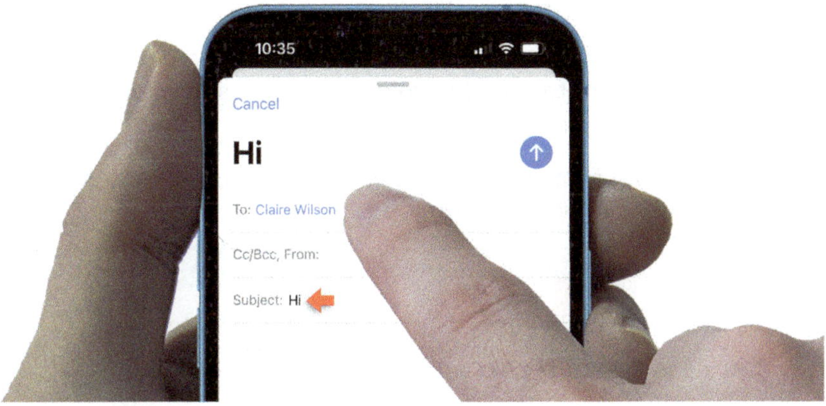


Tap in the message body underneath and type your message using the pop up on screen keyboard.

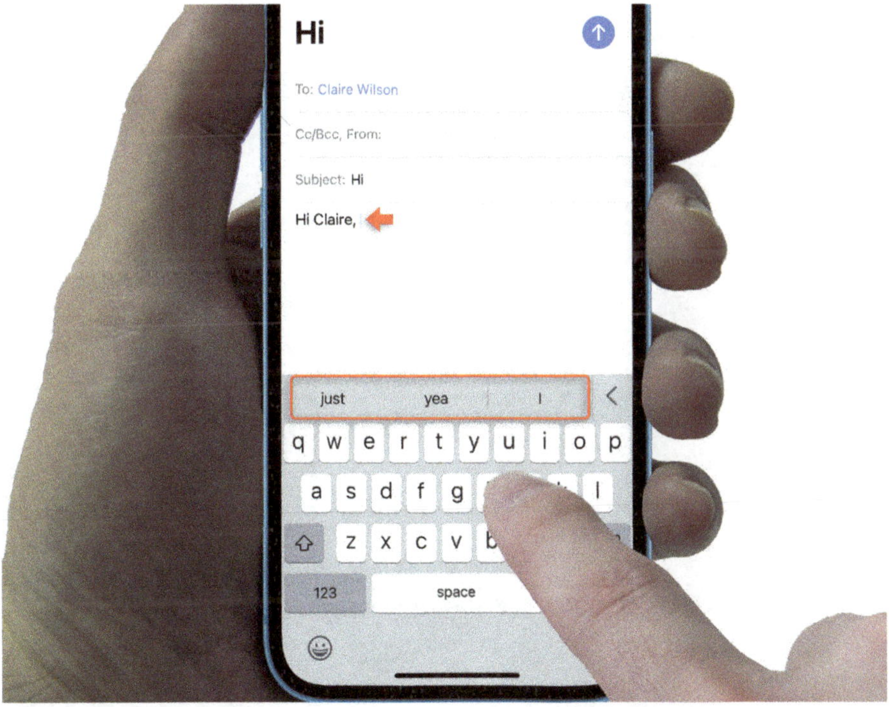


Along the top of the on-screen keyboard, you'll see some text predictions. These are words your iPhone thinks you're most likely to type while writing your email - tap on a word to insert into your message

## Insert Photos

If you look on the right of the on-screen keyboard you'll see a left arrow. Tap on this to reveal your formatting and insert options.

You can insert a photo directly from your photos app, or take a picture with your camera.

To insert a photo from photos you've taken, tap the photos icon. Then select a photo from your album.

If you want to take a photo, tap on the camera icon.

Take the picture with your camera

Tap 'use photo' to insert it into your message.

## Formatting

Tap the left arrow on the right hand side to reveal your formatting and insert options.

If you want to change the font, text size or colour, tap the text icon.

Here, you can select bold, italic, underlined or strike text. You can change the font, size, and colour.

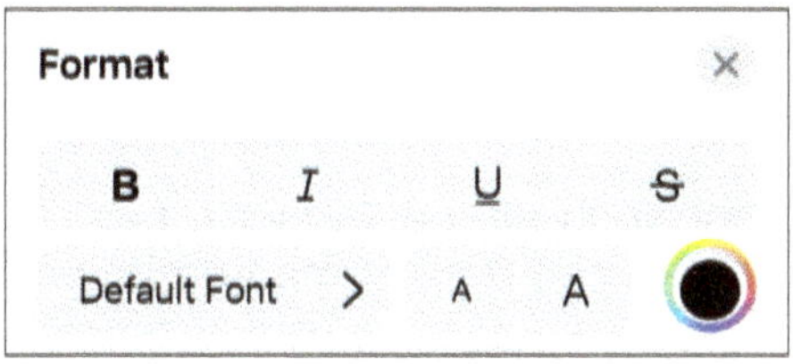


Underneath you can add an ordered list, or a bullet list. You can change the text alignment (left, center, right)

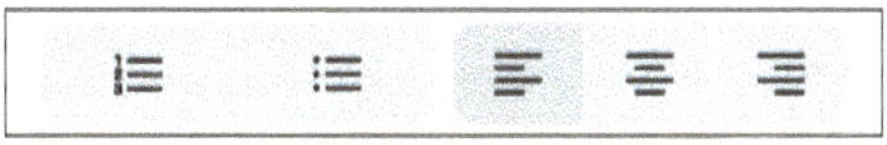

The two tools on the left indent and display text as a quote. This is useful if you're quoting something from another email and responding to it. It makes the email clearer to the reader.

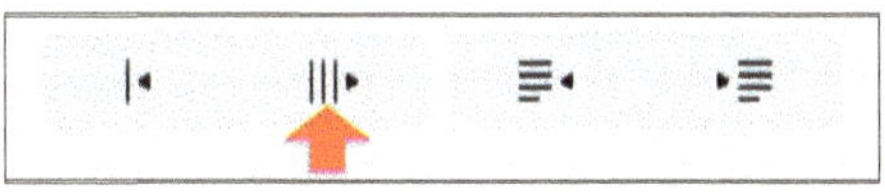

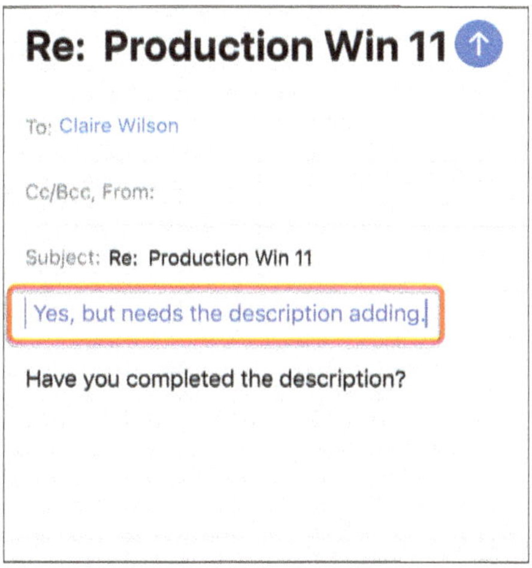

The two tools on the right increase or decrease the text indent.

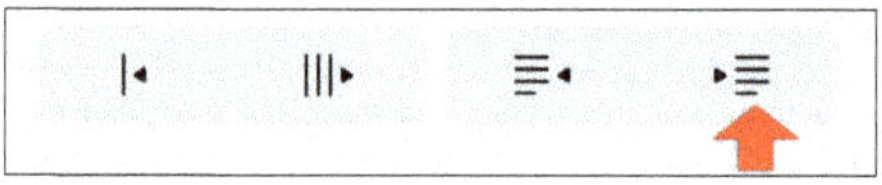

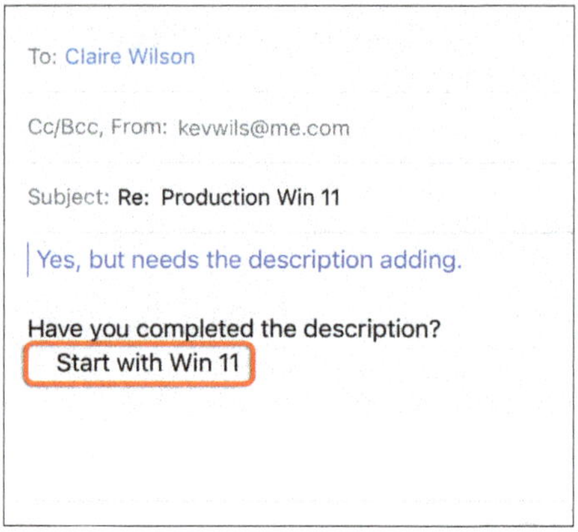


## Attachments

To add an attachment such as a document, tap the left arrow on the right hand side to reveal your formatting and insert options.

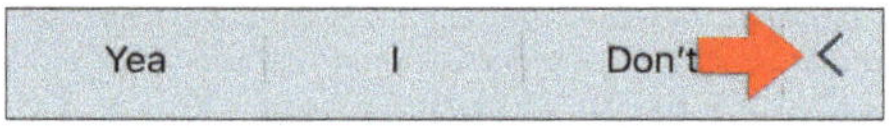


Tap on the document icon.

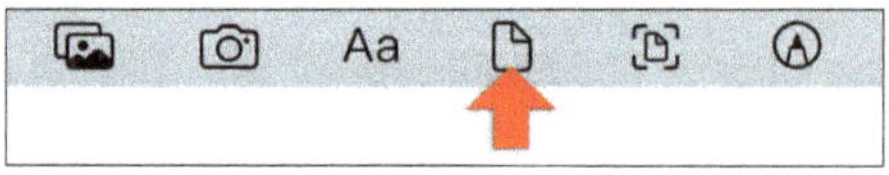


From the popup dialog box, select the document you want to attach to your email.

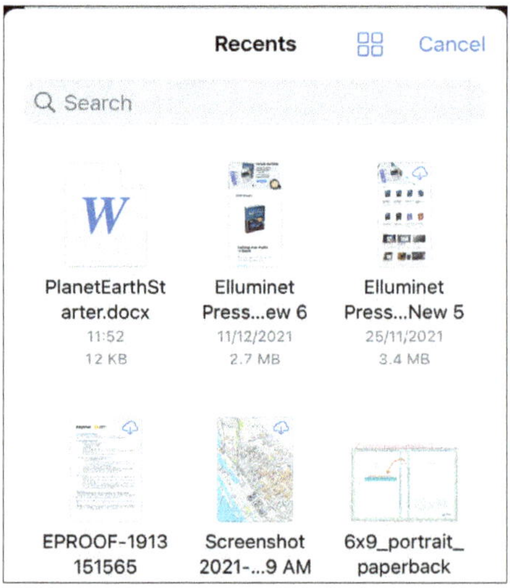

## Document Scanner

To scan a document to add to your message, tap the left arrow on the right hand side to reveal your formatting and insert options.

Tap on the scanner icon.

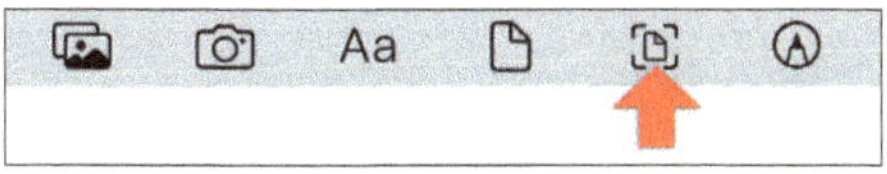


Frame the document with your camera.

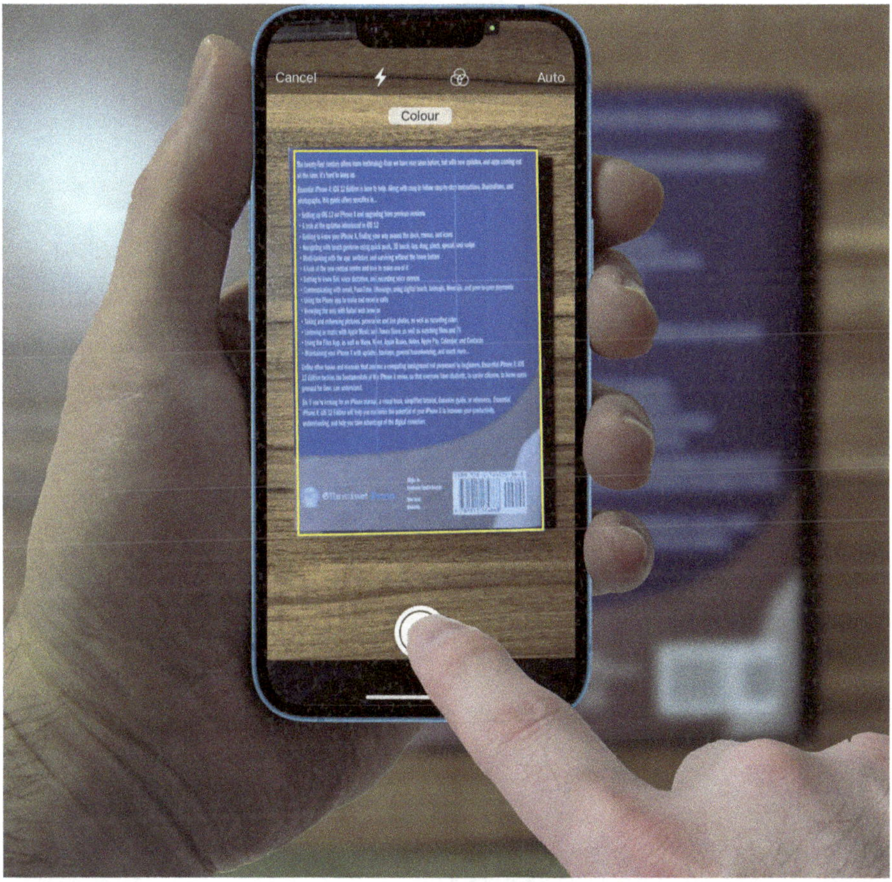


Frame the document inside the blue on-screen markers (I've highlighted these in yellow in the image above so you can see).

Tap the white circle at the bottom to take the scan.

## Markup

To insert a drawing, tap the left arrow on the right hand side to reveal your formatting and insert options.

Tap on the markup icon.

Here, you can draw an image. From the toolbar at the bottom of the screen, you can select a pen, size and colour

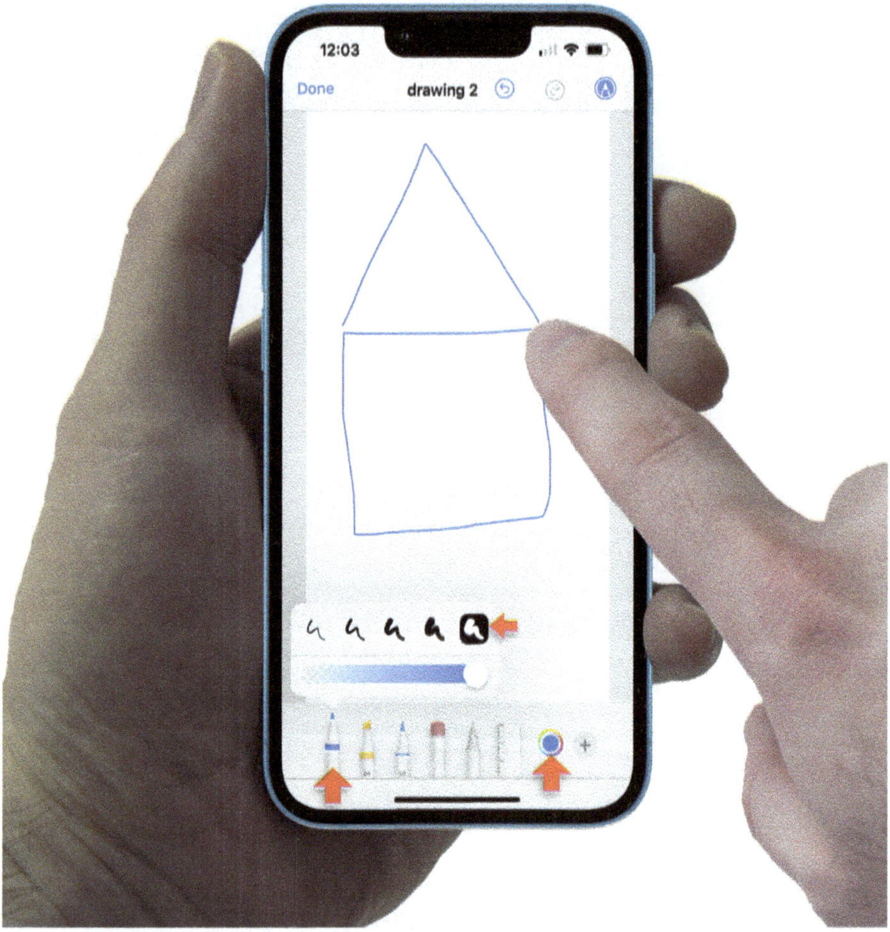


Use your finger to draw on the canvas.

## Flagging Messages

You can choose from a variety of colours when you flag an email message. Coloured flags are synced with iCloud to the Mail app on all your Apple devices.

To flag a message, swipe left over the message.

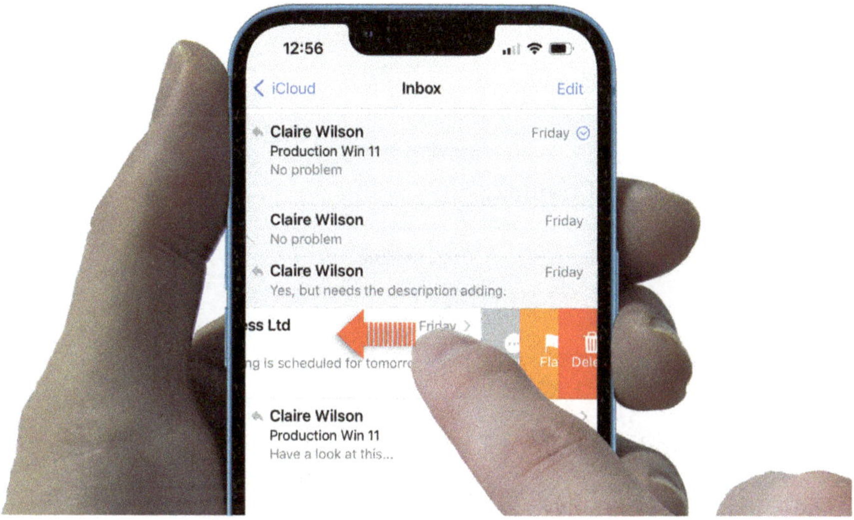


Tap 'flag' from the options.

## Create a Mailbox Folder

To create a mailbox, swipe inwards from the left hand edge to open the side panel.

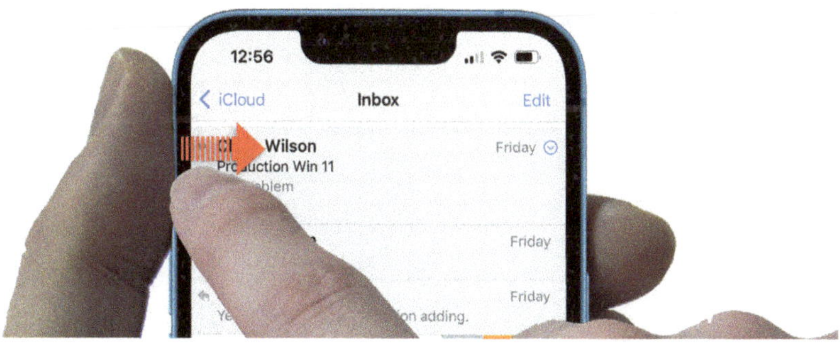

Tap 'edit' on the top right of the panel.

Tap 'new mailbox' on the bottom right of the panel.

Type in a meaningful name...

Tap the field under 'mailbox location'

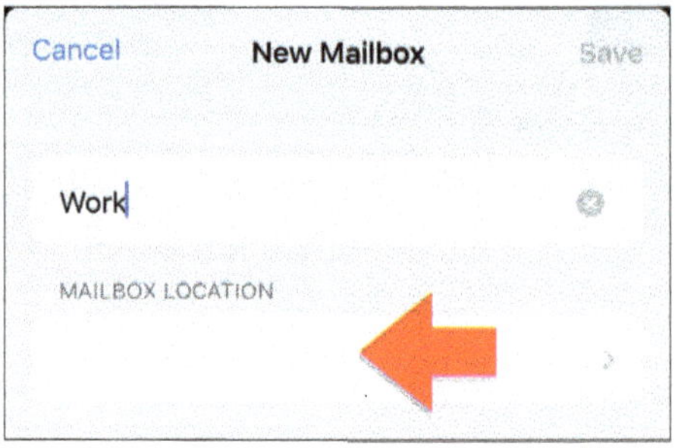


Select the location where you want to add the folder, eg in 'iCloud' or your email account . Tap 'save'.

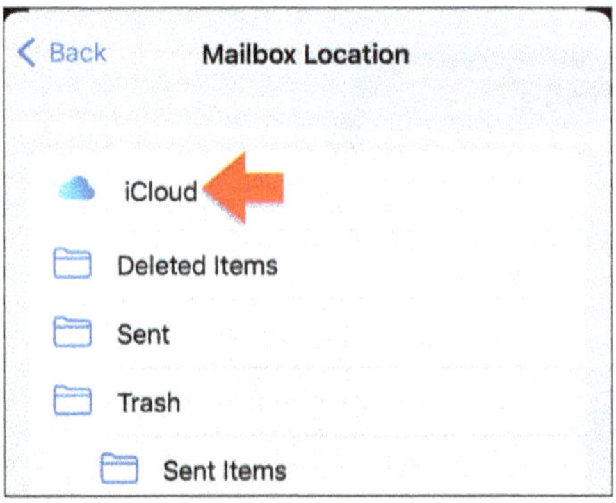


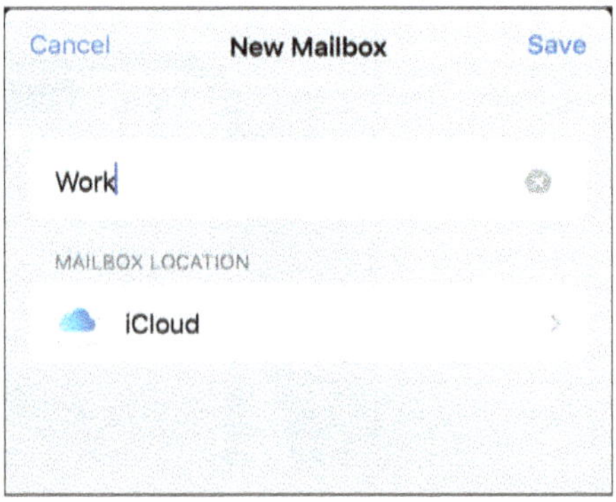

You'll find the new folder in the mailbox sidebar.

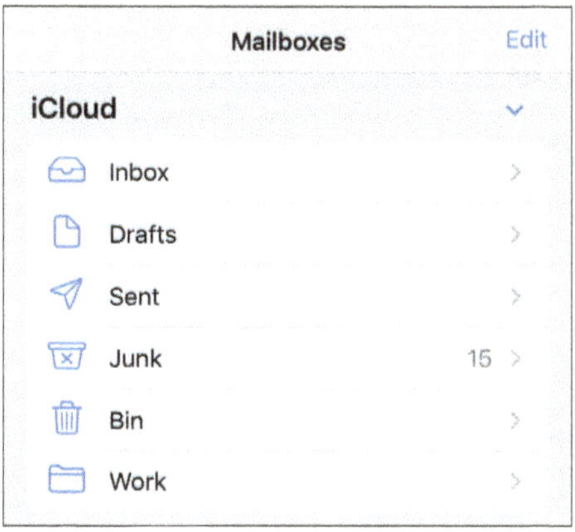


## Move Message

To move a message to another folder, swipe left over the message in your inbox

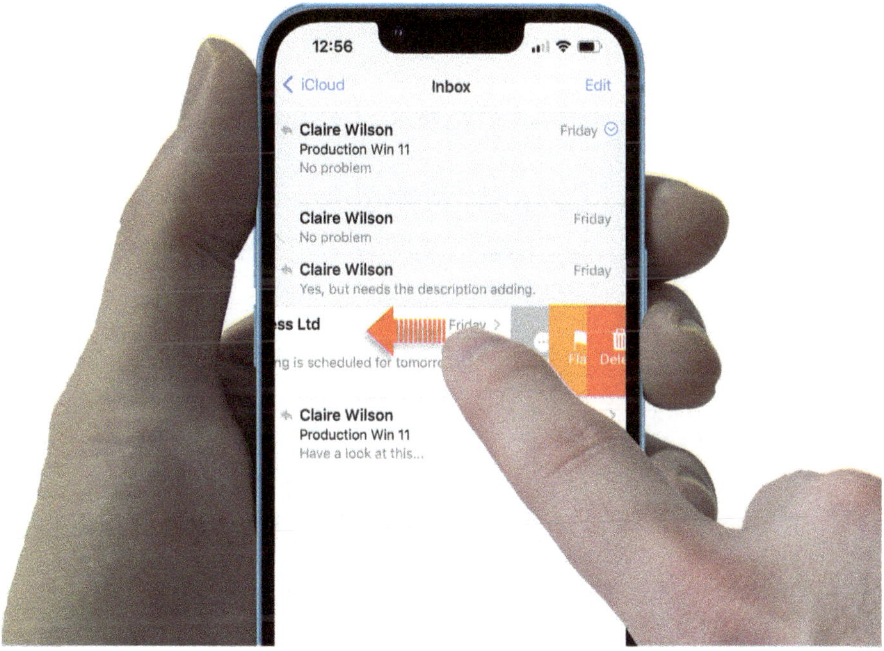


Tap 'more'.

From the popup panel, select 'move message'.

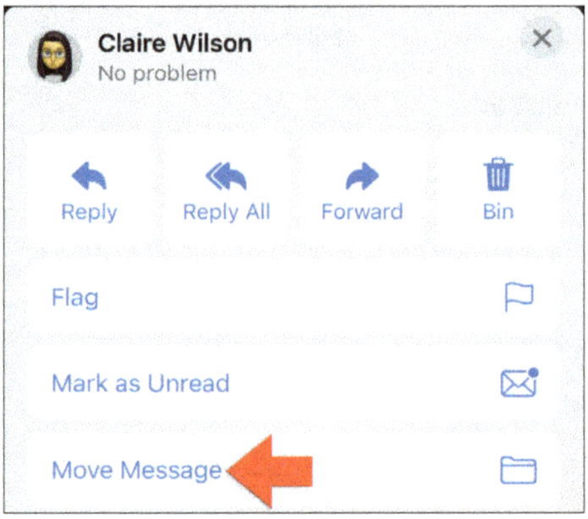


Select the mailbox to move the message to eg 'Work'

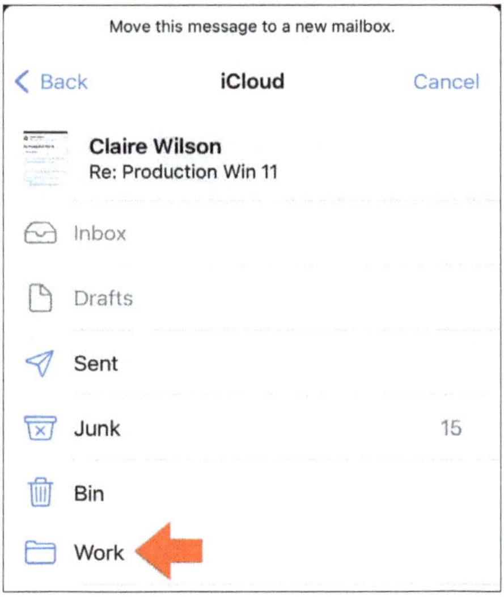


## Block Sender

You can have email from a specified sender blocked and put directly to the trash. Blocking a sender works across all your Apple devices. First, open the message.

Tap the sender's email address at the top.

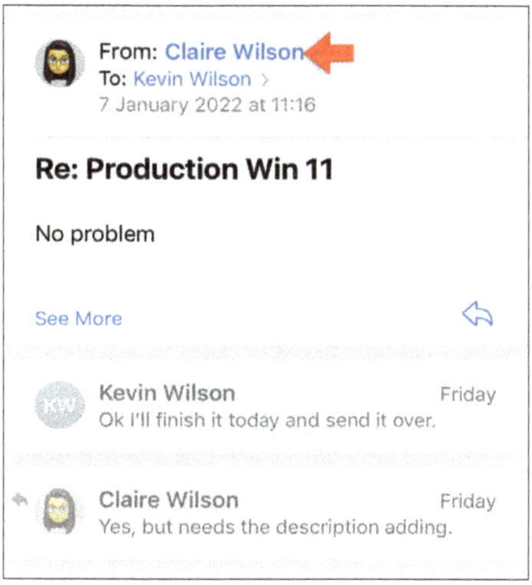


Select 'Block This Contact' from the popup panel.

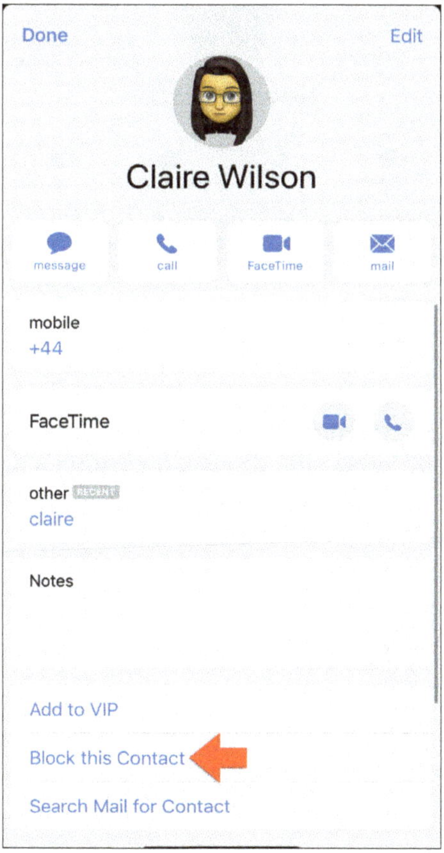

# Contacts

The Contacts App is your address book. It contains all the names, email addresses, phone numbers and addresses of the people you correspond with.

To launch your contacts app, tap the icon on the home screen.

This is the main screen. The app usually opens showing your contact info. To see all the contacts in your address book, tap 'contacts' on the top left.

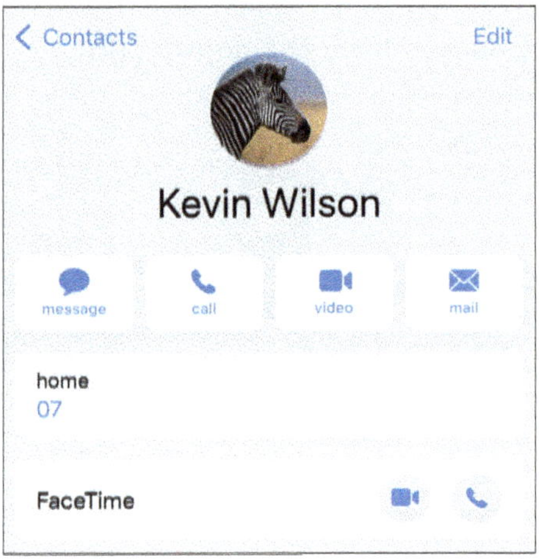


Here, you can browse contacts, or add new ones. Tap on a contact in the list down the left hand side to view a contact's details.

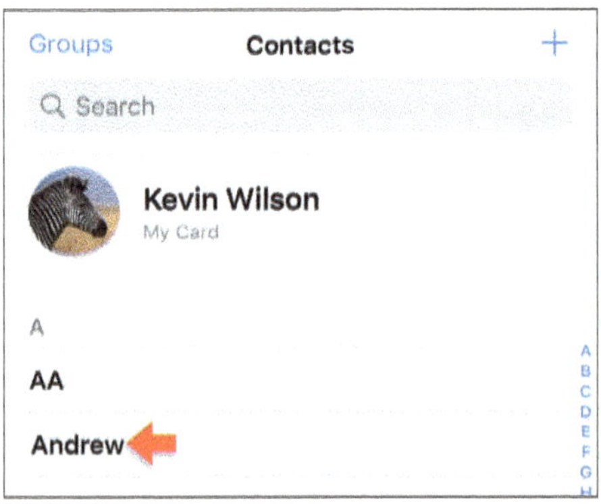

From here you can edit their details, send a message, email, FaceTime them if they have an iPhone, or give them a call.

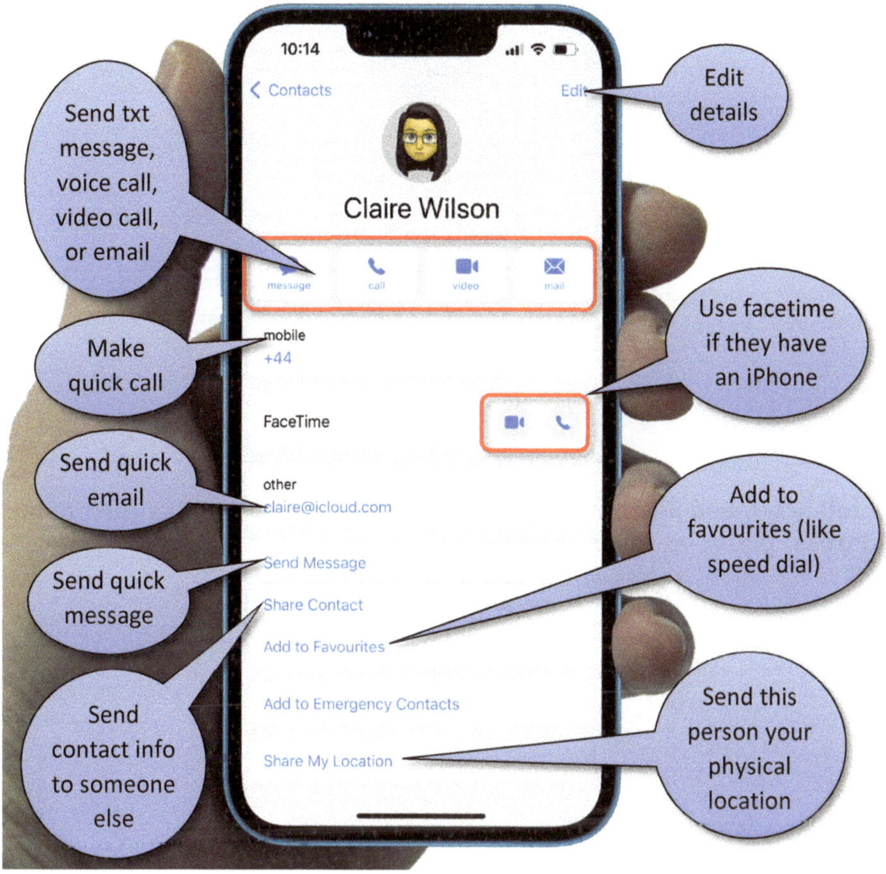


## New Contact

Tap the + sign on the top right of the left hand panel to add a new contact.

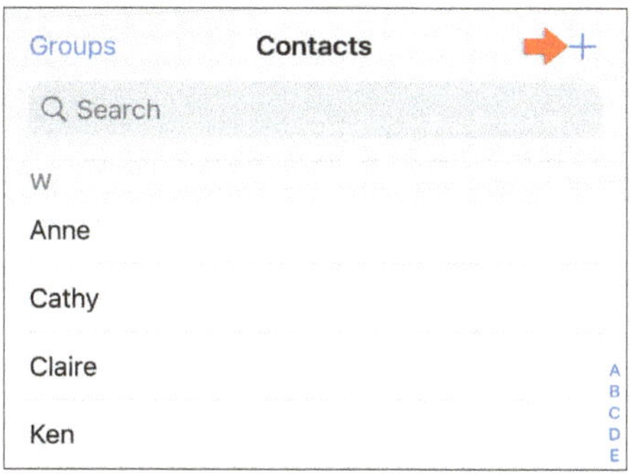

Add the contact's details. Tap 'add photo' if you want to assign a photo to the contact, then enter their first and second name.

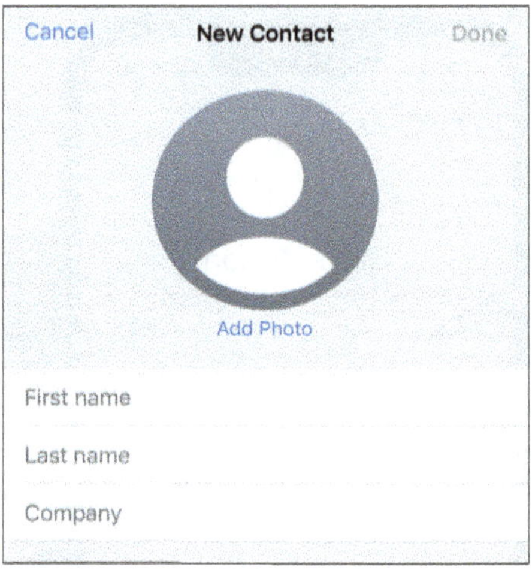


Scroll down and add any other details about them, such as their email address, phone number, address and so on.

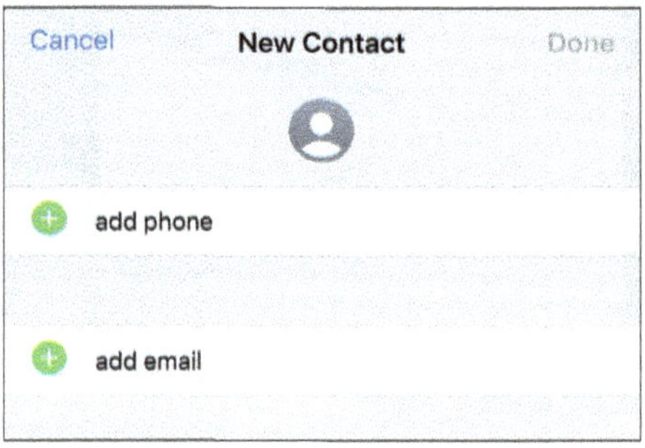


You can add a specific ring tone to this contact. This helps you identify a caller when they ring you or send you a message. Just tap on 'default' then select a tone.

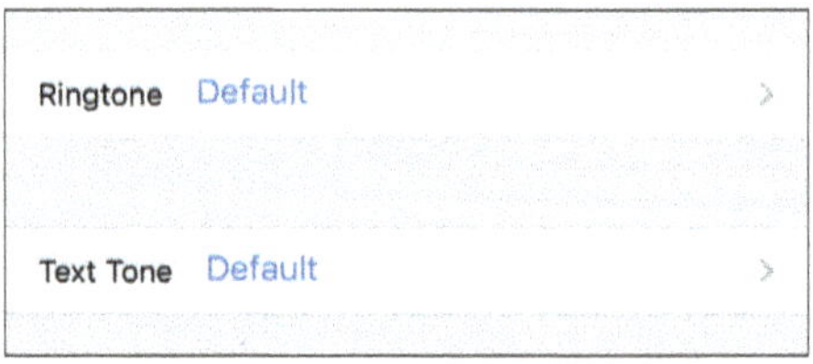


Next, add the person's physical address if required. Tap 'add address'.

Fill in the details. Tap 'home' to change this to 'work', 'school' or whatever the address is. To add another address, tap 'add address'.

Scroll down, add any other information you need.

## New Contact from a Message

You can also add a contact from an email message. Open the email message in the Mail App. Tap the link on person's name at the top of the email.

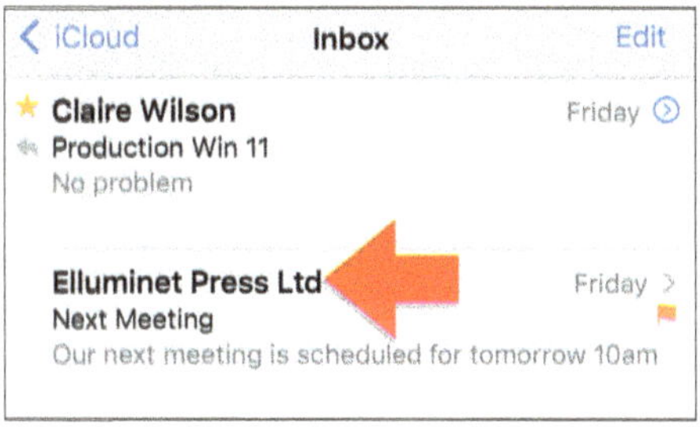


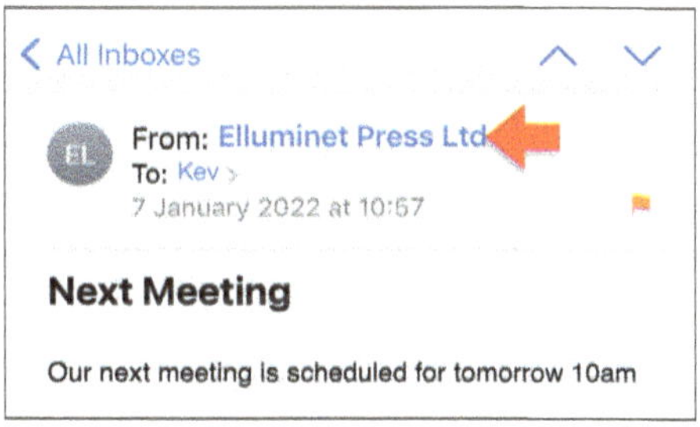


From the popup panel, scroll down, tap 'create new contact'.

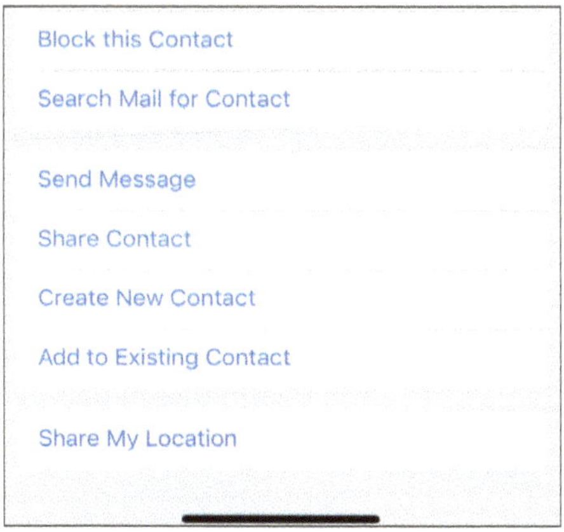

Your iPhone will automatically add the names and email address the message was sent from.

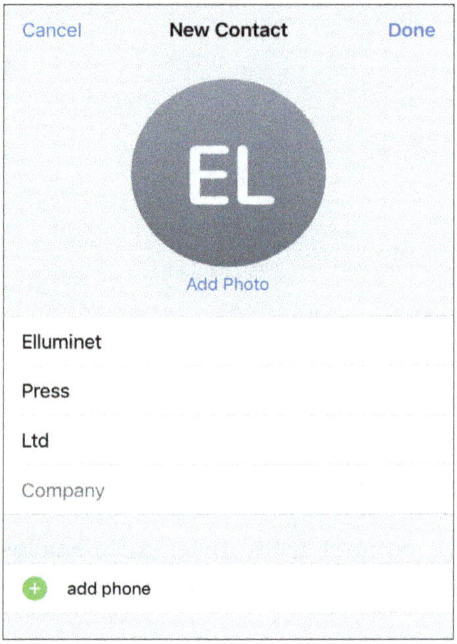


Add any other details if necessary. Tap 'done' when you're finished.

*You can do the same with text messages in Message. Tap on the message, then tap 'details', tap the 'i' icon (top right), tap 'create new contact'. Enter their name and details in the screen that appears.*

## Delete a Contact

To delete a contact, open your contacts app and select the person's name in the list.

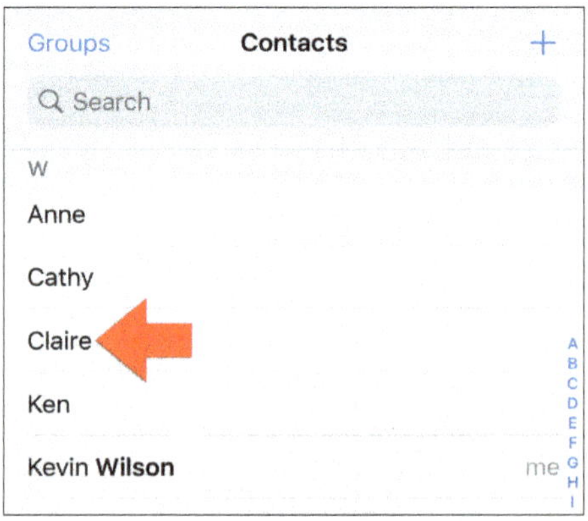

Tap 'edit' on the top right, then scroll down to the bottom of the page,

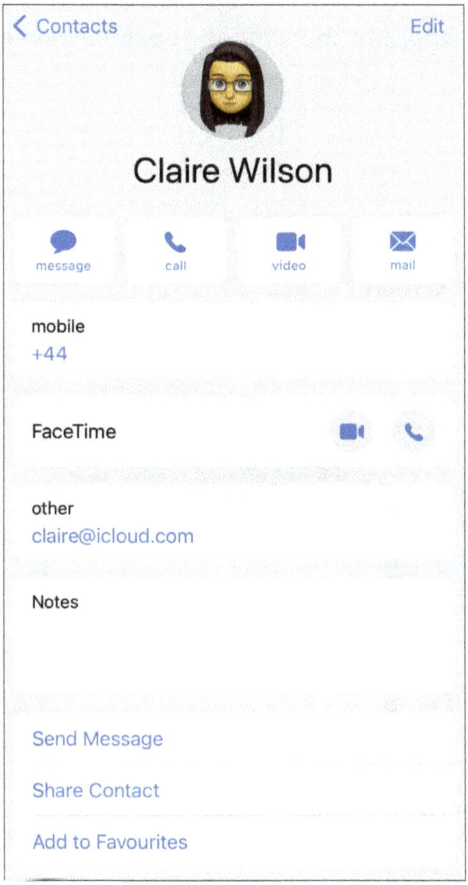


Tap 'delete contact'

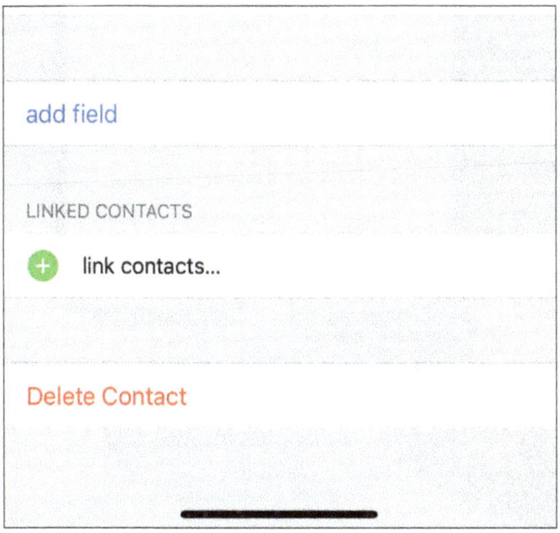

# Calendar App

To start calendar app, tap the icon on the home screen

This will bring up the calendar main screen. I found it easiest to view the calendar in month or week view. Below is in month view. Let's take a look around the screen.

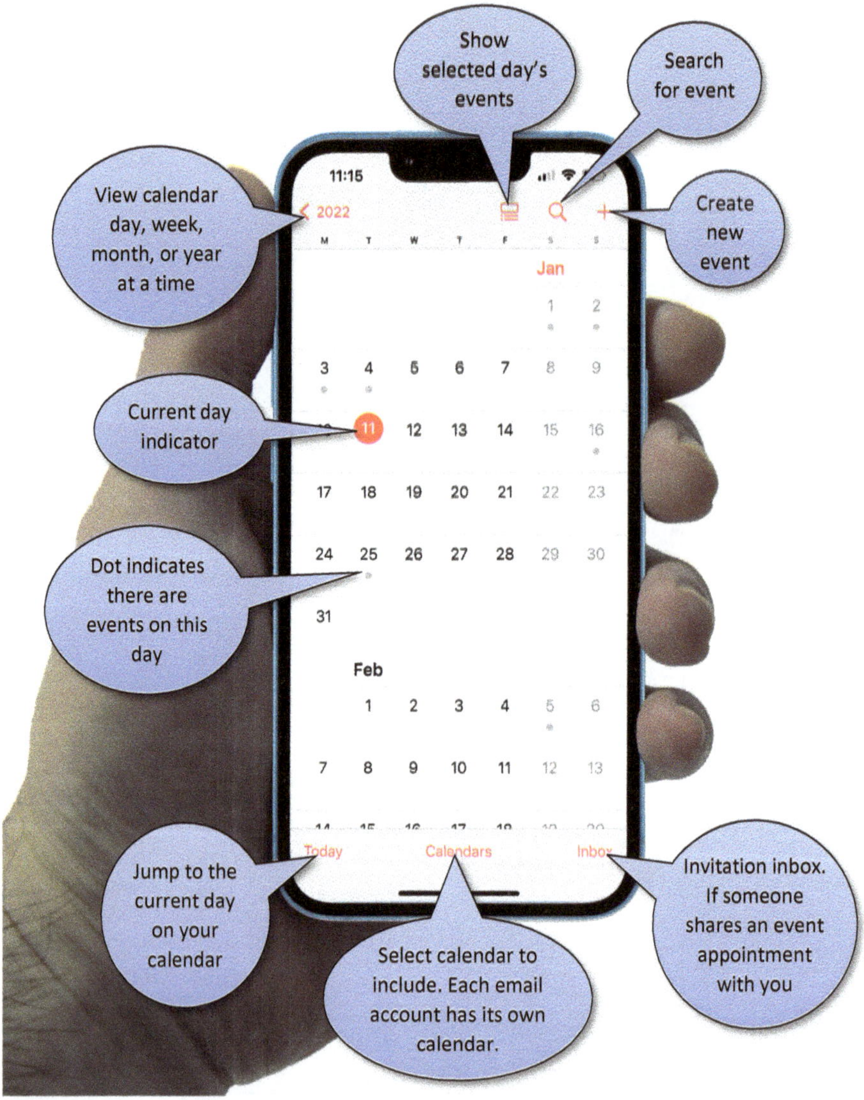

## Adding an Appointment

To add an event to the calendar, go to month view, then tap on the day the event or appointment falls on.

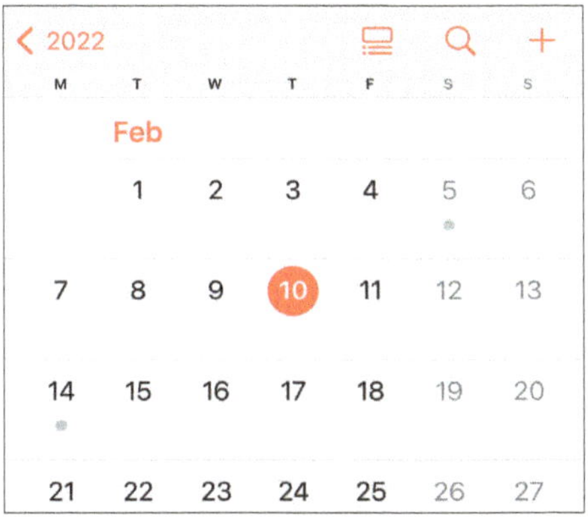


Tap and hold your finger on the calendar, you'll see a new event marker appear. Now drag this marker down the list until you see the correct start time of the event. In the example below, I want to add a new event at 11:30am. So I would drag the orange marker down past 11:00, until I see ':30' on the left hand side.

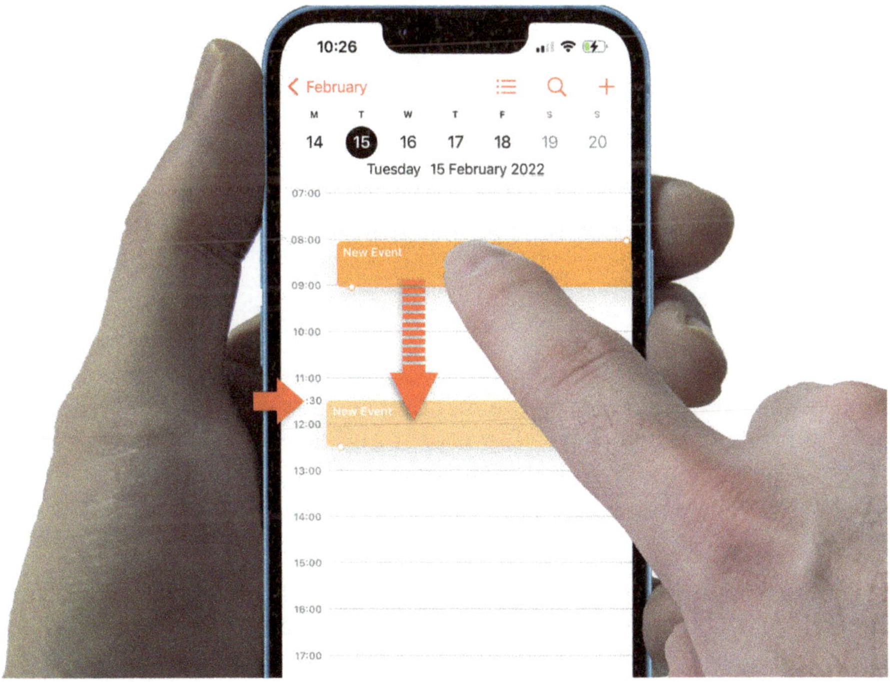


Once you see the correct start time, release your finger.

A new event window will appear. Here, at the top, add the name of the event. You can also add a location.

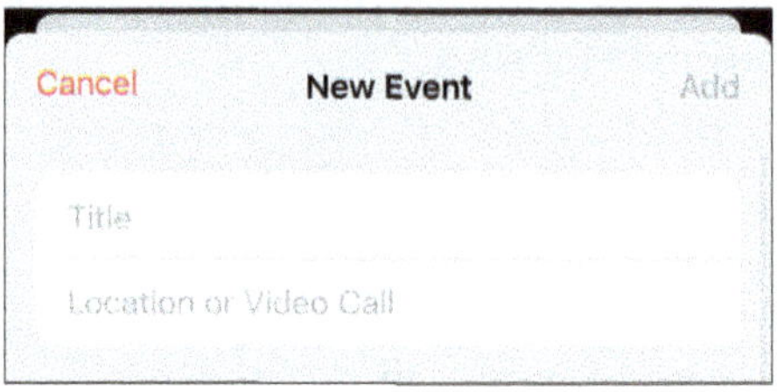


Next, you can adjust the start time if you need to, and change the end time. If the event is all day, then turn on 'all day'.

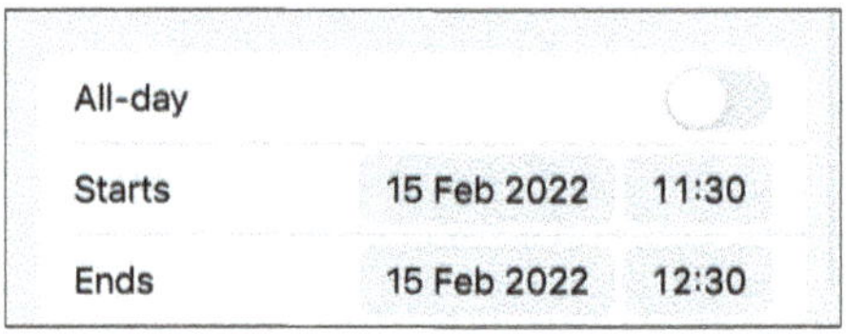


To do this, just tap on the time then adjust it using the rollers underneath.

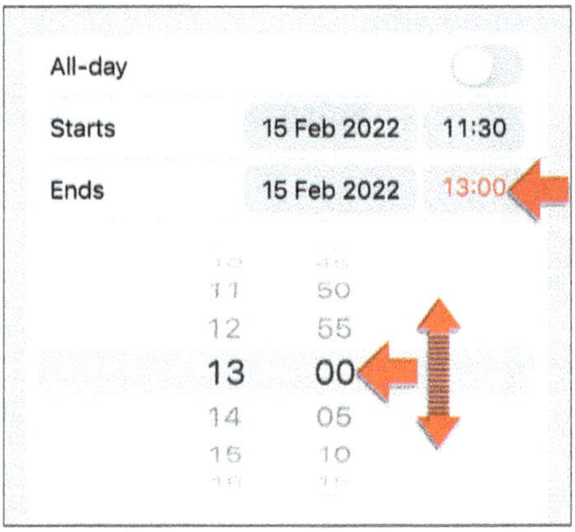


Next, if the event repeats, eg the meeting is weekly or monthly, you can set the event to repeat here. Tap repeat and select an option.

If you have multiple calendars one for work and one for personal, you can select which calendar to add the event to here.

You can invite others to the event which will allow them to add the event to their calendars. Just tap invitees then enter the person's email address or phone number.

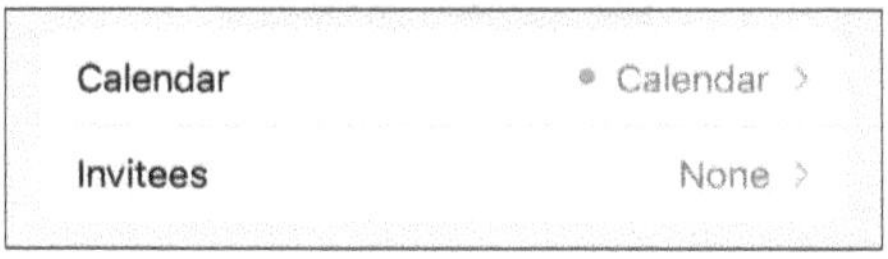


At the bottom, you can add an alert. This is a reminder that you can set to remind you of the event. To set a reminder, tap alert then select and option. You can also show others that you're busy during the event. To do this tap 'show as' then select an option.

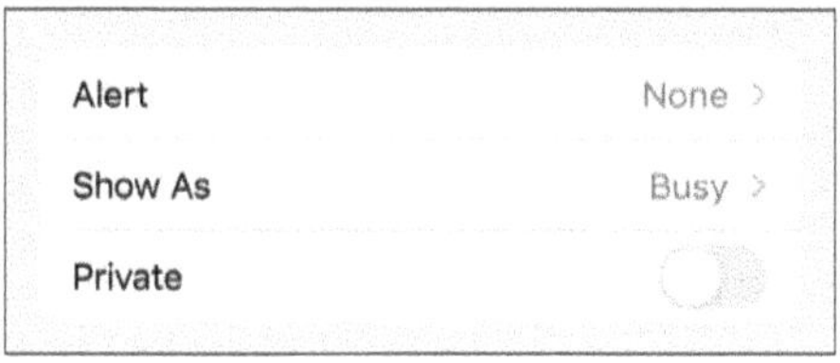


If you want the event to be private, turn on 'private'. This means that if you share the calendar, the event wont show up.

Underneath you can add any attachments such as meeting minutes, documents, website URLs and any notes that you might need.

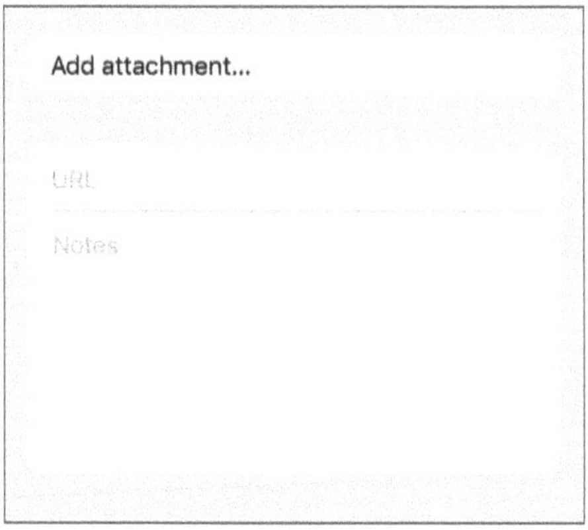


Tap 'add' on the top right when you're done.

## Adding an Appointment from a Message

Apple Mail, Message and FaceTime will scan your message for phrases that look like dates and times and will create a link in the email for you. These will be underlined in light grey.

To add the event from the email or text message, tap on this link.

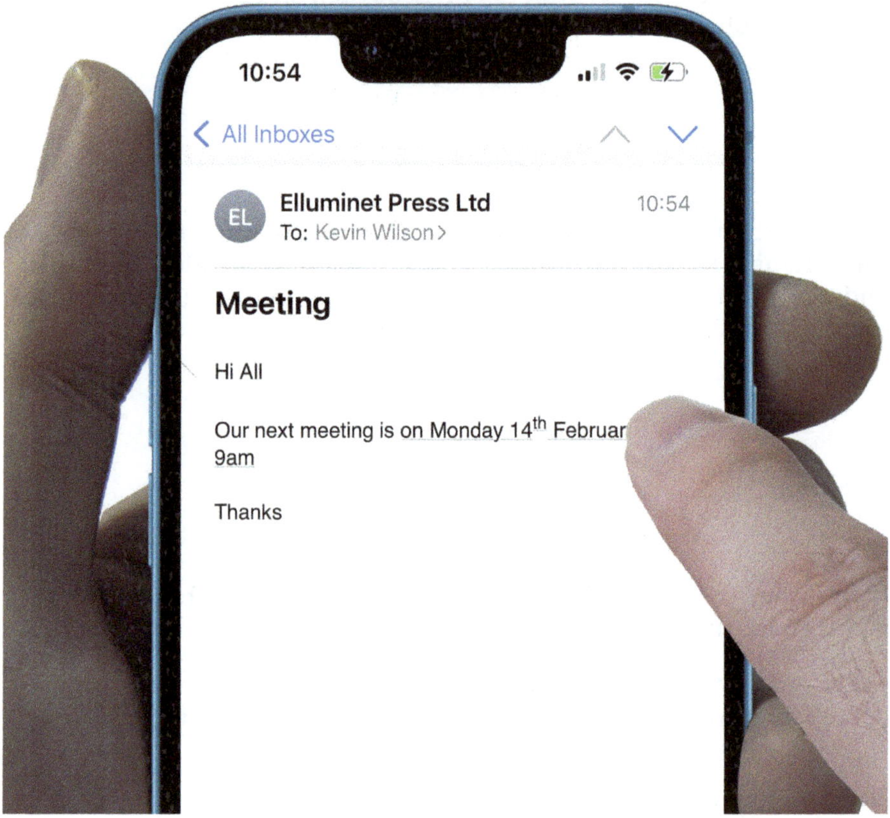


From the popup box tap 'create event'.

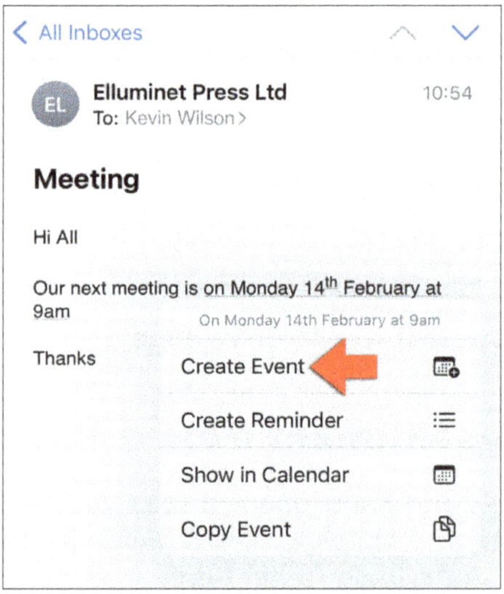

Enter a title and location if calendar didn't pick one up from the email. You can also tweak the information and add additional information if required.

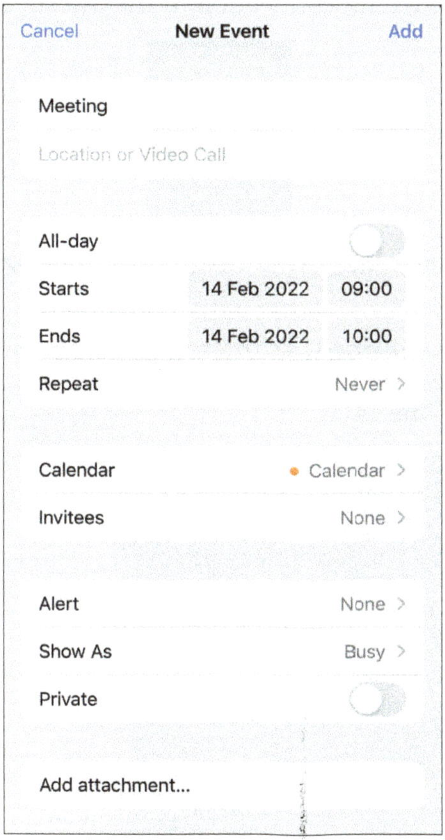


Once you have done that, tap 'add' to enter the appointment into your calendar.

# FaceTime

To use FaceTime, tap the icon on the home screen. You will need your Apple ID and a WiFi/data connection to the internet.

When you open FaceTime, you will be prompted to sign in if you haven't already done so.

Once FaceTime has opened, at the top you'll see two options, one to create a FaceTime link you can share with others, and the other to make a new FaceTime call.

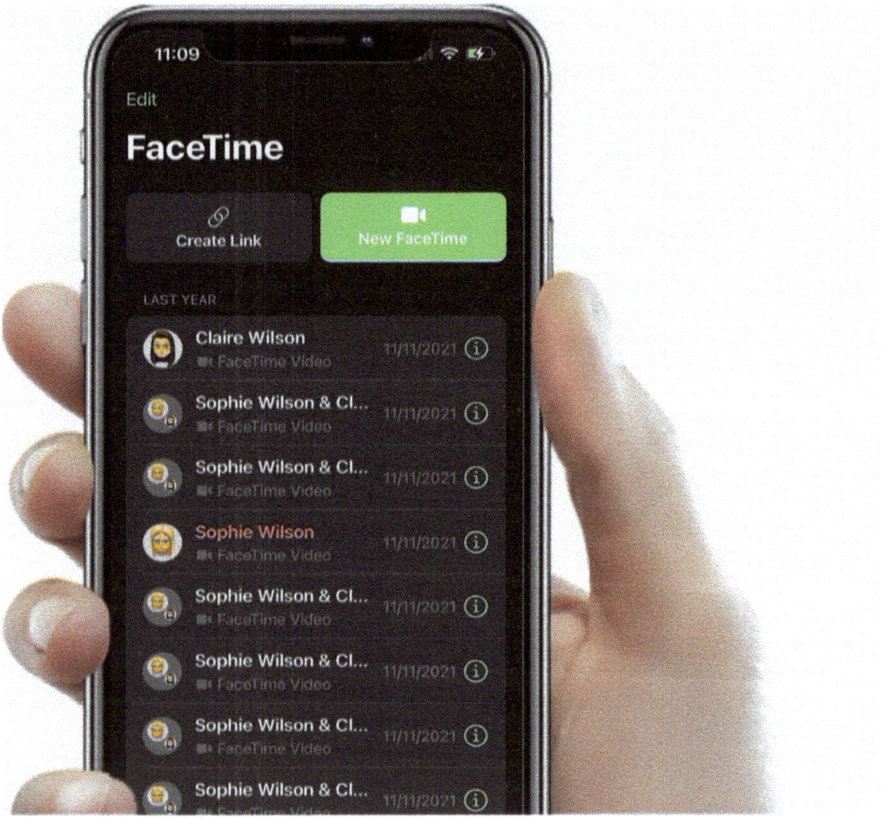


Listed down the bottom, you'll see a list of calls you've made. You can tap on any of these to make another call.

## Making a New Call

In this demonstration, Claire is going to FaceTime Sophie from her iPhone. To make a new call, tap the green 'New FaceTime' icon on the top right of the screen.

Start typing the person's name you want to FaceTime into the 'to' field on the top of the screen. If the name is in your contacts, then it will appear underneath. Tap the person's Apple ID email address, phone number or name. Or select one of the suggestions.

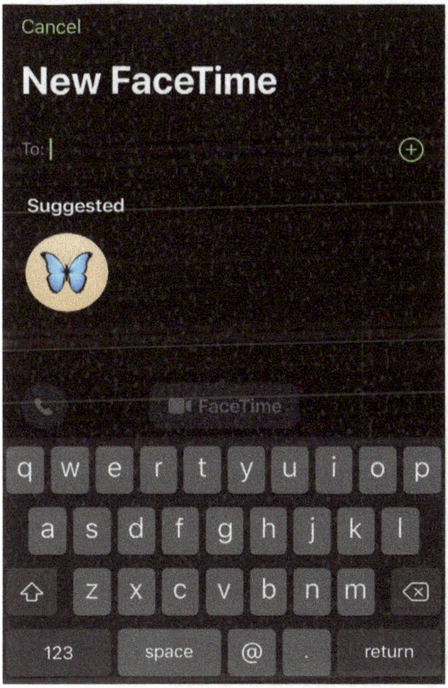


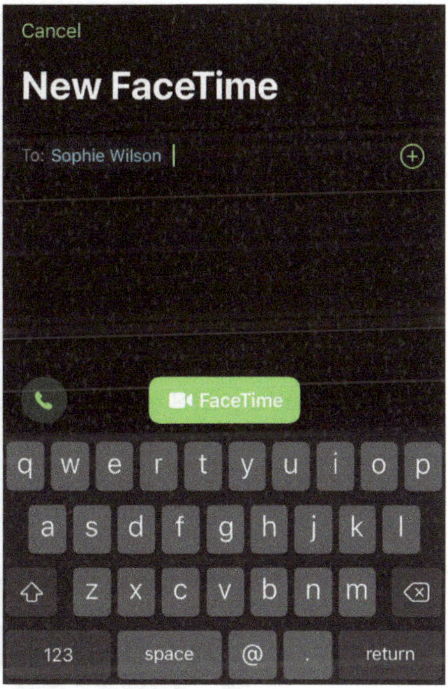


Tap the green FaceTime icon, then wait for the other person to answer.

In the background of your screen, or sometimes on the bottom right, you'll see a preview of your camera - so make sure you're squarely in the frame so when the call is answered, the other person can see you clearly.

Once the other person answers, the call will go full screen. You'll see the person you're calling in the main display, and you'll see a preview of your camera on the bottom right.

You'll also see a panel of other icons at the top of the screen. Let's take a look at what each icon does.

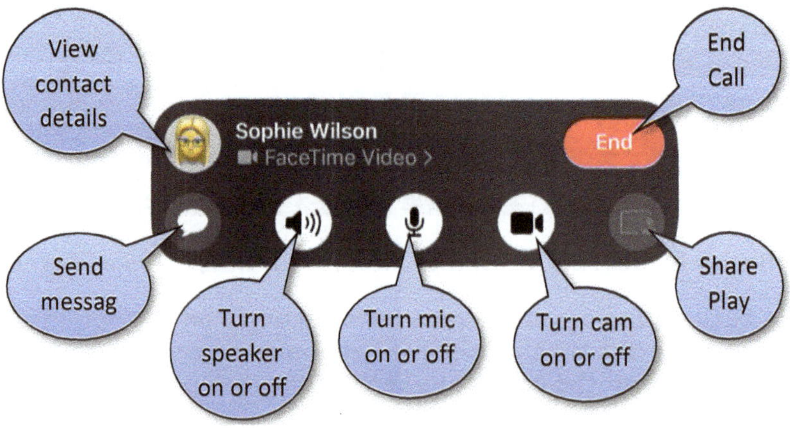

On the bottom right, you'll see a preview of your camera. On the bottom of the preview, you'll see two icons.

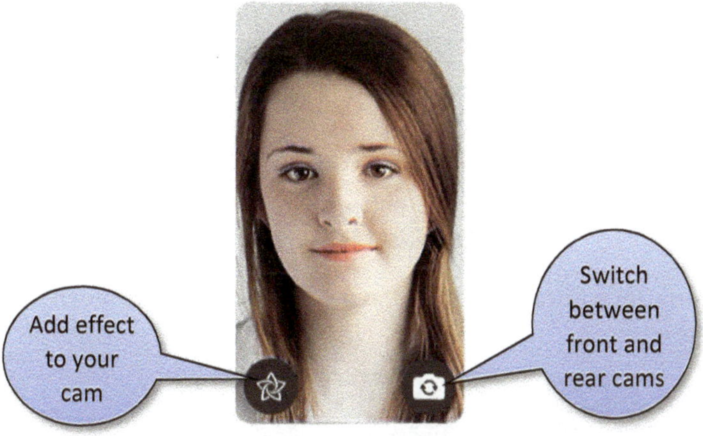


If the icons in the call screen disappear, tap the screen once and they'll re-appear. The white circle on the left hand side of the main call window will take a photo of the call.

## Adding Effects

During a call, you can add all sorts of effects to your image. To do this, tap the effects icon on the bottom left of your camera preview in the bottom right corner.

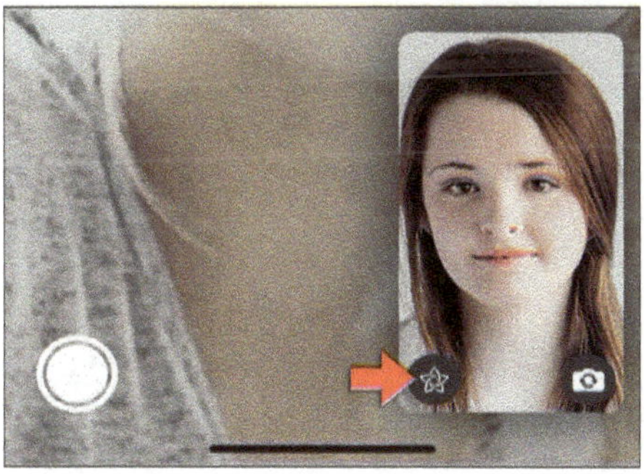

### Animojis & Memojis

To add a memoji, tap the effects icon on your camera preview.

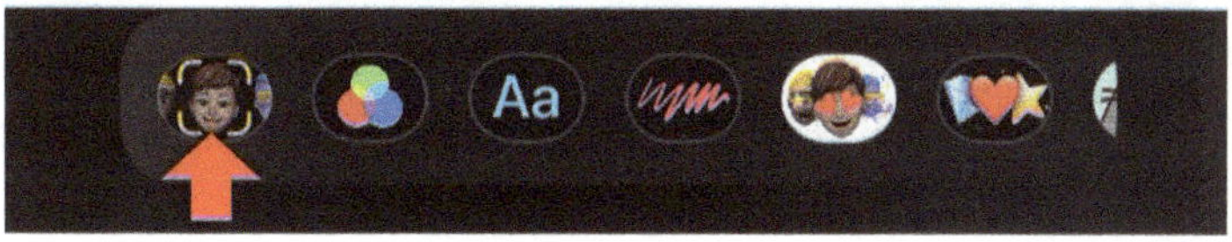

You can select from multiple animojis and memojis. Swipe left to right over the characters on the panel at the bottom of the screen. Select a character

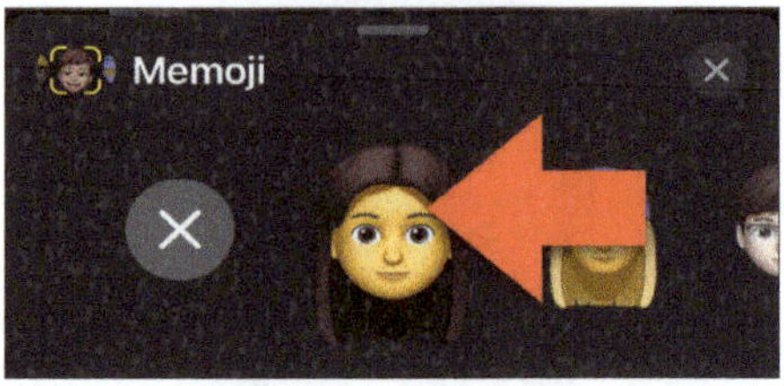


Bring your face into focus and position yourself between the yellow markers.

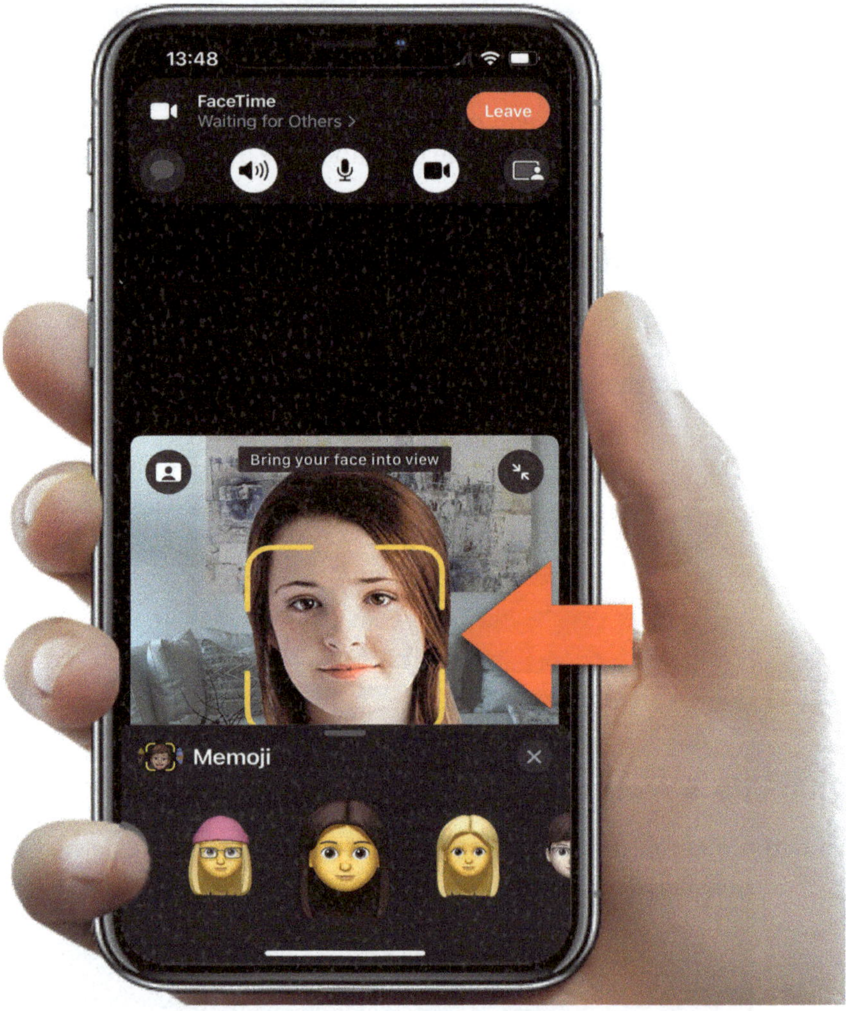

Your iPhone will map the memoji or animoji to your facial expressions, as demonstrated by Claire below.

Smile, the memoji will copy your facial expressions. "Making a Memoji" on page 295 for more info on how to create your own.

## Adding Text

Lets add a text effect. Tap the effects icon on your camera preview.

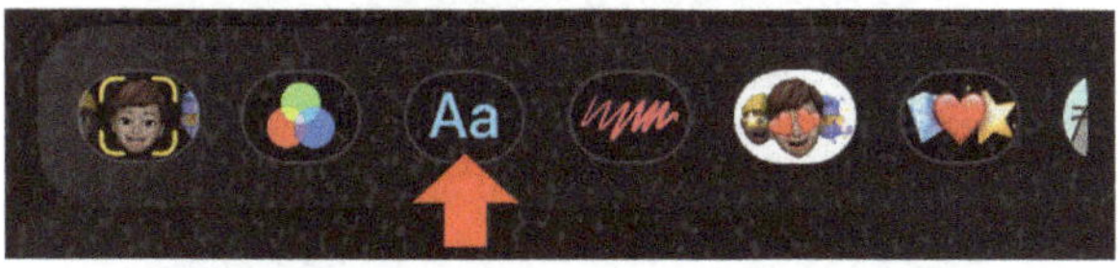


Tap the text icon.

If you want to add an object such as a speech bubble, tap the formatting icon on the left.

Select an object from the options.

Type in some text.

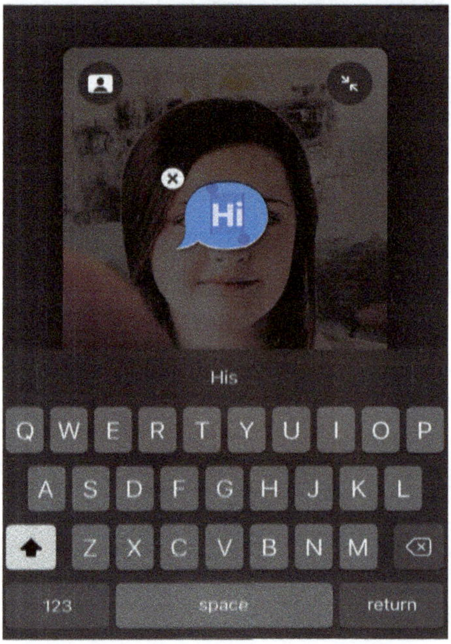

Tap and drag the speech bubble into position. If you want to resize the object, use your thumb and forefinger to stretch the object.

## Stickers

Stickers are pre-made graphics that you can add to your image. Tap one of the sticker icon on your camera preview.

If you tap the first of the three icons highlighted above, you can add some little animations. Tap and drag the sticker to reposition it. Use your thumb and forefinger to stretch the object.

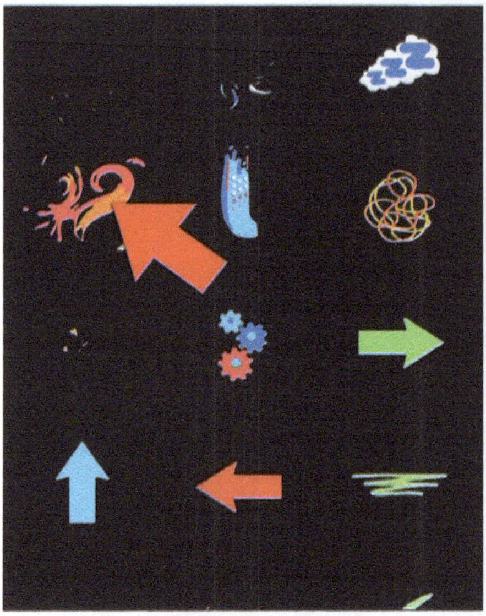

If you selected the memoji stickers (the second of the three icons highlighted above). Select a memoji type from the horizontal bar at the top, then select a memoji. "Making a Memoji" on page 295 for more info.

If you want to delete text or a sticker, just tap on it in the camera preview. You'll see a small 'x' appear. Tap on this to delete.

## Group FaceTime

Group FaceTime allows you to set up groups and chat to up to 32 people at a time. To use Group FaceTime, all participants must have iOS 12 or later and an iPhone 6s or later, otherwise you won't be able to add them to the group.

To place a group call, tap the green 'New FaceTime' icon on the top of the screen.

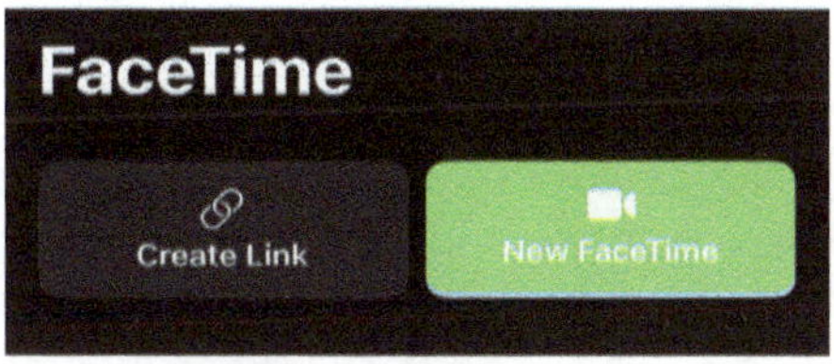


Type the names of the people you want to place a group call to in the 'to' field, or tap the + icon and add them from your contacts list.

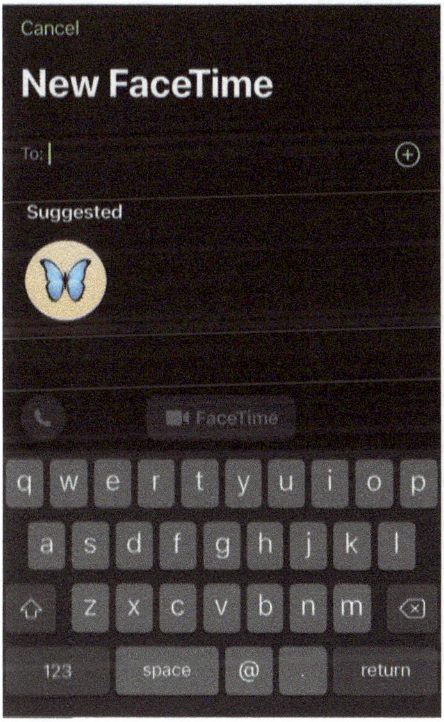


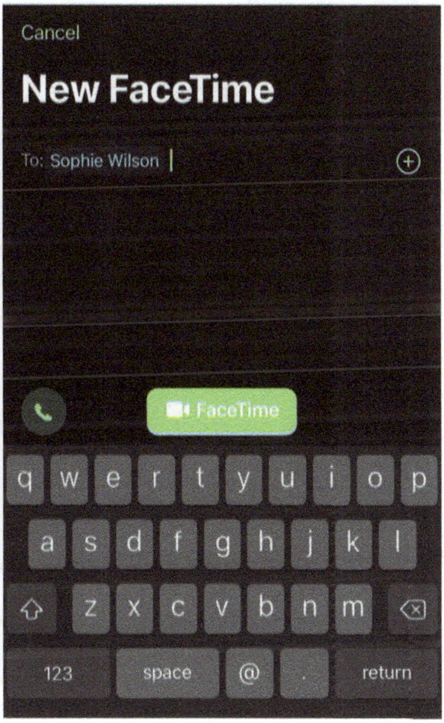


If they all have iOS 12 or later installed on their devices, you'll see two green buttons appear along the bottom of the side panel.

Tap on 'facetime' to place a group video call.

When your contacts answer, you'll see a thumbnail of each of them on your main display. Tap 'grid' on the top right if you want to change to grid view.

You'll see a thumbnail of your own camera in the bottom right of the screen. The other contacts in your group will show up in a thumbnail window in the main area of the screen.

With spacial audio, you'll hear each contact from a different position making it sound like the people are in the same room as you.

FaceTime is useful for keeping in touch with family and friends who don't live near by, or live in another country.

## Share Screen

If you want to share your screen, within a FaceTime call, tap the share icon on the bottom right

Now you can open another app as normal to show on your screen.

Tap back on the thumbnail preview of your camera to return to FaceTime

Tap the icon share again to stop sharing

## SharePlay

Within a FaceTime call, swipe up from the bottom edge of the screen, then open an app that supports SharePlay such as the TV app.

Choose a movie or TV show, and press play.

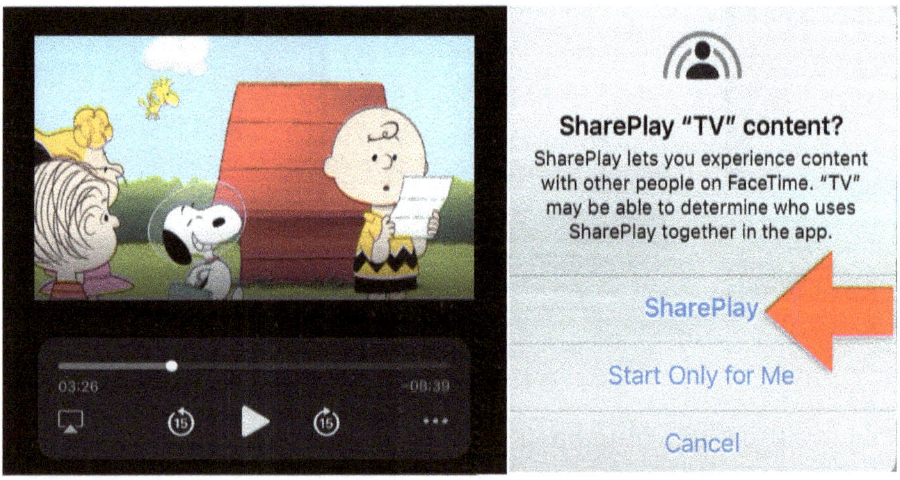


Select SharePlay from the prompt.

Now you can watch together... You'll still be table to hear everyone. Tap on the FaceTime preview on the bottom right to switch back to the chat. Here, the girls are enjoying Charlie Brown & Snoopy together.

In this particular setup, the iPhone is streaming the video to Apple TV which is connected to the TV screen in the background of the image above.

If you don't have Apple TV connected, you'll be able to see the video you're sharing on your phone's screen.

# Phone App

Making phone calls on the iPhone is quite straight forward. To open the phone, tap the phone icon on the dock along the bottom of the screen

Lets take a look at the phone app...

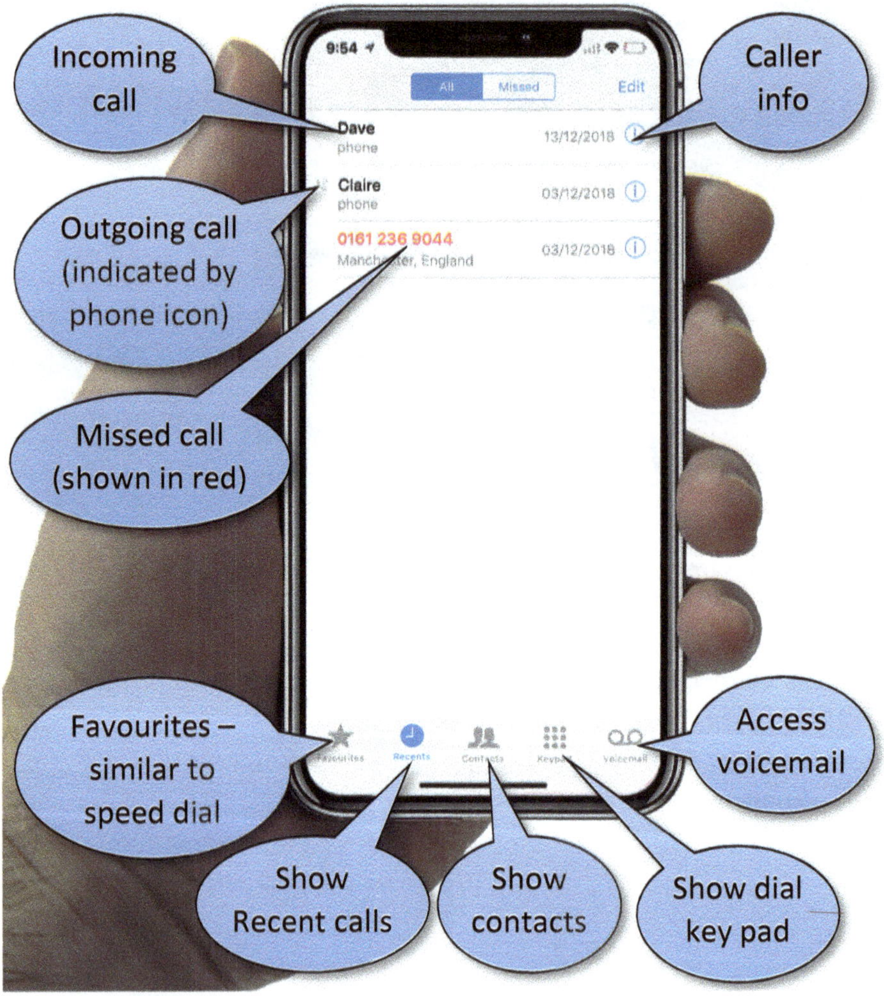


Along the bottom of the screen, you'll see a toolbar with some icons. Use these to navigate between the different sections.

## Answering Calls

Incoming calls will be displayed on your screen, your phone will also play a ringtone and/or vibrate.

Along the top, you'll see the caller's name if their number is in your contacts list, and where they're calling from. You'll just see a number if the caller isn't in your contacts list.

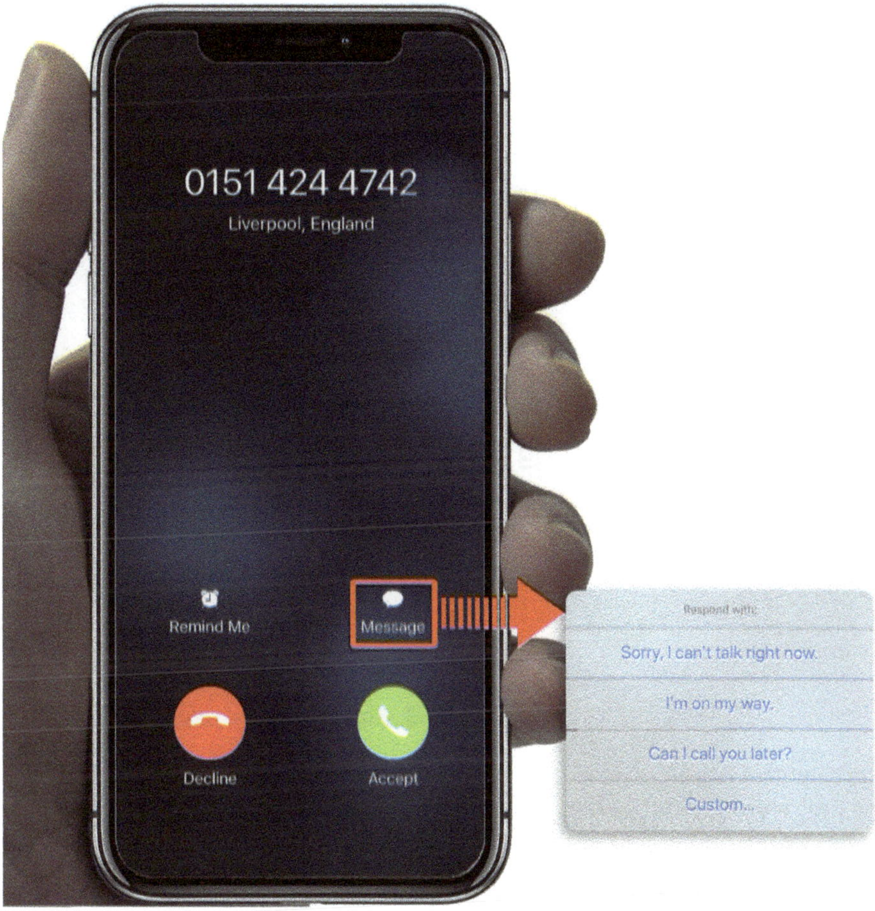


You'll be able to

- Tap 'accept' to answer the call
- Tap 'decline' to refuse call the call
- Tap 'message' to send a quick call decline message
- Tap 'remind me' to set a reminder to call them back

You can set custom quick messages in the settings app, which will appear in this list. These are called 'call decline messages'.

## Dialling Numbers

If you have a phone number for a friend, colleague, or a company, you can key it in using the keypad. To do this tap the keypad icon on the tool bar along the bottom of the screen

Tap in the number using the keypad. Tap the green icon to place the call.

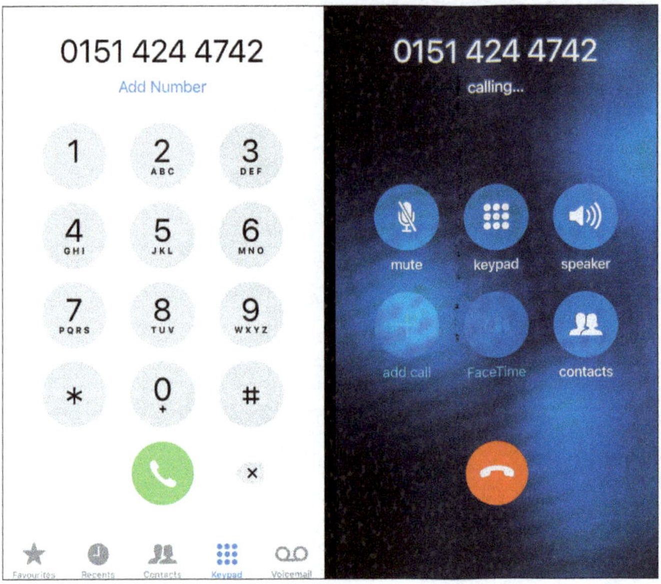


Wait for the other person to answer. When the other person answers, the call will be established. While in call...

- Tap **'mute'** to temporarily mute your microphone, so the other person can't hear you.
- Tap **'keypad'** to open up the keypad - useful if you need to make menu choices when calling some numbers.
- Tap **'speaker'** to put the call on speaker phone.
- Tap **'add call'** to add someone else to the call if the other person's phone supports this.
- Tap **'facetime'** to transfer the call to facetime video chat, if the other person has an iPhone.
- Tap **'contacts'** to view your contacts list.
- Tap the red icon at the bottom to end the call.

## Call Someone from Contacts List

Open the phone app, tap the 'show contacts' icon on the toolbar along the bottom of the screen.

Tap on the person you want to call.

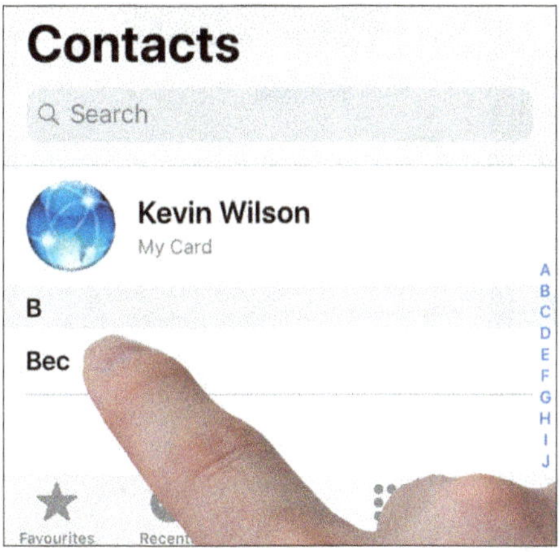


From the person's profile, tap 'call' to call them. If they have more than one phone number, tap on the number you want to call them on underneath.

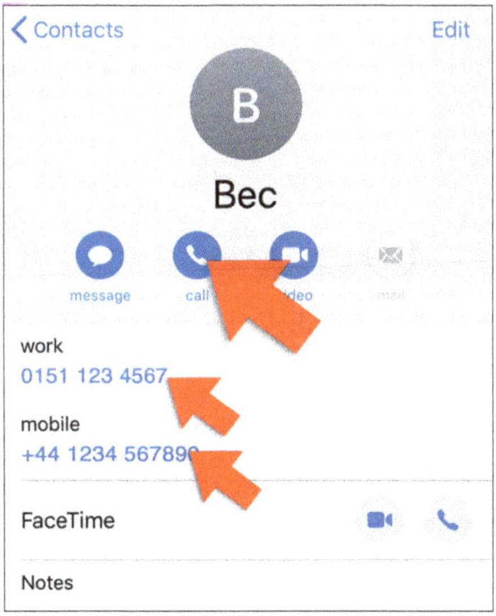

## Call Someone from Recent Calls List

Open the phone app, tap the 'recents' icon on the toolbar along the bottom of the screen.

Tap on the person you want to call.

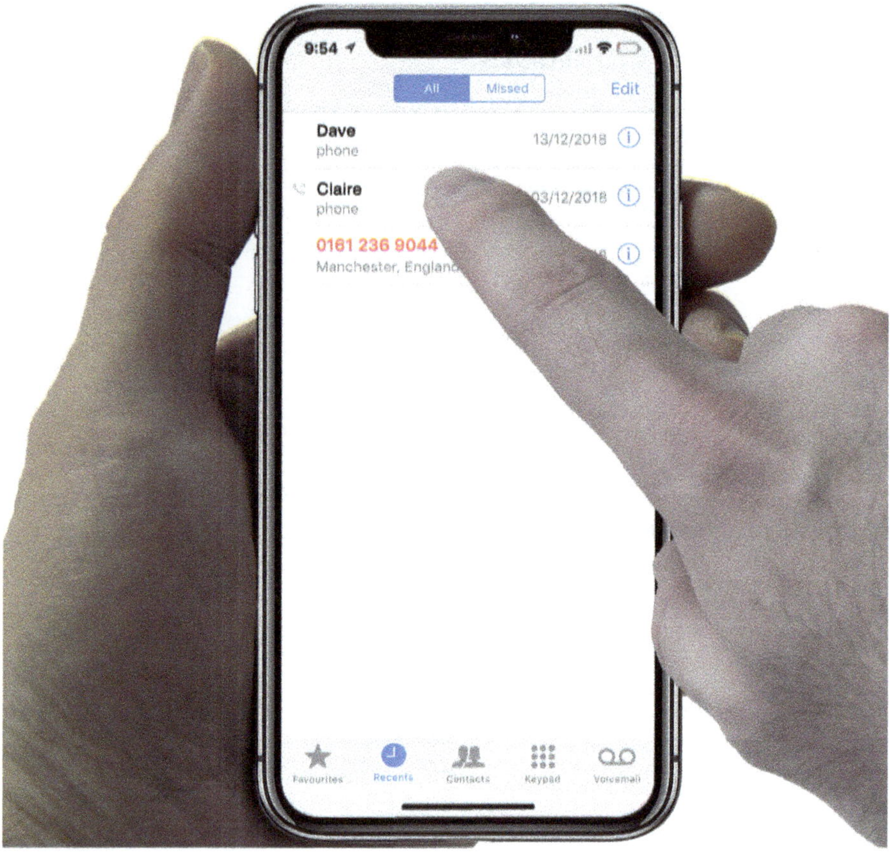


All missed calls show up in red. Calls you have placed, are indicated with a small phone icon.

All incoming calls you have answered show up in black text.

To see all calls you have placed & received, tap 'all' along the top of the screen. To only see missed calls, tap 'missed'.

Swipe right to left over the call in the list, and tap delete to remove it.

## Add Someone to Favourites

The favourites list is similar to speed dial. The idea is to put all your most used contacts on the favourites list, so you can access them easily.

To do this 'Favorites' on the toolbar along the bottom of the screen.

Tap the "+" sign in the top right of your screen.

Select a contact from your contacts list

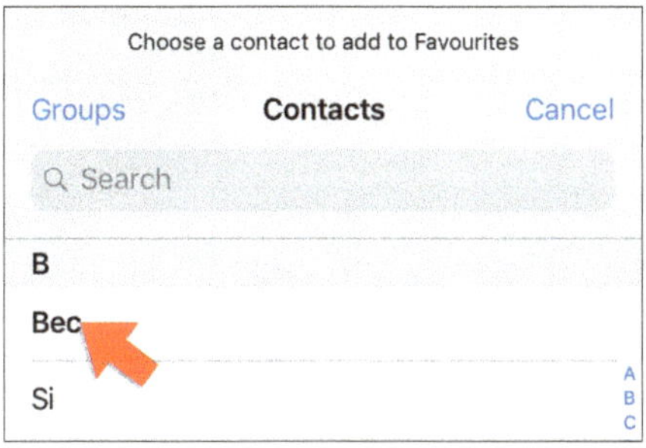


Now select the method you want to contact them with. This could be a phone call, text message, or facetime. Select the method you most likely use to contact this person. In this example, I'm going to call them

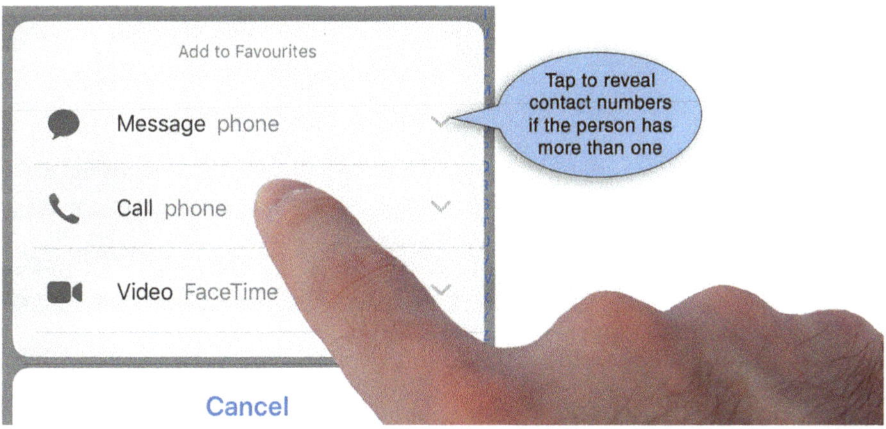

If the person has more than one contact number, eg home, work, or mobile, tap the small down arrow next to the method of contact to reveal all the person's contact numbers

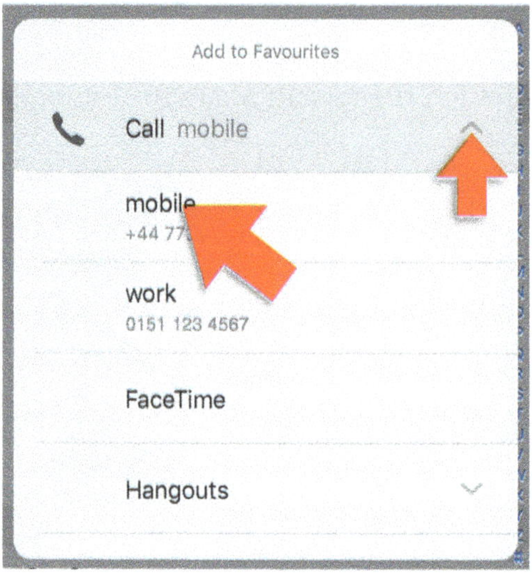


The numbers will appear on your favourites section. Tap on one to call the person.

To delete a favourite, swipe right to left over the name in the list, then tap 'delete'.

## Voice Mail

If someone has left you a voice message, you can check those here. To check, tap 'voice mail' on toolbar along the bottom of the screen

You'll see a list of phone numbers or names of people who have left you a voice message. Tap on one of these.

From the voice message screen, tap play icon to listen to message, tap 'call back' to return call.

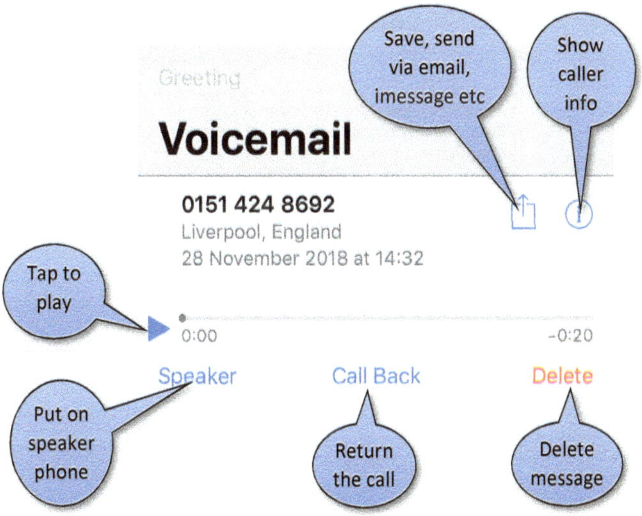


You can also put the message on speaker phone, or send the message to someone else using the share icon on the top right. You can send the message via email, Messages App, etc

## Custom Call Decline Messages

Open the Settings app from your home screen, scroll down the list and tap 'phone'.

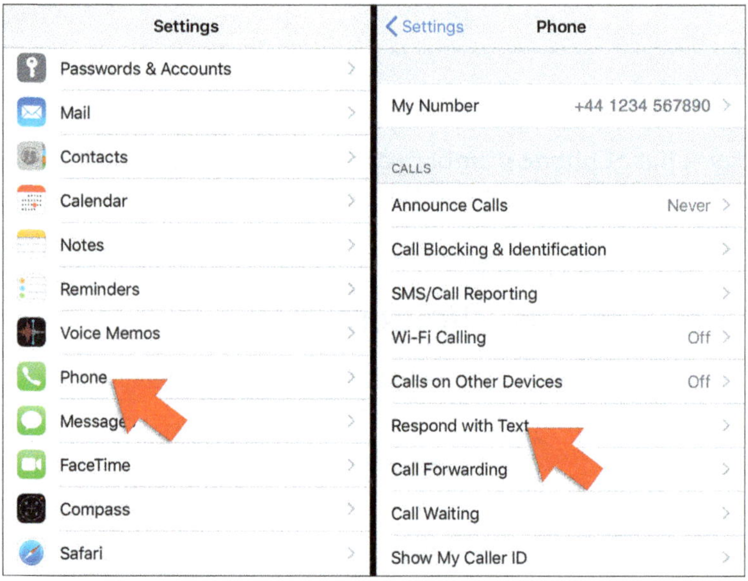


Tap 'Respond with Text'.

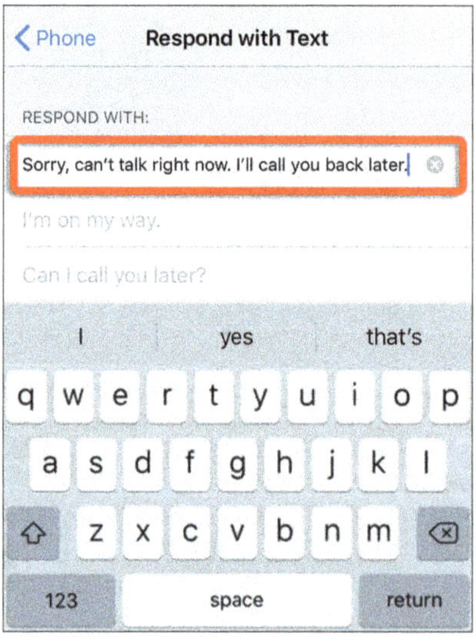


Tap any field you want to replace or customize and type your message. Your message will automatically appear as an option from now on when you tap the message button to decline a call.

## Ringtones and Text Tones

You can set individual ring tones for different people - this helps you identify people when they call. You can assign a different ring tone to each of your friends.

To do this, open the contacts app on your home screen, and tap on the person's name. In their contact details, tap 'edit' on the top right of the screen.

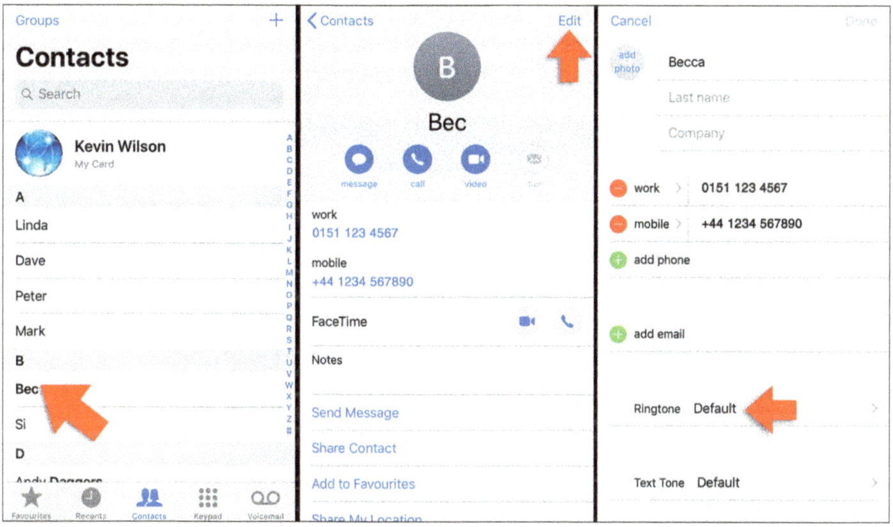


Scroll down and select 'ringtone'.

Select a ringtone from the list.

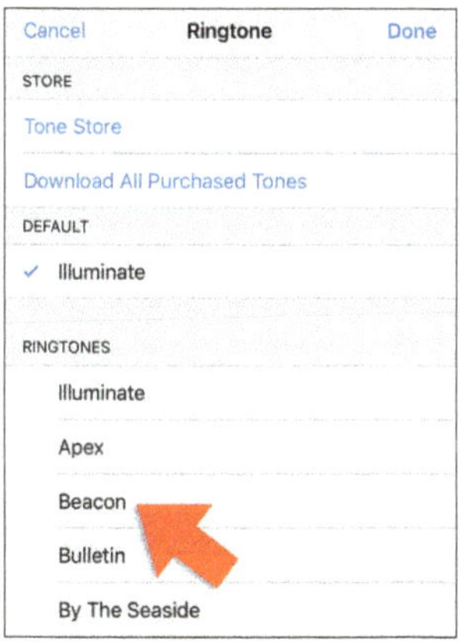


You can also purchase more ringtones from the tone store. To do this tap 'tone store'.

# Messages App

You can send photos and videos and also voice messages to anyone with an Apple device. To start Message, tap the icon on the dock on your home screen.

When you open Messages App, you will see a list of all your received messages. Tap on a message to read and reply.

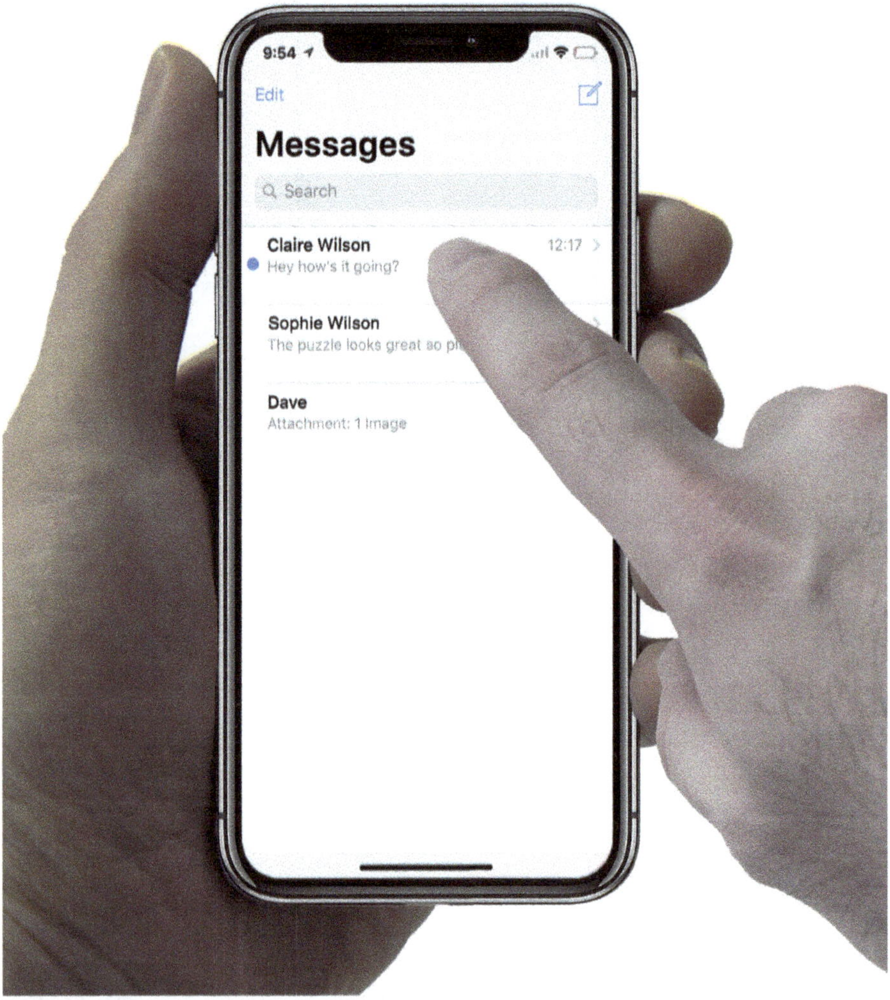


Tap the new message icon on the top right of the screen.

## New Message

Go back to the messages screen, then tap the new message icon on the top right.

Tap the + sign to add an address or phone number from your contacts. Or start typing the person's name or phone number into the 'to' field.

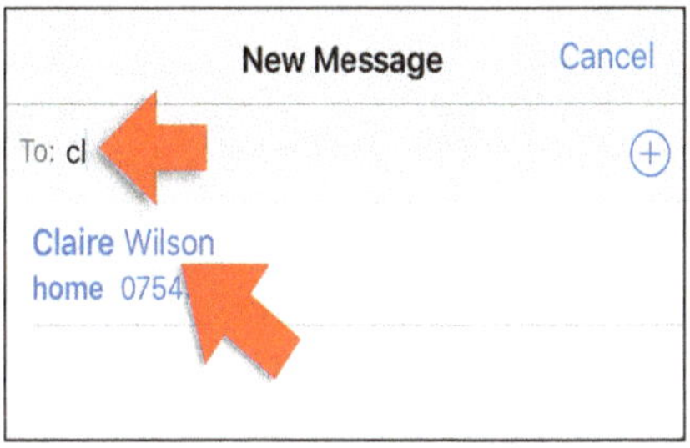


Type your message in the box indicated with the red arrow.

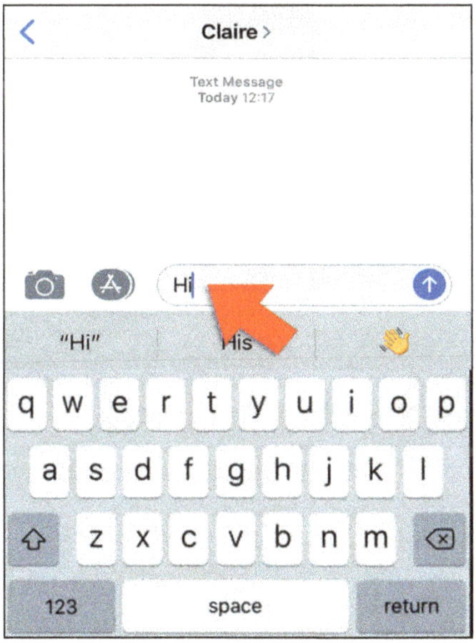


Tap the blue arrow on the right hand side to send the message

## Send a Voice Message

To send a voice message, in the message window tap and hold your finger on the audio icon to the right of the message field. Record your message, then release your finger to stop.

From the options that appear, tap the play icon to hear the recorded message. Tap the send icon to send the message.

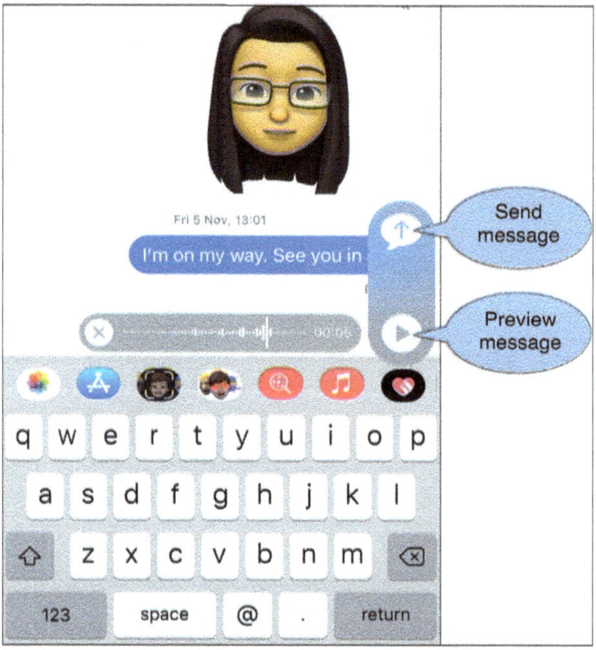

## Sending Photos from Photos App

To send a photograph or video you've taken previously, tap the small app icon on the bottom left of your message window.

Tap the 'photos' icon.

Select the photo you want to send from your photos. Tap 'all photos' to see more.

Type in a message where it says 'add comment or send'.

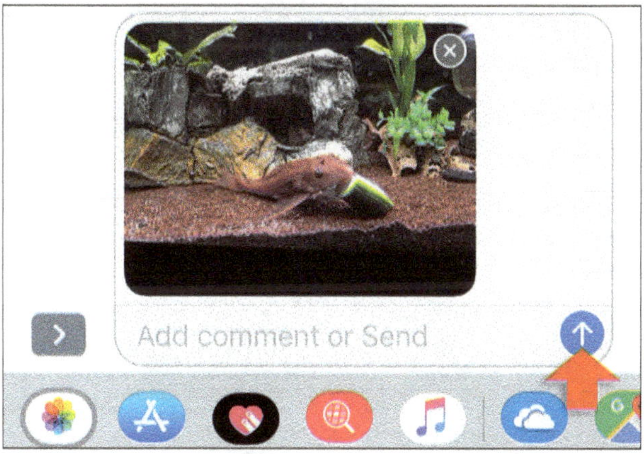


Tap the blue icon on the right hand side to send the image.

## Sending Photos from Camera

To send a photograph or video, tap the small camera icon on the bottom left of your message window.

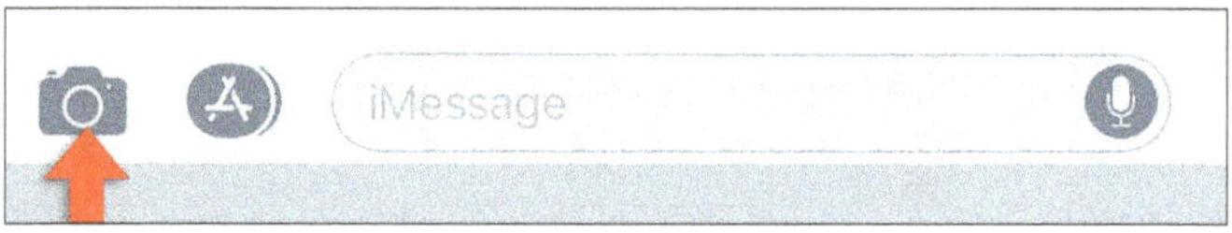


Your camera app will open up. Select 'photo' from the list on the bottom right, then tap on the white circle to take the picture.

Once you've taken your photo, you can add effects and annotate the image before you send it. Just tap the markup icon on the right hand side of the screen.

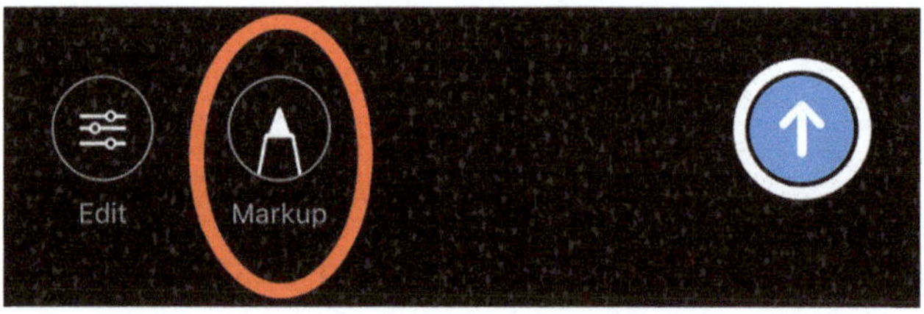

Draw directly onto the photo with your finger or pencil.

Tap 'save' on the top right hand side of your screen.

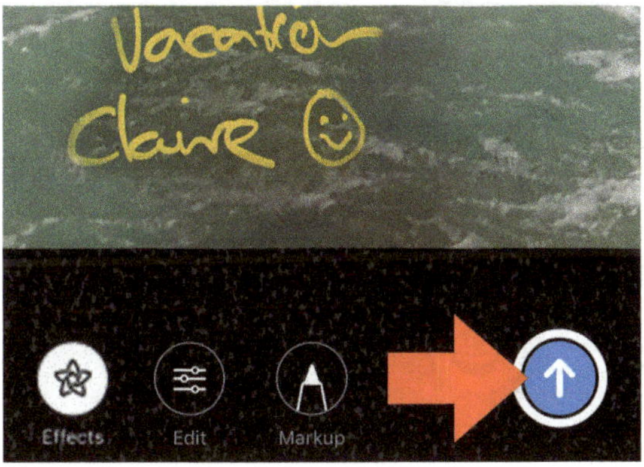


Tap the blue arrow to send

## Effects

You can also add effects to a photo or video. To do this, select 'photo' from the list on the bottom right, then tap on the white/red circle to take the picture.

Once you've taken your picture, select the effects icon from the panel on the bottom of the screen. Then select an effect from the panel that appears.

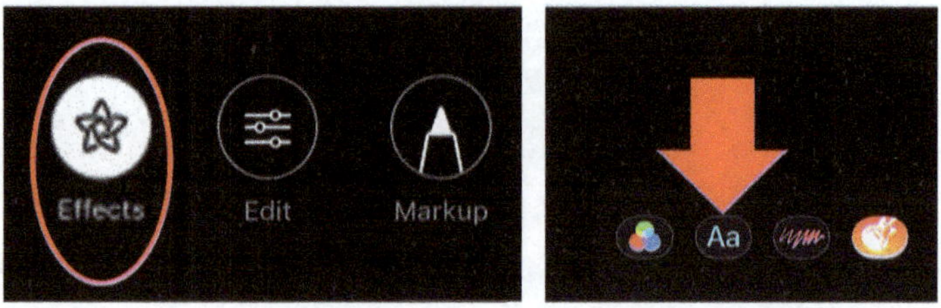


Add some text and effects to your image. Tap and drag the effect into place.

Try a few of the other effects.

Tap the blue arrow on the right hand side to send immediately, or tap 'done' on the top right of the screen to return to the message window.

If you returned to the message window, enter a message in the text field, tap the blue arrow to the right of the text field to send.

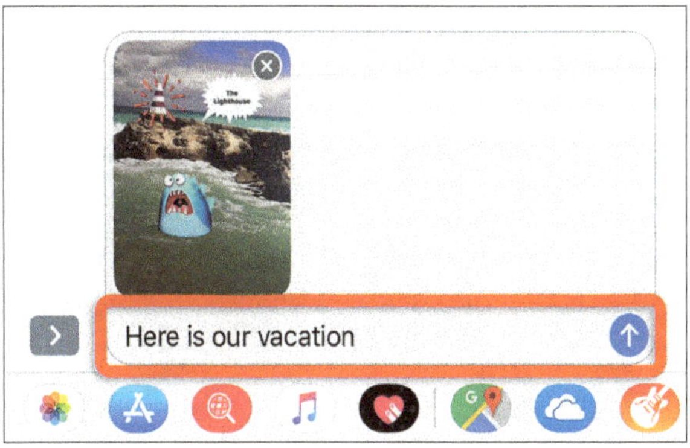

## Digital Touch

In digital touch mode, you can draw with your finger and send animations.

Tap the app icon to the left side of the text field to reveal additional options.

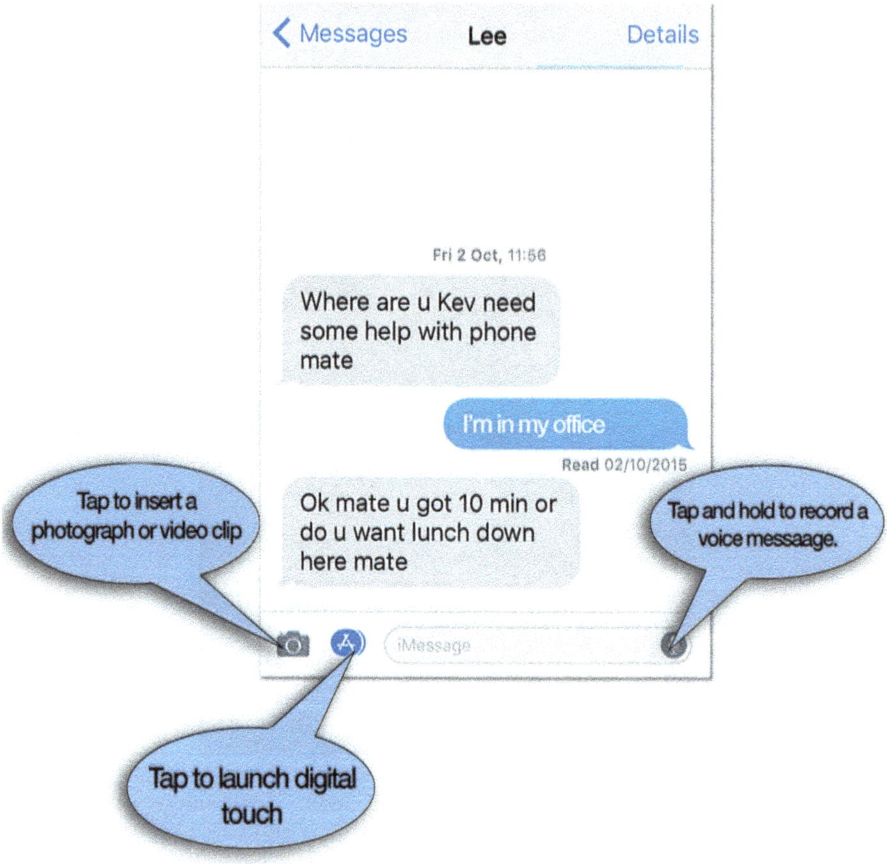


Then tap the digital touch icon. This opens up the digital touch interface.

Tap the blue circle on the left hand side. This will open up the digital touch panel

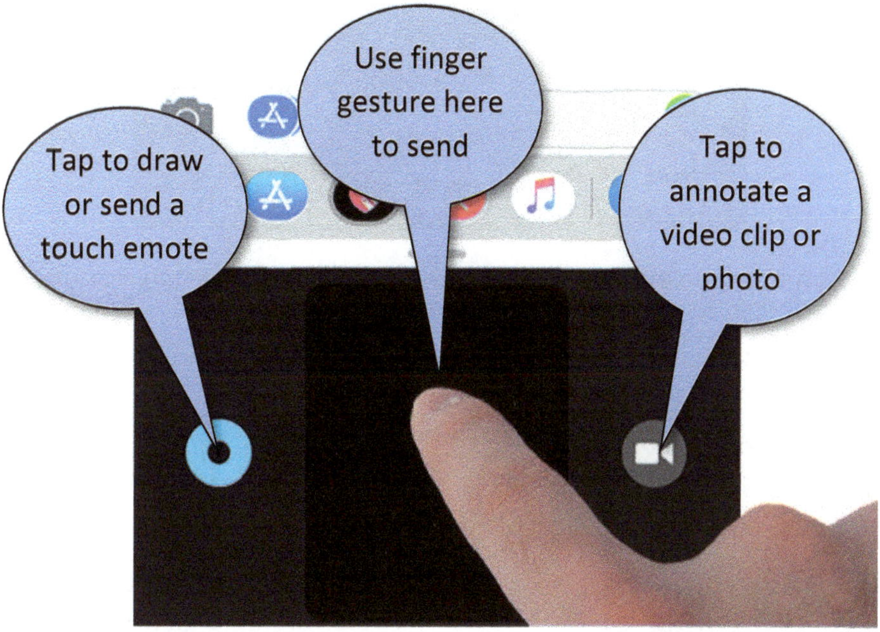


You can use certain finger gestures to send different emotes. For example, you can use one finger to draw or write something, press with one finger to send a fireball effect, tap with two fingers to send a kiss and so on. Here's a list of a few of the good ones...

You can also draw using your finger. Tap on the dot on the left hand side to open up the colours.

Tap on a colour along the left hand side, then draw a diagram on the black screen in the centre.

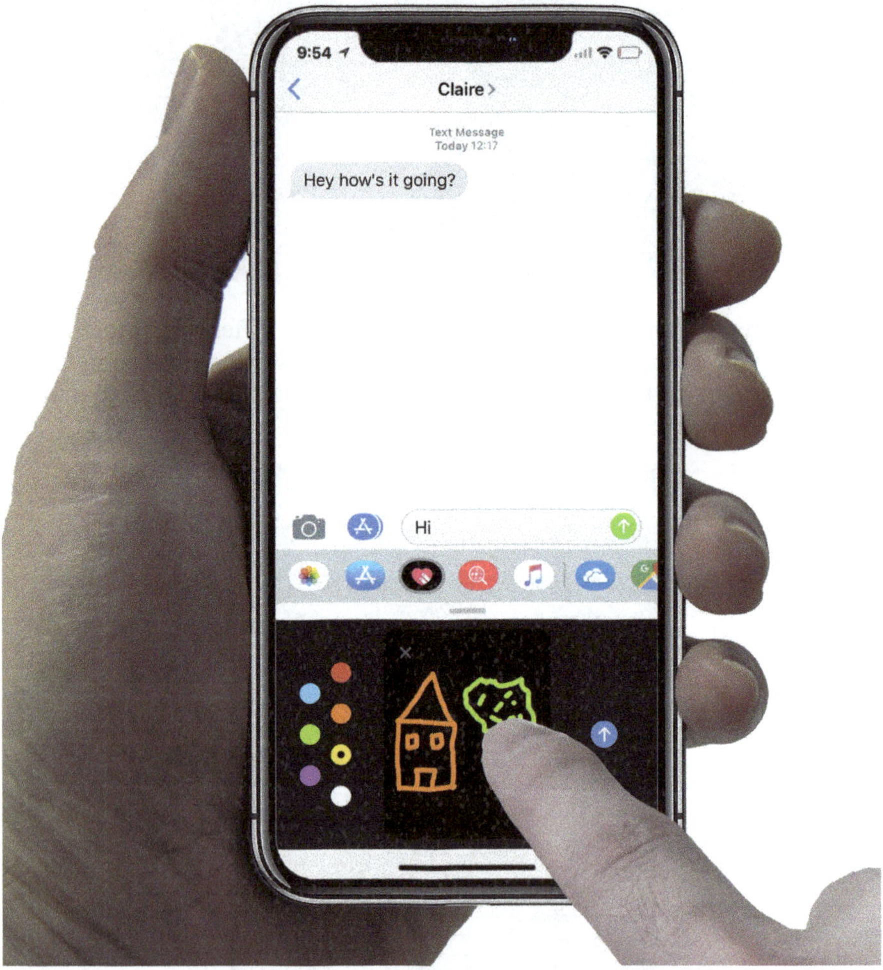


Tap on the blue arrow to the right to send.

You can also annotate a video or photograph using digital touch. To do this, from digital touch interface, tap the camera icon.

Tap the red button to start recording. While the video is recording, use the digital touch tools to draw on it. Tap a colour, then draw or write on the image with your finger.

*The white button at the bottom left takes a photo, while the red button in the centre records a video.*

Try a few 'tap and holds' with two fingers to add a few hearts. Or tap with two fingers to send a kiss.

Tap the record button again to stop recording.

Tap the blue arrow at the bottom right to send your finished piece.

## Animated Gifs

You can add gifs which are short animations. Select the app icon. Then select the gif icon. Tap on a gif to add it to your message or type in to the 'find images' field to search for something specific.

## Music

You can also share what music you are listening to on the Music App. Select the app icon. Then along the bottom of the screen, select the 'Music' icon.

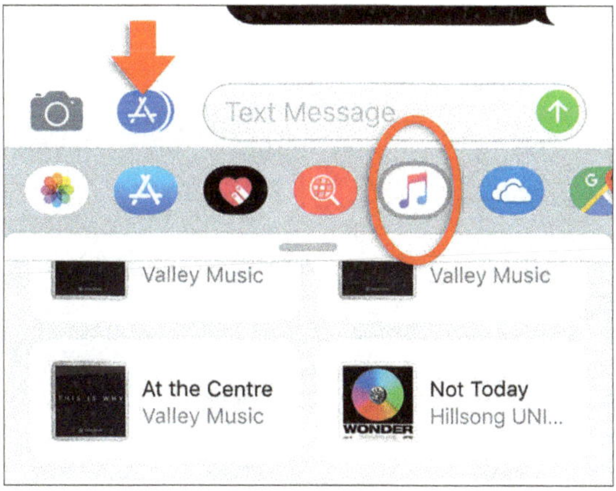


You'll see all the music you have been listening to or currently listening to on your iPhone. Tap on a track to share.

## Sending Payments

You can send payments to contacts on Messages App using Apple Pay. This only work between Apple devices at the moment, so you can't send payments to users of other phones or tablets. This feature is not available in some countries yet.

Tap the app icon to the left side of the text field to reveal additional options. Then tap the Apple Pay icon.

Enter the amount. Either use the + and - buttons to increase/decrease the amount, or tap 'show keypad' and tap in the amount. Once you're done hit 'pay'.

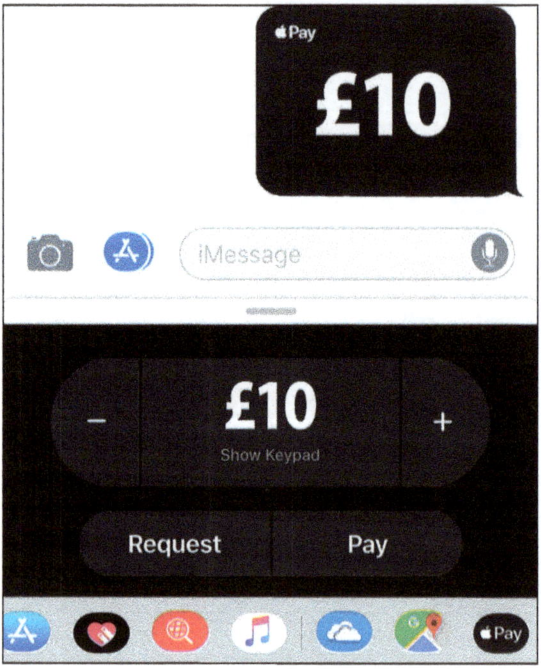


If people are owing you money, you can enter the amount as above and tap 'request' to send them an invite to pay you the amount.

## Emojis

Also known as emoticons, emojis are little ideograms used to express emotion in a text based world. These ideograms could be facial expressions such as smilies, common objects, places, and animals. You can use them in Messages App, text messaging, and email.

You'll find the emoji panel on your on screen keyboard. To open the panel, tap the small 'smiley' icon on the bottom left.

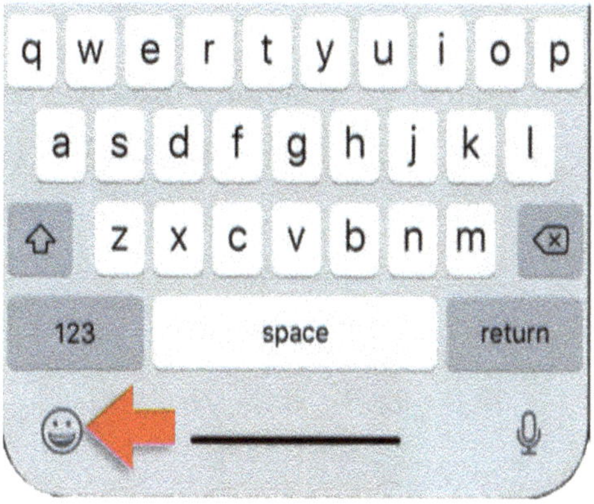


Swipe left to scroll through the list of emojis. You can also tap the grey icons along the bottom to jump to different categories, eg food, places, sports, and so on.

Tap on the emoji you want to insert.

Tap 'abc' on the left hand side to close the emoji panel.

## Sending Memojis

To find your memojis, tap the app icon to open the panel if it isn't already open. Then from the list of icons, tap the memoji icon

Swipe left and right to select your memoji from the list.

Now, look at the screen. You'll notice that the animoji will copy your facial expressions. Tap the red record icon on the bottom right to start recording. Make some head movements, facial expressions or record a message. Your iPhone's microphone will pick up your voice.

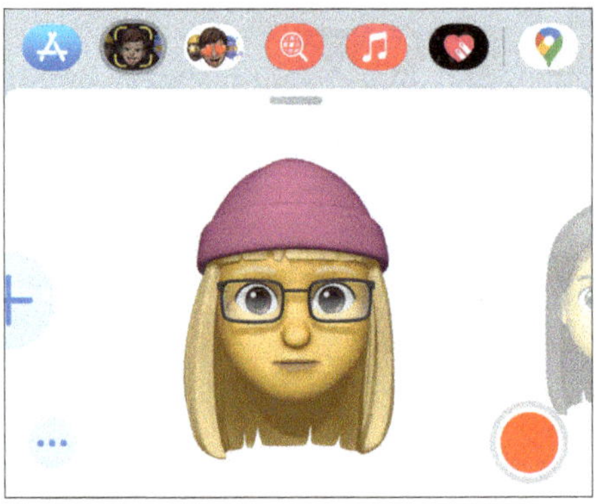

Tap the red record icon again to stop recording. Tap the blue arrow to send the memoji. See

## Stickers

Stickers are little characters you can use to send to your friends.

To find your stickers, tap the app icon to open the panel if it isn't already open. Then from the list of icons, tap the sticker icon

Select a character from the line up at the top, then select a sticker from the characters.

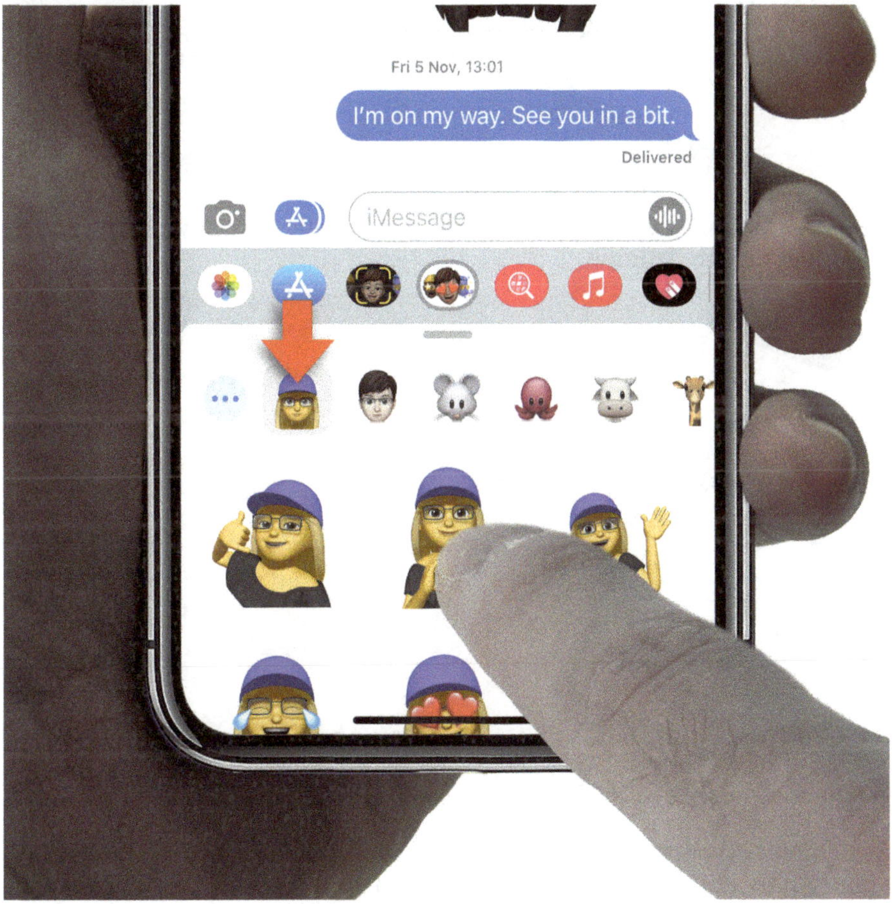


Tap on the sticker you want.

# Animojis and Memojis

An animoji uses a 3D graphic that maps to your face, allowing you to play an animated character, animal, robot, or dragon. As you smile, blink open your mouth or talk, the animoji moves with you.

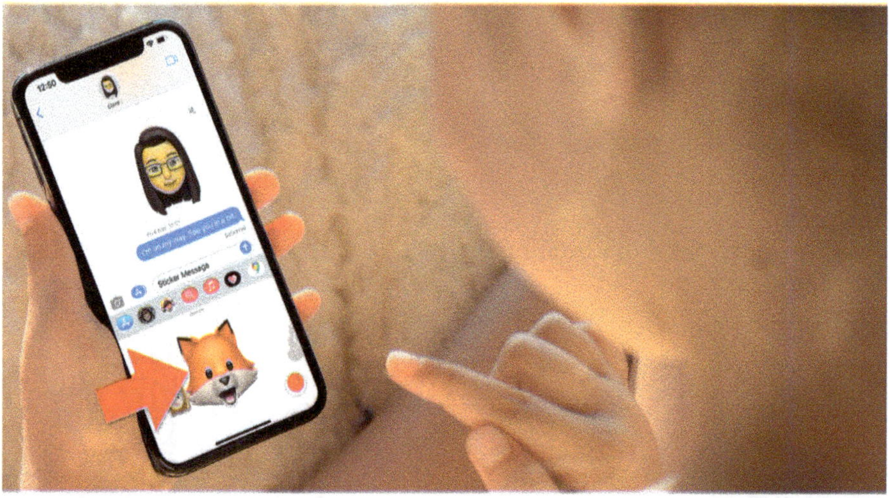

Memoji lets users create 3D avatars of themselves that you can use in a similar way to Animoji.

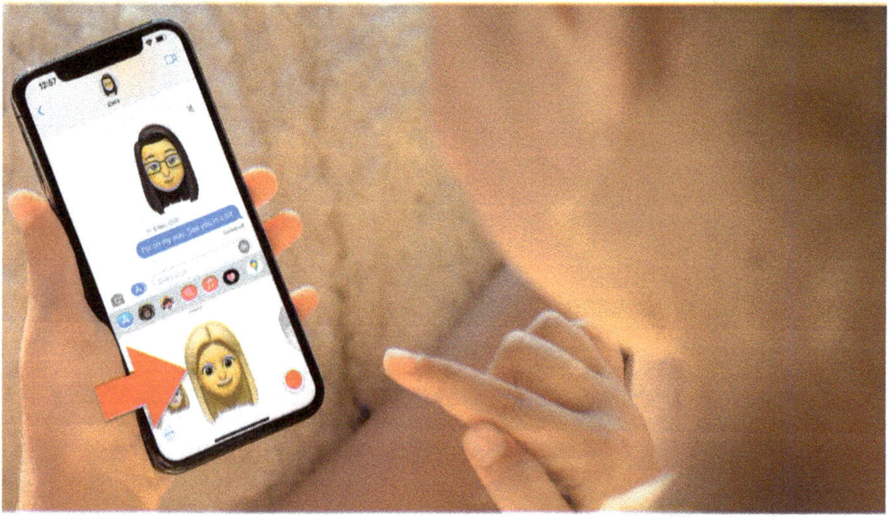

A memoji is a customised graphic that looks like the user. Your face shape, hair colour, eye colour, and skin tone can be personalized to look and feel just like you. With the iPhone's True Depth camera and face tracking technology, the memoji will mimic your facial expressions.

## Making a Memoji

To find your memojis, tap the app icon to open the panel if it isn't already open. Then from the list of icons, tap the animoji icon

Swipe to the right over the animojis until you see the 'new memoji' icon. Tap the '+' icon in the centre of the panel to create a new memoji.

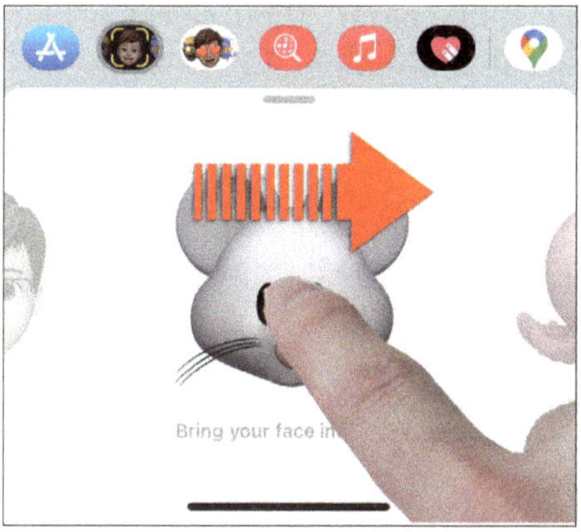

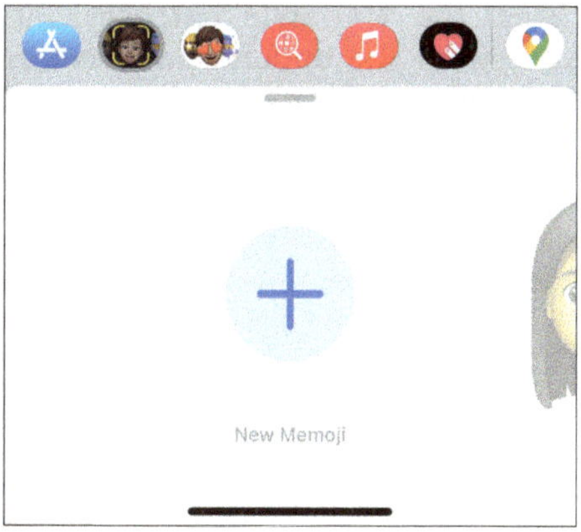


Start with skin. Choose your skin tone. Select a colour, then use the slider underneath to make the colour darker or lighter.

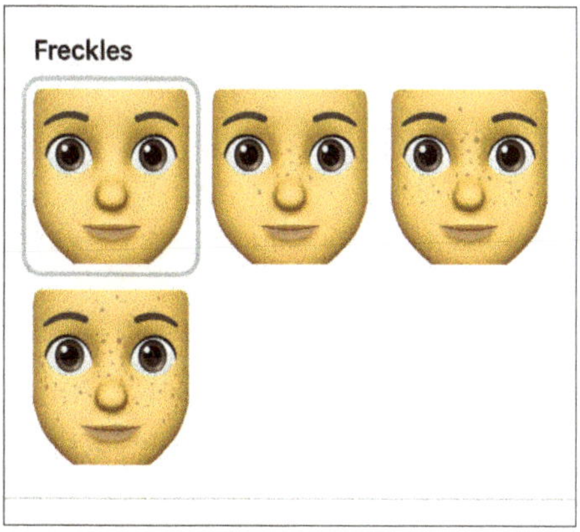


Scroll down, add some freckles, change your cheek shape, and add a beauty spot if you want.

Now, customise and start to build your memoji. Swipe through the categories in the centre of your screen.

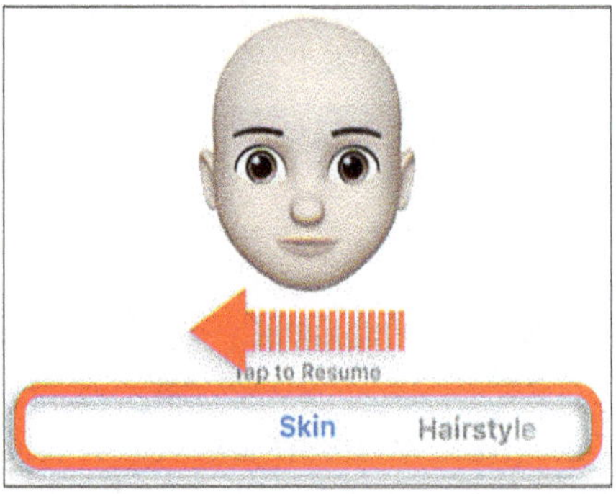


Select the 'Hairstyle' category. Pick a hair colour, then select a hair style from the options underneath. Tap 'highlights' if you want add highlights to your hair.

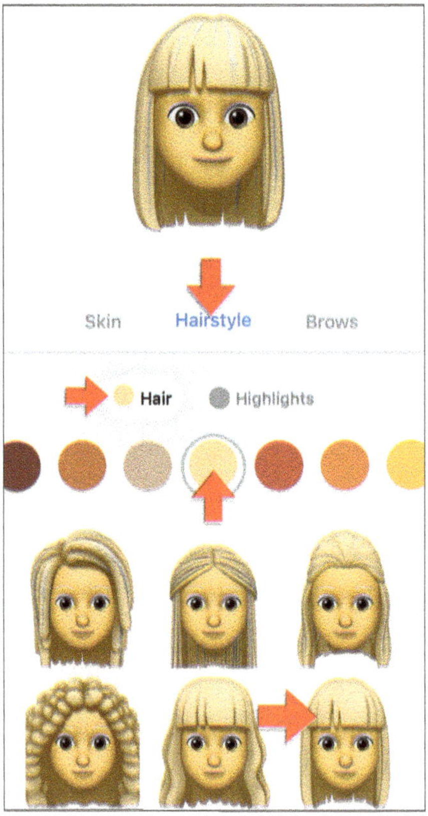


Swipe left across the list in the middle of the screen to reveal the rest of the categories.

Go through these categories as you did before and customise the other features.

- Eyes: Select eye colour and eyelashes.
- Brows: Select shape and different thickness.
- Nose and Lips: Choose size of nose, lip colour and shape.
- Ears: Choose size of ears and add any earrings or jewellery if you wish.
- Facial Hair: Add any facial hair.
- Eyeware: Add a style of glasses.
- Headwear: Add a hat or beanie to your memoji.
- Clothing: Pick an outfit. Tap 'main' to change main colour, tap 'second' and 'third' to change the other colours.

Once you have your memoji, tap 'done' on the top right of your screen.

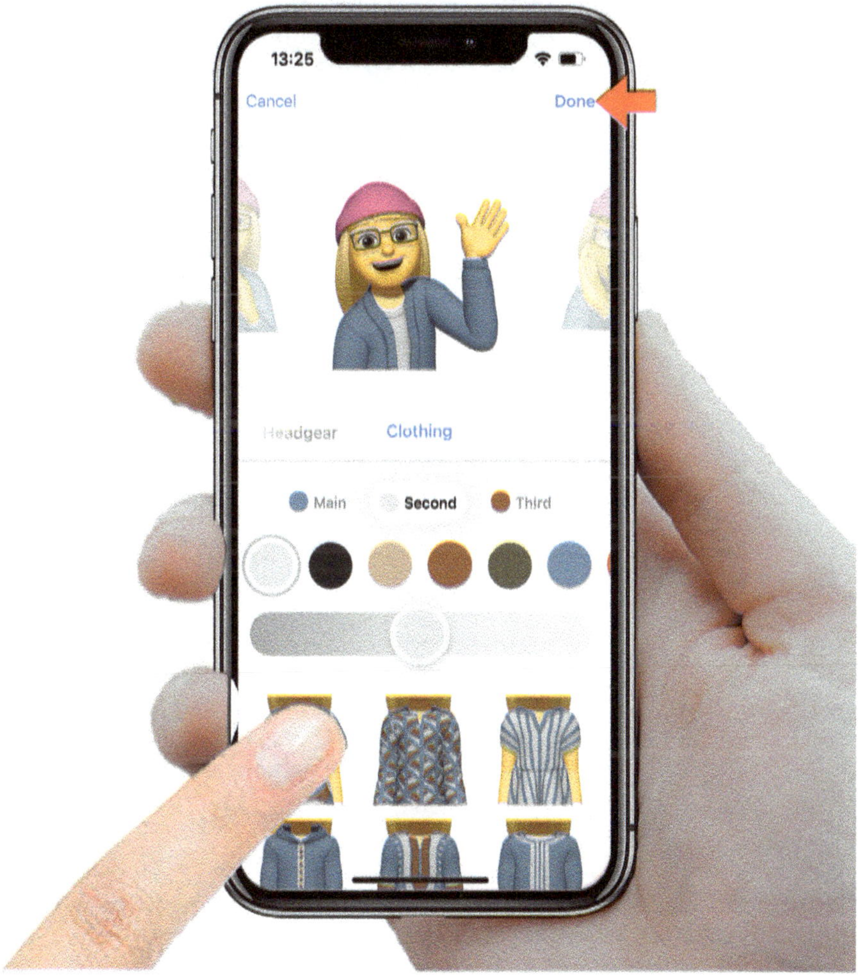

# AirDrop

AirDrop allows you to transfer files from one device to another wirelessly using bluetooth.

To use AirDrop you will need a compatible device, such as the iPhone 5 or later, fourth-generation iPhone, iPhone mini, and fifth-generation iPod touch, and have both Bluetooth and Wi-Fi enabled.

Swipe your finger downwards from the top right edge of your screen to open control center. Make sure your WiFi and bluetooth is turned on. If these are on, the icons will be blue.

To enable AirDrop open the settings app, go to 'general'. Tap 'airdrop'. From the AirDrop settings, select 'contacts only'.

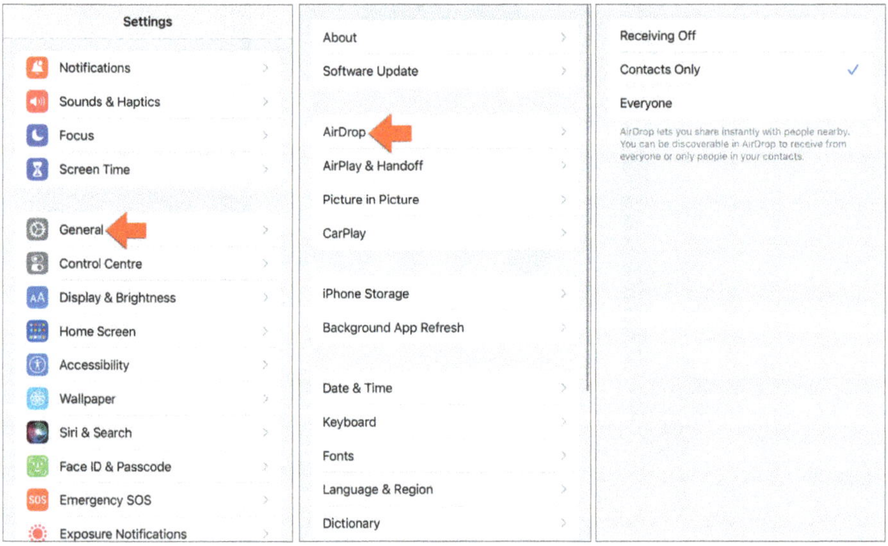


Be careful if you select 'everyone' as this means anyone in your vicinity that has an AirDrop enabled device can connect to and send files to your device, which could be a possible security risk.

## To Send a file to Someone using AirDrop

You can send a file or photo from your iPhone to another iPhone, Mac, or iPad.

Open the app you want to share a file from. In this example, I am going to send a photo from the Photos app.

Tap the image or video you want to share from your albums, tap next.

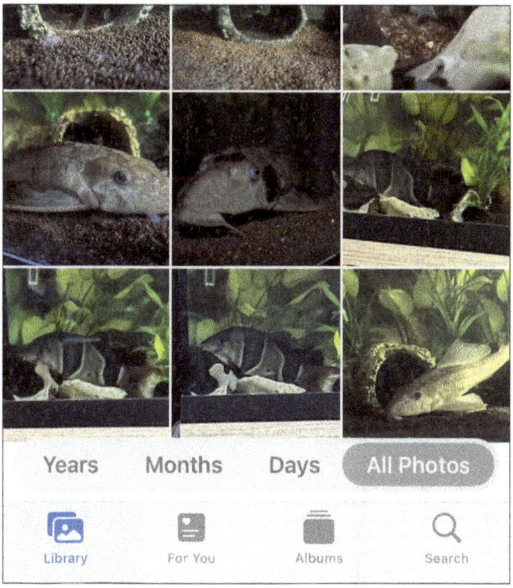


Tap on the Share icon. Then select 'airdrop'.

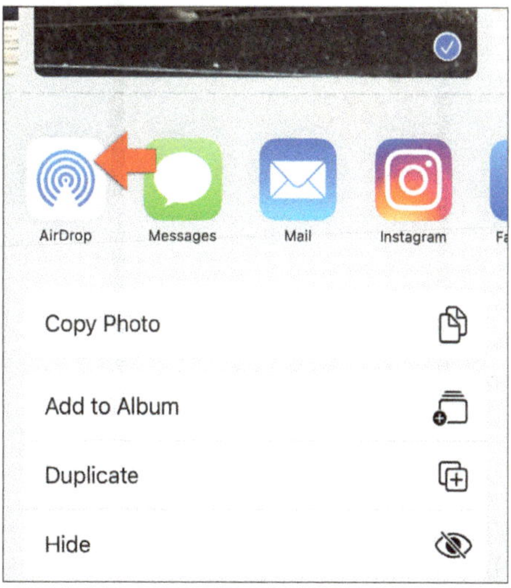

AirDrop will detect other devices in the vicinity. In this example, AirDrop has detected Sophie's iPhone. This is the one I want to share with. Tap the icon of the person/device you want to send to.

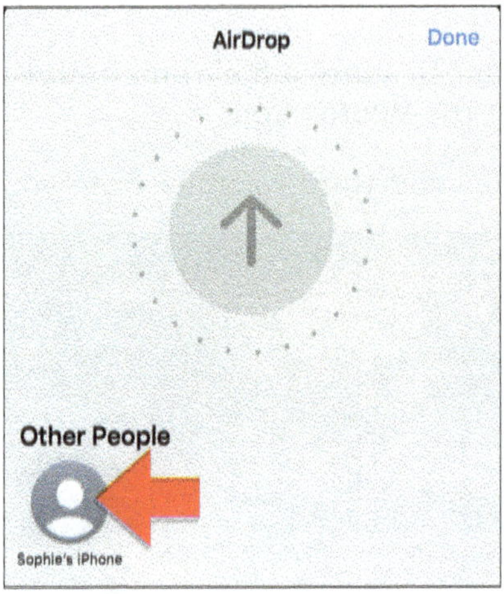


Now when you send the photo, the other person will get a prompt to download the image. Accept the confirmation and your image will download.

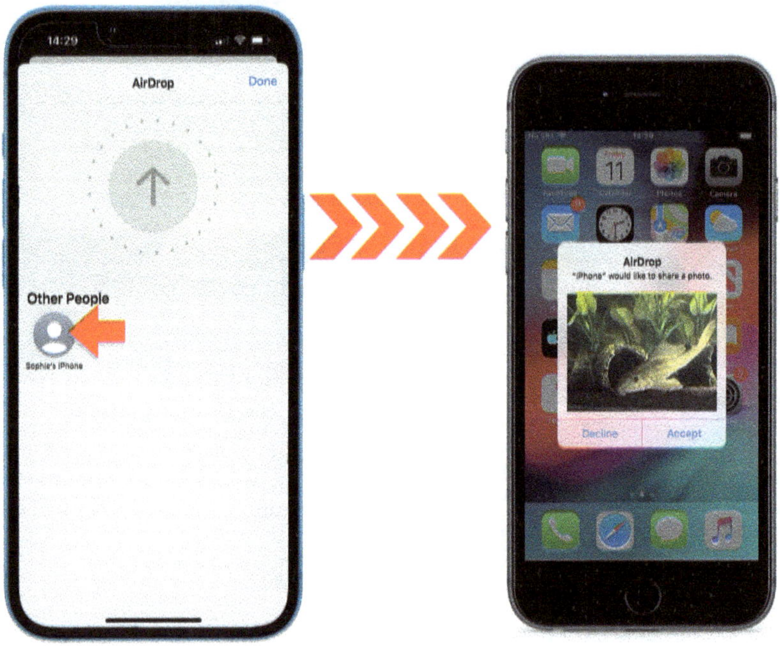


The image/video will be added to your photo library. The photo sent has appeared in photos app on the other iPhone.

## To Receive a File from Someone using AirDrop

Make sure your AirDrop is enabled on your device. Open settings app, tap general, tap AirDrop.

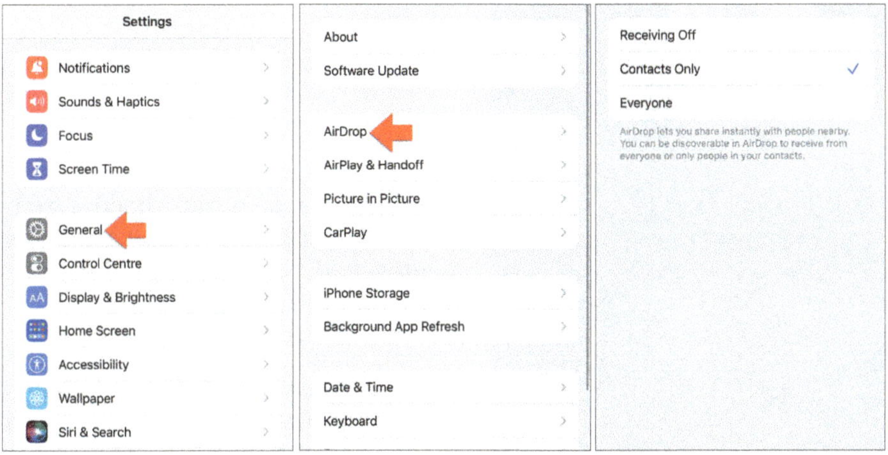


Select 'contacts only'. If the person you're receiving a file from isn't in your contacts list, select 'everyone'. It's a good idea to turn this off when you're not using AirDrop.

AirDrop will try to negotiate the connection with near by devices.

More often than not, the file will automatically download. If you get a prompt, tap on 'accept' when the photo comes through

Go into your photos app and the photo will be stored in there.

# 6

# Using Multimedia

Your iPhone is a multimedia rich device, meaning you can take photos and record videos. You can even edit and enhance your photos, correct colour and brightness.

You can post your photographs to your favourite social media account for the world to see. You can create slide shows, edit your videos, download and watch TV programmes and films. You can download and play any kind of music you can think of, all from your iPhone.

In this chapter, we'll take a look at:

- Photos App
- Camera App
- Music & Podcasts App
- Apple Music
- iTunes Store
- Apple TV App
- Airplay
- Apple Pencil
- Scribble
- Document & QR Code Scanner

Take a look at the video resources

elluminetpress.com/iphone-mm

# Photos App

Using the photos app, you can browse, organise, edit and share photos taken with the on board cameras on your iPhone.

To open the photos app tap the photos icon on your home screen.

When you open the photos app, you'll land on the home screen. Let's take a look around.

## Opening a Photo

To open a photo, tap on the thumbnail in your library of photos.

This will open the photo full screen. You can view the photo in portrait mode as show below, or you can rotate your phone 90° and view it in landscape mode.

## Edit a Photo

You can do some basic editing on your iPhone. You can lighten up dark images, crop and rotate your photos.

To do this, tap on the photo you want to adjust.

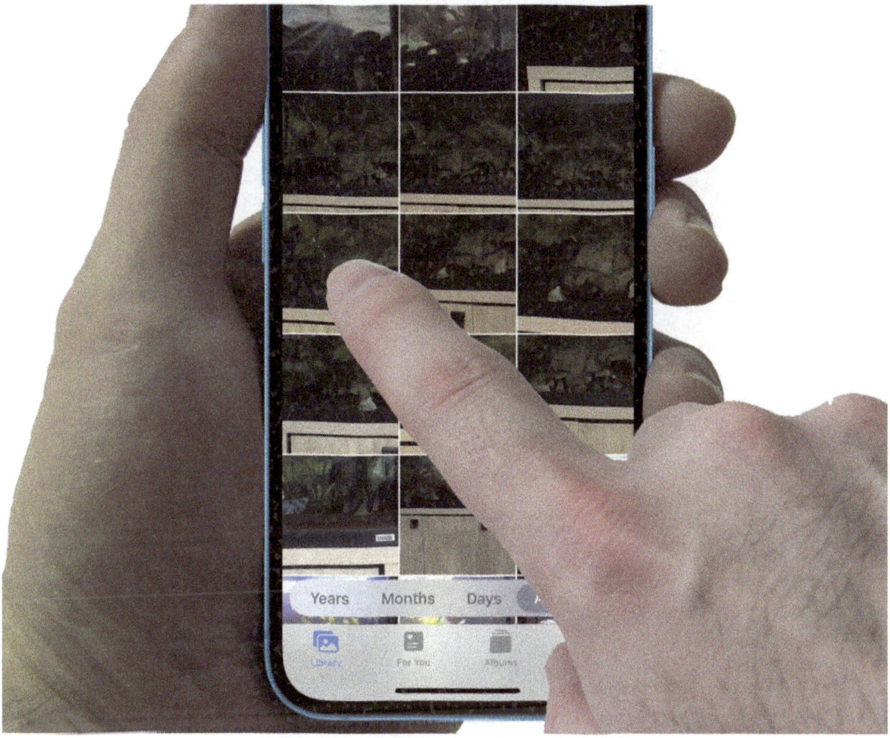


When your photo opens up, tap 'edit' on the top right of the screen.

When the adjustment screen appears, you'll see some icons along the bottom.

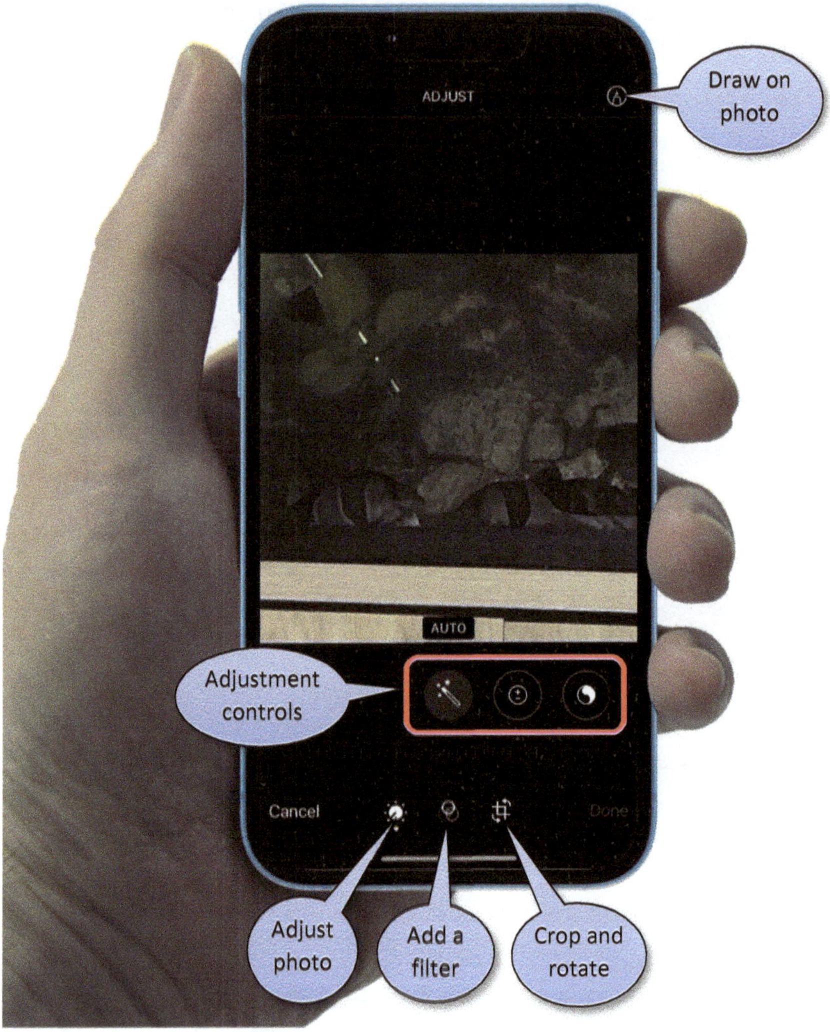


## Adjusting Images

To adjust images, tap the image adjustment icon from the three along the bottom of the screen. The image adjustment controls will appear under the photograph.

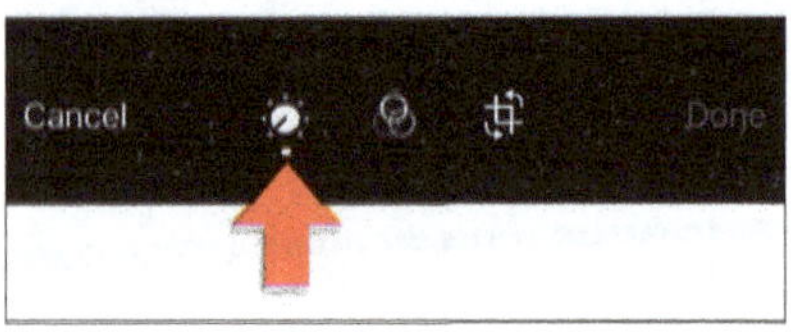

Swipe right over the controls to reveal the rest of the controls.

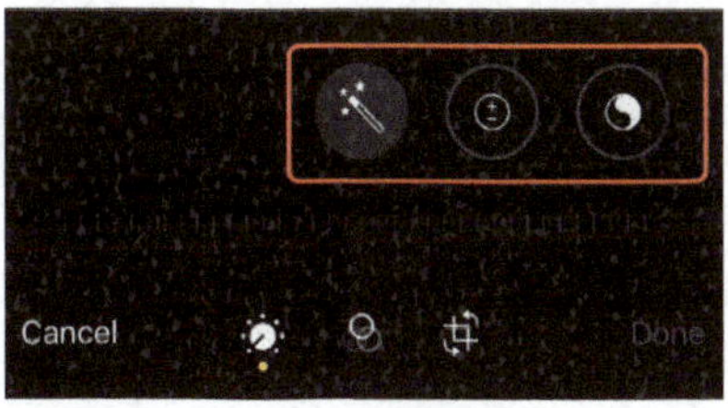


Let's take a look at what each icon does.

- **Auto**
- **Exposure**
- **Brilliance**
- **Highlights (bright or white parts of image)**
- **Shadows (dark or black parts of image)**
- **Contrast**
- **Brightness**
- **Black Point (brightness of the black parts of image)**
- **Color saturation (intensity of the colors)**
- **Color vibrance**
- **Warmth (white balance - bluish or orange tint to photo)**
- **Tint**
- **Sharpness**
- **Photo definition**
- **Noise reduction (removes noise from photo)**

To adjust the image, select one of the tools on the panel. For example, to brighten up the whole image, select brightness.

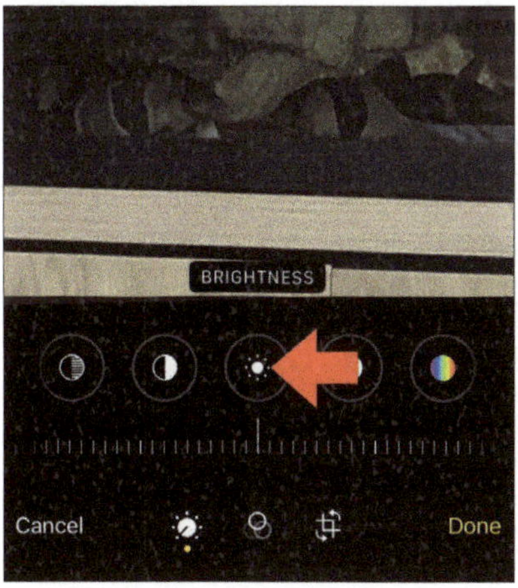

You can drag the panel upwards with your finger to see all the icons. Tap the icon you want, then drag the dial up or down to adjust.

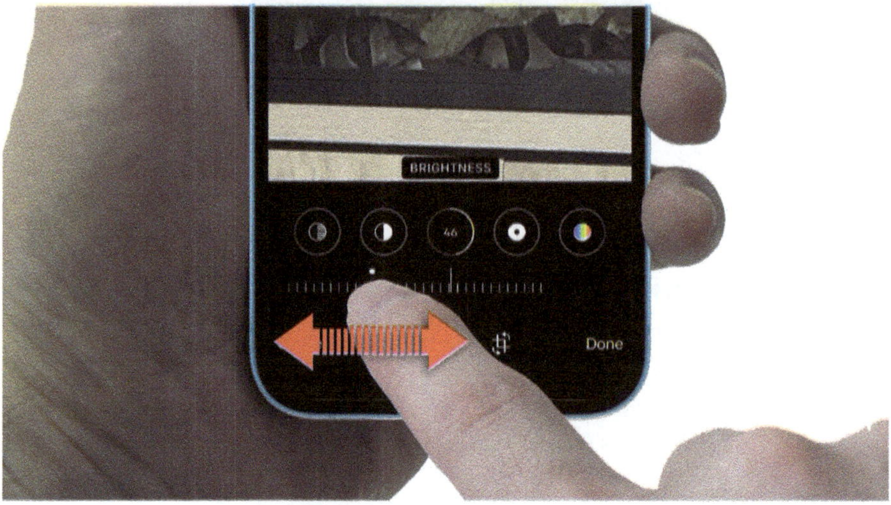


Select another icon to adjust.

Tap 'done' on the top right when you're finished.

## Crop an Image

To crop an image, tap the 'crop and rotate' from the three icons at the bottom.

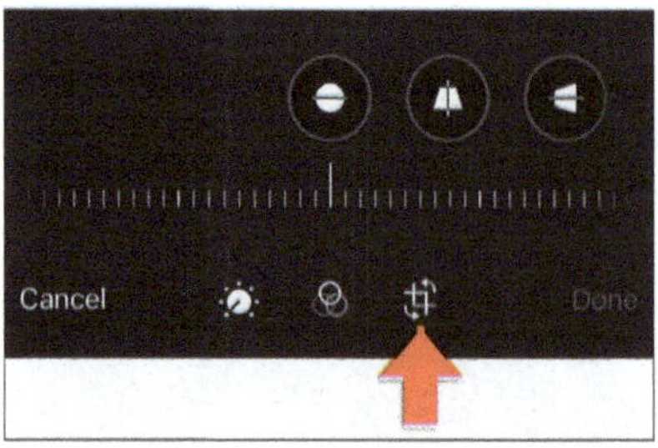

The image crop dials will appear.

Around the edges of your image you'll see some crop handles.

Tap and drag these around the part of the image you want to keep.

## Rotate an Image

To rotate an image, tap the 'crop and rotate' icon from the three on the bottom of the screen.

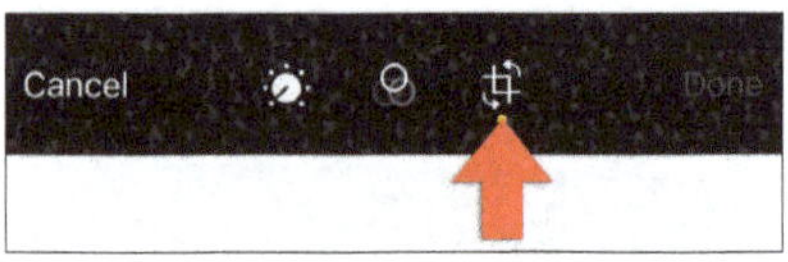


Tap the rotate icon from the adjustment controls.

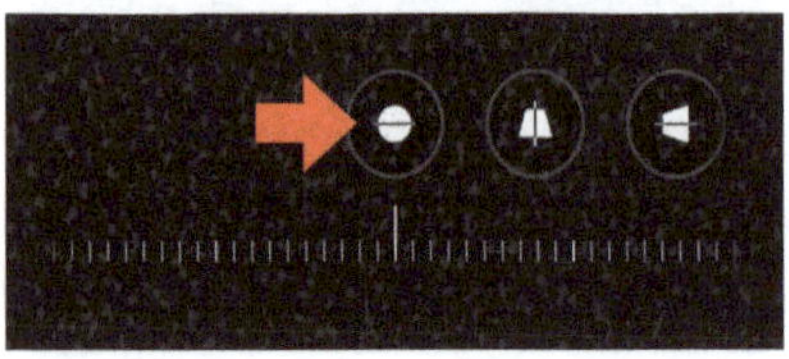

Tap and drag the dial up and down to rotate the image.

You can also adjust the horizontal and vertical distortion. This is useful if you want to straighten lens distortion.

Tap 'done' on the top right when you're finished.

## Creating Albums

You can create albums to organise your photos. To do this, from the bottom panel, select 'albums'.

Tap '+' on the top left

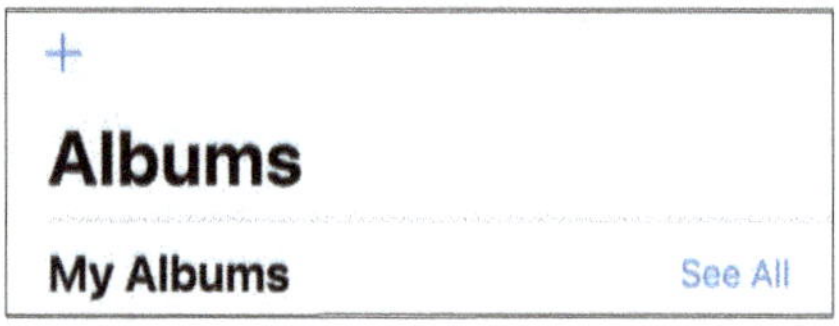


Select 'new album' from the drop down menu.

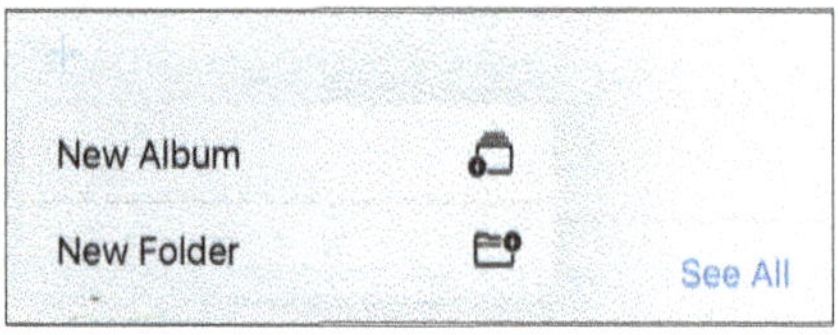


Give the album a name, then tap 'save'.

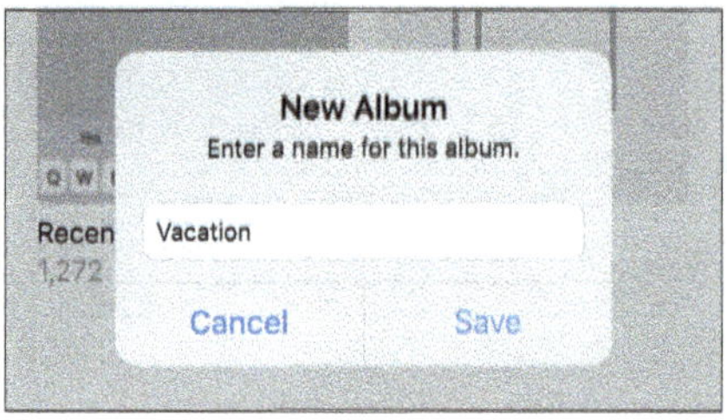


Tap on the photos you want to add to your album. Tap 'done'.

## Add Photos to Album

Select the photo or photos from your library.

Tap the share icon on the bottom left. Scroll down, select 'add to album'

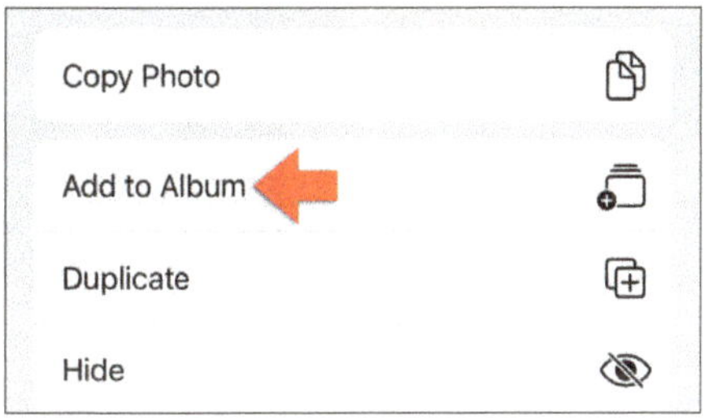


Select the album you want to add the photos to. Or select 'new album' if you want to add the photos to a new album.

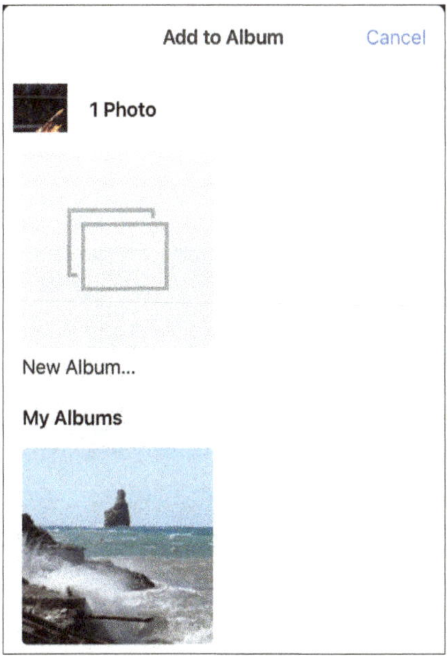

## Search for Photos

The photos app automatically scans your photos for recognisable objects, animals, places and people. To search, tap 'search' on the on the bottom panel.

Type in your keywords in the search field at the top of the screen.

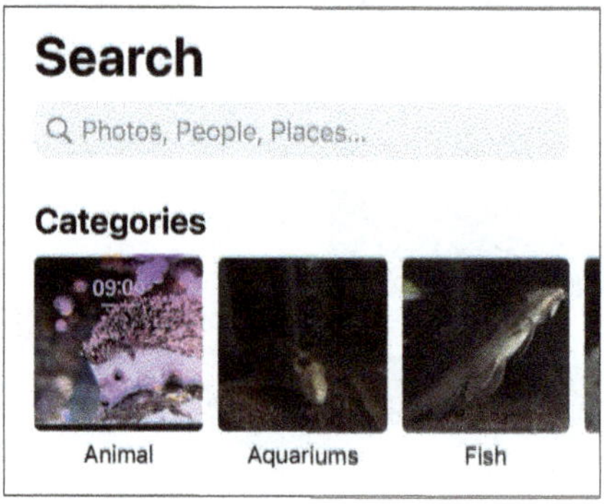


Scroll down the search results.

## Sharing Photos

To share a photo with a friend, or on social media, first tap 'library' on the bottom panel. Select the photo you want to share.

Once the photo opens up, tap the share icon in the bottom left corner.

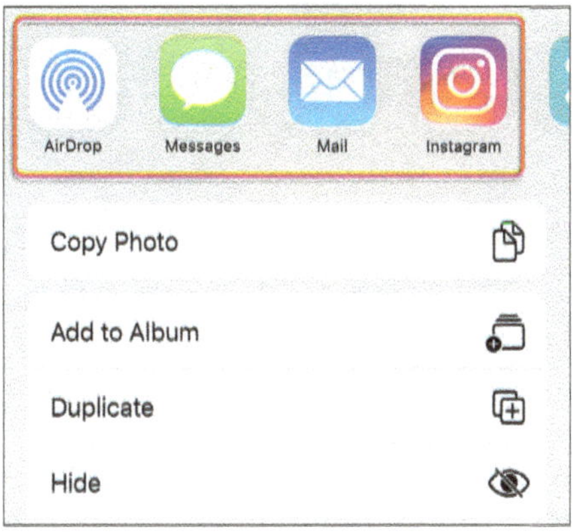


Select the app you want to use to share your photo. You can share the photo via email, messages, or social media (if you have the app installed). For example, select 'Instagram' from the list of icons to post on Instagram.

Type a message in your post, then hit 'post'.

You can use the same procedure for AirDrop, email, iMessage and any other social media you use. Just select the app from the icons.

# Camera App

Tap the camera icon on the home screen.

You can use your iPhone as a camera to take photos and record video. Lets have a look at the camera app...

Along the left hand side of your screen you have some icons. At the top, you can enable or disable live photos (a live photo captures what happens just before and after you take your photo, including the audio). On the bottom left, you can change the shutter speed and exposure time - useful if you're taking photos in low light. The icon below that, enables and disables the flash.

On the right hand side you can select the type of video or photo you want to take: time lapse, slomo, cinematic, video, photo, portrait, and panoramic photo.

The white circle takes the photo, the icon next to it swaps your cameras.

You can adjust the zoom using the slider on the right hand side of the image, or use your forefinger and thumb to zoom - just spread your two fingers out over the glass using a pinch & spread gesture, as shown in the illustration below.

If you're having trouble focusing, tap and hold your finger on the object you want to focus on. This will lock the exposure and focus on that object, so it doesn't change, making it easier to take the photo.

You can also adjust the brightness before you take a photo. To do this tap on the screen and you'll see a yellow square show up with a vertical line with a slider on it.

Drag the slider upward to brighten up the image, slide it downward to darken the image.

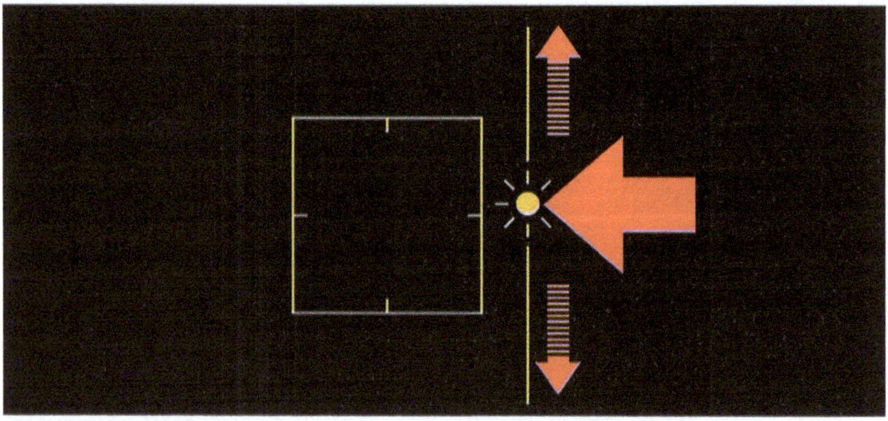

Tap the white circle to take the photo.

Once you have taken your photo you can you can adjust, crop or rotate the image, and add filters..

To do this tap the image preview thumbnail on the bottom left of the screen..

See page 306 for information on how to adjust images.

You'll find all the photos you've taken in the Photos App.

## Panoramic Photos

Panoramic shots are great for scenery and landscapes. Photos app allows you to automatically take a series of photos and it stitches them together into a long panoramic image.

To take panoramic photos, open your camera app. Swipe across the list along the bottom of the screen, then select pano.

Now, move your iPhone to the start of the scene and tap the white circle. You'll notice in the centre of the screen a rectangular box, this will start to fill as you move your iPhone across the scene. In this demonstration, I'm taking a panoramic photo of a mountain range.

Position your iPhone camera at the beginning of the mountain range on the left, tap the white 'take photo' icon on the right of your screen. Now move your camera along the mountain range until you get to the end. You'll see the rectangular box in the centre of the screen fill up as you do so. Tap the white circle again to finish.

Make sure you stand in one spot, the panoramic photos don't work if you walk along with it.

## Recording Video

You can record video using the camera app. Select 'video' from the list on the bottom right of your screen.

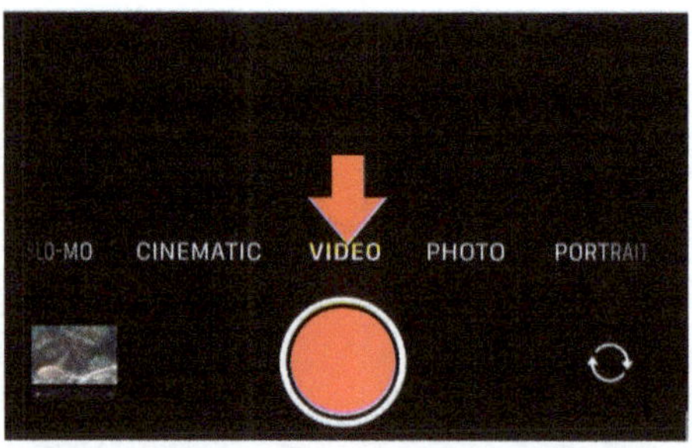

To take the best looking video, use your iPhone in a horizontal orientation as shown below.

Tap the red circle icon on the right hand side of the screen to start recording.

Tap on any part of the screen to focus on that point during the video.

Use a pinch & spread gesture to zoom in and out. Tap the red circle icon on the right hand side to stop recording. Try slo-mo and time-lapse and see what happens.

## Cinematic

In cinematic mode, you can create focus shifts from one object to another. For example, shift the focus from an object in the distance to an object closer by. Start recording, then tap on the object to focus.

Then tap on the object you want the focus to shift to.

Double tap your finger on the subject to enable auto focus tracking lock. This is useful for keeping fast moving objects in focus

## Slomo

Slow motion clips are a great way to capture fast moving objects in a scene and you can create some pretty spectacular shots. Here are the kids running in slow motion.

You can select the portion of a video that appears in slow motion. To do this, tap the preview thumbnail on the bottom left, then tap 'edit' on the bottom right.

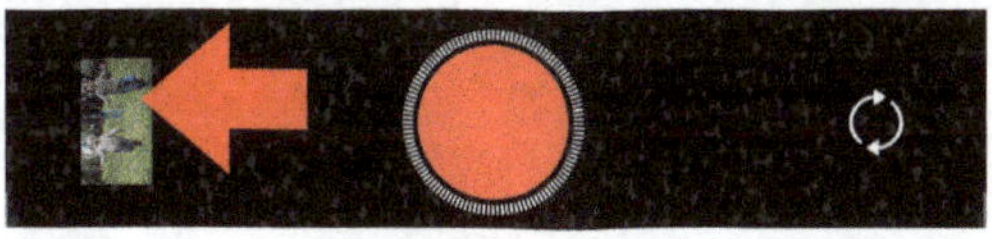

To select the portion of the video you want to appear in slow motion, tap and drag the start and end markers in the video time line along the bottom of the screen.

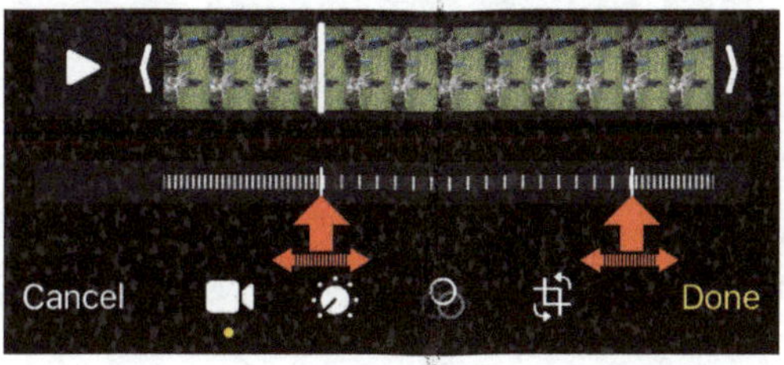


### Time Lapse

Time lapse video involves capturing a scene over a long period of time. To begin select time lapse from the options. Frame the scene, tap the red button, then leave your iPhone to capture the shot.

## Live Photos

Live Photos capture 1.5 seconds of motion before and after the photo. This feature is only available on the iPhone 6s and later.

To take a live photo, from the Camera app, tap the Live Photo icon on the top right of the screen. This turns live photos on and off.

Make sure the icon doesn't have a line through it - this means live photos are turned off.

Tap the shutter button to take your Live Photo.

You'll find your live photos in the photos app. Tap on the photo thumbnail on the bottom left of the screen.

To see the live photo, tap and hold your finger on the photo.

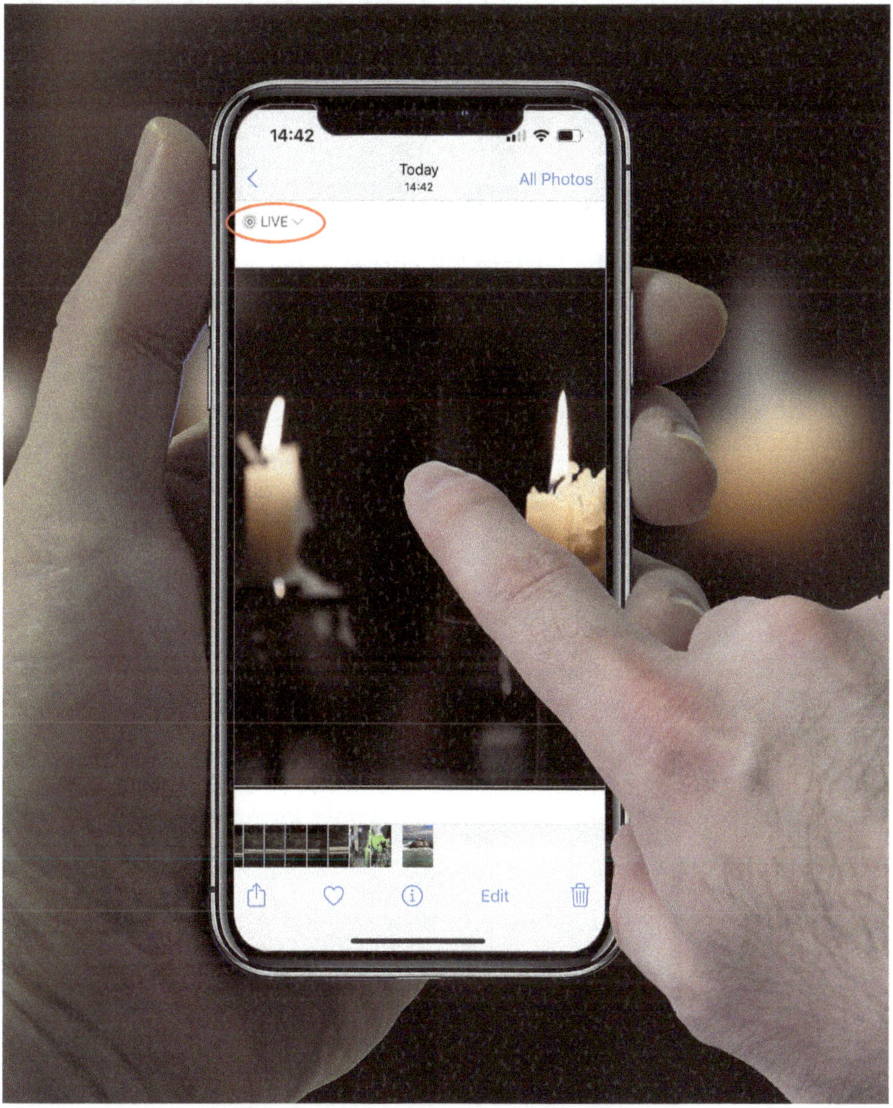


You can share photos via email, iMessage, Facetime in the usual way using the share icon on the bottom left.

## Share Photos on Social Media

First, you will need to have the appropriate app such as Facebook, Instagram, or Twitter installed. You can download these from the app store.

In this example I'm going to share a photograph on Facebook of the two girls. Once you have taken the photo, tap the small thumbnail in the bottom right hand corner.

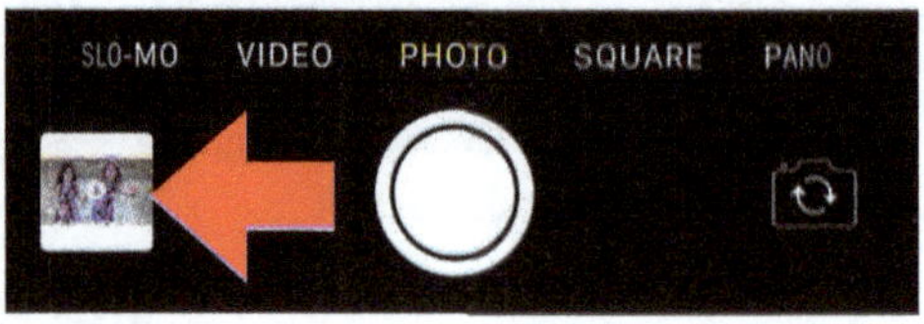


Tap the share icon in the bottom left corner.

From the share sheet, select the app you want to use to share your photo. Eg Facebook.

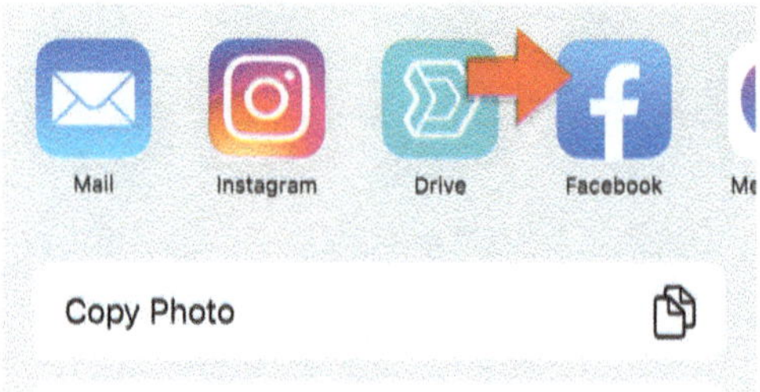


Type a message in your post, then hit 'post'.

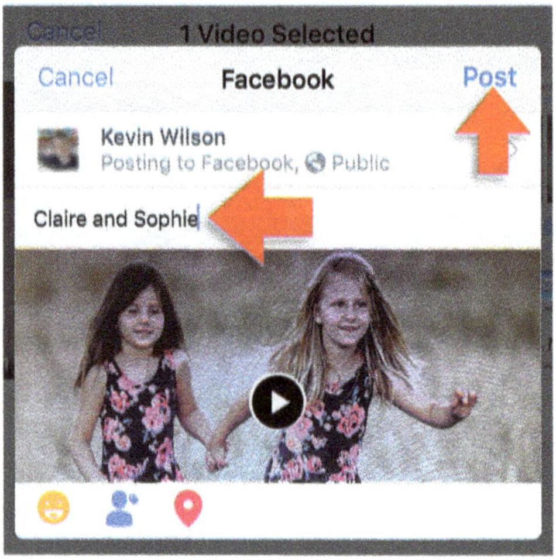


You can use the same procedure for Instagram, Twitter, email, iMessage, AirDrop, and any other social media app you use. Just select the icon from the icons list on the share sheet.

## Enhancing Video

You can use many of the same adjustments and filters for enhancing photos on your videos. Video editing supports all video formats captured on iPhone.

To edit a video, in the photos app select 'library' from the bottom panel, then tap on the video clip you want to adjust. If you've just taken a video with your phone, tap the thumbnail preview icon on the bottom left.

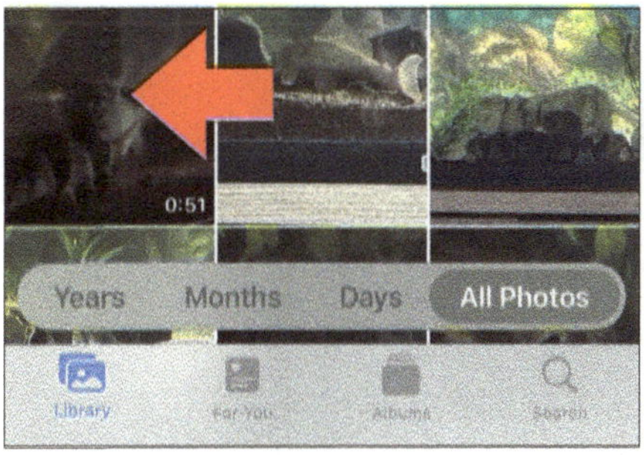

When your video opens up, tap 'edit' on the top right of the screen.

Tap the adjustment icon.

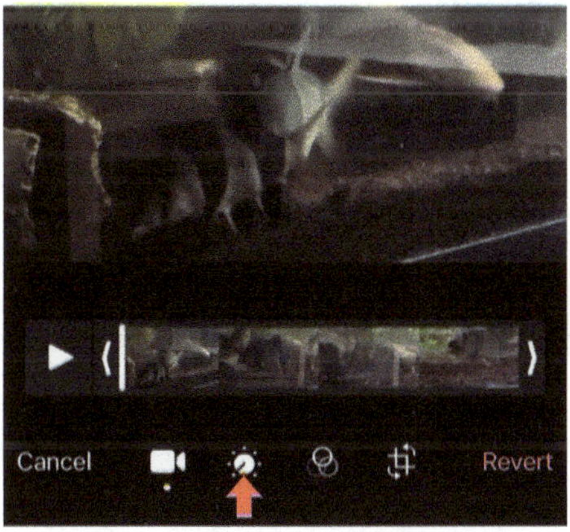


When the adjustment screen appears, you'll see three icons on the left hand side. On the bottom, you'll see some adjustment dials. These are the same as for photos. See page 306 for more info on how to adjust your images.

# Music App

To start the music app, tap the icon on your home screen.

Once music app has loaded you can see all the albums that are currently on your iPhone. Let's take a look at the main screen.

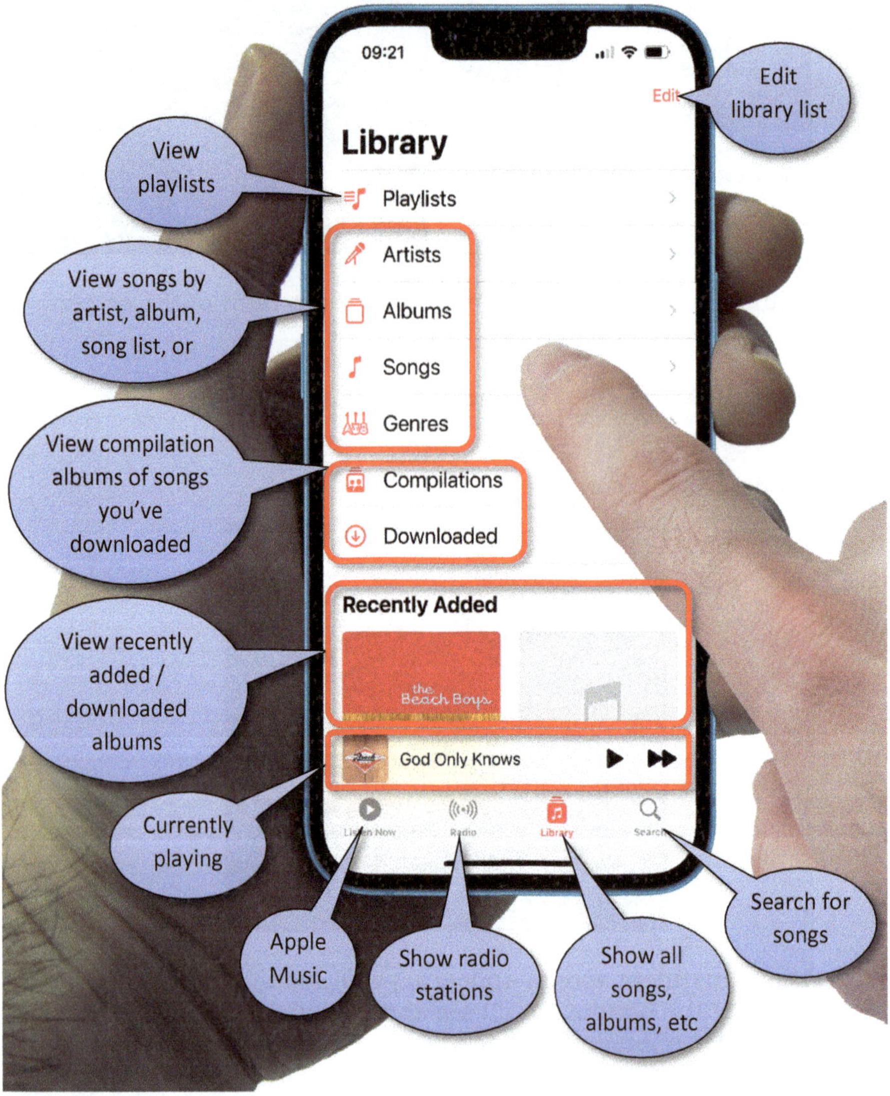

## Setting Up Apple Music Streaming

Apple Music is a music streaming service that allows you to stream music from the music library for a monthly subscription fee.

- £4.99 a month gives you full access to the music library and is only available for University/College students.
- £9.99 a month gets you full access to the music library and many radio stations available.
- £14.99 a month gets you full access to the music library and radio stations and allows up to 6 people to sign in and listen to their music. This is ideal for families.

To sign up, open the Music App, then from the bottom panel select 'listen now'.

To get started with the individual plant, tap 'try for free'.

Authorise the payment using FaceID (or *enter your Apple ID username and password, or confirm with Touch ID, if you have this enabled, by placing your finger on the home button).*

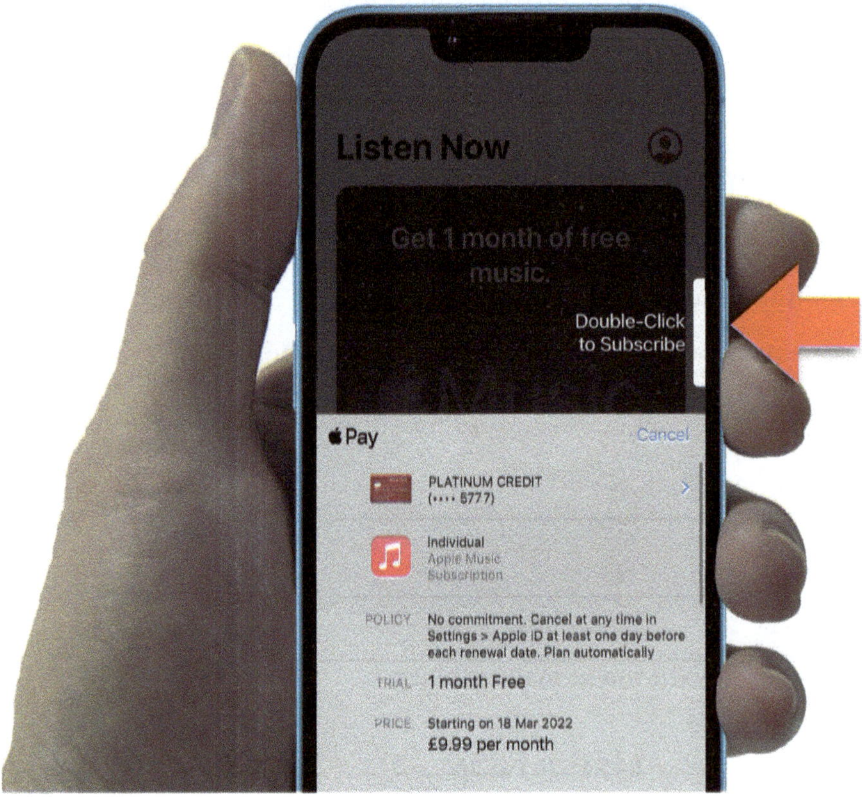


Tap the genres you like. Tap 'next' when you're done on the top right.

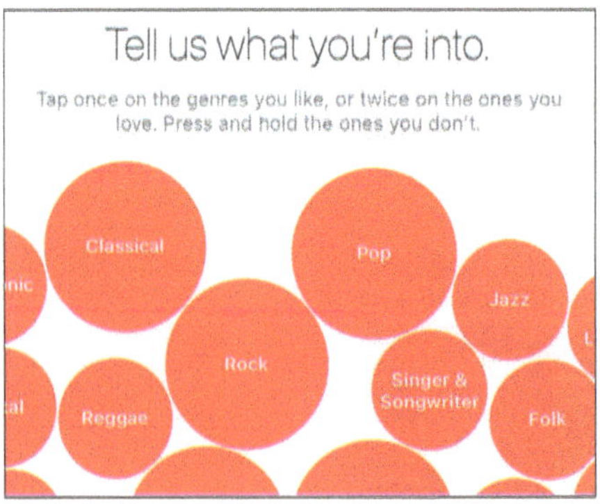

This gives Apple Music an idea of what kind of music you're into, so it can show you more music, albums and artists that you're interested in.

Once you've done that, you'll land on the Apple Music main screen.

If you want to cancel the trial, or change to a different subscription such as student or family, tap the profile icon on the top right.

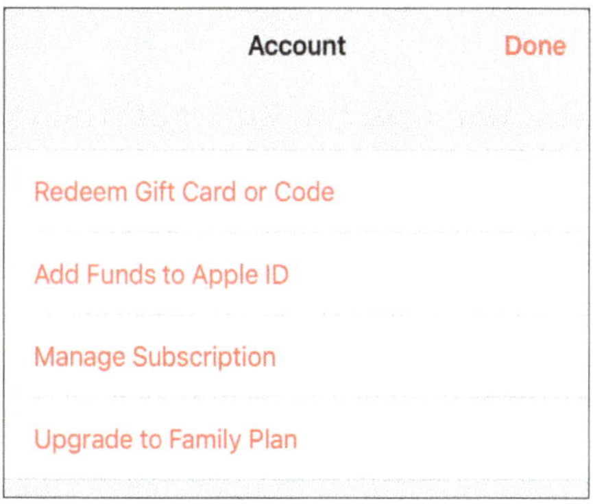


Tap 'manage subscription'.

Here at the top under the 'options' section, you can select a subscription plan.

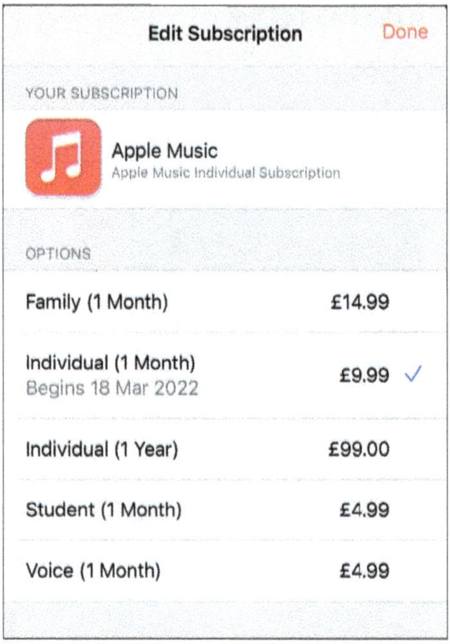


At the bottom, you can cancel the subscription if you want to.

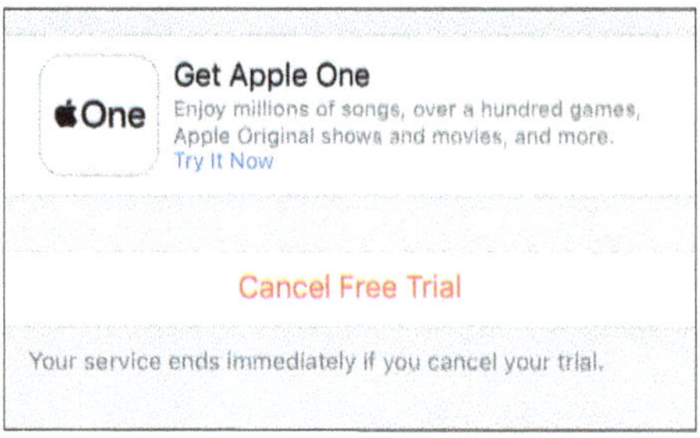


Tap 'done' on the top right when you're finished.

## Searching for Music

You can search for any artist, band or song you can think of. To do this, on the Music App's home screen, select 'search' from the sidebar on the bottom of the screen.

Type an artist's/album name into the search field at the top. Select the closest match from the search results.

Filter your search using the list along the top of the search results: 'artists', 'albums', 'songs'....

Tap on an album to open it up, or song name to play it.

Tap on a song in the album play list.

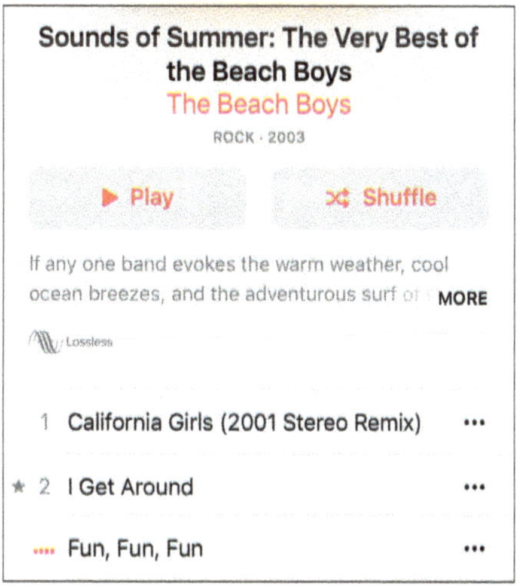


Tap the ... icon next to the song, then select 'add to library' to add it to your library.

The song will play. You'll see the title show up at the bottom of the screen. Here you can tap the pause icon to pause, etc. Tap the album cover to open it up in full.

You'll see the song open up in full.

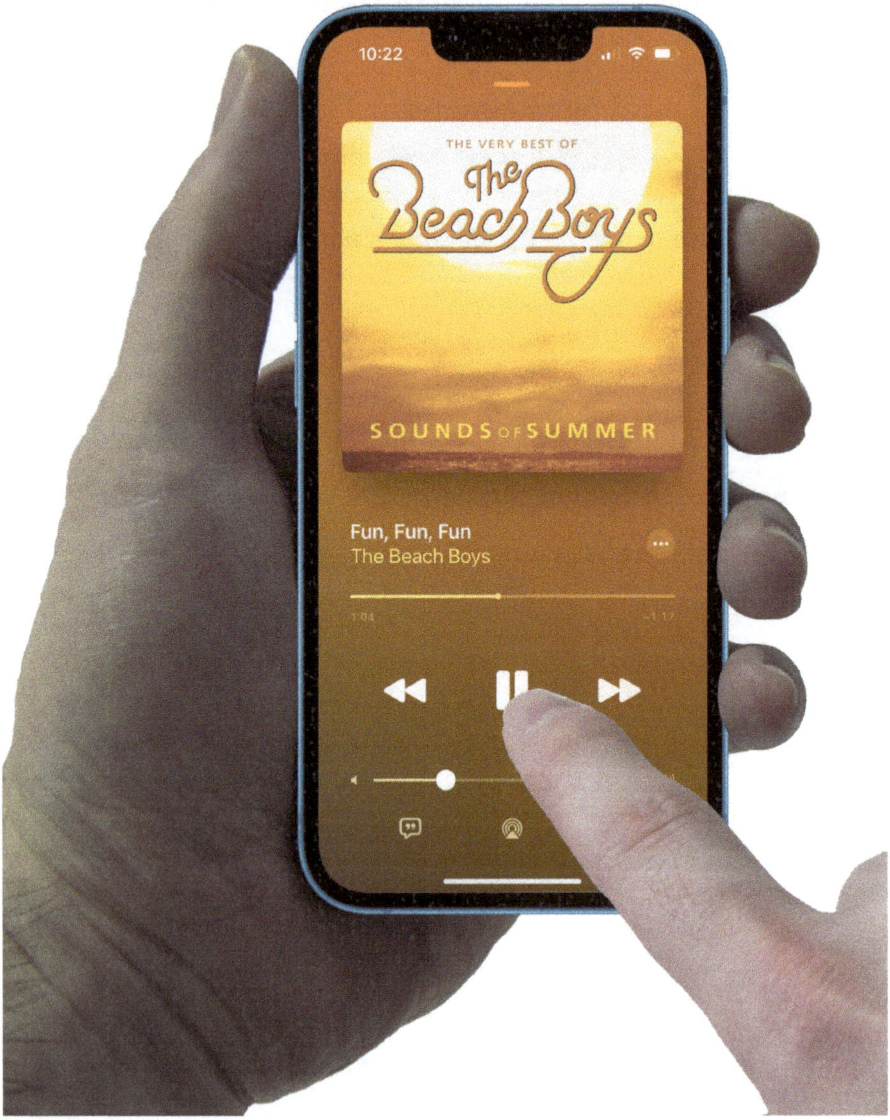

Here, you can find lyrics - just tap the lyrics icon on the bottom left of the screen.

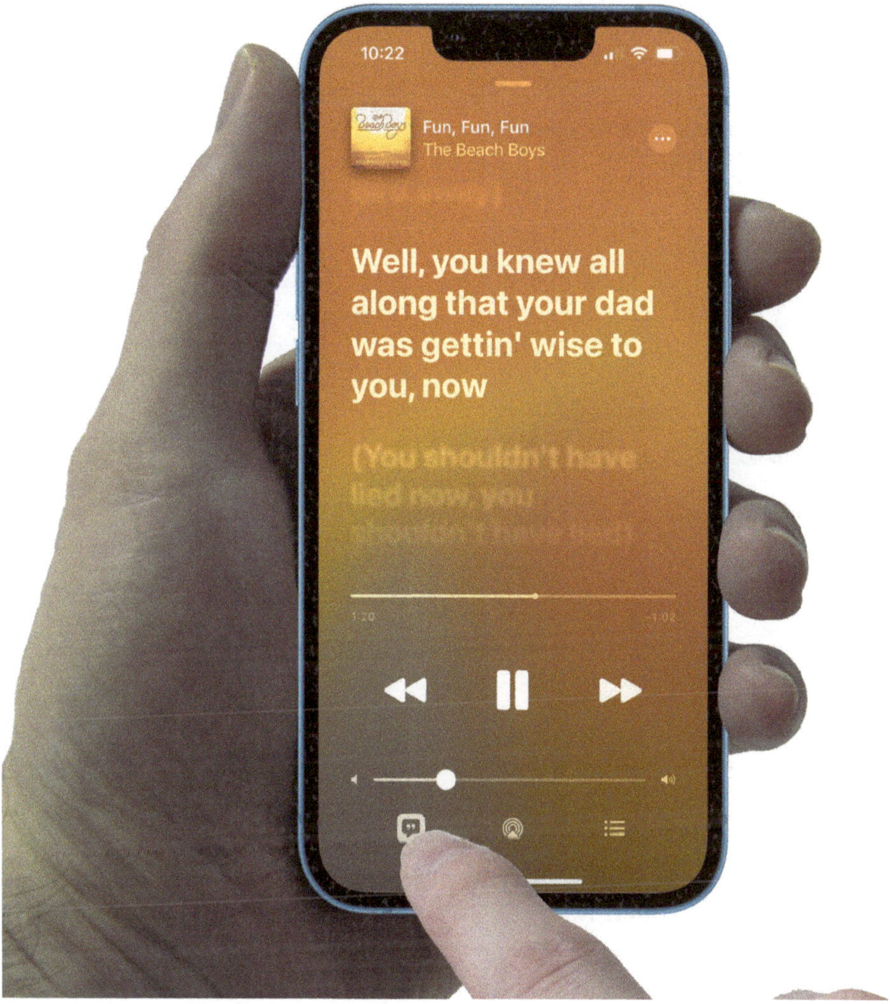


You can also cast the music to Apple TV or another Mac. Just tap the cast icon in the middle of the bottom panel, then select a device.

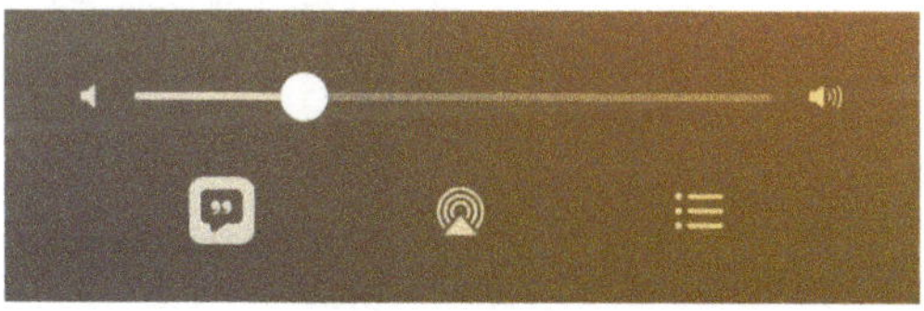

The icon on the bottom right, lists all the tracks in the album you've opened.

## Add to Library

You can start to create a library of your favourite music, so it's easy to find. To do this, tap the + sign next to the song you want to add to your library.

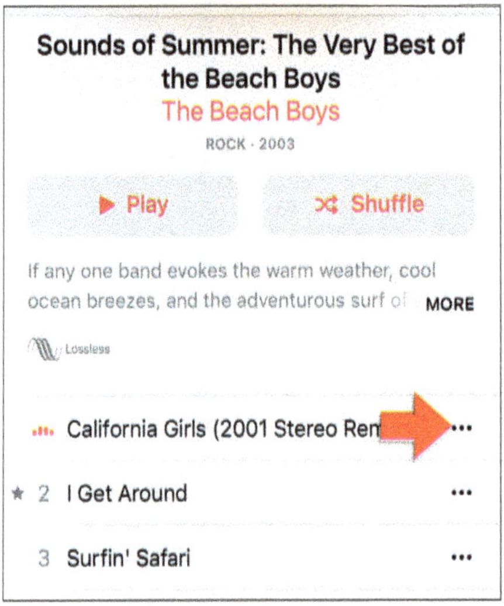


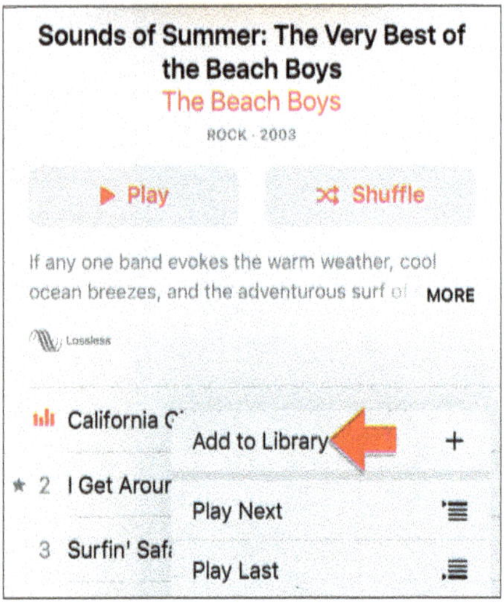


You can access your music library using the sidebar on the bottom of the screen.

To see the songs in your library, tap 'songs'. If you want to see albums, tap an albums to open it.

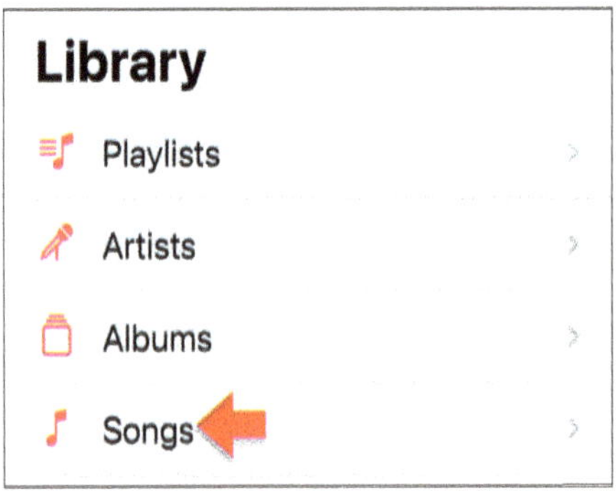

You'll see the songs you've added to your library. Tap on a track to play it.

## Creating Playlists

You can create playlists to play all your favourite tracks from any album or artist.

To add a track to a playlist, tap the three dots next to the track in your list of songs, then from the popup menu, select 'add to a playlist.

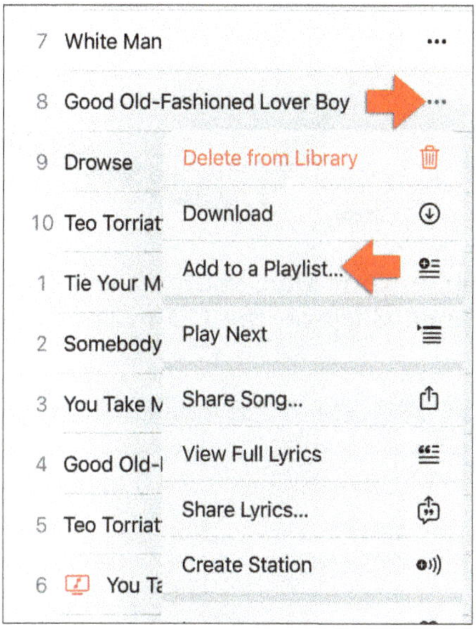


Select the playlist you want to add the track to, if it exists. Or tap 'new playlist' to add the track to a new playlist.

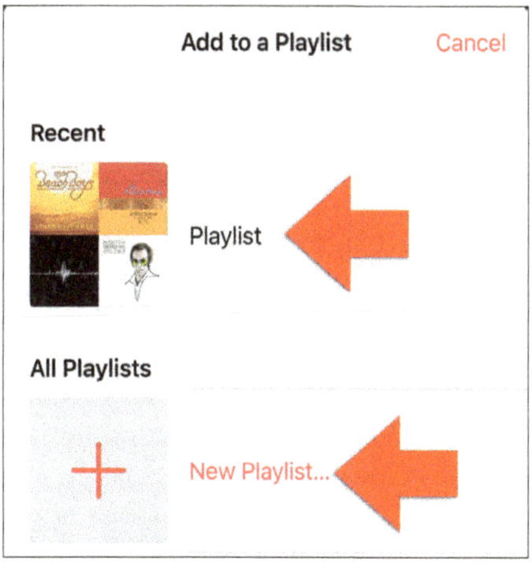


You'll find your playlists in your library. Tap 'library' on the panel along the bottom. Select 'playlists'.

## Importing CDs

Somewhat outdated technology nowadays, but if you still have audio CDs, you can import them. First you'll need an external CD drive. Plug the drive into a USB port on your Mac and insert a CD.

Open the music app on your Mac, your CD will appear under 'devices' on the left hand panel. Click on the CD to open. Click 'import CD' to begin.

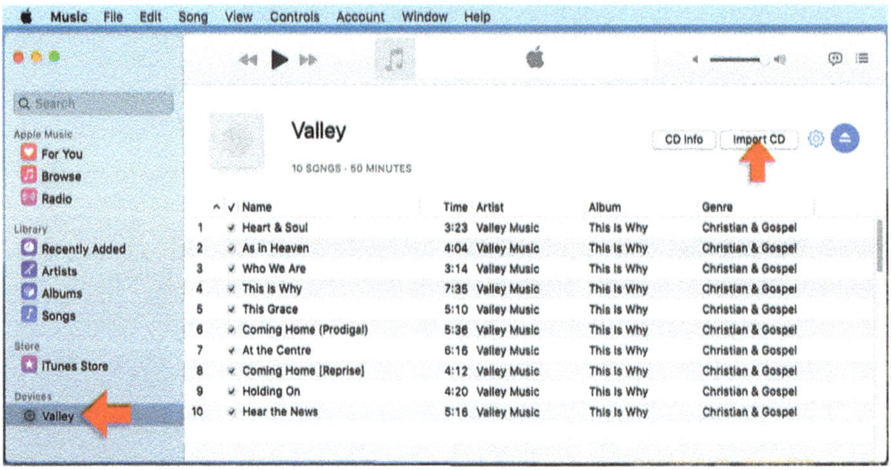


Click 'ok' on the 'import settings' popup.

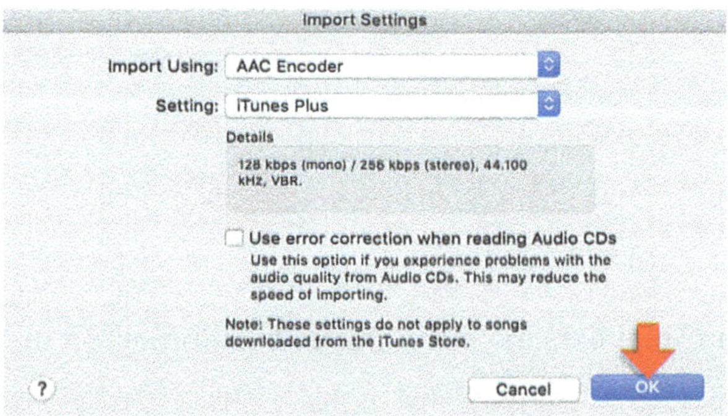

## Adding Tracks to your iPhone Manually

Tracks you download from the iTunes Store or stream from Apple Music will automatically synchronise across your devices. If you want to add music you've imported from a CD or other source you can add the tracks to your device. To do this, plug your iPhone into your Mac using the lightning to USB cable.

Open the music app on your Mac.

Select your iPhone from the left hand pane. Click 'trust' if prompted on your Mac and iPhone.

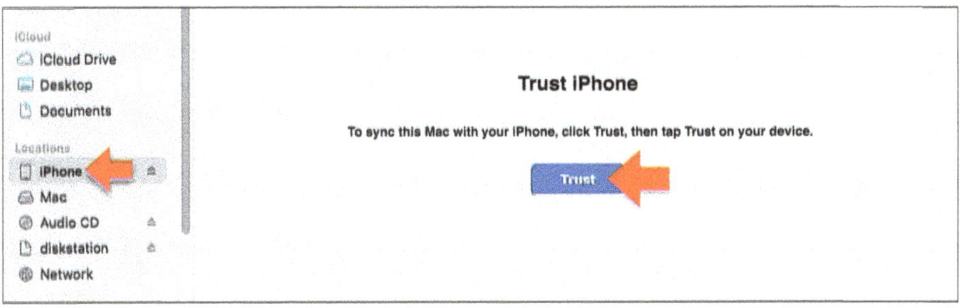

Select the tracks you want, then drag them to your iPhone under the devices section on the left hand side.

# Podcasts App

You can listen to all sorts of podcasts. To begin, tap the podcasts icon on your home screen.

Once the app starts, you can browse through the latest podcasts. Along the bottom of the screen you'll see a panel.

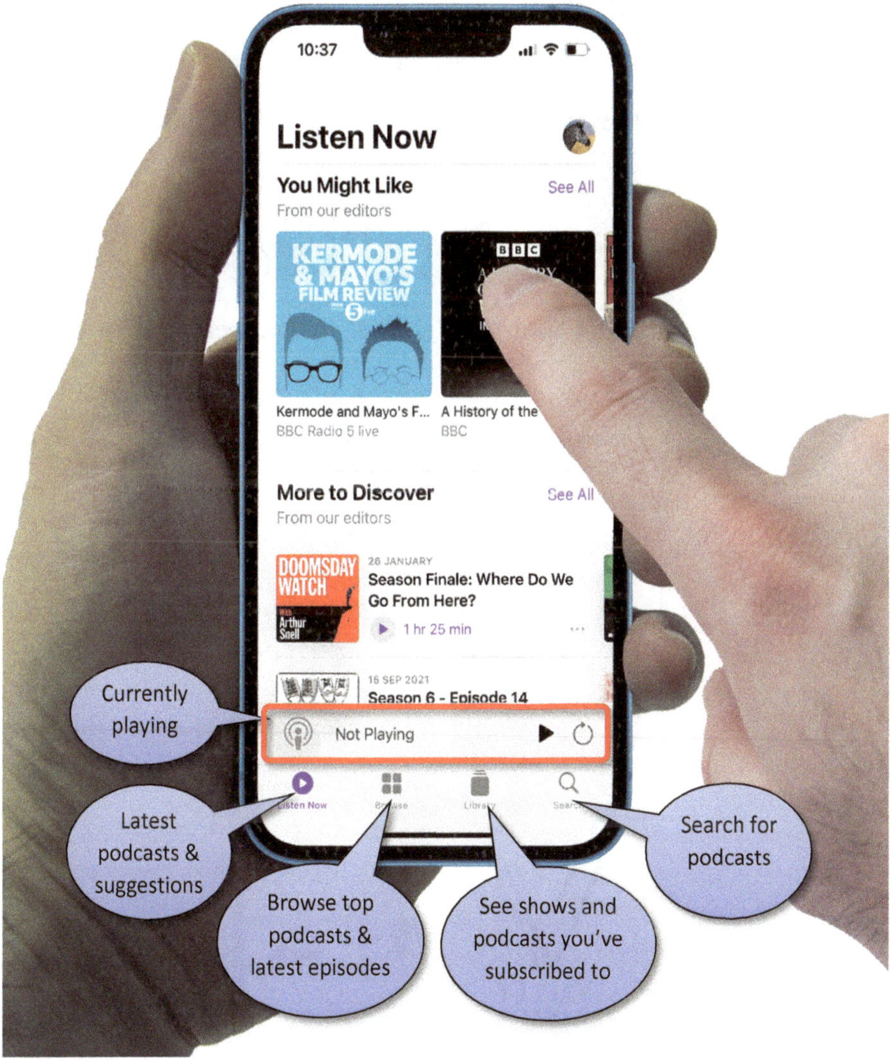

The best way to find your podcasts is to search for them. You can search for artist name, program name, or any area of interest. To search, tap the search icon on the panel along the bottom of the screen.

Type the podcast you're looking for in the search field at the top of the screen, the select the podcast you want from the results. *You can also tap through the categories underneath.*

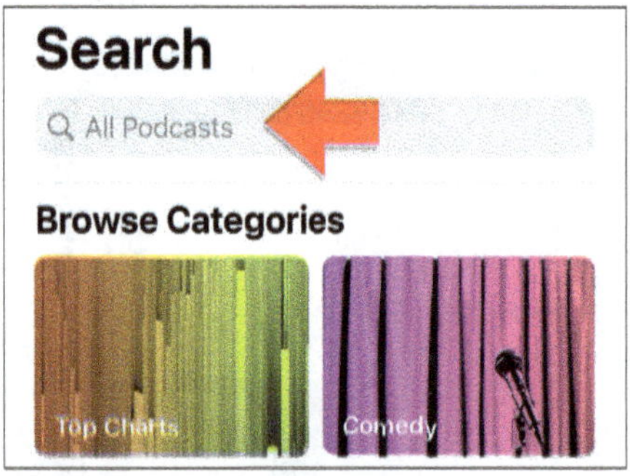


Select the closest match from the 'shows' that appear in the search results.

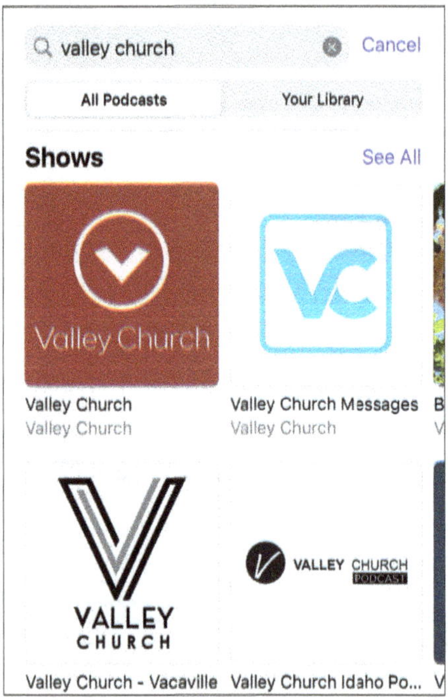

You'll land on the podcast's home page. From here, you can see the latest episodes. Scroll down to the bottom to see a list of all the podcast's published episodes.

To subscribe to the podcast, tap the plus icon on the top right of the screen.

You'll find all your subscribed podcasts in your library or on the 'listen now' tab. Tap the podcast cover to open it up.

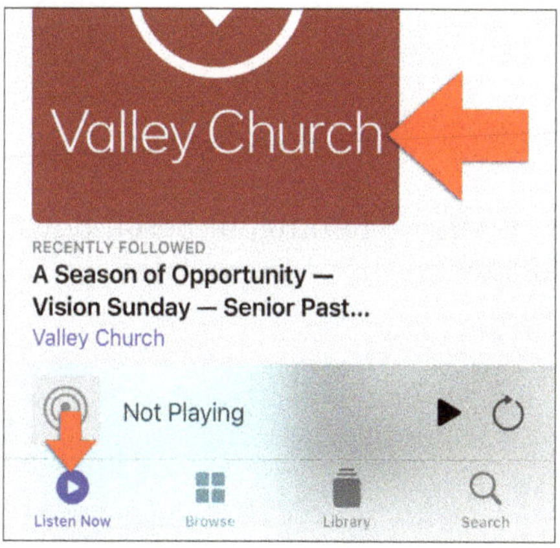


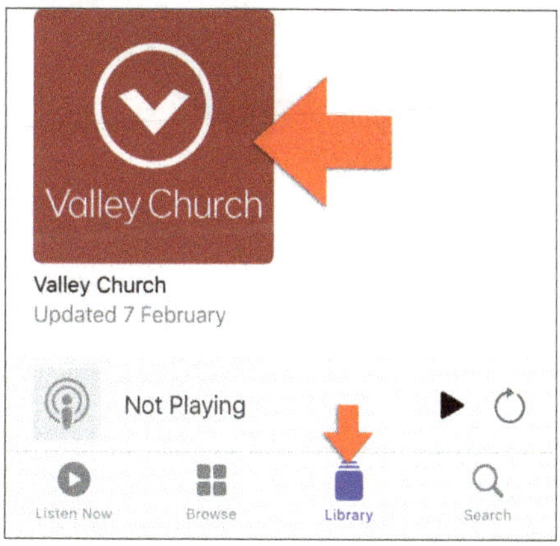

Tap the podcast icon to open the episodes. Tap play or resume at the top to play the latest episode.

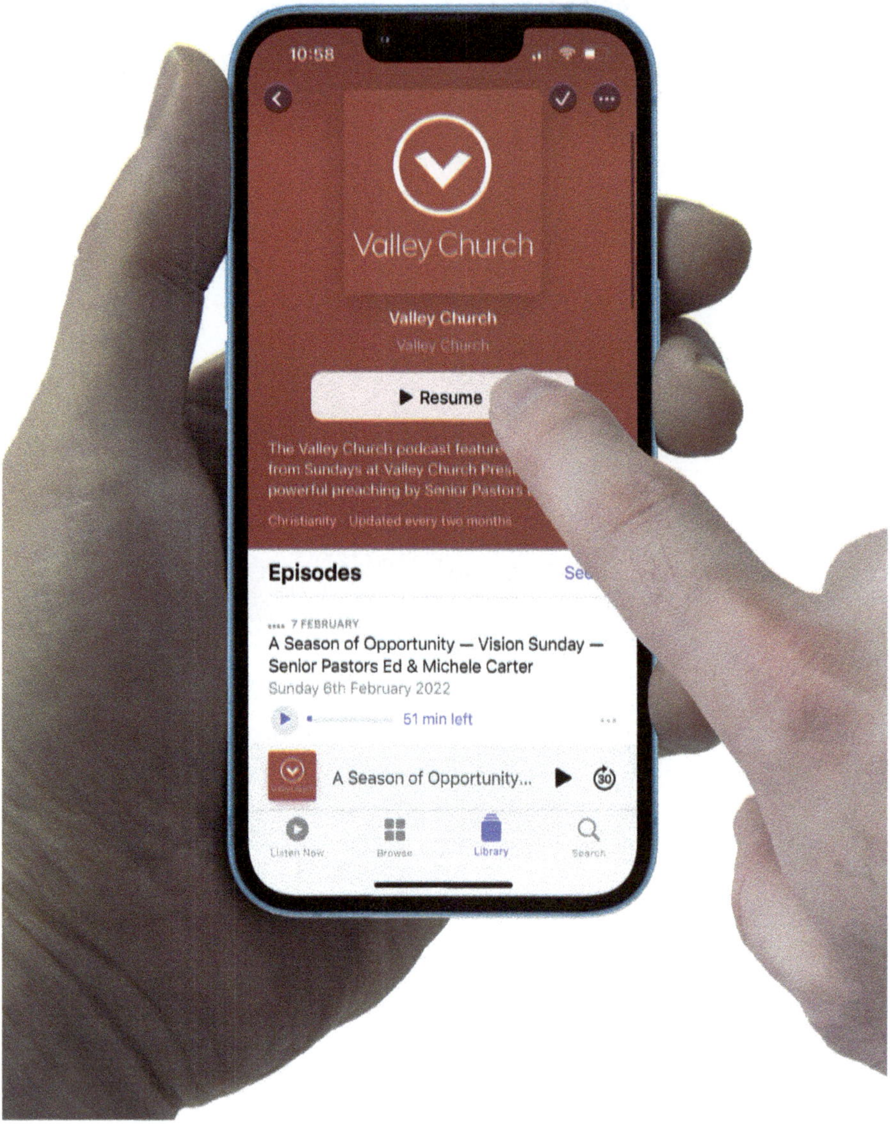


Tap the play icon next to the episode to start listening, or scroll down to see all available episodes for the podcast.

# iTunes Store

To access the iTunes Store, tap the 'iTunes Store' icon on your home screen.

Once the app has loaded you can browse through music, movies and tv shows - tap the icons across the bottom of the screen. You can also search for media - tap the search icon on the bottom right of the screen.

## Music

Within the music section of the iTunes Store, you can browse through the latest releases, charts and different genres. Tap 'genres' on the top left, then select your favourite type of music genre. Along the top, you can browse by 'featured' albums and artists, or see the 'charts'.

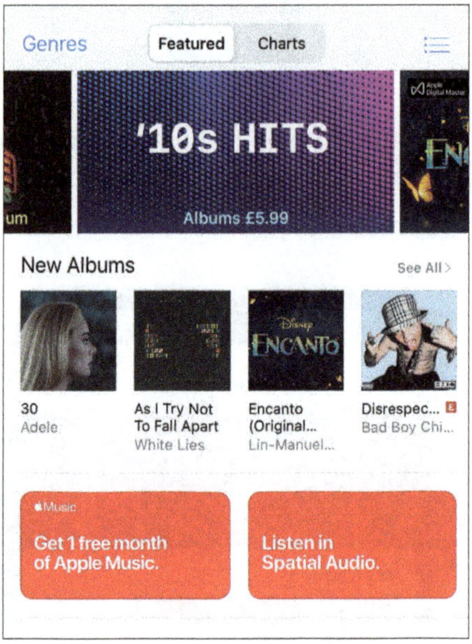


To search for your favourite tracks, artists and albums, tap the search icon on the bottom right.

Type your search into the field at the top. Then select the closest match from the suggestions.

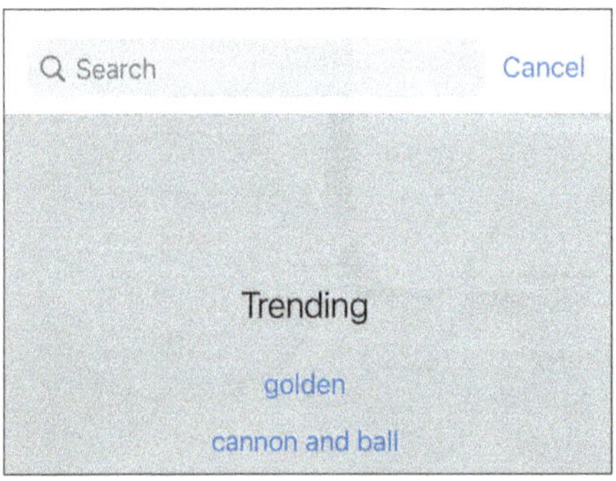


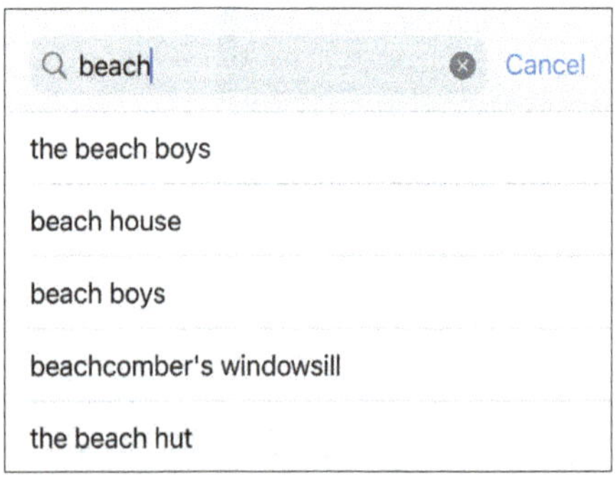

Along the top of the search results, you can view by song or album. Scroll up and down the list to see the songs and albums.

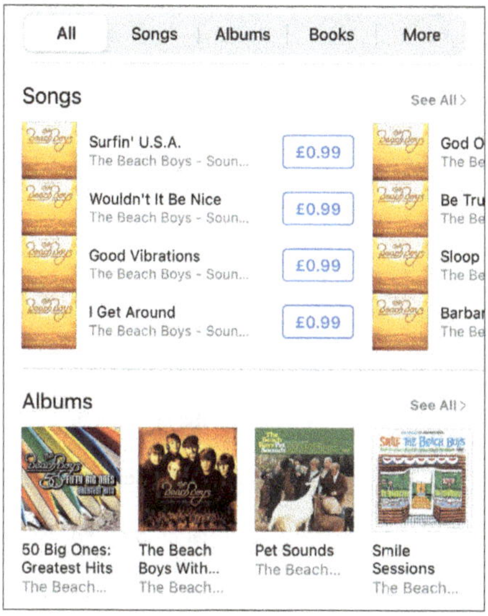


Tap on the price tag to download the song. Once the songs are downloaded you will find then in your recently added playlist in the music app.

## Movies & TV

You can stream movies and TV programmes directly to your iPhone from the iTunes Store. You can buy or rent what you want to watch. To to this, select 'movies' or 'TV programmes' from the panel along the bottom of the screen.

Browse through the selections. Tap 'genres' on the top left to change genre.

You can also search for a specific title using the search icon on the bottom right of the screen.

Type in the movie or TV show you want to watch. Select the closest match from the search suggestions.

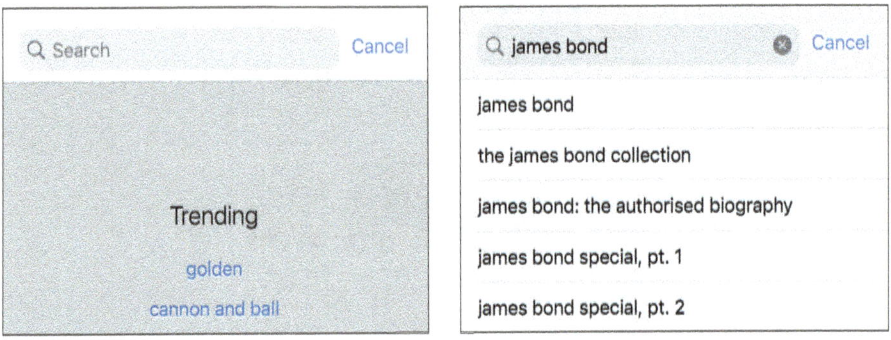


On the film details screen you'll be able to read details about the film, reviews and ratings. Tap 'rent' or 'buy'. Verify your purchase using the Touch ID, or your Apple ID username and password.

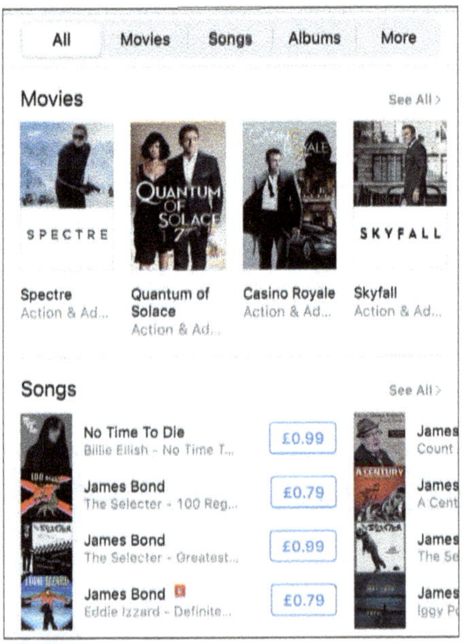


You'll find your downloaded films and TV programmes in the library section of the TV App.

# Apple TV App

Gearing up for Apple's new streaming service Apple TV+, the Apple TV App becomes your entertainment hub where you'll find all your purchased or rented films, music, and TV programmes. You'll find the app on your home screen.

Here, you'll be able to subscribe to Apple's streaming service and stream the latest TV Programmes and movies direct to your iPhone.

## Watch Now

When you first start the app, you'll land on the 'watch now' page.

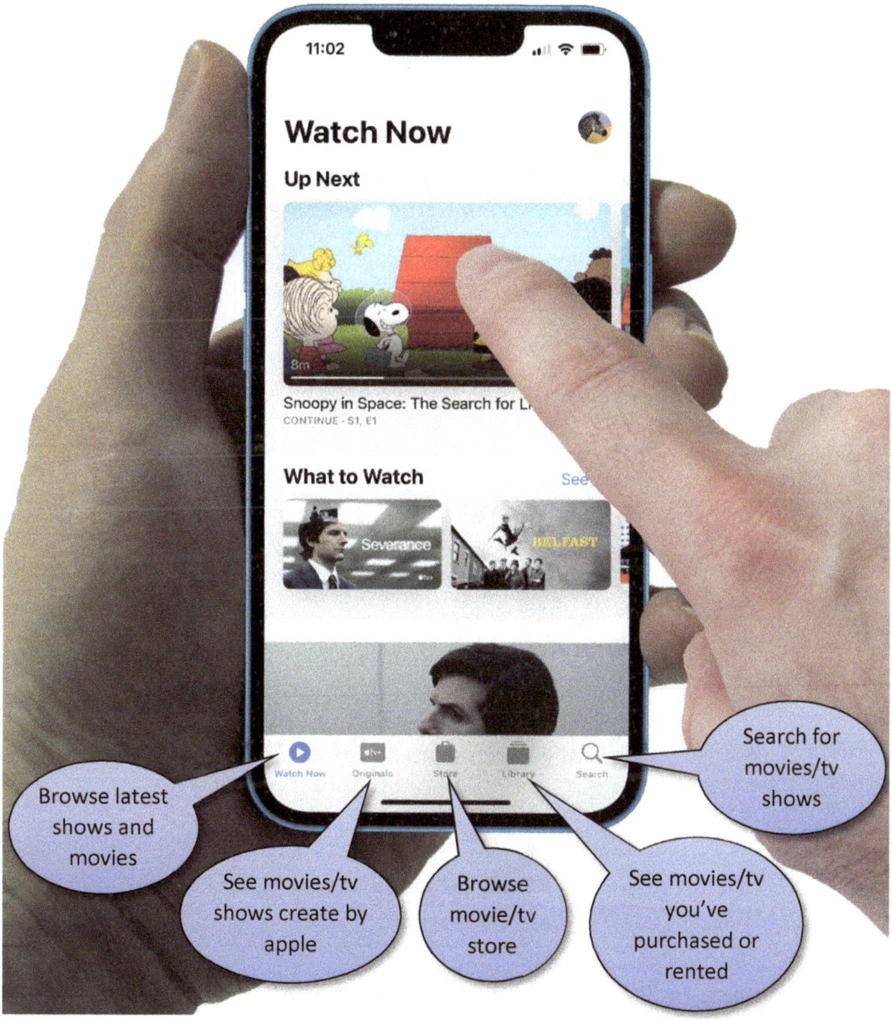

Along the top of the screen you can select movies, TV shows or kids shows.

Along the bottom of the screen you can browse with 'watch now', see your library of media you've purchased or rented, or search for a particular artists, actor, or title.

In the middle of the screen, you'll be able to scroll through current TV Shows and movie releases. Tap on the thumbnail icons to view details, or tap 'see more' on the top right to see more content.

## Library

Select 'library' from the panel along the bottom of the screen.

Select 'movies' to see movies you've rented or purchased, similarly select 'TV shows' if you've downloaded a TV show.

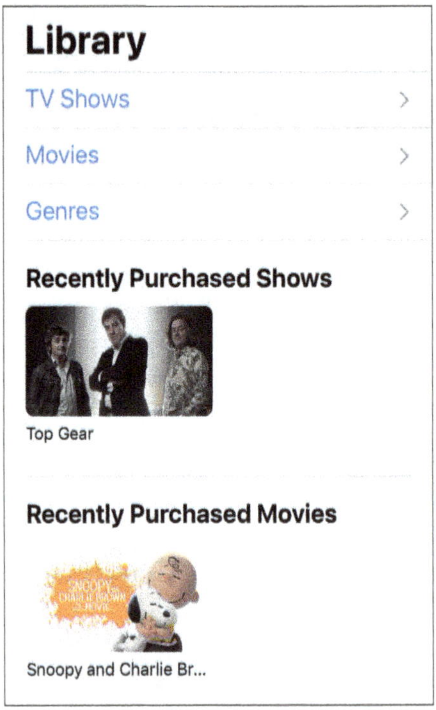


Tap on the film or TV programme to begin playback.

You'll see the film play back on your iPhone. It's best to view the film in horizontal mode as shown below.

You can also stream your movie to a compatible TV, Apple TV, or your Mac.

# Airplay to Apple TV

Airplay allows wireless streaming of audio and video data to an Apple TV, a Mac, or compatible receiver on your TV.

For this to work, both your iPhone and Apple TV will need to be on the same WiFi network. This is usually the case in most homes.

To mirror your iPhone, play the film or movie, then tap the cast icon on the bottom right edge of your screen.

Select the device you want to cast the video to.

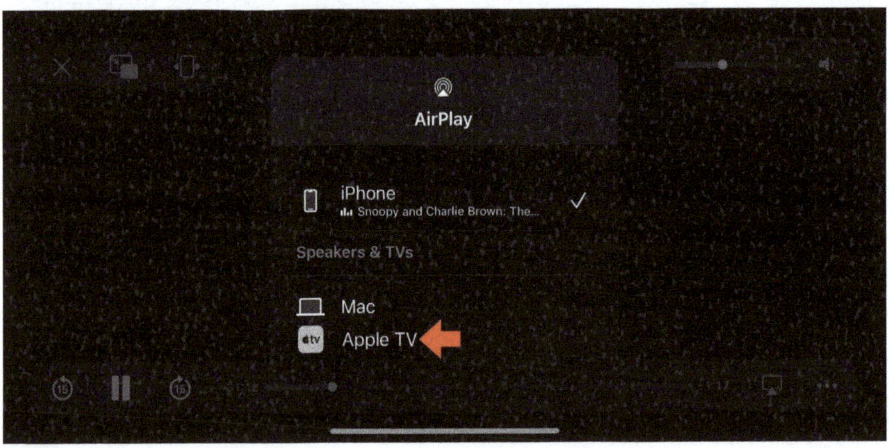

# Airplay to your Mac

You can stream music and video from an iPhone to your Mac. To do this, open a video or music track.

Tap the 'airplay' icon at the bottom left of the screen. On the music app, the icon looks like the image below on the left. In the TV app it looks like the image below on the right.

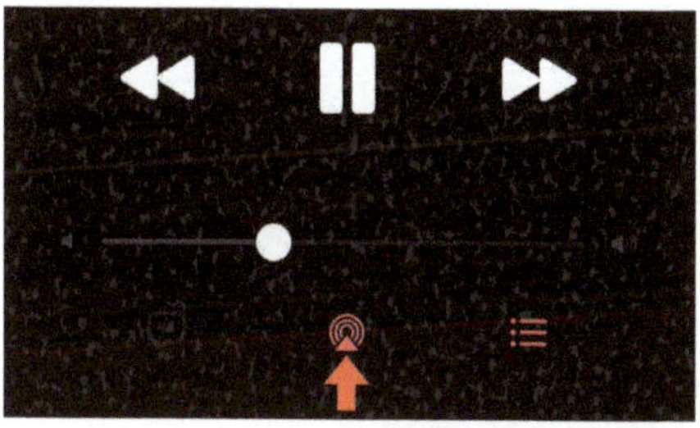

Select your Mac from the popup menu.

You'll hear the media play on your Mac.

## Setup Airplay on your Mac

This feature turns your Mac into an AirPlay receiver. This means you can stream music and video from an iPhone or iPhone to your Mac.

To activate 'AirPlay to Mac', on your Mac, open the system preferences

Select 'sharing' from the system preferences window.

Click the lock icon on the bottom left, then enter your mac username and password.

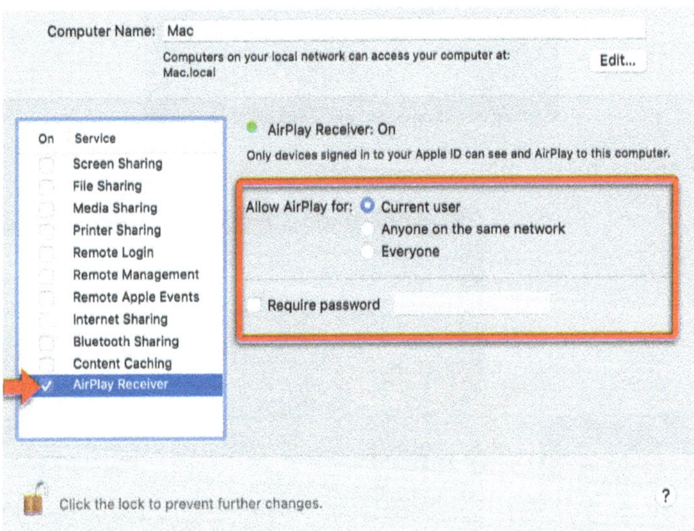


Select 'airplay receiver'. Then select who you want to allow access. Current user is your own Apple ID. Selecting 'anyone on the same network' will allow anyone connected to the same WiFi network to stream media. Selecting 'everyone' will allow anyone to stream media. You can also set a password.

AirPlay will stream from any iPhone running iOS 15 or later. This feature works on all Macs released in 2018 or later.

# Document Scanner

Within the Notes App, you can scan documents and convert them. From the Notes App, open a new note, tap the camera icon on the bottom right of your screen, or on the top of the on-screen keyboard.

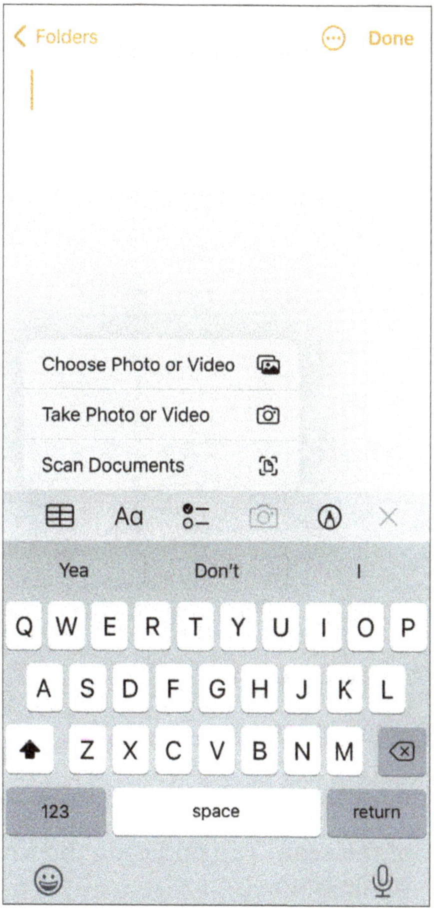


Tap 'manual' on the right hand side, this is so you can take a photo of each of your pages and gives you more control than auto mode.

Line up the document in the window as shown below, make sure the yellow box covers the whole document.

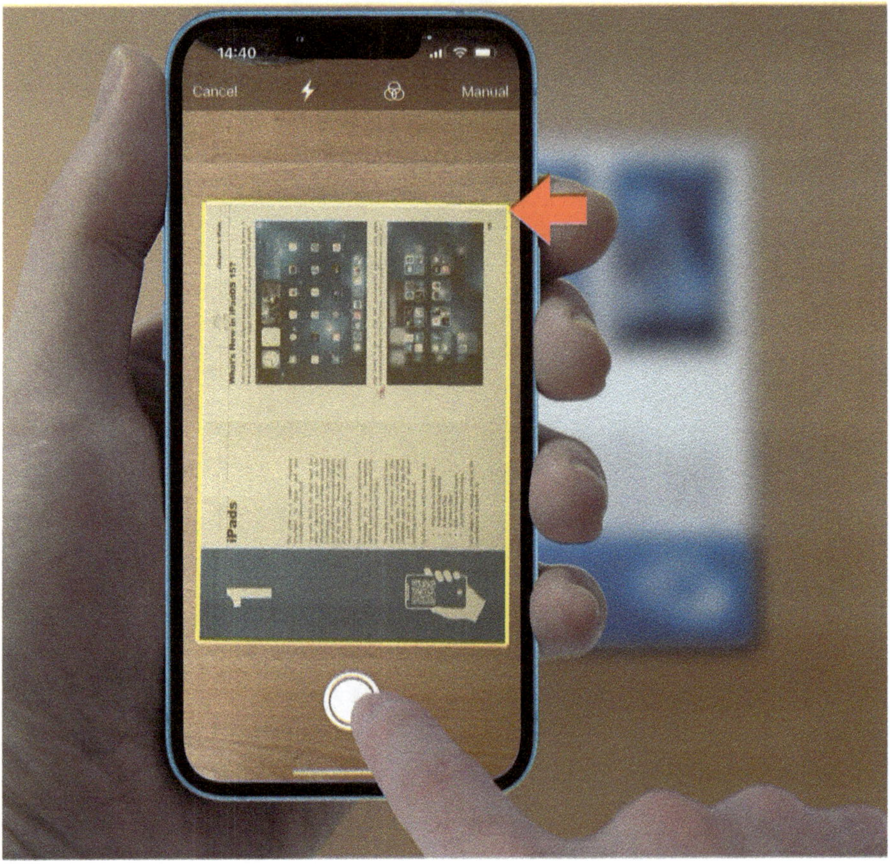


Tap the white button on the right hand side to 'scan the document'.

You'll see a preview of the scan. Tap and drag the white markers if they are not around the whole scan.

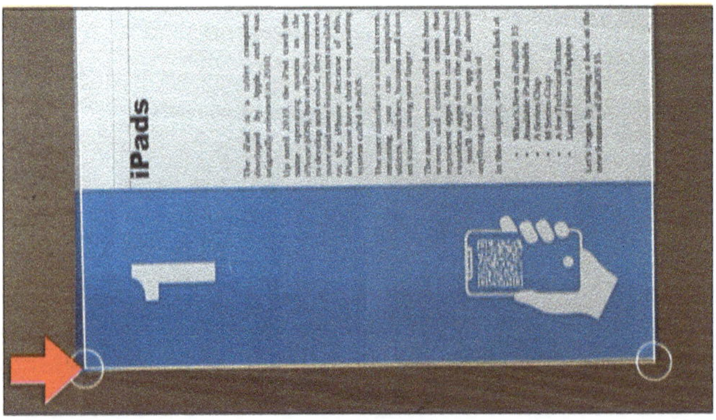

If you're happy with the scan, tap 'keep scan'. If it didn't scan propery, tap 'retake'.

If you have more pages, repeat the process and 'scan' them as well using the white button. Once you have 'scanned' all your pages, tap 'save' on the bottom right corner.

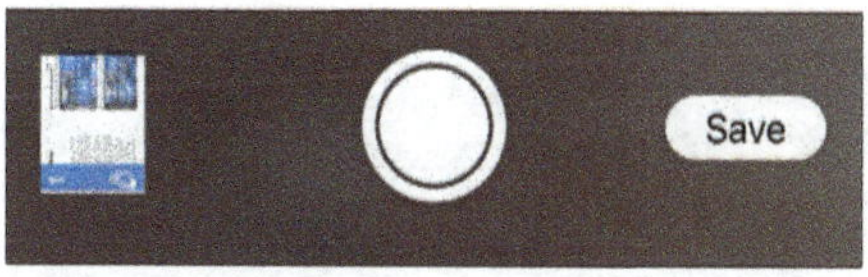


The pages will be added to your note. Tap on the thumbnail to open it up full screen.

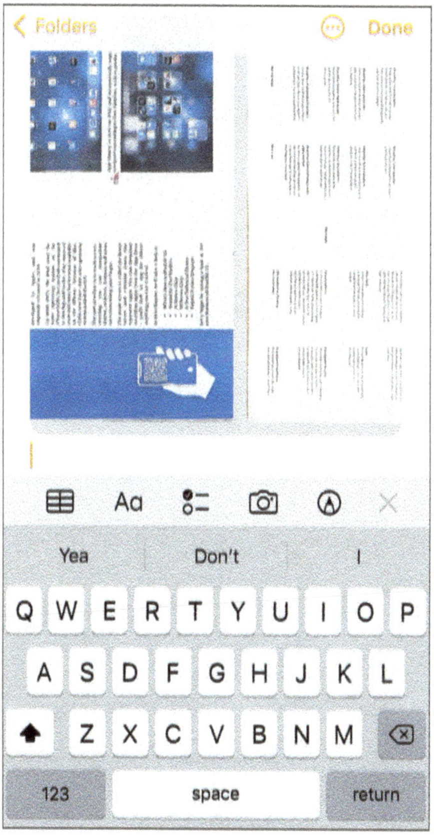


Now you can send the document via email, save it as a PDF, print it or write directly onto the scan with markup.

# QR Code Scanner

A QR code (or quick response code) is a 2D bar code used to provide easy access to information through your iPhone. This could be a link to a website, a pay code and so on. These codes are usually printed on signs, flyers, and other printed material.

To scan a QR code, open your camera app, point it at a QR code, tap the code on the screen to focus.

When the camera reads the code, you'll see a prompt under the code telling you what the code is and where it links to.

You also see a QR code icon on the bottom right of the screen. You can tap this to share the code, copy the code's link, add the site to your reading list or open the code.

Tap the code to go to the website or execute the code.

# 7

# iPhone Accessories

There are thousands of different accessories available for the iPhone and you can buy them from a number of different manufacturers, not only Apple.

You can buy various accessories from Apple, as well as universal bluetooth accessories such as cases, and headphones.

You just need to keep in mind the size and model of your iPhone when shopping for accessories. Make sure it will fit the model you have - iPhone mini, air, pro, etc.

In this chapter we'll take a look at

- Covers & Stands
- AirPods
- Bluetooth Headphones
- Wired Headphones

Take a look at the video resources

`elluminetpress.com/using-iphone`

# Covers

A cover is a must. You can get hundreds of different types. The covers I find best are the ones that cover the back and screen allowing easy access to the phone's features without getting in the way. Make sure you get the correct cover for your phone as these are often moulded to the phone's size and shape.

The edges are usually cut out to allow access to the phone's buttons

# Stands

You can also get stands that allow you to stand your iPhone up making it great for watching movies.

# Power Chargers

You can get a whole range of chargers from all different manufacturers. The most useful ones I have found are the ones that have a powered USB port on the side, that allows you to plug in your iPhone and any other tablet for that matter, using the cable that came with it.

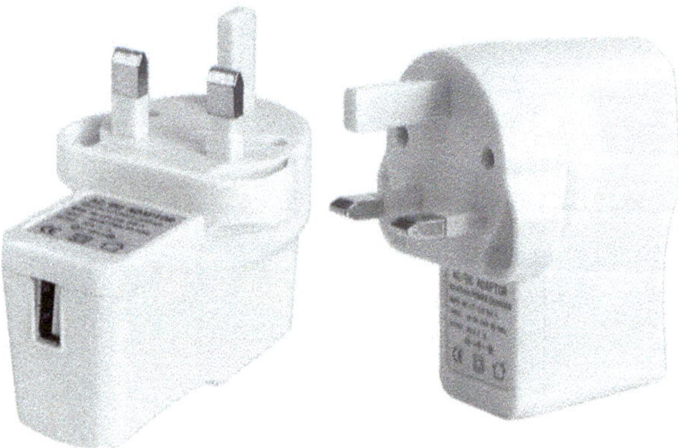

Your iPhone will come with a charger so you won't need to buy one unless you need a replacement.

# AirPods

AirPods are essentially bluetooth headphones. There are two types of AirPods. The AirPods (shown below left) and AirPod Pro (shown below right).

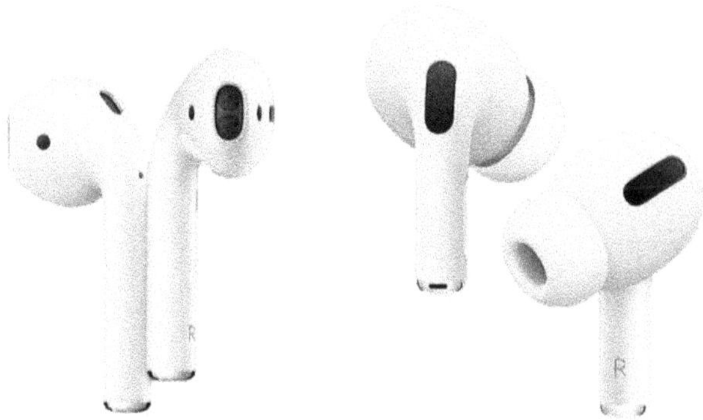

AirPods do have some additional features over other bluetooth headphones. For example, if you're listening to music on your iPhone, you can pick up your iPhone to watch a TV show and the AirPods will connect automatically. AirPods Pro also have noise cancelling features, have custom eartips and are water resistant.

## Setup

Open the case with your AirPods inside, then place them next to your iPhone. You'll see a prompt on your iPhone asking you to connect. Tap 'connect'.

Run through the tips and settings on screen. Tap 'done' when you're finished.

## Charge

To charge your AirPods, put them in the case and close the lid. Plug your cable from your charger into the power port on the bottom of the case.

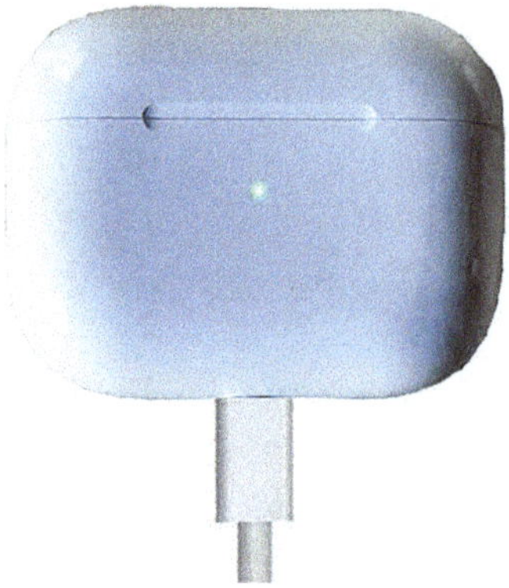

## AirPod Controls

You can control various functions using the stem of your AirPod.

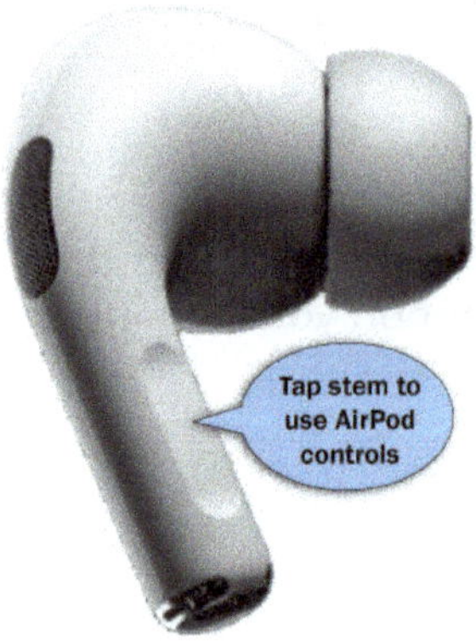


Here are the controls for the standard AirPods.

- Double-tap to play, skip forward, or answer a phone call.

The AirPod Pro has some additional controls:

- Tap once to play, pause, or answer a phone call
- Tap twice to skip forward
- Tap three times to skip back
- Tap and hold to switch between Active Noise Cancellation and Transparency mode

# Bluetooth Headphones

You can use any bluetooth headphones on your iPhone. First, you need to put your headphones in to pairing mode. You'll need to refer to the device's instructions to find specific details on how to do this. On most devices, press and hold the pairing button until the status light starts flashing. See "Bluetooth" on page 72.

# Wired Headphones

iPhones no longer come with a 3.5mm (1/8") headphone jacks. If you want to connect wired headphones or speakers, you'll need an adapter. For the iPhone you'll need a Lightning to 3.5mm headphone jack adapter such as the one shown below.

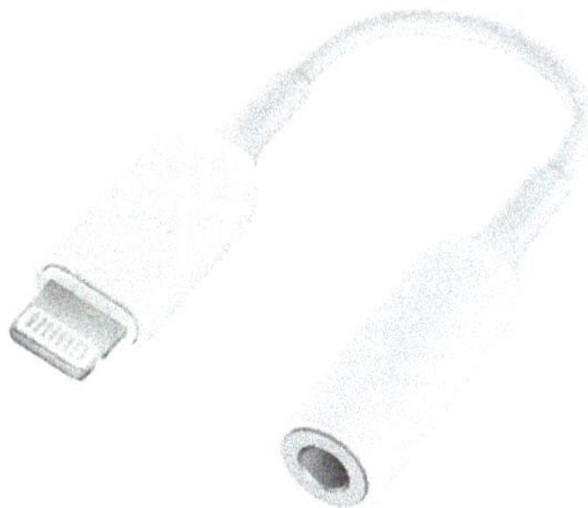

Plug one end into the port on the bottom of your iPhone, then plug the headphones into the adapter.

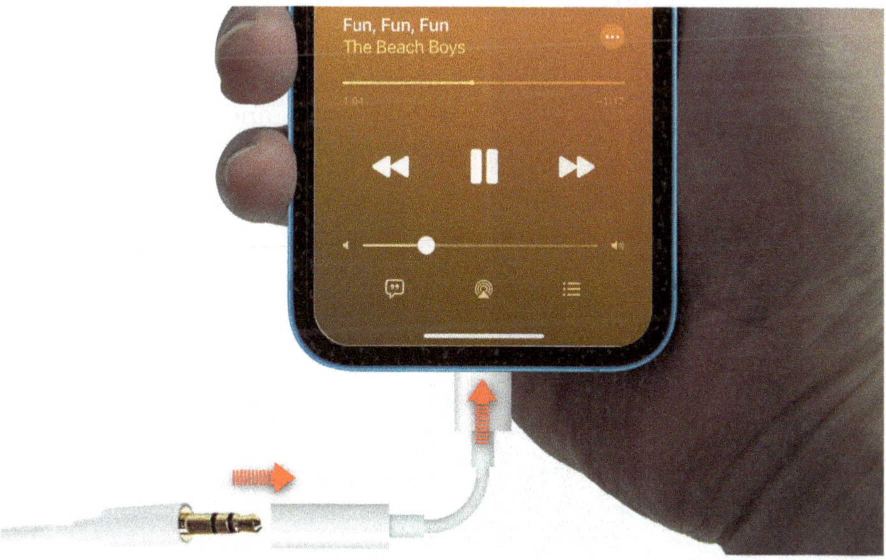

# 8 Maintaining your iPhone

New iPhones will ship with iOS, but if you can upgrade a previous model. iOS will install on the following devices.

- iPhone Backups
- System Updates
- App Updates
- Deleting Apps
- iPhone Storage Maintenance
- iPhone Recovery
- Connecting to a Computer
- Erase iPhone

Before upgrading, make sure you have some time where you don't need to use your iPhone as it will be temporarily inoperative while the installation takes place.

For this chapter, take a look at the maintenance section. Open your web browser and navigate to the following site

`elluminetpress.com/iphone-sys`

# iPhone Backups

You can backup your settings, apps and files to your iCloud account. Go to Settings, Tap on your account name at the top.

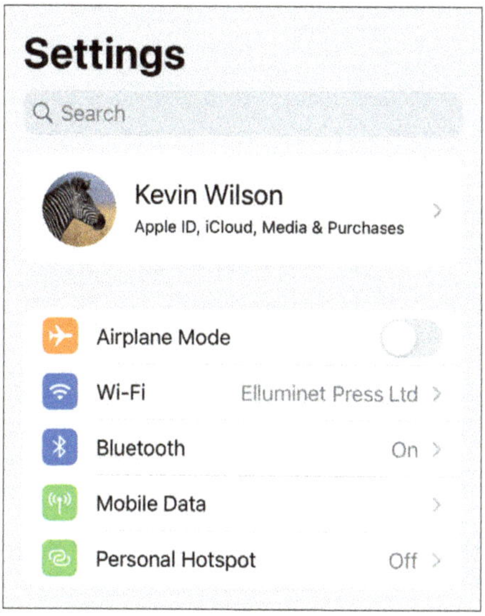


Select 'iCloud', then sign in if you haven't already done so.

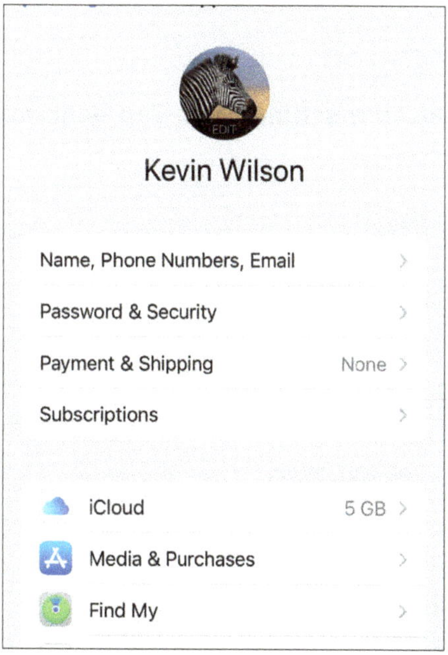


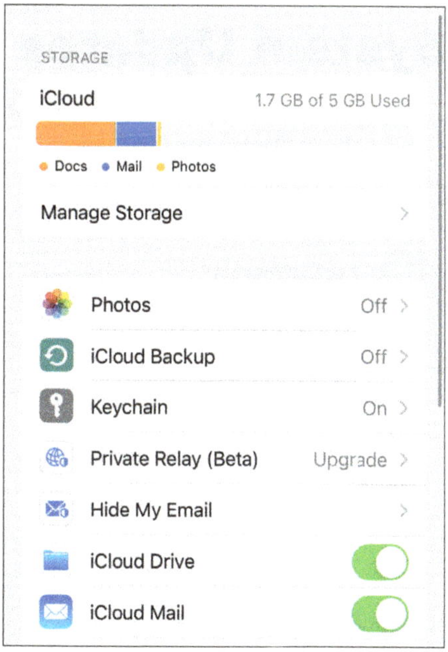


Select 'iCloud Backup'.

Turn on iCloud Backup if it isn't already.

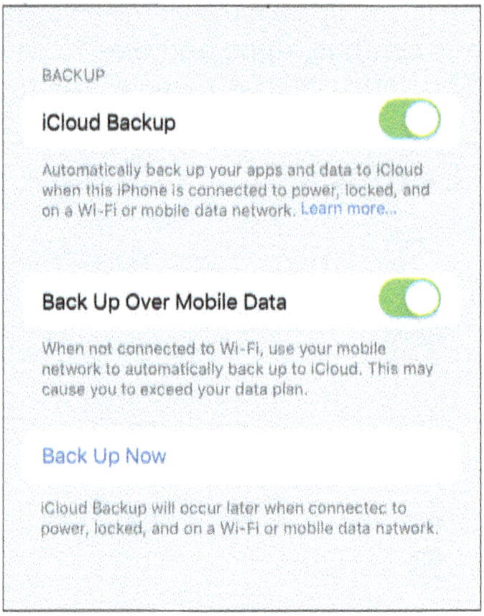


Turn off 'backup over mobile data' to restrict backups to only run when you're connected to WiFi

Tap 'Back Up Now' to start backing up your data.

# System Updates

To run the update, on your iPhone open your settings app. Tap 'general' then select 'Software Update'.

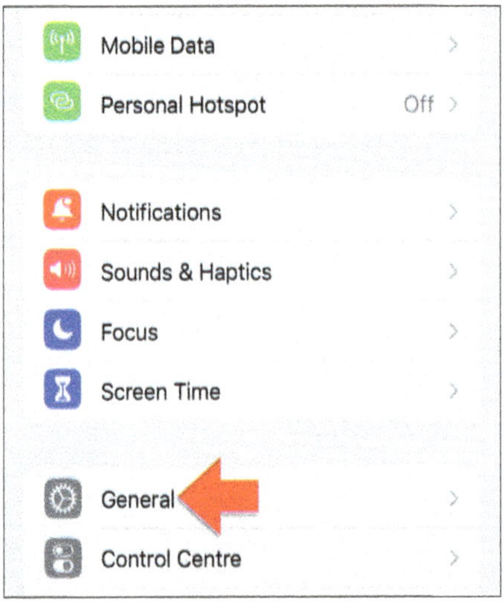


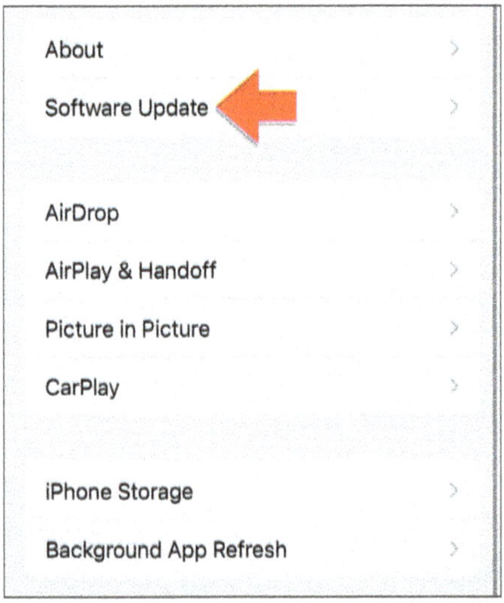

Make sure your device is connected to both Wi-Fi and a power supply, then tap 'download and install' to begin. If you want your iPhone to automatically take care of system updates for you, tap 'automatic updates' and turn the option on.

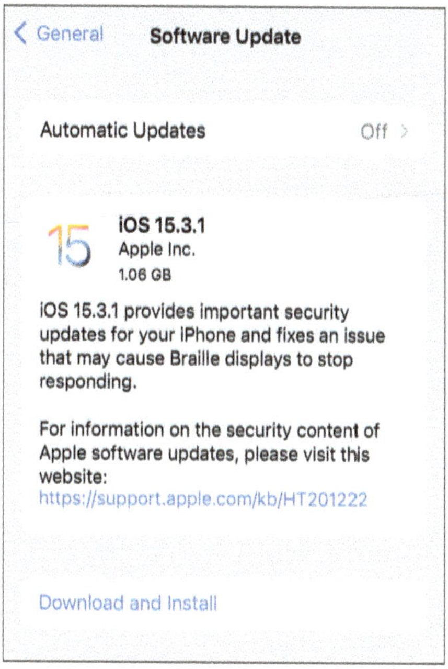


The installation will take a while.

# App Updates

To check for app updates, open the app store

Tap your Apple ID icon on the top right of the screen.

Scroll down to 'available updates'. You'll see a list of updates that are pending for the apps you have installed.

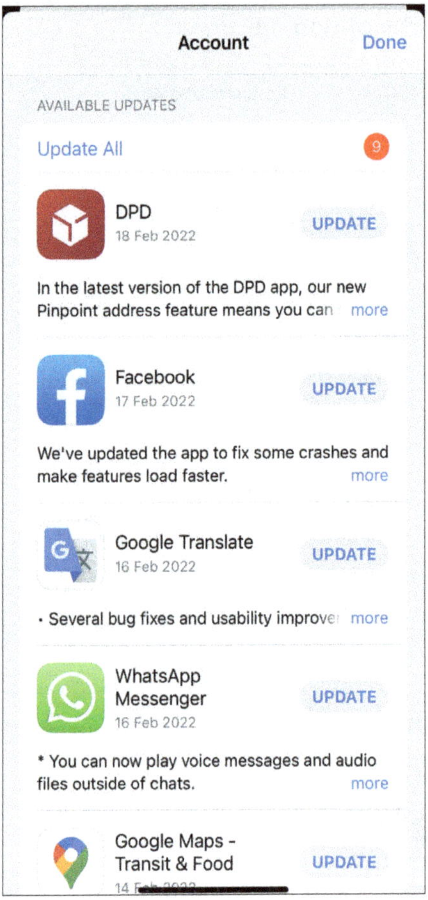


Tap 'update' next to the app to update it, or tap 'update all' to apply all the updates that are available.

# Deleting Apps

To delete apps, tap and hold your finger on an app, until the X appears on the top left of the icon.

Tap on the X to delete the app. Tap 'done' on the top right when you're finished.

You can also delete any of the pre-installed apps you don't use, in the same way as above.

# iPhone Storage Maintenance

You can see what apps an data are stored on your iPhone's physical storage. First open your settings app, select 'general', then 'iPhone storage'

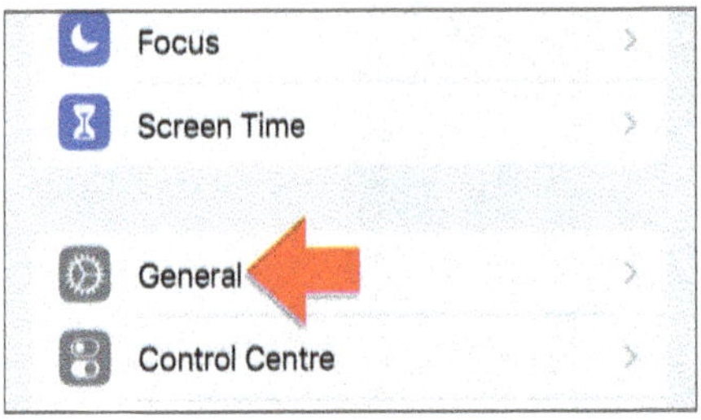


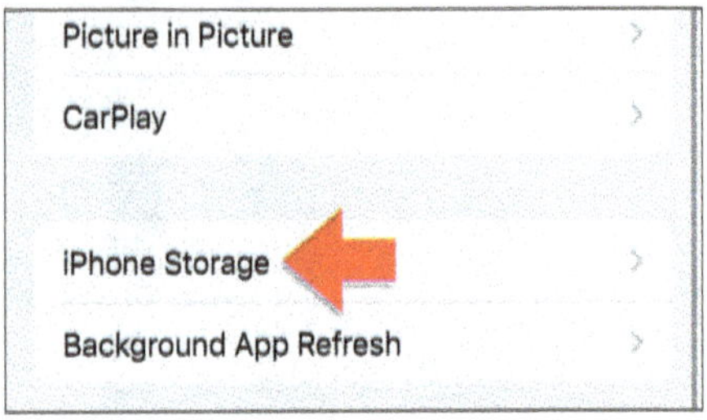


From here, you can see all the apps installed on your iPhone. You can also delete or offload apps that you don't use.

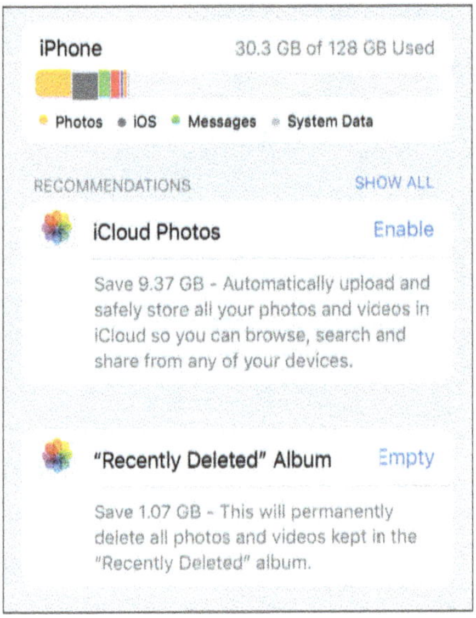


Tap 'enable' next to 'offload unused apps'. This will automatically offload apps you don't use but only when you run out of storage. When apps are offloaded, the app itself is deleted from your iPhone freeing up space, but any associated documents and data remain. The app icon remains on the home screen, so you can still access it.

Tap 'empty' next to 'recently deleted album'. This will clear deleted photos from your photos app.

When you tap on an offloaded app it will automatically re-install and any documents and data will still be there.

Listed below that on the 'iPhone storage' screen are all the apps installed on your iPhone. Tap on an app name to see details.

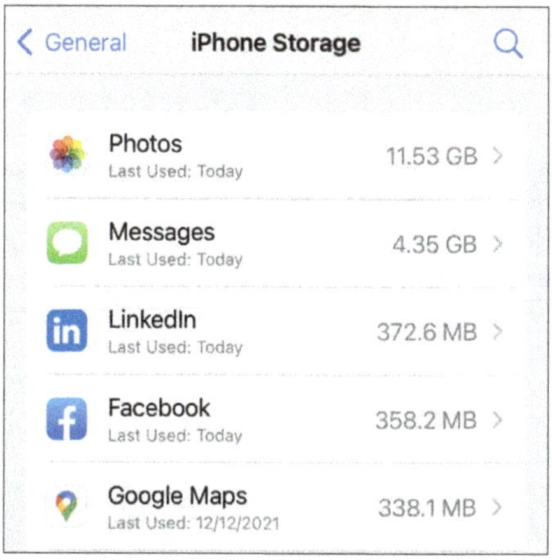


At the top you'll see the amount of space the app takes up (the app size), and the space used for documents and data. From here you can manually offload the app, or delete it. To do this, tap 'offload app' to offload, and 'delete app' to delete.

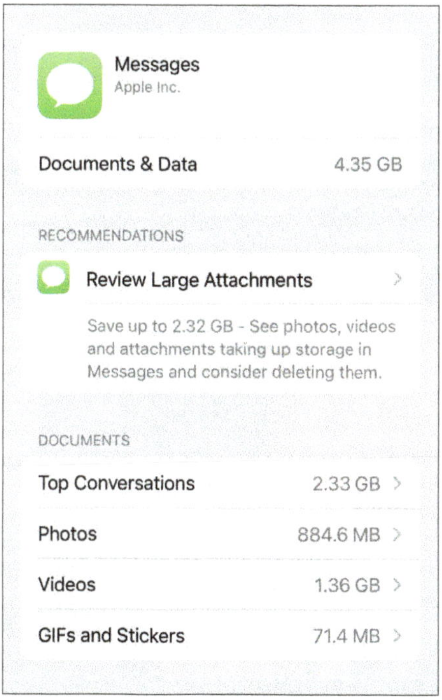


On some apps you'll see any media you've sent, received or downloaded. Tap on these to view details.

# iPhone Recovery

First power off your iPhone (hold side button and volume down button, then slide the slider to the right to power off).

Plug the other end of the lightning cable into your Mac or PC.

Open the Music App on your Mac, or iTunes on your PC

Now, press and hold the side button while you plug the end of the lightning cable into the charge port on the bottom of the phone. This will force your iPhone into recovery mode. Ignore on-screen the sliders. Hold the side button down until you see the recovery screen.

On your mac, you'll see a prompt appear in the finder app. If you don't see the prompt, open finder, then select your iPhone from the list on the left.

Tap 'update' to update to the latest iOS then restore your iPhone to factory defaults.

Tap 'restore' to restore your iPhone to factory defaults without updating iOS.

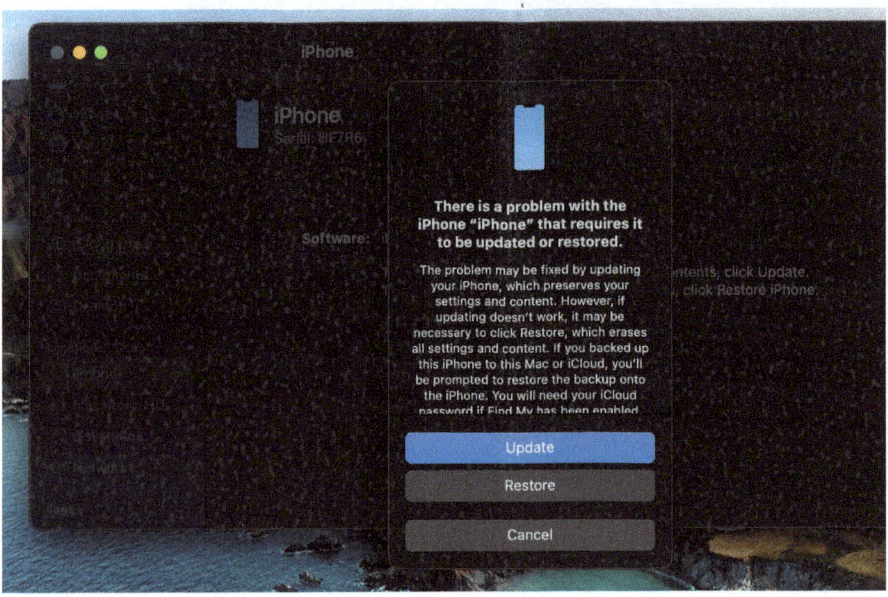

# Connecting to a Computer

To access iPhone from your PC you will need to have iTunes installed. If you are using a Mac, iTunes is now called the Music App and will already be installed.

Tap the Music App icon on your dock or on Launch the app.

*If you are on a PC then you will need to download iTunes from the Microsoft Store. You'll find the Microsoft Store on your start menu.*

*Type 'itunes' into the search field on the top right, then select 'iTunes' from the drop down menu.*

*Click 'install'.*

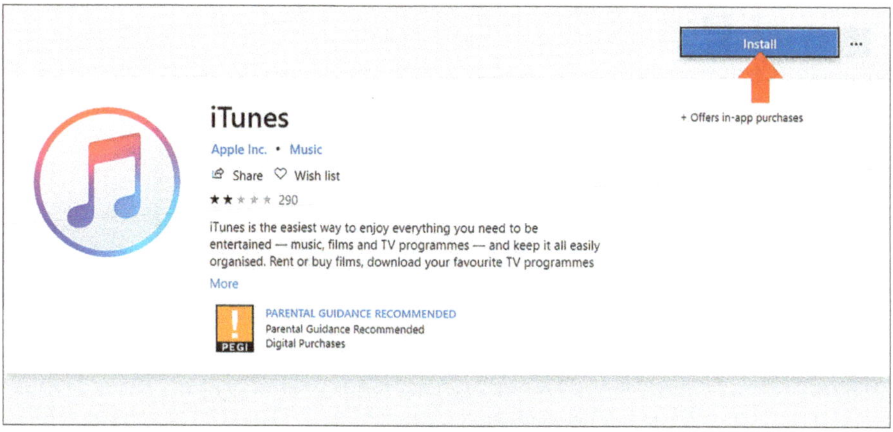


*You'll find the iTunes app on your start menu.*

Select the 'account' menu, click 'sign in...', then enter your Apple ID and password. Click 'sign in'.

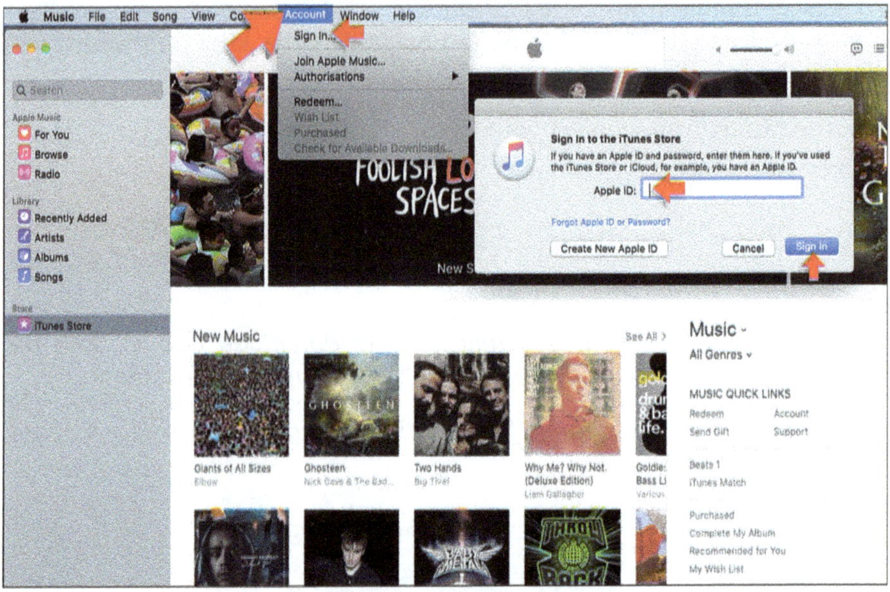


## Sync your iPhone with your Mac

Plug your iPhone into your Mac. Tap 'trust' on your iPhone/iPhone if prompted. Open the finder app. Your iPhone/iPhone will appear under 'devices' on the left hand panel. Click on your device.

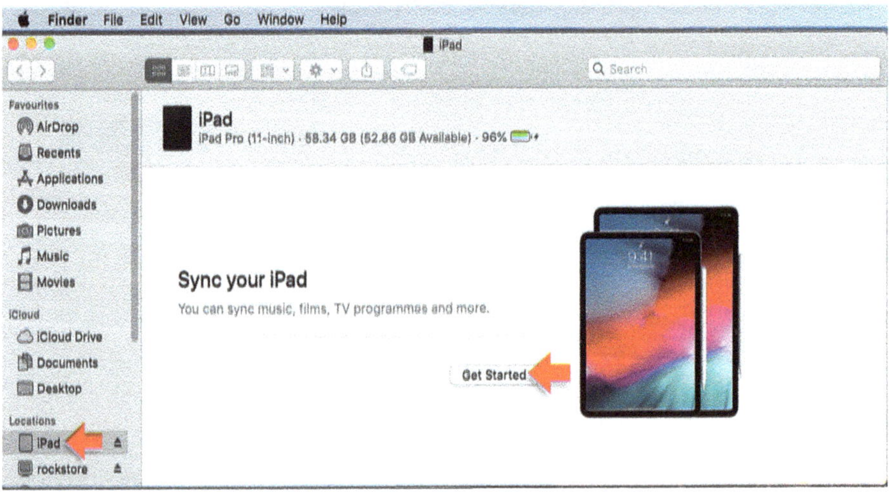


If this is the first time you have connected your device to your mac, click 'get started'.

Here you can manage your iPhone. Select 'general' for general settings, click 'music', 'films', 'tv programs', 'podcasts', 'audio books', and 'books' tabs to set auto sync between your mac to device,

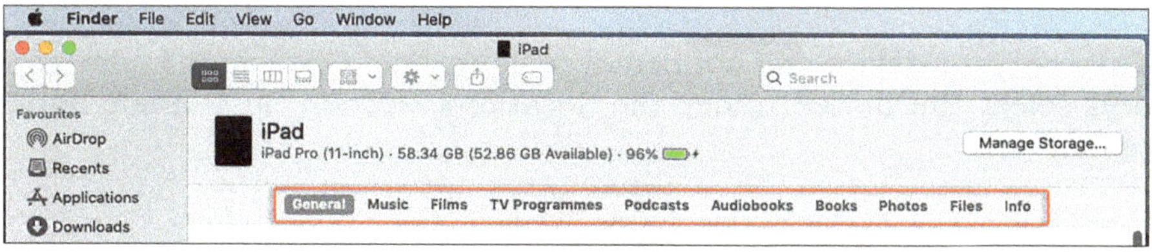


From the 'general' tab, you can check for updates, or restore iPhone if you're having problems. You can also back up your iPhone to your computer or restore your iPhone from a backup.

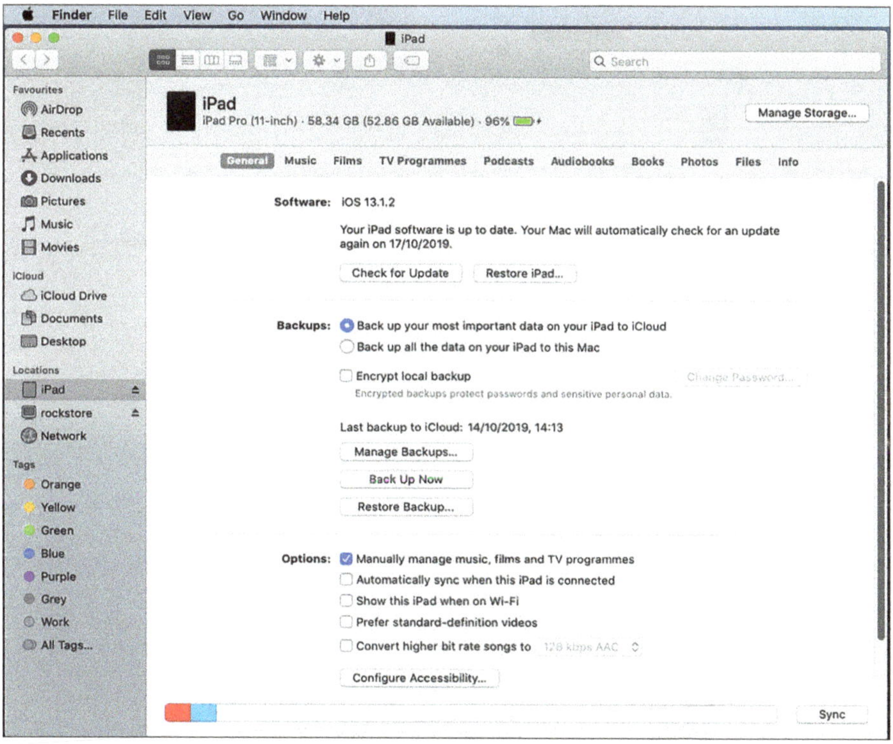


In the 'options' section further down the page, you can 'manually manage your music'. This allows you to drag and drop the music you want on your iPhone from your mac. This is better if you prefer to choose what you to sync rather than syncing your whole music library on your mac.

Along the bottom, you'll see a data bar. This shows you how much space has been used on your device.

# Restore iPhone

You can restore your device to its factory settings if you have problems with it.

Turn on your device and connect it to your mac. Open your finder app and select the device under the 'locations' section on the left hand panel.

On 'general' settings, click 'Restore iPhone'. *If you have downloaded a restore image (IPSW), hold the option key and click 'restore' then select the image file.*

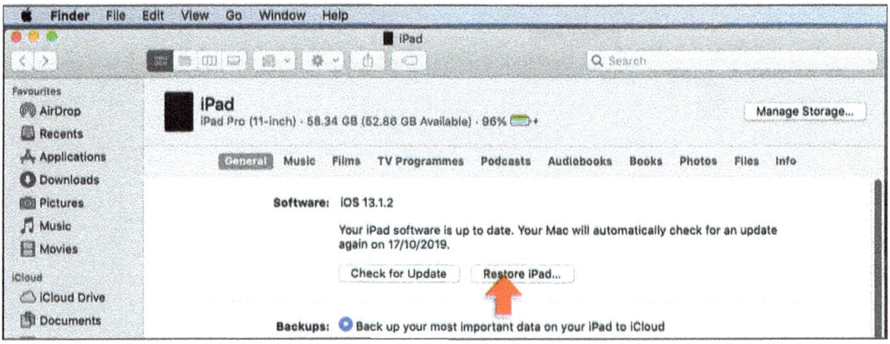


Click 'back up'.

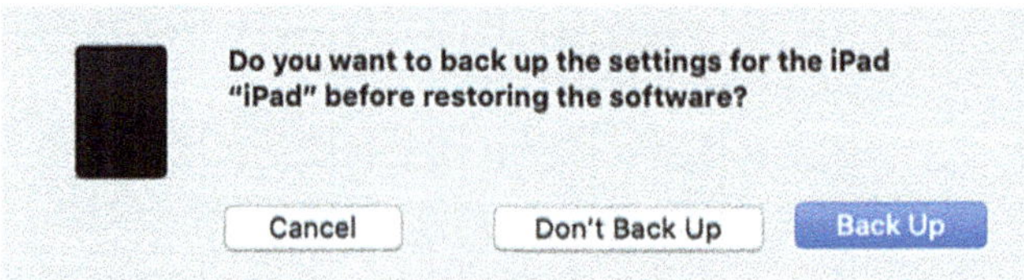


Click 'restore and update'

This will wipe your data, apps, music and settings, so you'll need to restore from a previous backup if you do this.

# Erase iPhone

If you want to erase your iPhone, this will delete all your data and personal information. This is useful if you are selling your iPhone or giving it to someone else. To erase your iPhone, open the settings app, select 'general' then tap 'transfer or reset iPhone'.

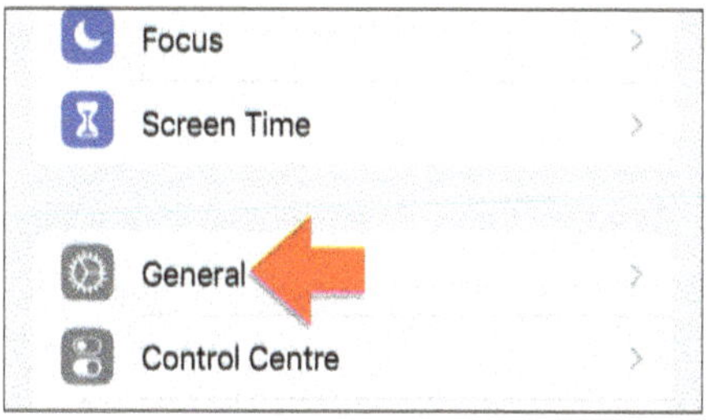


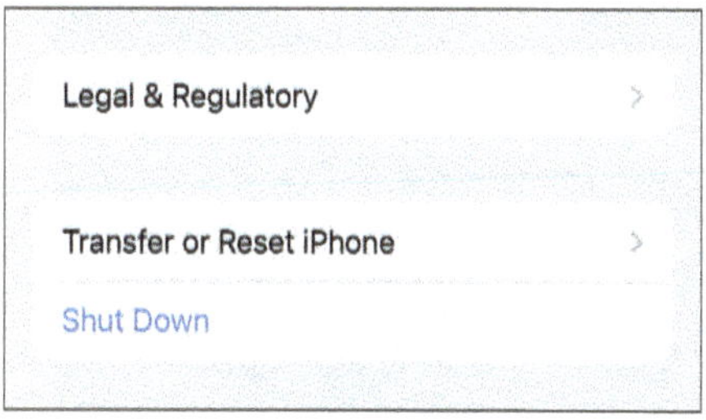


Tap 'Erase All Content and settings'.

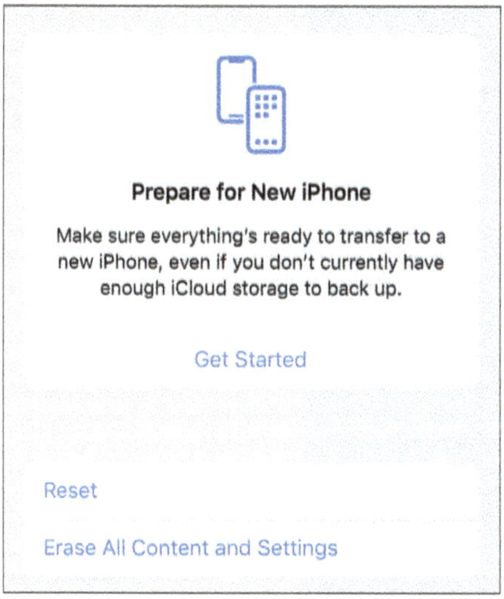


*Reset all Settings removes things like your Wifi password and settings you've set on your iPhone for Apps, mail, messages, FaceTime etc. Erase All Content and Settings restores a device to its factory defaults, and is useful if you want to completely wipe your phone, or give/sell it to someone else..*

Tap 'erase all content and settings', then enter your iPhone's passcode.

Follow the instructions on screen. Enter your Apple ID password to turn off the Activation Lock and remove the device from the 'Find My' app and your Apple ID Account. Your iPhone will reset. You'll land on the 'hello' screen when the reset is complete. From here you will need to run through the initial setup to set the iPhone up again.

# Video Resources

To help you understand the procedures and concepts explored in this book, we have developed some video resources and app demos for you to use, as you work through the book.

As well as the video resources, you'll also find some downloadable files and samples for exercises that appear in the book.

To find the resources, open your web browser and navigate to the following website

`elluminetpress.com/iphone`

Do not use a search engine, type the website into the address field at the top of the browser window.

At the beginning of each chapter, you'll find a website that contains the resources for that chapter.

# Using the Videos

When you open the link to the video resources, you'll see a thumbnail list at the bottom.

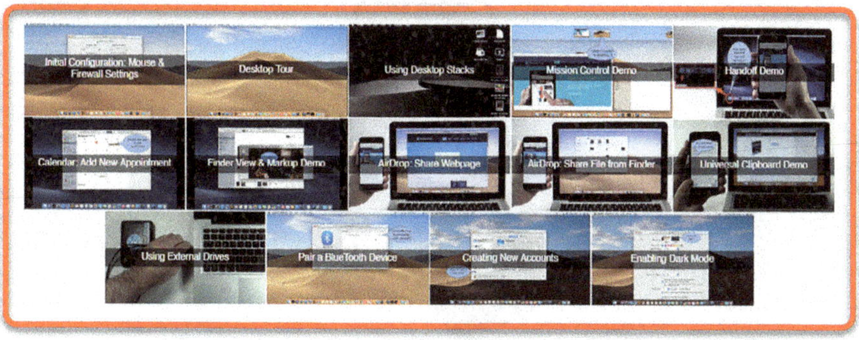


Click on the thumbnail for the particular video you want to watch. Most videos are between 30 and 60 seconds outlining the procedure, others are a bit longer. When the video is playing, hover your mouse over the video and you'll see some controls...

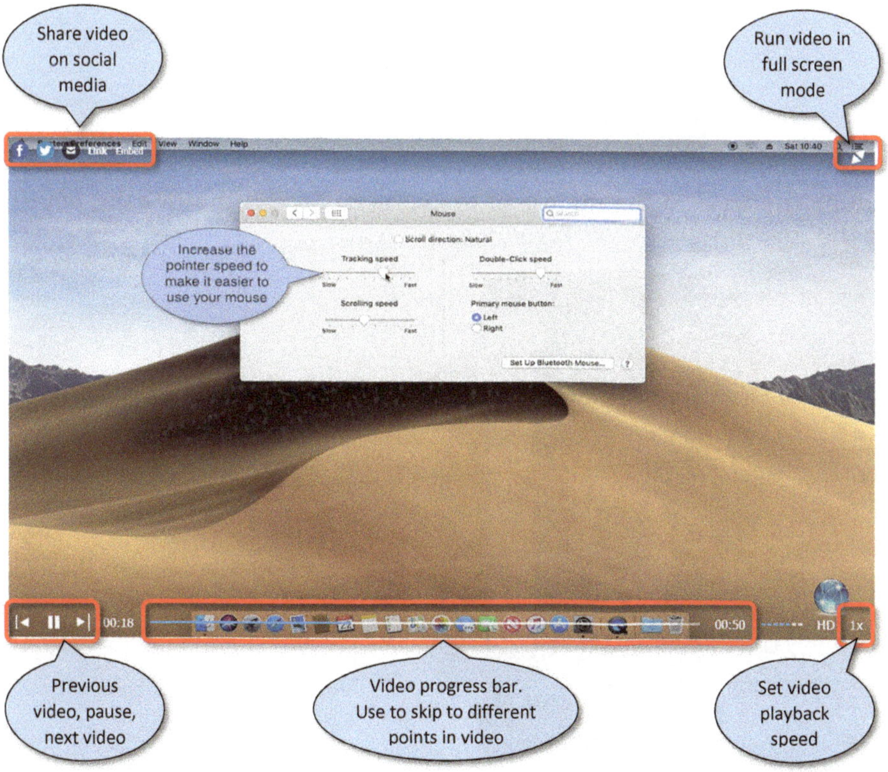

# Scanning the Codes

At the beginning of each chapter, you'll a QR code you can scan with your phone to access additional resources, files and videos.

## iPhone

To scan the code with your iPhone, open the camera app.

Frame the code in the middle of the screen. Tap on the website popup at the top.

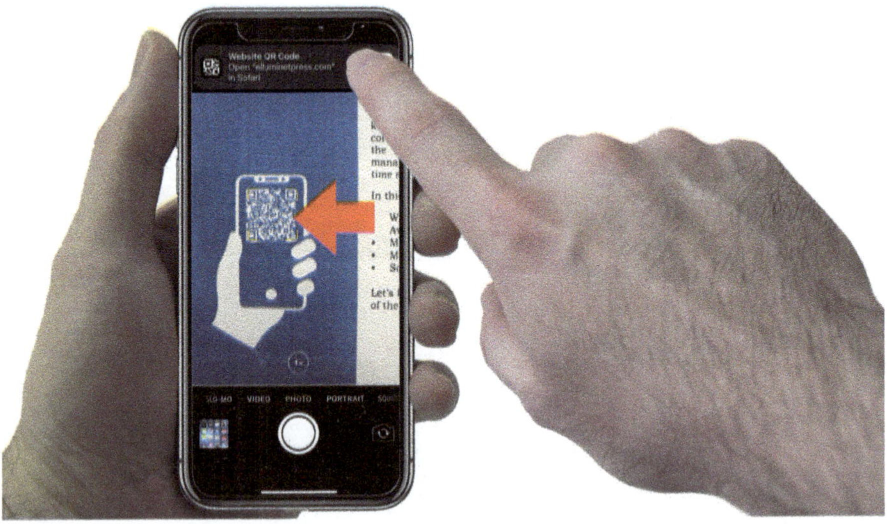

## Android

To scan the code with your phone or tablet, open the camera app.

Frame the code in the middle of the screen. Tap on the website popup at the top.

If it doesn't scan, turn on 'Scan QR codes'. To do this, tap the settings icon on the top left. Turn on 'scan QR codes'.

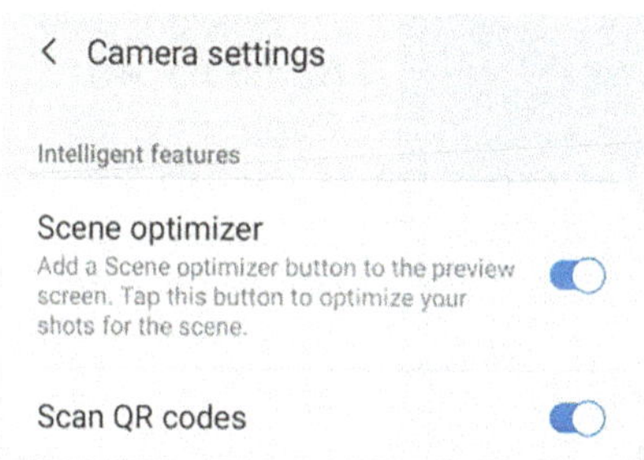


If the setting isn't there, you'll need to download a QR Code scanner. Open the Google Play Store, then search for "QR Code Scanner".

# Index

## Symbols



## A

## D



## E



## F

## G



## H



## I

## O



## P

## Q



## R



## S

## T

# SOMETHING NOT COVERED?

We want to create the best possible resources to help you learn and get things done, so if we've missed anything out, then please get in touch using the links below and let us know. Thanks.

SCAN ME

office@elluminetpress.com

elluminetpress.com/feedback

Milton Keynes UK
Ingram Content Group UK Ltd.
UKHW022045071223
433993UK00009B/65

9 781913 151676